The Future
as a
Social Problem

The Future as a
Social Problem

edited by Ronald Fernandez
Central Connecticut State College

Goodyear Publishing Company, Inc.
Santa Monica, California

Library of Congress Cataloging in Publication Data
Main entry under title:

The Future as a social problem.

   Includes bibliographical references.
   1.   Social history—20th century—Addresses, essays, lectures.
2.   Social problems—Addresses, essays, lectures.   3.   Social
change—Addresses, essays, lectures.   I.   Fernandez, Ronald.
HN18.F86   309.1'04   76-8150
ISBN 0-87620-340-3

Copyright © 1977 by
Goodyear Publishing Company, Inc.
Santa Monica, California 90401

Y-3403-6

Current printing (last digit):

10 9 8 7 6 5 4 3 2 1

Printed in the United States of America

cover and interior design: Jacqueline Thibodeau

To Adam and Carrie

Contents

Preface

DISCOVERING THE FUTURE

Like all words, "future" is a symbol. Today it represents a conception of time that points us toward tomorrows filled with change and imaginable disasters. But some human societies have expected their future to closely resemble their past and present. Preliterate societies, the majority in human history, apparently lack the idea of future. To preliterates, time is not a line extending infinitely into increasingly hazy tomorrows. Instead, preliterates represent time in cycles that always direct thought *back* to a point of origin, not forward to a point of what may be no return.[1]

Our own values intervene when we try to decide if life is better without a future. But since we have no choice—as an idea, the future is here to stay—perhaps we can turn from the question of better or worse and try instead to gain a broader perspective of our own future by looking at societies who manage to live without one.

Preliterate societies are dominated by religion. In fact, because myths, gods, spirits, and rituals are so pervasive in primitive life, Mircea Eliade believes that preliterates live in a thoroughly sacred and enchanted world. Nothing exists in and of itself. Every act, from hunting and fishing to harvests and wars, bears the special stamp of the sacred. Every act somehow participates in or is shrouded by the mysterious and awesome power of the world of the gods.

Although the word "every" covers a lot of territory, it is crucial to Eliade's argument that *all* is sacred because primitive life is guided by the gods, spirits, or ancestors who "founded" the society. They direct everyday life, and the preliterates' actions are "nothing but a ceaseless repetition of gestures initiated"[2] by the gods and spirits. For example, the Yąnomamö fight ceaselessly because their myth of origin says that the Yąnomamö were born in and from blood; the Ancient Greeks kept a sacred fire lit in order to please and appease their ancestors; and the Australian aborigines practiced circumcision with a stone knife because that is how their ancestors did it.[3]

The most important consequence of living in a world overwhelmingly dominated by the sacred is that preliterates live without historical (lineal) time. History is, after all, the realm of the unique: June 5, 1920, was a once and only phenomenon, a day that will never be repeated. But how can primitives think of history when their lives are inextricably rooted in the world of the gods? Their daily actions continually repeat the gestures of others, and even in their special rituals they imitate the world first established by the gods. In effect, there is no room for the unique or for a view of time that points toward a relatively unknown tomorrow. There is only room for the never-ending, always backward-looking world of the gods.

Today we live in historical time. And since we can look out toward the unknown, the obvious question is how we got from there to here, from a world without a future to one in which the future is a major social problem.

Although religious scholars trace the beginnings of history as an idea to ancient Judaism,[4] others point to what is perhaps a more basic root: literacy.[5] Goody and Watt argue that preliterates shape their cultures orally; facing everyday life they lack dictionary definitions and the accumulated meanings of history. Their only alternative is to develop language and meaning "in intimate association with the experience of the community"[6] and to teach and learn "in face-to-face contact with others."[7] Coincidentally, this type of learning has profound effects on the society, for although change takes place, say in the culture's myths of origin, it is easily assimilated. After all, since preliterates lack a "body of chronologically ordered statements to which reference can be made,"[8] they need not recognize contradictions between what is said "today" and what was said fifty years ago. Life is now, "and as the individuals of each generation acquire their vocabulary, their genealogies, and their myths, they are unaware that various words, proper-names and stories have dropped out, or that others have changed their meanings or been replaced."[9]

Like a fenced enclosure, then, illiteracy pens in skepticism. Preliterates sink roots in the gods' world, shape their myths in intimate association with experience, and lack the chronological records that might otherwise indicate their contradictions and inconsistencies. So, they are able to digest change without letting it seriously affect their ties to the gods or cyclical time.

Literacy forces contradictions into the open. Faced with written records of the past, people see the differences between past and present. Some may run from their insights, but others courageously confront the past and embrace "a much more conscious, comparative, and critical attitude to the accepted world picture, and notably to the notions of God, the universe, and the past."[10] In ancient Greece this attitude reached a climax in the "dogmatic doubt" of the Skeptics,[11] but the crucial point is that although written records made "the pastness of the past" an obvious fact of human life, they also held out the promise of a future pregnant with possibilities. For example, in *The Republic,* Plato dared to imagine something startlingly new: Utopia.

Between them, Skeptics and Utopians provided the polar reactions to the discovery of past, present, and future. On one hand, Skeptics looked at the past, became disgusted with it, and decided to build their future on a foundation of doubt. Utopians, on the other hand, although also dissatisfied with the past, came to the conclusion the future could be different. Captivated by the possibilities of tomorrow, Utopians walked into the future with a perfect plan.

We need not take sides to see that the onset of lineal time was a mixed blessing. Looking back, it is easy to embrace doubt. For example, viewing *our* future, the following questions immediately come to mind. Can a species that has fought nearly sixty wars since 1945 have any hope?[12] Can a world already filled with starving people hope for a better future when the earth's human population threatens to add a billion people every decade? Finally, even if we make provisions for population control, what kind of environment will exist in twenty-five years? Can people stop treating the planet as a dump?

Clearly, the Skeptics had a point, but so did the Utopians. Social reality— our past, present, and future—is humanly constructed[13] and if one result of discovering history is doubt, the other is power, the power of people to shape their own destinies. Preliterates apparently lacked this ability on a conscious level. Locked into religious cycles and lacking written records, preliterates only looked back. But with written records to guide them, people can view the past more objectively, see the relevance of the past to the present, and then proceed to the future on the basis of their insights and corrections. Naturally people need not look back in order to move forward. But the power is there to be used; rooted in history, we have the potential to consciously build our future on the basis of a collectively shared and corrected past.

However, since any reconstruction takes place in the present, the ties between the three categories of time are quite intimate. In effect, to understand today, plus consciously shape tomorrow, we must know about yesterday. Seemingly, no choice exists if people wish to face the future with open eyes. For the future is still to come; it is preeminently the realm of probability, of the more or less likely. And the irony is that the only way to perceive what is likely—and perhaps decide against it—is to ask how much, and in what ways, past and present are determining future.

Now, a basic argument of this book is that a look back at the deepest levels of our beliefs and practices is urgently required. Our future is a major social problem because such factors as population growth, the arms race, and pollution threaten the continued existence of the human race. This is not prophecy; it is probability. It is the contention that the introduction of two billion more people on a planet already troubled by problems of food supply and distribution may cause, among other things, wars over the control of resources and the use of nuclear weapons by, if not America or Russia, perhaps India or China.

No one knows for certain this will occur. It is a good possibility but one we need not embrace. After all, if people have the ability to consciously shape their future, why accept the one that now seems before us?

As sociologists, our task is not to construct blueprints for tomorrow or our own version of the new society. However, sociologists can shed light on the future by sharing their insights about the constraints the past and present place on the future. For example, is any particular social problem (e.g., women's role in society) also a cultural problem, that is, a problem of values? If it is, can we solve social problems without first changing those values? And if we cannot change those values, what are the limits that the cultural past and present place on our construction of a new future?

Precise answers to these questions are impossible, but the main thesis of this volume is that social problems are always intimately related to cultural assumptions. Our goal is to highlight the nature of this relationship, and try to understand any cultural constraints on the solution of social problems.

THE FUTURE AS A SOCIAL PROBLEM

In a famous essay, Carl Von Clausewitz said that "war was nothing but a continuation of politics by other means."[14] In Clausewitz's system, politicans never need to resort to the ultimate weapon in their political arsenal, but if they do, war must always be guided by political realities. For example, if the aim is a limited war, military tactics are closely controlled by politicians. Orders are to avoid widening the war by antagonizing nearby countries (China, for example, in the case of Vietnam), and soldiers are forbidden to use weapons (nuclear weapons in Korea or Vietnam) that might damage the nation's image and lead to a political nightmare—total war.

Clausewitz was right; wars are political. But if we focus attention on the political aspects of war, we will miss what is perhaps a more important sociological point: Wars are fought by the masses of citizens, and the evidence indicates that political goals and ideals are relatively unimportant to the average soldier. World War II is an example. Conventional wisdom argues that soldiers fought to keep the world safe for democracy, but the volumes of *The American Soldier* show a conspicuous absence of political ideals and values.[15] Men were reluctant to talk about politics, which led the authors to conclude that the main motive keeping soldiers in the field was the close personal ties that developed among the ten or twelve men who fought together. More specifically, however, the authors noted that soldiers worried about their images. None wanted to appear cowardly because each was afraid of looking like a "fag." So, men often showed courage, not to defeat Hitler, but to prove to others that they were real men.[16]

I am not trying to prove that World War II began because soldiers wanted to be he-men. I am arguing that we will never abolish wars if we define them only in political terms. For one important reason men fought in World War II, Korea, and Vietnam was to assert their masculinity.[17] This value was learned in childhood. Essentially, it is the man's affirmation of his culture's definition of sex roles: Men are strong, men fight, and men show courage by knowing how to defend themselves. All the political analysis in the world will not change these beliefs because they are a basis for action in virtually *every* facet of a man's life. And in a different way, they are a basis for action in many facets of a woman's life. Women, after all, learn to applaud men who maul each other on a football field, to respect men who have the ambition and willingness to "get what they want," and to be ashamed of sons who refuse to fight. To paraphrase Will Rogers, look at the eyes of a woman when she shows you the picture of her son killed in an automobile crash and the picture of her son killed in a war.

Attitudes toward war constitute only one example of the impact cultural values have upon social phenomena. In a different way, similar factors influence population, pollution, and racism. For no social problem exists in a vacuum; each is rooted in a particular culture, in the special way a group of people decide what is proper (or improper) to think, do, and have as members of society.

Consider culture's power. Before we were born, institutionalized patterns of thought and action already existed. They were an arbitrary inheritance from the parents and teachers who taught us the "rules of the game." However, no one told us that. In fact, instead of telling us that our culture was one of many possible patterns of thought and action, others probably gave us little choice. Ideally, they told us our culture was the best of all possible worlds, but even that is unnecessary for us to accept the recipes of others. Children have no choice. Others tell them what is right and wrong, and even if those others find fault with culture, to the extent they see no alternatives, the children are likely to agree. For the essence of a successful socialization is that what exists "out there," in the minds of others, eventually finds its way "in here," into your mind and mine.

Culturally, children normally remain captive audiences until at least the age of thirteen of fourteen. For it is not until then that most people have the ability to think hypothetically, to think in terms of possibilities rather than realities. The Swiss psychologist Jean Piaget calls this "the stage of formal operations,"[18] the stage in intellectual development when people are finally able to look back at their own or their culture's development and say, "All other things being equal, I could have turned out this way," or "All other things being equal, American culture might have turned out differently."

Piaget argues correctly that the ability to think in terms of possibilities is an enormous qualitative advance in intellectual development. Anyone who thinks hypothetically has the ability to see how things got to be the way they are. The hypothetical thinker can step outside inherited patterns of thought and action, see how those patterns developed, and even decide if he wishes to continue believing as he does. Free of the bonds of culture, he can see his society as one of many alternative societies, and see his own life as a series of choices.

Since most people only begin thinking hypothetically as teenagers, any process of objective reevaluation takes place on a more or less solid cultural foundation. Although the new hypothetical thinker has the ability to rethink the process of his socialization, he enters this newly discovered world of possibility equipped with a host of assumptions about himself and society—about sex roles, the welfare system, various ethnic groups, scientists, and much more. So, successful socialization into a culture becomes a major barrier against using the new-found ability to think in terms of possibilities. For example, even in a period changing as rapidly as our own, careful studies of adolescence indicate that most young people do *not* disagree with their parents on basic values, do *not* want to radically change their culture, and do *not* want to join a commune tomorrow.[19]

Considering the barriers cultural assumptions erect against change, this attitude of the young is not surprising. Any substantial reevaluation of long-held beliefs—not to mention change itself—involves questions whose answers might topple those beliefs. For it is ironic but true that in order to change I must make what is often a frightening admission. I must admit, ''Perhaps I am not who I think I am,'' or ''Perhaps what other people told me about the nature and rights of women and men is untrue,'' or ''Perhaps one consequence of industrial progress is the wholesale destruction of the earth's environment.''

Adolescent or adult, we all normally turn a deaf ear to insights that threaten established cultural assumptions. It is easier to tolerate the accepted than accept the pain that accompanies change. However, despite the human tendency to avoid the uncomfortable, one question refuses to disappear—since any particular social problem is also a cultural problem, can we solve today's and tomorrow's social problems without radically rethinking the culture that sustains them?

My answer is no. The future may prove me wrong, but tomorrow is filled with such a host of profound problems (e.g., population, pollution, biological research, diminishing energy resources, and the arms race) many requiring immediate solutions, that it is hard to imagine a tolerable future without substantial voluntary change at the cultural level. For example, can we solve world pollution problems without major changes in our attitudes toward nationalism and sovereignty? Or can biological research in such areas as head grafting (see Chapter 15) be controlled without major changes in our attitude toward science and our worship of objectivity? Again, I argue no. We either attack problems at their roots now or we risk a future that says only, ''I told you so.''

As if survival were not a sufficient reason to begin our search for solutions at the cultural level, there are three others. First, if any particular social problem is also a cultural problem, long-range solutions are much easier if we begin at its roots. The concept of treating the cause instead of the symptom is an old argument, but grey hair fails to sap its potency. A second reason is that change at the cultural level is already taking place, whether or not we agree with it. From the women's movement to black power to the counterculture, large numbers of people are already reevaluating their cultural values at their roots, and tomorrow is likely to see even more of this reevaluation, if only because of increased educational opportunities. One possible way to avoid open conflict is to openly analyze the arguments made by advocates of substantial cultural change. Perhaps analysis will only strengthen our present beliefs? But no answer is possible without making the effort; and one good reason to make it is the conclusion that neither the women's movement nor black power is likely to ''wither away.''

Finally, and most important, a reevaluation of long accepted beliefs and values offers hope of a future without violence and crisis at every turn of the road. Third World populations are unlikely to starve quietly forever, and even large lakes and rivers can ''digest'' only so much human and animal waste.

So, why wait for catastrophe to induce change? Why wait for some individual or group to force it on us? With a thorough understanding of past and present, people have the ability to walk into the future with their eyes wide open. Peaceful yet substantial social change is not impossible; it is only very difficult and painful.

One point remains. Arguing in favor of basic reevaluation of our cultural underpinnings does not necessitate neglecting practical reform. Since the relationship between practical and cultural change is dialectical—one always acts back upon the other—the two are always intertwined in the most varied ways. For instance, *Brown* v. *The Board of Education,* the U.S. Supreme Court's 1954 desegregation decision, stimulated the civil rights activity of the late fifties. And from those legal battles many black activists turned to a reevaluation of their basic beliefs and values. One conclusion they reached was ''black is beautiful.''[20]

In sum, although cultural and practical changes are always intertwined, cultural questions are more basic. And that is my essential point. Our future is filled with profound problems and the best way to face them is to search for solutions which strike at their heart, at the level of cultural beliefs, values, and practices.

CHANCES FOR CHANGE

If the young remain tied to their parents' beliefs and values, why assume that either group will radically reevaluate its patterns for living and dying? If people normally run from threatening insights, why assume they will be different tomorrow? In short, if substantial and voluntary cultural change is so very difficult, what hope exists for its realization?

Some people believe there is none. In Part I of this book the selections by both Robert Heilbroner and Jacques Ellul embrace pessimism. For different reasons and from different perspectives both writers come to the conclusion that no hope exists. In their views, our problems are too great, our will too weak, our ability to change too limited. So, since nothing meaningful can or will be done, tomorrow can bring nothing but disaster. The future adds up to a series of zeros.

The black view of Heilbroner and Ellul may be accurate, but I believe that hope exists on three interrelated fronts. First, many modern societies, America in particular, are structurally conducive to change.[21] Opportunities for higher education, a free press, and free speech offer hope that serious discussions of the future will receive widespread publicity in an atmosphere open to change. Naturally, any reevaluation of beliefs and values will still be resisted, but without the chance to openly discuss future alternatives, one cause of hope vanishes.

Cultural crisis is my second source of hope. While welcoming difficulty may sound strange, my hope is based on Robert Nisbet's contention that wherever it exists in substantial degree, change is always associated with some form of crisis.[22] Of course, crisis need not lead to change, but given the human tendency to resist the new and different, crisis is always an important factor in producing change. Like a sharp slap in the face, crisis forces itself upon us and often leaves no alternative: We must make changes or suffer further crises.

Future crises can assume at least two forms. Like the Arab oil embargo or the famines in Bangladesh, crises can develop from very practical situations. But it is also possible to envision our future as a series of cultural crises that must be confronted if we wish to avoid a long series of practical crises (see Part II). If examination of the human prospect acts like a slap in the face, hope exists that our response will be a voluntary effort to find the root causes of such a problematic future.

My third cause of hope is factual: Since only people make culture, there is nothing to prevent them from remaking it. Naturally, the past and present impose certain limitations on our plans, but many possibilities for major change still exist. A dismal future is not inevitable. There is no insurmountable barrier that prevents people with the will and insight to achieve positive change from remaking culture and society in a form that offers hope for tomorrow.

NOTES

1. Discussions of the preliterate conception of time can be found in Mircea Eliade, *Cosmos and History* (New York: Harper & Row, 1959); Claude Levi-Strauss, *The Savage Mind* (New York: Free Press, 1962); and Stanley Diamond, ed., *Primitive Views of the World* (New York: Free Press, 1963).

2. Eliade, *Cosmos and History*, p. 5.

3. Additional examples are contained in Napoleon Chagnon, *The Yanomanö* (New York: Holt, Reinhart and Winston, 1958); Fustel de Coulanges, *The Ancient City* (Garden City, N.Y.: Doubleday, 1963); and Eliade, *Cosmos and History*.

4. See Peter Berger, *The Sacred Canopy* (Garden City, N.Y.: Doubleday, 1967); and Max Weber, *Ancient Judaism* (New York: Free Press, 1962).

5. J. Goody and I. Watt, "The Consequences of Literacy," in *Comparative Studies in Society and History*, vol. 5 (Harper & Row, 1963), pp. 304–345.

6. Goody and Watt, "Consequences of Literacy," p. 321.

7. Goody and Watt, "Consequences of Literacy," p. 324.

8. Goody and Watt, "Consequences of Literacy," p. 325.

9. Goody and Watt, "Consequences of Literacy," p. 325.

10. Goody and Watt, "Consequences of Literacy," p. 329.

11. Bertrand Russell, *History of Western Philosophy* (New York: Simon & Schuster, 1961), p. 243.

12. George Thayer, *The War Business* (New York: Simon & Schuster, 1968).

13. Peter Berger and Thomas Luckmann, *The Social Construction of Reality* (Garden City, N.Y.: Doubleday, 1963).

14. Carl von Clausewitz, *On War* (Baltimore: Penguin, 1968), p. 119.

15. See Samuel Stouffer, et al., *The American Soldier* (New York: Wiley, 1948).

16. J. Glenn Gray, *The Warriors* (New York: Harper Torch Books, 1967); Bill Mauldin, *Up Front* (New York: Henry Holt and Company, 1945).

17. See Martin Russ, *The Last Parallel* (Chicago: Bobbs Merrill, 1957); and Michael Parks, *G.I. Diary* (New York: Harper & Row, 1968).

18. Jean Piaget, *The Child and Reality* (New York: Viking 1972); also "Intellectual Development from Adolescence to Adulthood," *Human Development,* Volume 15, 1972, pp. 1–12.

19. A more extensive treatment of this subject can be found in Elizabeth Douvan and Joseph Adelson, *The Adolescent Experience* (New York: Wiley, 1966); Ernest Q. Campbell, "Adolescent Socialization," in David Goslin, ed., *The Handbook of Socialization* (Chicago: Rand McNally, 1969); and Robert Conger, *Adolescence* (New York: Wiley, 1973).

20. See William Greer and Michael Cobbs, *Black Rage* (New York: Bantam, 1968); and Julius Lester, *Watch Out Whitey, Black Power Gonna Get Your Momma* (New York: Grove Press, 1968).

21. Neil Smelser, *Essays in Sociological Theory* (Englewood Cliffs, N.J.: Prentice-Hall, 1968).

22. Robert Nisbet, *The Social Bond* (New York: Alfred A. Knopf, 1970), p. 316–321.

The Future
as a
Social Problem

Part I
OVERVIEWS

Introduction

To walk into the future with open eyes, to begin the painful process of consciously reevaluating our past and present, we face one unavoidable task: We must thoroughly analyze the cultural assumptions and customs that sustain advanced industrial society. So, the purpose of Part One is to provide this background. None of the selections gives specific solutions to tomorrow's problems; none furnishes a precise program of what should be done. Instead, each selection focuses on the values that underlie modern societies. From different perspectives, and with contrasting hopes for tomorrow, each selection analyzes the various thought processes and values that will or could be the basis of our future society.

The philosophical emphasis of Part One provides a crucial foundation for the more specific confrontations with the future contained in Part Two. For if every social problem is rooted in culture, and if it is hard to imagine a tolerable future without radical changes in culture, we have no choice but to reevaluate and change our cultural assumptions and patterns for living. Otherwise we will walk into the future blindfolded, without conscious knowledge of the beliefs and values that direct our thought and action.

José Ortega y Gasset's reading from *Man and Crisis* appears first because it delineates the profoundly unsettling consequences of living through a period of radical social change. People may know that their traditional values are false, yet still be unable to move from the negative to the positive, to replace the worn-out with the new. So, my hope is that an outline of what we can expect from ourselves during periods of radical change will alert us to our condition. If we are familiar with the mistakes those before us have made, perhaps we can avoid making them ourselves.

Following the Ortega selection are those of Robert Heilbroner (from *An Inquiry into the Human Prospect*) and Daniel Bell (from *The Coming of Post-Industrial Society*). Heilbroner finds little hope, basing his conclusion on the observation that socialist and capitalist societies have the common problem of commitment to industrialization but that there is no future in industrialization. If pollution doesn't get us the exhaustion of fossil fuels will. Heilbroner finds no evidence that people are willing to reconsider the value they place on industrialization; to him, that unwillingness spells doom.

Daniel Bell focuses on bureaucratization, rationalization, and specialization—concepts that are part of the framework of industrial society and that eventually dominate it. He appears to be optimistic about a future in which these concepts are implemented by a host of technical experts.

Jacques Ellul is very unhappy about the ascendancy of the expert. In the selection from *The Technological Society,* Ellul ranks it high as a dehumanizing influence, placing it on a level with industrialization. Efficiency and impersonality rule in Ellul's version of tomorrow—this clearly signifies to him that the quality of life will be based on inhuman values. For different reasons, then, Ellul echoes Heilbroner's hopelessness.

Theodore Roszak's book, *Where the Wasteland Ends* (see Chapter 5), takes issue with science, which, like bureaucratization, teaches the value of objectivity. One frightening end of society's devotion to science has thus far been a world in which men and women build nuclear bombs and engage in potentially catastrophic biological research—all in the name of science. This folly can only be corrected, suggests Roszak, if we shift our emphasis from science to religion. We must construct a vision born of transcendent knowledge if we wish to radically change society.

Richard Falk follows with "two images of the future" (Chapter 6). He focuses on politics, asserting that citizens and political leaders must transcend their passionate nationalism and desire for sovereignty. The solution of world problems demands international political institutions; without international organization how can we, for example, regulate the use of the oceans or solve the problems created by multinational corporations?

Chapters 2 through 6 should be viewed as a unit. They discuss many of contemporary society's most important values, beliefs, and practices, and all together they provide a perspective on tomorrow. In general, I agree with Heilbroner, Ellul, Roszak, and Falk that we have little cause for hope unless we alter our commitments to nationalism, science, industrialization, and the other crippling concepts that, like weeds, take over industrialized societies.

This bleak conclusion is based on two facts. First is the number and magnitude of our problems. Since we are threatened by possible catastrophe on many fronts (e.g., increasing population, pollution, biological research, nuclear war), the crisis is now. We either make major changes or willingly embrace probable disaster. Second is the root causes of any social problem. As noted in the Preface, my argument is that while cultural and institutional changes are always intertwined, one is more basic than the other; one promises to attack the interior, the other the exterior, of a problem. Consider, for example, pollution of the oceans. This is an international problem. We all pollute the oceans, and only overall control by supranational institutions promises to effectively police the world's waterways. But are such institutions likely to be created, much less work effectively, until we change our beliefs about the value of nationalism? Is it possible to imagine meaningful control of ocean pollution unless countries allow international bodies to investigate and, if necessary, intervene in the internal affairs of a society that pollutes the oceans?*

To extend our example, even if ocean pollution could be controlled without major changes in our beliefs about nationalism, only part of the problem would be solved. Pollution is also fueled by our commitment to nonstop industrialization and our assumptions about the ultimate value of land and natural resources. We must also reevaluate these concepts if pollution of the ocean is to end, for even if strict and enforceable laws were passed, how effective would they be if most people did not believe in the reasons for their creation?

Pollution is, of course, only one example of a social problem that is ultimately linked to our most basic thoughts about ourselves and the nature of our society. Chapters 2 through 6 are a unit because each links basic beliefs and values to specific social problems. And, except for Daniel Bell, each links the overwhelming problems our future apparently holds for us to what the writer considers a particularly weak spot in our culture. Naturally, Heilbroner, Roszak, and Falk argue that if the problems are to be solved, there must be major changes in the cultural beliefs and values that are the ultimate sources of the problems.

The two remaining chapters in Part One share a common bond that sets them apart from Chapters 3 through 6—they are hopeful. It should be noted, however, that their optimism is not of the same type as that of Daniel Bell, who appears optimistic that increasing the efficiency of our present industrialized society will cure our ills. Reich and Daly, like the pessimistic writers, are unhappy with today and begin the process of reevaluation needed for a different tomorrow.

Charles Reich's plan for the future, explained in the selection from *The Greening of America* (Chapter 7), is simply that there is no plan. To construct one would be to fall into the trap that imprisons advanced industrial societies— too much organization. Reich's plan is to live with self-realization as the chief goal, and he believes that the rest will follow. Inspired by good examples, average people will reevaluate their lives, with the result being a new, green future.

Mary Daly is a feminist who demands a transvaluation of values that will eventually end in a feminist ethics (see Chapter 8). A feminist ethics is a set of values and beliefs, which is now only developing, that treats both sexes alike, and because it applauds the humanity of all tolerates the inhumanity of none.

Although each of these selections discusses specific problems more thoroughly dealt with in Part Two, their overall significance is as possible starting points for a reevaluation of our past, present, and future. Does either of them point us in the right direction? My view is that the women's movement is the most revolutionary and consequently the most promising. Our

---

*For a good analysis of these questions, see Noel Mostert, *Supership* (New York: Warner Books, 1976).

gender identity is for many of us the most basic identity we have, and if feminists can help us to change it in the process of gaining justice for themselves, perhaps they will open us to the possibility of further radical change.

Consider, for example, the traditional virtues of manhood. A Man is supposed to be strong, hard, tough, unwilling to be pushed around, and ready to fight anyone who treats him badly. Suppose that in the process of redefining Woman, feminists enable men to redefine their identities too. Perhaps someday a man will be defined as someone who, in his vulnerability, has the capacity to openly discuss his problems and weaknesses. Perhaps a man will be someone who thinks before he fights, and a coward someone who fights at the drop of a hat. Perhaps, too, if people learn to perceive the connection between traditional masculinity and war, they will reevaluate some of the present axioms of statecraft and there will be fewer wars. Equipped with new gender identities, future citizens might begin to seriously question the claim, often made by former President Nixon, that a nation must fight because it has never suffered defeat. And, their own genders redefined, future presidents might begin to reassess the virtues of a foreign policy rooted in convictions about strength and weakness, power and impotence. Conceivably, future presidents might evolve a foreign policy based on tenets of empathy, humanity, and a determined resistance to the use of force.*

War is only one of the social problems that feminists can help us see in a new light. For example, if the family is the first place that children learn to accept institutionalized social inequalities, perhaps feminists can, in the process of establishing nonsexist families, enable us to rethink our beliefs about Indians, Blacks, or Asians. Obviously, all this is only a possibility, but feminism has the potential to generate dramatic change. For in reassessing the function and importance of our long-established sexual roles, feminists are asking questions that, like ripples of water, lead one to another, and another, and another.

Part Two will extend our analysis by providing some specific, detailed information needed to understand and deal with particular problems discussed more generally in Part One. In essence, however, Part Two deals with the branches of our future dilemma; Part One attacks the roots. Although we must implement our theories by devising new institutions, laws, and proposals for change, the best way to ensure their success is to alter the assumptions underlying the problems we would like to solve.

---

*For an extended analysis of these questions see Ronald Fernandez, *The I, The Me, and You,* (New York: Praeger, in press).

1
People and Crisis

Ortega's reading is first because it stresses the unsettling consequences of radical social change. It is a crisis that often creates a negative reaction. In the extreme, people do not know what new thing to think; they only know that "the traditional norms are false and inadmissable."

"But human existence abhors a vacuum." People must have answers and definitions that permit them to adapt to today and tomorrow. For some, adaptation "is the conviction that everything is doubtful." But others, seeking to transcend the negative, approach change by generating a "new set of positive tendencies." Although these tendencies—only the germs of a new order—are initially obscure, they represent an attempt to stabilize life by looking beyond the pain and anxiety that always accompany radical social change.

It is possible to look at some of the readings in Part One as the "germs of a new order." Many of the writers are overwhelmingly negative, but some (Falk, Reich, and Daly) are definitely trying to generate positive tendencies. Ortega even argues that the positive grows out of the negative, suggesting that in order to rethink tomorrow, we must first believe that past and present provide a poor basis for the future.

Finally, an important feature of this reading is Ortega's warning that the pain associated with change often breeds despair and a consequent tendency to view complex issues simplistically. The despairing try to avoid difficult questions by embracing easy answers, or to answer difficult questions with the argument that no answers exist. Alerted to these human tendencies, we can hope to avoid them.

From Man and Crisis
—*José Ortega y Gasset*

It is my belief that the so-called Renaissance represents a great historical crisis. An historical crisis is a concept, or better, a predicament of history; thereby it is a fundamental form which the structure of human life is able to adopt. But the concepts which define this structure of human life are many because the dimensions of human life are many. So it is useful to make clear to which of those aspects the concept of crisis refers. It refers to the element of change in historical life. Crisis is a peculiar historical change. Which one?

. . . We find two classes of vital historical change: first, when something changes in our world; second, when the world changes.

The latter . . . occurs normally in every generation. Now we ask ourselves what is special and particular about the type of world change that we call an historical crisis.

And now I shall anticipate my own reply, so that you may know what facts to take hold of and may clearly observe the path my thought is taking. An historical crisis is a world change which differs from the normal change as follows: the normal change is that the profile of the world which is valid for one generation is succeeded by another and slightly different profile. Yesterday's system of convictions gives way to today's, smoothly, without a break; this assumes that the skeleton framework of the world remains in force throughout that change, or is only slightly modified.

That is the normal. Well, then, an historical crisis occurs when the world change which is produced consists in this: the world, the system of convictions belonging to a previous generation, gives way to a vital state in which man remains without these convictions, and therefore without a world. Man returns to a state of not knowing what to do, for the reason that he returns to a state of actually not knowing what to think about the world. Therefore the change swells to a crisis and takes on the character of a catastrophe. The world change consists of the fact that the world in which man was living has collapsed, and, for the moment, of that alone. It is a change which begins by being negative and critical. One does not know what new thing to think—one only knows, or thinks he knows, that the traditional norms and ideas are false and inadmissible. One feels a profound disdain for everything, or almost everything, which was believed yesterday; but the truth is that there are no new positive beliefs with which to replace the traditional ones. Since that system of convictions, that world, was the map which permitted man to move within his environment with a certain security, and since he now lacks such a map, he again feels himself lost, at loose ends, without orientation. He moves from here to there without order or arrangement; he tries this side and then the other, but without complete convictions; he pretends to himself that he is convinced of this or that.

This last is very important. During periods of crisis, positions which are false or feigned are very common. Entire generations falsify themselves to themselves; that is to say, they wrap themselves up in artistic styles, in doctrines, in political movements which are insincere and which fill the lack of genuine convictions. When they get to be about forty years old, those generations become null and void, because at that age one can no longer live on fictions. One must set oneself within the truth.

. . . I [have] said that there is no such thing as what is usually called "a man without convictions." Whether you like it or not, to live is always to have convictions, to believe something about the world and about one's self. Now those convictions, those beliefs, can be negative. One of the most convinced men who ever trod the earth was Socrates, and Socrates was convinced only that he knew nothing. Well then, life as crisis is a condition in which man holds only negative convictions. This is a terrible situation. The negative conviction, the lack of feeling certain about anything important, prevents man from deciding with any precision, energy, confidence, or sincere enthusiasm what he is going to do. He cannot fit his life into anything, he cannot lodge it within a specific destiny. Everything he does, feels, thinks, and says will be decided and achieved without positive conviction—that is to say, without effectiveness; it will be only the ghost of any real doing, feeling, thinking, or saying; it will be a *vita minima*—a life emptied of itself, incompetent, unstable.

Since at heart he is not convinced of anything positive and therefore is not truly decided about anything, man and indeed the masses of men will move from white to black with the greatest of ease. During periods of crisis one does not really know what each man is because in point of fact he is not anything with any decisiveness; he is one thing today and another tomorrow. Imagine a person who, when in the country, completely loses his sense of direction. He will take a few steps in one direction, then a few more in another, perhaps the exact opposite. The world and our convictions about the world make up our sense of direction, orient us, give us the compass points which direct our actions. Crisis man has been left without a world, handed over to the chaos of pure circumstance, in a lamentable state of disorientation. Such a structure of life opens a wide margin for very diverse emotional tonalities as a mask for life; very diverse, but all belonging to the same negative type. On feeling himself lost, man may respond with skeptical frigidity, with anguish, or with desperation; and he will do many things, which though apparently heroic, do not in fact proceed from any real heroism but are deeds done in desperation. Or he will have a sense of fury, of madness, an appetite for vengeance, because of the emptiness of his life; these will drive him to enjoy brutally, cynically, whatever comes his way—flesh, luxury, power. Life takes on a bitter flavor— we will soon meet the acidity of Petrarch, the first man of the Renaissance.

But human existence abhors a vacuum. All about this state of negation, this absence of convictions, there begin to ferment certain obscure germs of a new set of positive tendencies. More than this, in order that man may stop believing in some things, there must be germinating in him a confused faith in others. This new faith, I repeat, although misty and imprecise as the first light of dawn, bursts intermittently from the negative surface of man's life in a time of crisis, and provides him with sudden joys and unstable enthusiasms which, by contrast with his usual humor, take on the appearance of orgiastic seizures. These new enthusiasms soon begin to stabilize themselves in some dimension of life, while the rest of life continues in the shadow of bitterness and resignation. It is curious to note that almost always the dimension of life in which the new faith begins to establish itself is art. Thus it happened in the Renaissance. Why? Let us leave the explanation to another day. . . .

. . . The fact is that with respect to the things in my surroundings I need to know on what I can rely. This is the true and original meaning of knowing: my knowing on what I can depend. Thus the self, the being, of things would be an expression of the kind and extent of my reliance on them. A God who always has things at his disposal, who may or may not have need of them, or who creates them *ad hoc* when he does need them, does not require them to have a self, a being. But as for me, I am preoccupied with existing in the moment to come, in the future, and in what may happen to me then. The present does not worry me because I already exist in it. The serious thing is the future. In order to be tranquil now in regard to the minute that is coming, I need to be sure, for example, that the earth which now sustains me is something which is here. On the other hand, the earth of the time to come, of the immediate future, is not here, is not a thing, but something which I must now invent, imagine, construct for myself in an intellectual schema—in a belief about it.

Once I know on what I can rely in regard to the earth, whatever be the content of my belief, even though the most pessimistic, I will feel at peace because I will adapt myself to what I believe to be inevitable. Man adapts himself to everything, to the best and the worst. To one thing only does he not adapt himself: to being not clear in his own mind concerning what he believes about things. For example, one of the beliefs which man may hold is the conviction that everything is doubtful, that he cannot positively discover that self of things which he so badly needs. Even in that extreme case man will feel at peace, and neither more nor less than when he enjoys beliefs which are more positive. In this sense, skepticism is a form of human life like any other. And nevertheless there is in it no room for thought to come to agreement with the positive self of things, since it denies the possibility of discovering such a self. What is essential is that the skeptic be fully convinced of his skepticism, that it be in fact his own genuine form of thought; in short, that when thinking this he be in agreement with himself and have no doubt with respect to what he can depend on when he comes face to face with things. The evil thing is for the skeptic to doubt that he doubts, because this means that he fails to know not only what things are, but what his own genuine thought is. And this, this is the only thing to which man does not adapt himself, the thing that the basic reality which is life does not tolerate.

But then *problem* and *solution* take on a meaning which is completely different from that which they customarily have, a meaning which in its origin excludes the interpretation offered by the intellectual and the scientist. Something is a problem to me not because I am ignorant about it, not because I have failed to fulfil my intellectual duties with regard to it; but when I search within myself and do not know what my genuine attitude toward it is, when among my thoughts about it I do not know which is truly mine, the one which I really believe, the one which is in full accord with me. And vice versa; *solution of a problem* does not necessarily mean the discovery of a scientific law, but only being clear with myself about the thing that was a problem to me, suddenly finding, among many ideas about it, one which I recognize as my actual and authentic attitude toward it. The essential, basic problem, and in this sense the only problem, is to fit myself in with myself, to be in agreement with myself, to find myself.

At the moment of coming alive I am thrown into a set of surroundings, into a chaotic, stinging swarm of things; in them I lose myself, not because they are many and difficult and disagreeable, but because they take me out of myself, they make me someone else, they alter me, they confuse me, and I lose sight of myself. Then I do not know what it is that I really want or do not want, that I feel or do not feel, that I believe or do not believe. I lose myself *in* things because I lose *myself*. The solution, the salvation, is to find one's self, to get back into agreement with one's self, to be very clear about what one's sincere attitude is toward each and every thing. It does not matter what this attitude may be—wise or unlearned, positive or negative. What does matter is that each man should in each case think what he actually thinks. At best the humblest peasant is so clear about his actual convictions, so well coordinated within himself, so sure of what he thinks about the reduced catalogue of things which make up his environment, that he has hardly any problems. And the deep repose of his life amazes us, the dignified serenity with which he lets his fate flow on. There are very few of these countrymen left now; culture has reached them, and so has the topical, and that which we called socialization; and they are beginning to live on ideas received from the outside and to believe things they do not believe. Farewell to deep quietude, farewell to life enmeshed within itself, farewell to serenity, farewell to the genuine. As our slang puts it so acutely, take man away from his interests and you unhinge him, he is no longer in gear with himself.

For his part, the man who knows many things, the cultivated man, runs the risk of losing himself in the jungle of his own knowledge; and he ends up by not knowing what his own genuine knowledge is. We do not have to look very far; this is what happens to the modern average man. He has received so many thoughts that he does not know which of them are those he actually thinks, those he believes; and he becomes used to living on pseudo-beliefs, on commonplaces which at times are most ingenious and most intellectual, but which falsify his own existence. Hence the restlessness, the deep *otherness,* which so many modern lives carry in their secret selves. Hence the desolation, the emptiness, of so much personal destiny which struggles desperately to fill itself with one conviction or another without ever managing to convince itself. Yet salvation would be so easy! Although it would be necessary for modern man to do exactly the opposite of what he is doing. What is he doing? Well, insisting on convincing himself of that of which he is not convinced; he is feigning beliefs, and, in order to ease the pretense in which he lives, drugging himself with those attitudes which are easiest, most topical, most according to formula. Those attitudes are the radical ones.

I do not dwell on this because I want to speak about the present only as much as is strictly necessary for an understanding of the theme of this book, which is an historical theme, a vital episode in the human past.

May I sum up what I have said in sentences which are stripped and numbered so that they may fix themselves in your minds:

1. Man, whether he wants to or not, always subscribes to some genuine belief of his own concerning the things that make up his environment.

2. But at times he does not know or does not want to know which, among the many ideas that he can think, is the one that constitutes his own veritable belief.

3. The originating sense in which something becomes a problem for man has no intellectual character, much less a scientific character. On the contrary, because man finds himself and his life really lost among things and in the face of things, he has no other choice but to formulate for himself a repertory of personal opinions, beliefs, or intimate attitudes with respect to them. To this end, he mobilizes his mental faculties and constructs a plan of the points of reliability which tells him how far he can depend on each thing and on the entire body of things which make up his universe. This design for confidence, so to speak, is what we call the self, the being, of things.

4. It follows that man is not born in order to dedicate his life to intellectual pursuits, but vice versa; immersed willy-nilly in the task of living, we have to exercise our intellects, to think, to have ideas about what surrounds us; but we must have them in truth, that is, have our own. Thus life is not to be lived for the sake of intelligence, science, culture, but the reverse; intelligence, science, culture have no other reality than that which accrues to them as tools for life. To believe the former is to fall into the intellectualist folly which, several times in history, has brought about the downfall of intelligence because it leaves intelligence without justification at the very moment of deifying it and asserting that it is the only thing which does not need justification. Thus intelligence is left in the air, rootless, at the mercy of two hostile forces: on the one hand, the bigotry of culture; on the other, insolence against culture. Throughout history a period of cultural bigotry has always been followed by one of anticultural insolence. At a later date we will see how these two ways of life—to be bigoted and to be insolent—are two false and unreal fashions of existence; or to put it another way, man cannot, even if he wishes to, be in truth bigoted or in truth insolent. And when he is one or the other, he is being what he does not truly wish to be. Man makes a play actor of himself.

On the other hand, our interpretation, by which we refuse to recognize intelligence as the end of life, makes of it unavoidably a tool of life, by the use of which life is rooted irrevocably in the vital sod and granted an imperishable existence. The traditional intellectualist maintained that man *ought* to think; but he recognized that in fact man can live without using his intelligence, that his understanding is narrow and limited. Our concept denies that intelligence, intellectuality, is one of man's duties. It contents itself with showing that in order to live man has to think, whether it pleases him or not. If he thinks badly, that is, without a sense of personal and intimate veracity, he lives badly, in pure anguish, full of problems and uneasiness. If he thinks well, he is well adjusted within himself; and that is the definition of happiness.

5. Therefore our real thoughts, our strong beliefs, are an inescapable element in our destiny. I mean by this that it is not in man's power to think and believe as he pleases. One can want to think otherwise than one really thinks, one can work faithfully to change an opinion and may even be successful. But what we cannot do is to confuse our desire to think in another way with the pretense that we are already thinking as we want to. One of the giants of the Renaissance, the strange Leonardo da Vinci, coined for all time the adage: *"Chi non puo quel che vuol, quel che puo voglia"* —He who cannot do what he wants, let him want what he can do.

6. None of the foregoing even touches on the question of whether the historical evolution of human life carries with itself a meaning such that man may come to have no genuine beliefs except those that are scientific—that is, whether man's ultimate genuineness is not reason itself. I cannot now enter upon so enormous a subject. It is enough for me to remind you that in fact man has been coming through a period, beginning in 1600, during which he actually did not feel easy in himself, in his customary ways, did not feel himself on his hinges, so to speak, except when he thought in accordance with reason. That is to say, he did not genuinely believe except when he believed himself to be reasonable. Modern man, as I have said, started out by being the man of Galileo and the Cartesian man. Rationalism, having to think as a rationalist, whether he wanted to or not, was his fate. Will this type of man, this form of life which lives *on* reason, be definitive? . . .

2

Industrialization and the Human Prospect

Robert Heilbroner analyzes the chances that either capitalism or socialism have to meet our future problems. His conclusion is that neither system furnishes the solid foundations needed for long-range survival because both are committed to industrialization. In effect, given such factors as pollution and the exhaustion of fossil fuels, our future survival is dependent upon a cut in the level of industrialization.

Much of Heilbroner's pessimism is rooted in the belief that the citizens of advanced industrial societies will not tolerate the reduced standards of living likely to result from a slowing rate of industrialization. Either accustomed to or anxious to achieve the good life, all classes will resist changing beliefs and practices, but the fight should be fiercest in the lower classes and the underdeveloped nations. Neither group has had a real taste of industrialization's benefits, and both seem very much to want it. Neither will relish being told industrialization is a health hazard.

Remember too that the drive for changes in the level of industrialization often comes from members of the upper middle class. Educated and financially comfortable, they stress the quality of life (as represented by clean rivers, clean air, beautiful cities) to people who only seek food or decent housing. Often the one group fails to communicate with the other, and they must communicate if we are to avoid the dangers posed by industrialization. One obvious suggestion is that the rich demonstrate their good faith to the suspicious poor by offering to redistribute the world's wealth.

One last point: Heilbroner's potentially puzzling references to the heat of the earth follow from an earlier chapter's discussion of what he calls the "hot house effect." The essence of this controversial idea is that if we do not stop industrializing, the earth will become too hot for human habitation by about 2075.

From An Inquiry into the Human Prospect
—Robert Heilbroner

Do these dangers wholly account for the somber state of mind with which we look to the future? I think not. For the dangers do not descend, as it were, from the heavens, menacing humanity with the implacable fate that would be the consequence of the sudden arrival of a new Ice Age or the announcement of the impending extinction of the sun. On the contrary, population growth, war, environmental damage, scientific technology are all *social* problems, originating in human behavior, and capable of amelioration by the alteration of that behavior. Thus the full measure of the human prospect must go beyond an appraisal of the seriousness of these problems to an estimate of the likelihood of mounting a response adequate to them, and not least to some consideration of the price that may have to be paid to muster such a response.

The question is where to begin. I propose we start with an examination of the adaptive properties of the two great socio-economic systems that influence human behavior in our time: capitalism and socialism.

Our choice of approach requires us to begin with the seemingly simple, but actually very difficult, task of making clear what we mean by "capitalism" and "socialism." I do not think there will be much disagreement over the necessary elements that must go into our basic definition of capitalism. Capitalism is an *economic* order marked by the private ownership of the means of production vested in a minority class called "capitalists," and by a market system that determines the incomes and distributes the outputs arising from its productive activity. It is a *social* order characterized by a "bourgeois" culture, among whose manifold aspects the drive for wealth is the most important.

As we shall see, this deceptively simple definition has unexpectedly complex analytical possibilities. But it also calls our attention to the necessity of conducting our inquiry at a suitable level of abstraction. It is the behavior of general socio-economic *systems* in which we are interested, not the behavior of particular examples of those systems. This is a consideration that has special relevance for the political animus that we carry with us in an investigation of this sort. It is a common tendency, for example, for radical analysts to assume that the word "capitalism" is synonymous with the words "United States." "The United States is a capitalist society, the purest capitalist society that ever existed," according to Paul Sweezy, the foremost American Marxian critic.[1]

Serious problems arise from the choice of the United States, not as the richest or most powerful, but as the *typical* capitalist nation. The first is the assumption that certain contemporary attributes of the United States (racism,

Reprinted from *An Inquiry into the Human Prospect* by Robert L. Heilbroner. By permission of W. W. Norton & Company, Inc. Copyright © 1974 by W. W. Norton & Company, Inc.
[1]Paul M. Sweezy, "The American Ruling Class," in *The Present as History* (Monthly Review Press, 1953), p. 126.

militarism, imperialism, social neglect) are endemic to all capitalist nations—an assumption that opens the question why so many of these features are not to be found in like degree in all capitalist nations (for instance, in England or Sweden or The Netherlands), as well as why so many of them are also discoverable in noncapitalist nations such as the Soviet Union.

Second, the selection of the United States as the archetype of capitalism raises awkward issues with regard to socialism. For the logical question then is posed: if the United States is chosen to represent "typical" capitalism by virtue of its size, power, or global predominance, must we not designate the Soviet Union as the "typical" socialist nation for the same reasons?

The radical critic recoils at this logic and explains the repugnant features of Soviet Russia as the unhappy legacy of its past, a tragic instance of the socialist ideal fatally compromised by the institutional and historical setting in which it was first achieved. But if we take this argument to be valid—and surely it has serious claim to consideration—are we not forced to extend the same apologia to the United States? That is, does not the United States then appear not as a "pure" realization of capitalism, but as a deformed variant, the product of special influences of continental isolation, vast wealth, an eighteenth-century structure of government, and the terrible presence of its inheritance of slavery—the last certainly not a capitalist institution? Indeed, could we not argue that "pure" capitalism would be best exemplified by the economic, political, and social institutions of nations such as Denmark or Norway or New Zealand?

The point of this caution, which applies equally to the conservative who singles out the Soviet Union as the incarnation of socialism, is that we cannot analyze the adaptive properties of capitalism or socialism by confining our attention to the merits or shortcomings of any single example of either system. The range of social structures, traditions, institutions of government, and variations of economic forms is sufficiently great for both socio-economic orders that generalizations must be made at a very high level of abstraction—so high, in fact, that one may seriously question whether an analysis along these lines can shed much light on the adaptive capabilities of, say, "capitalist" Sweden or Japan versus "socialist" Hungary or East Germany. Why, then, pursue at all the elusive question of the capacities of these socio-economic orders? First, the words "socialist" and "capitalist" continually recur in day-to-day (or in scholarly) discussions of the future, and therefore it seems worthwhile to examine the specificity that can be given to these terms, even if it turns out to be very small. Second, I believe a socio-economic analysis is warranted because, for all the variety in national forms, both systems must cope with common problems rooted in their economic and social underpinnings. That their responses may differ widely does not lessen the importance of singling out these common problems and examining the challenges that they present to related societies in which they appear.

Can we make a plausible prognosis with regard to capitalism as an "ideal type"? Can a system whose identifying characteristics are a small propertied class, a powerfully determinative market system, and a social climate of acquis-itiveness be expected to adapt to, or survive, the challenges that are now familiar to us? Our first answer must be a disappointing one. On the basis of the bare specifications of capitalism two major historic projections for that system have been constructed, both of which have been proved inadequate. The first of these projections lies along the lines of the Marxian "scenario" for capitalist development, a scenario foretelling its gradual polarization into two bitterly inimical camps, its growing inability to maintain a smoothly func-tioning economic process, and its eventual collapse through revolution. Central to that prophecy was the expectation that the dynamics of the system would create a working class "ever increasing in numbers," and disciplined by its economic hardships into an instrument of revolutionary historic change.

Some of that prediction, it should be noted, has been validated. The dynam-ics of capitalism did bring about a steady forced migration of farmers and self-employed small proprietors into the ranks of wage and salary workers, and the pronounced instability of the system did generate recurrent severe economic hardships. What seems to have forestalled the final vindication of the Marxian prognosis, however, was a series of developments that offset the revolutionary potentialities envisaged by its author. One such offsetting tendency was the steady augmentation of per capita output, which effectively undercut the development of proletarian feelings of exploitation. A related development was the rise of "welfare," which also served to defuse the revo-lutionary animus of the lower classes. Last and perhaps most important was the gradual discovery—a discovery both in economic techniques and social viewpoint—that government intervention could be used to prevent a recur-rence of the near-catastrophic collapses suffered by the laissez-faire versions of capitalism characteristic of the late nineteenth and early twentieth centuries.

As we shall see, the Marxian conception of capitalism as a system inherently burdened with internal "contradictions" is far from being disproved by these events. But let us examine, first, the other major prognostication for the sys-tem. Unlike the radical scenario, the second prognosis has had no single major expositor. It is to be found, rather, in the generally shared expectations of such writers as Alfred Marshall and John Maynard Keynes, or indeed, of the main body of nonradical twentieth-century economists.

Their prediction, like that of the Marxists, was also based on the presumed behavior of a private-property, market-directed, profit-seeking system, but not surprisingly it emphasized elements that were overlooked in the radical critique. The basic prognosis of the conservatives was that the capitalist system would display a steady tendency to economic growth, and that the socially harm-ful results of its operations—poverty, social neglect, even unemployment—could be effectively dealt with by government intervention within the institutions of private property and the market. As a result, the conservative view pro-jected a trajectory for capitalism that promised the exact opposite of the Marxian: economic success coupled with a rising degree of social well-being.

Yet that prediction has also not fully materialized. As with the Marxian prophecy, certain of its elements were in fact attained, in particular an increase in per capita output and an expansion of social welfare policies. But the social harmony that was expected to result from these trends did not follow along. In the United States, for example, the economic transformation from the depressed conditions of the 1930s to those of the 1970s—a transformation that effectively doubled the real per capita income of the nation—failed to head off racial disturbances, an explosion of juvenile disorders among the affluent as well as among the poor, a widespread decay in city life, and a serious deterioration in national morale. And this disturbing experience has not been confined to the United States. Unprecedented economic growth in France and Germany and Japan has not prevented violent outbreaks of disaffection in those countries, especially among the young. Nor have Sweden and England and The Netherlands—all countries in which real living standards have vastly improved and in which special efforts have been made to reduce the economic and social distance between classes—been spared similar expressions of an underlying social discontent.

How can we explain this? We can only hazard a few guesses. One is that poverty is a relative and not an absolute condition, so that despite growth, a feeling of disprivilege remains to breed its disruptive consequences.[2] Another is that each generation takes for granted the standard of living that it inherits, and feels no gratitude to the past.[3] Finally, the failure of the conservative prognosis may simply tell us that whatever its economic strengths, the social ethos of capitalism is ultimately unsatisfying for the individual and unstable for the community. The stress on personal achievement, the relentless pressure for advancement, the acquisitive drive that is touted as the Good Life—all this may be, in the end, the critical weakness of capitalist society, although providing so much of the motor force of its economy.

The lesson of the past may then only confirm what both radicals and conservatives have often said but have not always really believed—that man does not live by bread alone. Affluence does not buy morale, a sense of community, even a quiescent conformity. Instead, it may only permit larger numbers of people to express their unhappiness because they are no longer crushed by the burdens of the economic struggle.

Does this confounding of two prognoses leave us with anything on which to base a general estimate of capitalism as a system capable of meeting the problems of the future? We will be able to answer that question more easily after we have looked at the other side of the coin, and applied to socialism the same "ideal-type" scrutiny that we have so far applied to capitalism.

Here we must begin by recognizing a serious difficulty. In discussing capitalism as an ideal type, we had in mind a variety of "advanced" nation-states that, however different in many aspects, shared a roughly similar social setting. No such unified image presents itself when we consider socialism. We can easily recognize socialism as an *economic system* by its replacement of private

---

[2] See Richard Easterlin, "Does Money Buy Happiness?" in *The Public Interest*, Winter 1973.
[3] See Paolo Leon, *Structural Change and Growth in Capitalism* (Johns Hopkins, 1967), p. 23f.

property and the market with some form of public ownership and planning. But socialism is much more difficult to specify as a social order than capitalism. Indeed, we can identify at least two, and possibly three, social orders that rest on public property and planned economic activity.

One of these is typified by the industrial "socialism" of present-day Russia and imposed by it on much of Eastern Europe. Characteristic of this type of socialism are two salient features: an industrial apparatus closely resembling that of capitalism, both in structure and in outlook, and a highly centralized, bureaucratic, and repressive social and political "superstructure." A second "socialist" order is represented by the societies that have arisen in the under-developed world, or that are likely to emerge there in the future. Here political centralization and social repression exist, but not the framework of industrialism characteristic of the first type.

A third type of socialism presents far more difficulties for our kind of analysis than the other two, because it exists mainly in the imagination. This is a socialist order that seeks to combine a high degree of industrialism with a considerable amount of political freedom and decentralization of control. This form of socialism has been perhaps most closely approximated in the brief tragic career of "socialism with a human face" in Czechoslovakia, and—to an extent difficult to determine—in contemporary Yugoslavia. Yet, because it exists in the minds of many socialist reformers as the kind of society toward which the West may hope to move in the foreseeable future, it exerts its influence as an historical force, even though its realization in fact is as yet very slight.

It will be necessary, therefore, to proceed with great caution in attempting to describe the dynamics of the family of socialist societies. Nonetheless we can at least start with a striking fact. It is that the two main prognoses with respect to actual *industrialized* socialism have proved as inadequate as did the corresponding prognoses with respect to industrial capitalism.

The first of these prognoses, frequently encountered only a generation ago, was that industrial socialism was "impossible," and that socialist economies would break down by virtue of their inherent irrationality. The resemblance of this prediction to that of the Marxian expectations with regard to the malfunction of capitalism is evident, and so is the failure of the prediction to come true. Despite the inability of industrial socialist economies to work with the smooth efficiency expected by their partisans—indeed, despite the frequent vindication of their critics' expectations of irrationality and malperformance—socialism did not break down. If economic discontent here and there reached threatening levels, the same can be said for the capitalist world in the 1930s. But in the one case as in the other, tendencies to growth overcame those of stagnation or crisis, so that by strictly economic criteria, industrial socialism proved as great a "success" as did capitalism.

But as the once confidently advanced prediction of a spontaneous collapse of socialist economies disappeared, there also faded the second prediction— the belief that the replacement of private ownership by public ownership, and the displacement of the market by planning, would usher in an age of high social morale as well as high economic performance.

Again in striking parallel to the disappointments that have attended the growth of economic output under capitalism, the "successful" workings of socialist economic institutions have not brought the hoped-for results. On the contrary, if we are to judge by the relentless campaigns in the Soviet or East European press against absenteeism, carelessness, bureaucratic tyranny, or "un-socialist" attitudes, or by the actual revolts of workers in Poland and Hungary against their working conditions, or by the widespread evidence of a sense of intellectual oppression in many of these nations, the social results of socialist economic growth have been very disappointing. If some of the more extreme forms of social disorder characteristic of the West, above all the anti-establishment mood and actions of youth, are much less to be observed, there seems good reason to credit this to the efficiency of the socialist police rather than to an absence of such tendencies on the part of the young. As for the growth of a communal spirit, one need only mention the continuous efforts of their citizens at all levels of society to emigrate to capitalist nations, and the equally damning refusal of their authorities to permit the free entry of ideas. Thus, at least so far as the existing type of industrial socialism is concerned, one cannot say that economic success has brought a corresponding rise in general "happiness" or social contentment, any more than in capitalist countries.

In saying this, I do not claim that industrial socialism has therefore failed: on the contrary, I imagine that in the minds of the majority of its citizens it has "succeeded," to much the same degree as capitalism. Rather, I call attention to the situation within the industrial socialist world to stress the surprising similarity of outcomes between two otherwise widely differing systems. Each has been marked with serious operational difficulties; each has overcome these difficulties with economic growth. Each has succeeded in raising its level of material consumption; each has been unable to produce a climate of social satisfaction. This leads to the suggestion that common elements of great importance affect the adaptability of both systems to the challenges of the human prospect.

In the light of our analysis, it will not come as a surprise if I identify these common elements as the forces and structures of scientific technology on which both systems depend for their momentum. This suggestion would least seem to need supporting argument to explain the ability of both systems to achieve economic growth, despite the malfunctions of the market in one case and of planning machinery in the other. All the processes of industrial production that are the material end products of scientific technology have one characteristic of overwhelming effect—their capability of enormously magnifying human productivity by endowing men with literally superhuman abilities to control the physical and chemical attributes of nature. Once an industrial system has been established—a historic process that has been as painful for capitalism as for socialism—it truly resembles a gigantic machine that asserts its productive powers despite the sabotage of businessmen or bureaucrats.

It is perhaps less self-evident that the common disappointments of capitalism and socialism in achieving "happiness" can also be traced to the presence of scientific technology and the industrial civilization that is built upon it. I have already pointed out the peculiar ills that may have their roots in the capitalist ethos; it is also clear that many of the socialist dissatisfactions arise from repressive political and social institutions. Nevertheless, if we look more deeply I think we can find a substratum of common problems in the industrial civilization of both systems.

For industrial civilization achieves its economic success by imposing common values on both its capitalist and socialist variants. There is the value of the self-evident importance of efficiency, with its tendency to subordinate the optimum human scale of things to the optimum technical scale. There is the value of the need to "tame" the environment, with its consequence of an unthinking pillage of nature. There is the value of the priority of production itself, visible in the care both systems lavish on technical virtuosity and the indifference with which both look upon the aesthetic aspects of life. All these values manifest themselves throughout bourgeois and "socialist" styles of life, both lived by the clock, organized by the factory or office, obsessed with material achievements, attuned to highly quantitative modes of thought— in a word, by styles of life that, in contrast with nonindustrial civilizations, seem dazzlingly rich in every dimension except that of the cultivation of the human person. The malaise that I believe flickers within our consciousness thus seems to afflict industrial socialist as well as capitalist societies, because it is a malady ultimately rooted in the imperatives of a common mode of production.

I am aware, of course, that it is questionable to assert that technology has "imperatives," for technology is no more than a tool in the hands of man. If the industrial apparatus has imposed its dehumanizing influence on capitalist and socialist industrial societies alike, there remains the possibility that in another milieu that apparatus could be turned to human account. It may be that extensive decentralization, workers' control, and an atmosphere of political and social freedom could better reconcile a socialist industrial system with individual contentment.

I will not hide my doubts, however, that these reforms can wholly undo the dehumanizing requirements of the industrial process. Modes of production establish constraints with which humanity must come to terms, and the constraints of the industrial mode are peculiarly demanding. The rhythms of industrial production are not those of nature, nor are its necessary uniformities easily adapted to the varieties of human nature. While surely capable of being used for more humane purposes than we have seen hitherto, while no doubt capable of greater flexibility and much greater individual control, industrial production nonetheless confronts men with machines that embody "imperatives" if they are to be used at all, and these imperatives lead easily to the organization of work, of life, even of thought, in ways that accommodate to machines rather than the much more difficult alternative.

The suggestion that a common industrial organization of life is responsible for certain parallels in the development of capitalism and industrial socialism can be no more than a speculation. More pressing are the immediate challenges that both great socio-economic orders will have to face.

We have already seen that the problem of population growth must be discussed in terms of the differential rates of growth of the developed and the underdeveloped lands. The question to be considered, then, is whether the dangerous consequences of the population problem in the underdeveloped world will, in the end, affect industrial socialist nations, such as the Soviet Union or East Germany, differently from capitalist nations, such as the United States or West Germany. These consequences, we will recall, resided in the encouragement given to the emergence of revolutionary regimes, and in the temptation—or necessity—for these regimes to use nuclear blackmail as a means of inducing the developed world to transfer its wealth on an unprecedented scale to the underdeveloped regions.

In this impending drama, it seems likely that the advanced socialist world will be the initial beneficiary of feelings of comradeship from the new revolutionary nations, and will probably be their immediate benefactor as well. Conversely, the rise of revolutionary governments presents the danger that capitalist nations will be tempted to use force to keep the spread of revolutionary socialism within bounds. The Indochina war is an all too clear example of precisely this form of counterrevolutionary activity. Thus, the population problem brings as an immediate consequence an increased risk of aggressive behavior on the part of the threatened capitalist world.

These reflections apply, however, mainly to the short run, when the setting of international existence will be much as we find it today. In the longer run the prospect alters considerably. To begin with, over a longer span we must resist the temptation to generalize from the United States' belligerence in the past decade as firmly as we must resist similar generalizations based solely on the behavior of the Soviet Union. Looking over the record of capitalist nations during the past century, one does not discover a universal tendency toward military activity. The pacific attitude of the Scandinavian bloc, or of the smaller countries of Europe, the antimilitary record of the United States until World War II (despite being punctuated by limited imperialist adventures), the recent disappearance of traditional warlike attitudes from the cockpit of capitalist conflict in Europe make one cautious in declaring that capitalism is ''inherently'' a warprone system. Moreover, in examining the motives that provoked the major capitalist wars during the past century, one discovers, in addition to the specifically capitalist drives for economic expansion, powerful considerations of national prestige, strategic geographic advantage, or simply ideological enmity—all motives that have driven nations long before the advent of capitalism as a system, and that continue to manifest themselves visibly in the behavior of socialist nation-states.

More important yet, there is reason to believe that the pressures of the population explosion will come to bear increasingly on all industrial nations alike, socialist as well as capitalist. The initial congruence of political interests between young revolutionary regimes and the older socialist ones must contend with a growing conflict over their economic aims. Given the closing vise of resource and energy supplies, and the gradually approaching barriers to growth imposed by the environment, it is clear that control over the planet's resources and claims on its output will be increasingly vital for all industrial systems. In the inescapable competition for dwindling resources and for the right to maintain, if not increase, the level of national output, I can see no reason why the imperatives of self-preservation should not operate as strongly among the socialist industrial nations as among capitalist ones. In both cases, wars of "preemptive seizure" would be a possible strategy. Barring such undertakings, I do not see why demands for a more equitable sharing of the world's output should not be as peremptorily directed by the poor countries against their rich socialist brothers as against their rich capitalist enemies.

The long-run problem then will be that of coping with a "two-level" world. It cannot be foreseen whether or not that problem can be resolved without recourse to war, initiated by the poor countries or by the rich ones. Much hinges on the degree of reason, compassion, or flexibility with which one endows the imaginary capitalist and socialist nations or ruling classes of the future, a matter in which our political presuppositions strongly affect our judgments.

This estimate need not be wholly subjective, however. For it becomes ever more apparent that the central issue of the future will lodge in the capability of dealing with the environment. Let us therefore inquire into relative abilities of capitalist and socialist systems in coping with that challenge.

To start with the capitalist side, there is no doubt that the threatened depletion of resources, and the drastic ecological dangers that loom at a somewhat greater distance, directly threaten a main characteristic of capitalism—its strong tendency to expand output. This tendency serves three main functions for the system. It expresses the drives and social values of its dominant class. It provides the means by which a market-coordinated system can avoid the dangers of a "general glut." And finally, it accommodates the striving of its constituents for larger rewards. Thus expansion has always been considered as inseparable from capitalism, whether as a necessary condition for its operation, as Marxian critics would claim, or as a justification for the institutions of private property and the market, as the conservative protagonists of capitalism have maintained. Conversely, a "stationary," nonexpanding capitalism has always been considered either as a prelude to its collapse or as a betrayal of its historic purpose.

Is a stationary capitalism therefore unworkable? Is it a contradiction in terms? The answers depend on various sociological assumptions into which, I need hardly add, our subjective evaluations can hardly help entering. To begin with the first of the functions served by expansion, I do not think that we can make a dogmatic assertion that the social values and drives of its dominant class could not be accommodated within a largely static framework. Here we have the evidence of the extremely defensive economic posture characteristic of French or English capitalists just before and after World War II, respectively, and of the curiously bureaucratic complexion of Japanese capitalism, run by an extraordinarily "passive" and conformist managerial elite.

The expansive drive of capitalism springs, however, not only from the "animal spirits" of its dominant class, but also from the restless self-aggrandizing pressures of its corporations. Here as well, however, a solution is imaginable. Much of the aggressive drive of firms arises from their continuous striving for a larger share of the market. A deceleration in growth, enforced by government decree, could include provisions for leaving market shares relatively undisturbed. Such a solution would be no more than a full-fledged transformation of "private" capitalism into planned "state" capitalism—a transformation already partially realized in Japanese capitalism.

It is perhaps less simple for a stationary capitalism to avoid a severe economic crisis. As economists from Adam Smith and Marx through Keynes have pointed out, a "stationary" capitalism is subject to a falling rate of profit as the investment opportunities of the system are used up. Hence, in the absence of an expansionary frontier, the investment drive slows down, and a deflationary spiral of incomes and employment begins.

Yet I do not think it can be maintained that a stationary capitalism is therefore "impossible." Expansion serves an indispensable purpose in maintaining a socially acceptable level of employment and demand in laissez-faire capitalism. It is by no means so certain that expansion is indispensable in a managed state capitalism. There seems no inherent reason why the deflationary tendencies of such a system could not be offset by a variety of measures. A nigh level of public demand could be provided by government investment in housing, education, and the like, or by transfer payments within the nation, or by the distribution of "surplus" goods, if any existed, to the underdeveloped nations. All these measures are already in use in various parts of the capitalist world. Thus a stationary state would not seem to present insuperable problems for a managed capitalism, in so far as those problems concerned the maintenance of employment or aggregate purchasing power.

It may be argued that I have leaned over much too far in projecting such an optimistic prognosis for capitalist adaptation to a nonexpansionary situation. I have done so deliberately, however, because there remains an aspect of the transition to a stationary system that strikes me as far more taxing with respect to capitalist powers of accommodation. This is the problem of finding a means of managing the social tensions in a capitalist system in which growth had ceased or was very greatly reduced.

Central to capitalism, as we have already noted, is a bourgeois ethos of economic advancement. Previously we have suggested that this ethos may be partly responsible for the failure of capitalist expansion to produce high social morale. But the pervasive values of competitive striving and expected personal advancement also present another problem—how to satisfy the demands of the lower and middle classes for higher living standards, while protecting the privileges of the upper groups. The solution has been to increase the output of the economy, thereby providing absolute increases in income to all classes, while leaving the share of the upper groups relatively undisturbed.

The prospect of a stationary economy directly challenges this traditional solution. For under a stationary (or even a slow-growing) capitalism, continued efforts of the lower and middle classes to improve their positions can be met only by diminishing the absolute incomes of the upper echelons of society. A stationary capitalism is thus forced to confront the explosive issue of income distribution in a way that an expanding capitalism is spared.

In this connection we must bear in mind that we are not merely talking about the dismantling of a few vast fortunes or the curtailment of a handful of swollen incomes, although that might be difficult enough. What is at stake are the incomes of the upper middle classes, which include something like the upper fourth or fifth of the nation. This upper stratum is by no means composed of millionaires alone, but also includes teachers, shopkeepers, professional and technical workers: in the United States in the early 1970s a family entered the upper fifth with an income of about $15,000. This stratum of society enjoys about 40 percent of the nation's total income. If the pressure from below were to eliminate its advantages over the "average" family, the upper stratum would have to yield a large fraction of its income, from perhaps a third at its lower levels to well over half at its upper levels. This gives one some appreciation of the magnitude of the political strain to which a massive pressure for income redistribution would give rise.

One saving possibility must, however, be considered. Growth might be permitted to continue for an indefinite period, provided that it were confined to outputs that consumed few resources and generated little heat. An expansion in the services of government, in the administration of justice, in the provision of better health and education, arts and entertainment, would not only rescue the system from a fatal encounter with the environment, but might produce enough "growth" to ease the income distribution problem.

If capitalism is to survive for a considerable period this is the road along which it will assuredly have to travel. Perhaps in some cases it may successfully manage such a shift in the composition of its output. But we must not lose sight of the environment in which this shift must be made. A transition to a more equitable distribution of income within the capitalist nations will have to take place at a time when the larger struggle will focus on the distribution of resources among nations. If this struggle is gradually decided in favor of the underdeveloped world, whether out of humanitarian motives, the pressure of nuclear blackmail, or simply by the increased political cohesion and bargaining power of the poorer regions, the citizenries of the wealthy nations will find themselves in a long period of declining physical output per capita. This is apt to be the case, even without an international redistribution, if the many constraints of the environment exert their expected effect, beginning perhaps as soon as the coming decade.

Thus the difficulty of managing a socially acceptable distribution of income in the capitalist nations is that it will have to contend with the prospect of a decline in the per capita output of material goods. The problem is therefore not merely a question of calling a halt to the increasing production of cars, dishwashers, or homes, while encouraging the output of doctors' services or theatrical activities, but of distributing a shrinking production of cars, appliances, homes. The experience of a limited oil shortage is bringing home to many Americans the hitherto unimaginable possibility that their way of life might not be indefinitely sustainable. If that shortage is extended over the next generation or two to many other kinds of material outputs, a climate of extreme "goods-hunger" seems likely to result. In such a climate, a large-scale reorganization of social shares would have to take place in the worst possible atmosphere, as each person sought to protect his place in a contracting economic world.

I am inclined to the belief, therefore, that the problem of income distribution would pose extreme difficulties for capitalism of a political as well as an economic kind. The struggle for relative position would not only pit one class against another, but also each against all, as lower and middle groups engaged in a free-for-all for higher incomes. This would bring enormous inflationary pressures of the kind that capitalism is already beginning to experience, and would require the imposition of much stronger control measures than any that capitalism has yet succeeded in introducing—indeed, than any that capitalist governments have yet imagined.

In bluntest terms, the question is whether the Hobbesian struggle that is likely to arise in such a strait-jacketed economic society would not impose intolerable strains on the representative democratic political apparatus that has been historically associated with capitalist societies.

It is, of course, foolish to suggest that capitalism is the *sine qua non* of democracy, or to claim that democracy, with its commitment to political equality, does not conflict in many ways with the inequalities built into capitalism. Nonetheless, it is the plain historic fact that bourgeois societies have so far succeeded to a greater degree than any other social order in establishing parliamentary procedures, independent judiciaries, and constitutionally limited executives, all essential elements in a democratic political system. The question to be faced, then, is whether these political institutions can be expected to cope with the social and economic transformations whose extensive character we have indicated.

Here prediction along the lines of an "ideal type" cannot bring us very far. It is possible that some capitalist nations, gifted with unusual political leadership and a responsive public, may make the necessary structural changes without surrendering their democratic achievements. At best, our inquiry establishes the approach of certain kinds of challenges, but cannot pretend to judge how individual nations may meet these challenges. For the majority of capitalist nations, however, I do not see how we can avoid the conclusion that the required transformation will be likely to exceed the capabilities of representative democracy. The disappointing failure of capitalist societies to create atmospheres of social harmony, even in expansive settings, does not bode well for their ability to foster far-reaching reorganizations of their economic structures and painful diminutions of privilege for their more prosperous citizens. The likelihood that there are obdurate limits to the reformist reach of democratic institutions within the class-bound body of capitalist society leads us to expect that the governments of these societies, faced with extreme internal strife or with potentially disastrous social polarization, would resort to severe authoritarian measures. To the extent that these measures would necessarily include the national management of corporations and the non-market determination of income levels, the direction of change might be described as a movement toward "socialism," although in a manner very different from that of the classic revolutionary scenario and with implications that will distress the partisans of socialism as a democratic form of government.

These reflections raise a question that may have been impatiently waiting in the reader's mind. After all, the ecological threat is still some distance into the future. Hence long-term speculations about the feasibility of a stationary capitalism may seem hopelessly academic in the face of nearer-term risks of war, or of the disruption of capitalism from other causes, such as its inability to generate a high enough social discipline and morale. That may indeed be the case. But if capitalism collapses, what next?

As we have already seen, the successor may well be an authoritarian regime that is not easy to analyze according to our socio-economic ideal types. But let us suppose that the collapse of capitalism would usher in socialism—that is, a society built on the public ownership of goods and the replacement of the market by widespread planning. What can we say about the abilities of such a system to cope with the demands of the environmental challenge?

Here the possibilities of applying a socio-economic analysis seem much simpler. It appears logical to conclude that socialism, with its direct commitment to a planned economy and with its freedom from the ideological blockages of private property, could manage the adaptation of an industrial society to a stationary equilibrium much more readily than capitalism.

I believe this is true in the short run. Over a longer period, however, grave problems would emerge. A socialist society would also have to achieve a politically acceptable distribution of its income among its people. The task of arriving at such a division of income would be much more difficult in a period of shrinking physical output than in an economy where all levels expected their real incomes to rise. Hence a democratically governed socialism would very likely face the same Hobbesian struggle for goods as a democratically governed capitalism; and whereas an authoritarian socialism could certainly enforce some kind of solution, it seems likely that this would entail a degree of coercion that would make "socialism" virtually indistinguishable from an authoritarian "capitalism."

The similarity of the problems of and responses to the stationary state for both socialism and capitalism brings us finally to confront a question that has persisted throughout these pages. This is the relation of the two systems to the industrial civilization that has again and again emerged as a root cause for the dangers of the human prospect and as the common basis for the economic successes (and perhaps the social failures) of capitalism and industrial socialism. Is it now possible to maintain, on the grounds of our socio-economic analysis, that socialism will have a significant advantage over capitalism in asserting the necessary controls over the runaway forces of science and technology?

Once more I believe we must differentiate between the short run and long run capacities for response. In the short run, as in the case of international tensions and in the initial stages of coping with the pressures of a stationary economy, I would think that industrial socialism would possess important advantages. The control over the direction of science, over its rate of incorporation in technology, and over the pace of industrial production as a whole should be much more easily achieved in a society that does not have to deal with the profit drive than in one that does. To be sure, socialist systems have their own handicaps in the bureaucratic inertias of planning. But the absence of a necessity to heed the pull of commercial considerations should nonetheless confer an additional degree of social flexibility to the socialist control over the industrial process.

In the long run, however, I believe that once more there is a convergence of problems. For what portends, in that longer run, is a challenge of equal magnitude for industrial socialism and for capitalism—the challenge of drastically curtailing, perhaps even dismantling, the mode of production that has been the most cherished achievement of both systems. Moreover that mode of production must be abandoned in a mere flash of time, as historic sequences are measured. Given the present pace of industrial growth—which will take prodigies of science to maintain in the face of dwindling resources—the edge of the heat emission danger zone may be reached as quickly as three or four generations. Failing the achievement of the needed scientific breakthroughs, we will be spared the heat barrier simply because we will be unable to produce the energy or to process the resources to maintain our present growth rates. Thus, *whether we are unable to sustain growth or unable to tolerate it,* there can be no doubt that a radically different future beckons. In either eventuality, it seems beyond dispute that the present orientation of society must change. In place of the long-established encouragement of industrial production must come its careful restriction and long-term diminution within society. In place of prodigalities of consumption must come new frugal attitudes. In these and other ways, the ''post-industrial'' society of the future is apt to be as different from present-day society as the latter was from its pre-industrial precursor.

Can we expect an industrial socialist society, be it characterized by authoritarian or by democratic government, to weather such a transformation more easily than a capitalist society, ''private'' or state? I doubt it. Both socioeconomic systems are committed to a civilization whose most striking aspect is its productive virtuosity.

3

Control by Expertise

Focusing on social structure, Daniel Bell sees four major changes in our future. First, "science and cognitive values" will gain increased importance as "institutional necessities." Second, as decisions become more technical, scientists and economists will gain political power; decision makers will need their expertise. Third, increasing bureaucratization will create "a set of strains for the traditional definitions of intellectual pursuits and values." Scholars will find it difficult to maintain their stance of intellectual freedom if they are harnessed to the goals of large organizations. Fourth, giving great power to a "technical intelligentsia" raises "crucial questions about the relation of the technical to the literary intellectual." Will the literary intellectual pull society in one direction while the technical expert pulls it in another? Bell says yes. He predicts a cultural stress on self-realization, an organizational stress on efficiency, and conflict when people try to live by these two sets of incompatible "ideals."

Bell's analysis of the future stems from the past and present. Technology, industrialization, rationality, bureaucracy, and specialization are already the values that dominate our society. Tomorrow they will be even more important; they will completely dominate advanced industrial societies. Bell is not certain what the effects of that domination will be, but he appears optimistic. He believes politicians will successfully mediate the inevitable conflicts between advocates of the counterculture and advocates of post-industrial society.

I think Bell is wrong. The future he envisions is probable, but, like a straight line, it follows yesterday and today. I see no hope for tomorrow in mere extensions of the technological, institutionalized course we are on at present, regardless of how efficient those extensions may render us.

From The Coming of Post-Industrial Society
—Daniel Bell

THE DIMENSIONS OF POST-INDUSTRIAL SOCIETY

Analytically, society can be divided into three parts: the social structure, the polity, and the culture. The social structure comprises the economy, technology, and the occupational system. The polity regulates the distribution of power and adjudicates the conflicting claims and demands of individuals and groups. The culture is the realm of expressive symbolism and meanings. It is useful to divide society in this way because each aspect is ruled by a different axial principle. In modern Western society the axial principle of the social structure is *economizing*—a way of allocating resources according to principles of least cost, substitutability, optimization, maximization, and the like. The axial principle of the modern polity is *participation,* sometimes mobilized or controlled, sometimes demanded from below. The axial principle of the culture is the desire for the *fulfillment and enhancement of the self.* In the past, these three areas were linked by a common value system (and in bourgeois society through a common character structure). But in our times there has been an increasing disjunction of the three and . . . this will widen.

The concept of the post-industrial society deals primarily with changes *in the social structure,* the way in which the economy is being transformed and the occupational system reworked, and with the new relations between theory and empiricism, particularly science and technology. These changes can be charted, . . . But I do not claim that these changes in social structure *determine* corresponding changes in the polity or the culture. Rather, the changes in social structure pose *questions* for the rest of society in three ways. First, the social structure—especially the social structure—is a structure of roles, designed to coordinate the actions of individuals to achieve specific ends. Roles segment individuals by defining limited modes of behavior appropriate to a particular position, but individuals do not always willingly accept the requirements of a role. One aspect of the post-industrial society, for example, is the increasing bureaucratization of science and the increasing specialization of intellectual work into minute parts. Yet it is not clear that individuals entering science will accept this segmentation, as did the individuals who entered the factory system a hundred and fifty years ago.

Second, changes in social structure pose "management" problems for the political system. In a society which becomes increasingly conscious of its fate, and seeks to control its own fortunes, the political order necessarily becomes paramount. Since the post-industrial society increases the importance of the technical component of knowledge, it forces the hierophants of the new society—the scientists, engineers, and technocrats—either to compete with politicians or become their allies. The relationship between the social structure and the political order thus becomes one of the chief problems of power

From the Introduction of *The Coming of Post-Industrial Society: A Venture in Social Forecasting* by Daniel Bell, © 1973 by Daniel Bell, Basic Books, Inc., Publishers, New York, pp. 12–32.

in a post-industrial society. And, third, the new modes of life, which depend strongly on the primacy of cognitive and theoretical knowledge, inevitably challenge the tendencies of the culture, which strives for the enhancement of the self and turns increasingly antinomian and anti-institutional.

. . . I am concerned chiefly with the social structural and political consequences of the post-industrial society. In a later work I shall deal with its relation to culture. But the heart of the endeavor is to trace the societal changes primarily within the social structure.

"Too large a generalization," Alfred North Whitehead wrote, "leads to mere barrenness. It is the large generalization, limited by a happy particularity, which is the fruitful conception."[1] It is easy—and particularly so today—to set forth an extravagant theory which, in its historical sweep, makes a striking claim to originality. But when tested eventually by reality, it turns into a caricature—viz. James Burnham's theory of the managerial revolution thirty years ago, or C. Wright Mills's conception of the power elite, or W. W. Rostow's stages of economic growth. I have tried to resist that impulse. Instead, I am dealing here with *tendencies,* and have sought to explore the meaning and consequences of those tendencies if the changes in social structure that I describe were to work themselves to their logical limits. But there is no guarantee that they will. Social tensions and social conflicts may modify a society considerably; wars and recriminations can destroy it; the tendencies may provoke a set of reactions that inhibit change. Thus I am writing what Hans Vahinger called an "as if," a fiction, a logical construction of what *could* be, against which the future social reality can be compared in order to see what intervened to change society in the direction it did take.

The concept of the post-industrial society is a large generalization. Its meaning can be more easily understood if one specifies five dimensions, or components, of the term:

1. Economic sector: the change from a goods-producing to a service economy;
2. Occupational distribution: the pre-eminence of the professional and technical class;
3. Axial principle: the centrality of theoretical knowledge as the source of innovation and of policy formulation for the society;
4. Future orientation: the control of technology and technological assessment;
5. Decision-making: the creation of a new "intellectual technology."

Creation of a service economy. About thirty years ago, Colin Clark, in his *Conditions of Economic Progress,* analytically divided the economy into three sectors—primary, secondary, and tertiary—the primary being principally agriculture; the secondary, manufacturing or industrial; and the tertiary, services. Any economy is a mixture in different proportions of each. But Clark

---

[1] Alfred North Whitehead, *Science and the Modern World* (New York, 1960; original edition, 1925), p. 46.

argued that, as nations became industrialized, there was an inevitable trajectory whereby, because of sectoral differences in productivity, a larger proportion of the labor force would pass into manufacturing, and as national incomes rose, there would be a greater demand for services and a corresponding shift in that slope.

By this criterion, the first and simplest characteristic of a post-industrial society is that the majority of the labor force is no longer engaged in agriculture or manufacturing but in services, which are defined, residually, as trade, finance, transport, health, recreation, research, education, and government.

Today, the overwhelming number of countries in the world (see Tables 1 and 2) are still dependent on the primary sector: agriculture, mining, fishing, forestry. These economies are based entirely on natural resources. Their productivity is low, and they are subject to wide swings of income because of the fluctuations of raw material and primary-product prices. In Africa and Asia, agrarian economies account for more than 70 percent of the labor force. In western and northern Europe, Japan, and the Soviet Union, the major portion of the labor force is engaged in industry or the manufacture of goods. The United States today is the only nation in the world in which the service sector accounts for more than half the total employment and more than half the Gross National Product. It is the first service economy, the first nation, in which the major portion of the population is engaged in neither agrarian nor industrial pursuits. Today about 60 percent of the United States labor force is engaged in services; by 1980, the figure will have risen to 70 percent.

The term "services," if used generically, risks being deceptive about the actual trends in the society. Many agrarian societies such as India have a high proportion of persons engaged in services, but of a personal sort (e.g. household servants) because labor is cheap and usually underemployed. In an industrial society different services tend to increase because of the need for auxiliary help for production, e.g. transportation and distribution. But in a post-industrial society the emphasis is on a different kind of service. If we group services as personal (retail stores, laundries, garages, beauty shops); business (banking and finance, real estate, insurance); transportation, communication and utilities; and health, education, research, and government; then it is the growth of the last category which is decisive for post-industrial society. And this is the category that represents the expansion of a new intelligentsia—in the universities, research organizations, professions, and government.

The pre-eminence of the professional and technical class. The second way of defining a post-industrial society is through the change in occupational distributions; i.e. not only *where* people work, but the *kind* of work they do. In large measure, occupation is the most important determinant of class and stratification in the society.

The onset of industrialization created a new phenomenon, the semi-skilled worker, who could be trained within a few weeks to do the simple routine operations required in machine work. Within industrial societies, the semi-skilled worker has been the single largest category in the labor force. The expansion of the service economy, with its emphasis on office work, education, and government, has naturally brought about a shift to white-collar occupations. In the United States, by 1956, the number of white-collar workers, for the first time in the history of industrial civilization, outnumbered the blue-collar workers in the occupational structure. Since then the ratio has

TABLE 1

*The World's Labor Force by Broad Economic Sector,
and by Continent and Region, 1960**

REGION	TOTAL LABOR FORCE (MILLIONS)	PERCENTAGE DISTRIBUTION BY SECTOR		
		AGRICULTURE	INDUSTRY	SERVICES
World	1,296	58	19	23
Africa	112	77	9	14
Western Africa	40	80	8	13
Eastern Africa	30	83	7	10
Middle Africa	14	86	6	8
Northern Africa	22	71	10	19
Southern Africa[a]	6	37	29	34
Northern America[a]	77	8	39	53
Latin America	71	48	20	32
Middle America (mainland)	15	56	18	26
Caribbean	8	53	18	29
Tropical South America	37	52	17	31
Temperate South America[a]	12	25	33	42
Asia	728	71	12	17
East Asia (mainland)	319	75	10	15
Japan[a]	44	33	28	39
Other East Asia	15	62	12	26
Middle South Asia	239	71	14	15
South-East Asia	90	75	8	17
South-West Asia	20	69	14	17
Europe[a]	191	28	38	34
Western Europe[a]	60	14	45	41
Northern Europe[a]	34	10	45	45
Eastern Europe[a]	49	45	31	24
Southern Europe[a]	47	41	32	27
Oceania[b]	6	23	34	43
Australia and New Zealand	5	12	40	49
Melanesia	1	85	5	10
USSR[a]	111	45	28	27

SOURCE: *International Labour Review* (January–February, 1967); ILO estimates based on national censuses and sample surveys.

Note: Owing to independent rounding, the sum of the parts may not add up to group totals.

[a]More developed regions.

[b]Excluding Polynesia and Micronesia.

*An ILO survey for 1970 is due to be published later in the decade. In 1969, however, the OECD in Paris published a breakdown of the labor force in West Europe, by sectors, which provides for the comparisons in Table 2.

TABLE 2

Labor Force and GNP in Western Europe and United States by Sectors, 1969

COUNTRY	AGRICULTURE PERCENT- AGE OF GNP	AGRICULTURE PERCENT- AGE OF LABOR	INDUSTRY PERCENT- AGE OF GNP	INDUSTRY PERCENT- AGE OF LABOR	SERVICES PERCENT- AGE OF GNP	SERVICES PERCENT- AGE OF LABOR
West Germany	4.1	10.6	49.7	48.0	46.2	41.4
France	7.4	16.6	47.3	40.6	45.3	42.8
Britain	3.3	3.1	45.7	47.2	51.0	49.7
Sweden	5.9	10.1	45.2	41.1	48.9	48.8
Netherlands	7.2	8.3	41.2	41.9	51.6	49.8
Italy	12.4	24.1	40.5	41.1	51.7	45.1
United States	3.0	5.2	36.6	33.7	60.4	61.1

SOURCE: Organisation for Economic Co-operation and Development (Paris, 1969).

been widening steadily; by 1970 the white-collar workers outnumbered the blue-collar by more than five to four.

But the most startling change has been the growth of professional and technical employment—jobs that usually require some college education—at a rate twice that of the average. In 1940 there were 3.9 million such persons in the society; by 1964 the number had risen to 8.6 million; and it is estimated that by 1975 there will be 13.2 million professional and technical persons, making it the second-largest of the eight occupational divisions in the country, exceeded only by the semi-skilled workers (see Table 3). One further statistical breakdown will round out the picture—the role of the scientists and engineers, who form the key group in the post-industrial society. While the growth rate of the professional and technical class as a whole has been twice that of the average labor force, the growth rate of the scientists and engineers has been triple that of the working population. By 1975 the United States may have about 550,000 scientists (natural and social scientists), as against 275,000 in 1960, and almost a million and a half engineers, compared to 800,000 in 1960. Table 4[2] gives the breakdown of the professional and technical occupations— the heart of the post-industrial society.

The primacy of theoretical knowledge.   In identifying a new and emerging social system, it is not only in the extrapolated social trends, such as the creation of a service economy or the expansion of the professional and technical class, that one seeks to understand fundamental social change. Rather, it is through some specifically defining characteristic of a social system, which becomes the axial principle, that one establishes a conceptual schema. Industrial society is the coordination of machines and men for the production of

---

[2]In Table 3 the projected figure for the number of professional and technical persons in 1975 is given as 13.2 million and in Table 4 as 12.9 million. The discrepancies are due in part to the fact that the figure in Table 4 was calculated five years later, and also because different assumptions about the unemployment rate were made. I have let the figures stand to indicate the range.

TABLE 3

Employment by Major Occupation Group, 1964, and Projected Requirements, 1975[a]

MAJOR OCCUPATION GROUP	1964		1975		PERCENTAGE CHANGE, 1964–1975
	NUMBER (IN MILLIONS)	PERCENT	NUMBER (IN MILLIONS)	PERCENT	
Total employment	70.4	100.0	88.7	100.0	26
White-collar workers	31.1	44.2	42.8	48.3	38
Professional, technical, and kindred workers	8.6	12.2	13.2	14.9	54
Managers, officials, and proprietors, except farm	7.5	10.6	9.2	10.4	'23
Clerical and kindred workers	10.7	15.2	14.6	16.5	37
Sales workers	4.5	6.3	5.8	6.5	30
Blue-collar workers	25.5	36.3	29.9	33.7	17
Craftsmen, foremen, and kindred workers	9.0	12.8	11.4	12.8	27
Operatives and kindred workers	12.9	18.4	14.8	16.7	15
Laborers, except farm and mine	3.6	5.2	3.7	4.2	b
Service workers	9.3	13.2	12.5	14.1	35
Farmers and farm managers, laborers, and foremen	4.4	6.3	3.5	3.9	−21

SOURCE: *Technology and the American Economy,* Report of the National Commission on Technology, Automation, and Economic Progress, vol. 1 (Washington, D.C., 1966), p. 30; derived from Bureau of Labor Statistics, *America's Industrial and Occupational Manpower Requirements, 1964–1975.*
Note: Because of rounding, sums of individual items may not equal totals.
[a]Projections assume a national unemployment rate of 3 percent in 1975. The choice of 3 percent unemployment as a basis for these projections does not indicate an endorsement or even a willingness to accept that level of unemployment.
[b]Less than 3 percent.

TABLE 4

*The Make-up of Professional and Technical Occupations,
1960 and 1975 (in thousands)*

	1960	1975
Total labor force	66,680	88,660
Total professional and technical	7,475	12,925
Scientific and engineering	1,092	1,994
Engineers	810	1,450
Natural scientists	236	465
Chemists	91	175
Agricultural scientists	30	53
Geologists and geophysicists	18	29
Mathematicians	21	51
Physicists	24	58
Others	22	35
Social scientists	46	79
Economists	17	31
Statisticians and actuaries	23	36
Others	6	12
Technicians (Except medical and dental)	730	1,418
Medical and health	1,321	2,240
Physicians and surgeons	221	374
Nurses, professional	496	860
Dentists	87	125
Pharmacists	114	126
Psychologists	17	40
Technicians (Medical and dental)	141	393
Others	245	322
Teachers	1,945	3,063
Elementary	978	1,233
Secondary	603	1,160
College	206	465
Others	158	275
General	2,386	4,210
Accountants	429	660
Clergymen	200	240
Editors and reporters	100	128
Lawyers and judges	225	320
Arts and entertainment	470	774
Architects	30	45
Librarians	80	130
Social workers	105	218
Others (Airline pilots, photographers, personnel relations, etc.)	747	1,695

SOURCE: BLS Bulletin no. 1606, "Tomorrow's Manpower Needs," vol. IV (February 1969), Appendix E, pp. 28–29.

goods. Post-industrial society is organized around knowledge, for the purpose of social control and the directing of innovation and change; and this in turn gives rise to new social relationships and new structures which have to be managed politically.

Now, knowledge has of course been necessary in the functioning of any society. What is distinctive about the post-industrial society is the change in the character of knowledge itself. What has become decisive for the organization of decisions and the direction of change is the centrality of *theoretical* knowledge—the primacy of theory over empiricism and the codification of knowledge into abstract systems of symbols that, as in any axiomatic system, can be used to illuminate many different and varied areas of experience.

Every modern society now lives by innovation and the social control of change, and tries to anticipate the future in order to plan ahead. This commitment to social control introduces the need for planning and forecasting into society. It is the altered awareness of the nature of innovation that makes theoretical knowledge so crucial.

One can see this, first, in the changed relationship between science and technology. Almost all the major industries we still have—steel, electric power, telegraph, telephone, automobiles, aviation—were nineteenth-century industries (although steel begins in the eighteenth century and aviation in the twentieth), in that they were mainly the creation of inventors, inspired and talented tinkerers who were indifferent to science and the fundamental laws underlying their investigations. Kelly and Bessemer, who (independently) created the oxidation process that makes possible the steel converter and the mass production of steel, were unaware of their contemporary, Henry Clifton Sorby, whose work in metallurgy disclosed the true microstructure of steel. Alexander Graham Bell, inventor of the telephone, was in Clerk Maxwell's opinion a mere elocutionist who "to gain his private ends [money] has become an electrician." Edison's work on "etheric sparks," which led to the development of the electric light and generated a vast new revolution in technology, was undertaken outside the theoretical research in electromagnetism and even in hostility to it. But the further development of electrodynamics, particularly in the replacement of steam engines, could only come from engineers with formal training in mathematical physics. Edison, as one biographer has written, lacked "the power of abstraction."[3]

What might be called the first "modern" industry, because of its intricate linking of science and technology, is chemistry, since one must have a theoretical knowledge of the macromolecules one is manipulating in order to do chemical synthesis—the recombination and transformation of compounds.[4]

---

[3]Matthew Josephson, *Edison* (New York, 1959), p. 361.
[4]Aviation is an interesting transition. The first inventors were tinkerers, but the field could develop only through the use of scientific principles. Langley (1891) and Zahm (1902–1903) started the new science of aerodynamics by studying the behavior of air currents over different types of airfoils. At the same time, in 1900, the Wright brothers began tinkering with gliders, and in 1903 put a gasoline-powered engine into an airplane. But further work was possible only through the development, after 1908, of experiments (such as models in wind tunnels) and mathematical calculations (such as airflows over different angles of wings) based on physical laws.

In 1909 Walter Nerst and Fritz Haber converted nitrogen and hydrogen to produce synthetic ammonia. Working from theoretical principles first predicated by the Frenchman Henri Le Chatelier in 1888, the two German chemists provided a spectacular confirmation of Kant's dictum that there is nothing so practical as a good theory.[5] The irony, however, lies in the use of the result.

War is a technological forcing house, but modern war has yoked science to technology in a radically new way. Before World War I, every General Staff calculated that Germany would either win a quick, smashing victory or, if France could hold, the war would end quickly in a German defeat (either in the field or at the negotiating table). The reasoning was based on the simple fact that Chile was Germany's (and the world's) major source of the natural nitrates needed for fertilizer and for explosives and, in wartime, Germany's access to Chile would be cut off by the British Navy. In 1913 Germany used about 225,000 tons of nitrogen, half of which was imported. Stocks began to fall, but the Haber-Bosch process for the manufacture of synthetic ammonia developed so rapidly that by 1917 it accounted for 45 percent of Germany's production of nitrogen compounds. By the armistice Germany was almost self-sufficient in nitrogen,[6] and because she was able to hold out, the war became a protracted struggle of static trench warfare and slaughter.

In the latter sense, World War I was the very last of the "old" wars of human civilization. But with the new role of science it was also the first of the "new" wars. The eventual symbolic fusion of science and war was, of course, in World War II the atom bomb. It was a demonstration, as Gerald Holton has written, "that a chain of operations, starting in a scientific laboratory, can result in an event of the scale and suddenness of a mythological occurrence." Since the end of World War II the extraordinary development of scientific technology has led to hydrogen bombs, distant-early-warning networks coordinated in real time through computer systems, intercontinental ballistics missiles, and, in Vietnam, the beginning of an "automated" battlefield through the use of large-scale electronic sensing devices and computer-controlled retaliatory strikes. War, too, has now come under the "terrible" dominion of science, and the shape of war, like all other human activity, has been drastically changed.

In a less direct but equally important way, the changing relation between theory and empiricism is reflected in the formulation of government policy, particularly in the management of the economy. During the Great Depression of the 1930s, almost every government floundered about and had no notion

---

[5]See Eduard Farber, "Man Makes His Materials," in Kransberg and Pursell, eds. *Technology and Western Civilization,* vol. 2 (New York, 1967).

[6]See L. F. Haber, *The Chemical Industry, 1900–1930* (Oxford, 1971), chap. 7, pp. 198–203. As Haber writes:

"The Haber process . . . was still largely an unknown factor when the Great War broke out. The synthesis of ammonia . . . represents one of the most important advances in industrial chemistry. . . . The process, discovered by Fritz Haber and developed industrially by Carl Bosch, was the first application of high-pressure synthesis; the technology of ammonia production, appropriately modified, was used later in the synthesis of methanol and the hydrogenation of coal to petroleum. Its influence extends to present-day techniques of oil refining and use of cracker gases from refining operations for further synthesis." Ibid., p. 90.

of what to do with any confidence. In Germany in 1930, the socialist economists who determined government policy insisted that the depression would have to "run its course," meaning that the "overproduction" which caused it, by their Marxist reasoning, would be sopped up. In England, there was a similar sense of hopelessness. Tom Jones, a confidant of Stanley Baldwin and a member of the Unemployment Assistance Board, noted in a letter to Abraham Flexner on March 1, 1934: "On the home front we have favourable if slight evidence of improved trade, but nothing that will make any dent in the unemployment figures. It is slowly but surely being realized by more and more that the great majority of these will never work again, and people like Lindsay of Balliol, T. J., and that ilk, are facing up to big and permanent developments of these occupational and training centres."[7]

In the United States, Franklin D. Roosevelt tinkered with a wide variety of programs. Through the National Recovery Administration he set up an elaborate price-fixing and regulative set of codes which resembled a corporate state. On the advice of George Warren, he manipulated the gold content of the dollar in order to raise the price level. To do something for the idle, he began a large campaign of public works. Few of these policies derived from any comprehensive theory about economic recovery; there was none at hand. As Rexford Tugwell, one of Roosevelt's economic advisors, later observed, Roosevelt simply was trying one "magical formula" after another in the hope of finding some combination that would get the economy moving.[8]

It was largely through the joining of theory and policy that a better understanding of economic management was achieved. Keynes provided the theoretical justification for the intervention of government into the economy as the means of bridging the gap between saving and investment.[9] The work of Kuznets, Hicks, and others in macro-economics gave government policy a firm framework through the creation of a system of national economic accounts— the aggregations of economic data and the fitting of such components as investment and consumption into product accounts and income accounts—so that one could measure the level of economic activity and decide which sectors needed government intervention.

The other major revolution in economics has been the attempted use of an increasingly rigorous, mathematically formalized body of economic theory, derived from the general equilibrium theory of Walras and developed in the

---

[7]Thomas Jones, *A Diary with Letters* (New York, 1954), p. 125. Lindsay is A. D. Lindsay, Master of Balliol College for twenty-five years until 1949. T. J. is an ironic reference by Jones to himself.

[8]See Rexford G. Tugwell, *The Democratic Roosevelt* (New York, 1957), chap. 15, esp. pp. 312–313.

[9]The Keynesian revolution in economics actually occurred after most of the economies had recovered from the depression even though many policies, particularly so-called unbalanced budgets or deficit financing, were adopted by trial-and-error and had "Keynesian" effects. The most self-conscious effort to use the new economics was in Sweden, where the socialist finance minister, Ernest Wigforss, broke away from Marxist thinking and, on the advice of the economists Erik Lindahl and Gunnar Myrdal, pursued an active fiscal and public-works policy which was Keynesian before Keynes, i.e. before the publication of Keynes' *General Theory* in 1936.

last three decades by Leontief, Tinbergen, Frisch, and Samuelson[10] for policy purposes. In the past, these concepts and tools—production functions, consumption functions, time preferences, and discounting—though powerful as abstractions were remote from empirical content because there was no appropriate quantitative data for testing and applying this body of theory.[11]

The development of modern economics, in this respect, has been possible because of the computer. Computers have provided the bridge between the body of formal theory and the large data bases of recent years; out of this has come modern econometrics and the policy orientation of economics.[12] One major area has been the models of interdependencies among industries such as the input-output matrices developed by Wassily Leontief, which simplify the general equilibrium system of Walras and show, empirically, the transactions between industries, or sectors, or regions. The input-output matrix of the American economy is a grid of 81 industries, from Footwear and other Leather Products (1) to Scrap, Used, and Secondhand Goods (81) grouped into the productive, distributive, and service sectors of the economy. A dollar-flow table shows the distribution of the output of any one industry to each (or any) of the other 80 sectors. The input-output matrix shows the mix and proportions of inputs (from each or several industries) which go into a specific unit of output (in dollar value or physical production terms). An inverse matrix shows the indirect demand generated by a product as well as the direct demand. Thus, one can trace the effect of the final consumer demand say for automobiles on the amount (or value) of iron ore, even though the automobile industry buys no iron ore directly. Or one can see what proportion of iron ore, as a raw material, goes into such final products as autos, ships, buildings, and the like. In this way, one can chart the changes in the nature of final demands in terms of the differential effects on each sector of the economy.[13] Input-

---

[10]Thirty years ago few, if any, graduate schools taught mathematical economics. The turning point, probably, was the publication of Paul Samuelson's *Foundations of Economic Analysis* in 1947, which presented a mathematically formalized version of neoclassical economics. Today, no one can work in economic theory without a solid grounding in mathematics.

[11]It is striking that during the depression there was no real measure of the extent of unemployment because of the confusion over a conceptual definition and the lack of sample survey techniques to make quick counts; the government relied on the 1930 census and some estimates from manufacturing establishments. In 1921, when President Harding called a conference of experts to discuss the unemployment that accompanied the postwar depression, estimates ranged widely and the final figure published was decided, literally, by majority vote. The confusions about who should be counted, or what constituted the "labor force," continued through the 1930s and a settled set of definitions and figures emerged only in the 1940s. Nor were there, of course, the Gross National Product and national-income accounts to give a view of the economy as a whole. This came into public-policy use only in 1945. (I am indebted to an unpublished dissertation at MIT by Judith de Neufville, on social indicators, for the illustration on unemployment statistics.)

[12]Charles Wolf, Jr., and John H. Enns have provided a comprehensive review of these developments in their paper "Computers and Economics," Rand Paper P-4724. I am indebted to them for a number of illustrations.

[13]Mathematically speaking, an input-output matrix represents a set of simultaneous linear equations—in this case 81 equations with 81 variables which are solved by matrix algebra. See Wassily Leontief, *The Structure of the American Economy: Theoretical and Empirical Explorations in Input-Output Analysis* (New York, 1953). Ironically, when the Bureau of Labor Statistics tried to set up an input-output grid for the American economy in 1949, it was opposed by business on the ground that it was a tool for socialism, and the money was initially denied.

output tables are now the basic tools for national economic planning and they have been applied in regional planning, through computerized models, to test the effect on trade of changes in population distributions.

The large econometric models of the economy, such as the Brookings model discussed earlier, allow one to do economic forecasting, while the existence of such computer models now enables economists to do policy "experiments," such as the work of Fromm and Taubman in simulating eight different combinations of fiscal and monetary policy for the period 1960–1962, in order to see which policy might have been the most effective.[14] With these tools one can test different theories to see whether it is now possible to do "fine tuning" of the economy.

It would be technocratic to assume that the managing of an economy is only a technical offshoot of a theoretical model. The overriding considerations are political, and set the frames of decision. Yet the economic models indicate the boundaries of constraint within which one can operate, and they can specify the consequences of alternative political choices.[15] The crucial point is that economic policy formulations, though not an exact art, now derive from theory, and often must find justification in theory. The fact that a Nixon administration in 1972 could casually accept the concept of a "full employment budget," which sets a level of government expenditures *as if* there were full utilization of resources (thus automatically accepting deficit financing) is itself a measure of the degree of economic sophistication that government has acquired in the past thirty years.

The joining of science, technology, and economics in recent years is symbolized by the phrase "research and development" (R & D). Out of this have come the science-based industries (computers, electronics, optics, polymers) which increasingly dominate the manufacturing sector of the society and which provide the lead, in product cycles, for the advanced industrial societies. But these science-based industries, unlike industries which arose in the nineteenth century, are primarily dependent on theoretical work prior to production. The computer would not exist without the work in solid-state physics initiated

---

[14]Their conclusions: that the largest impact on real GNP came from increases in government nondurable and construction expenditures. Income-tax cuts were less of a stimulant than increase in expenditures. Gary Fromm and Paul Taubman, *Policy Simulations with an Econometric Model* (Brookings Institution, Washington, D.C., 1968), cited in Wolf and Enns, op. cit.

[15]With modern economic tools, Robert M. Solow argues, an administration can, within limits, get the measure of economic activity it wants, for the level of government spending can redress the deficits of private spending and step up economic activity. But in so doing, an administration has to choose between inflation or full employment; this dilemma seems to be built into the market structure of capitalist economies. An administration has to make a trade-off—and this is a political choice. Democrats have preferred full employment and inflation, Republicans price stability and slow economic growth.

In the last few years, however, there has been the new phenomenon—simultaneous high unemployment and high inflation. For reasons that are not clear, unemployment no longer "disciplines" an economy into bringing prices down, either because of substantial welfare cushions (e.g. unemployment insurance), wage-push pressure in organized industries, or the persistent expectation of price rises that discounts inflation.

The two turning points in modern economic policy were President Kennedy's tax cut in 1964, which canonized Keynesian principles in economic policy, and President Nixon's imposition of wage and price controls in 1971. Though mandatory controls were relaxed in 1973, the option to use them now remains.

forty years ago by Felix Bloch. The laser came directly out of I. I. Rabi's research thirty years ago on molecular optical beams. (One can say, without being overly facile, that U. S. Steel is the paradigmatic corporation of the first third of the twentieth century, General Motors of the second third of the century, and IBM of the final third. The contrasting attitudes of the corporations toward research and development are a measure of these changes.)

What is true of technology and economics is true, albeit differentially, of all modes of knowledge: the advances in a field become increasingly dependent on the primacy of theoretical work, which codifies what is known and points the way to empirical confirmation. In effect, theoretical knowledge increasingly becomes the strategic resource, the axial principle, of a society. And the university, research organizations, and intellectual institutions, where theoretical knowledge is codified and enriched, become the axial structures of the emergent society.

The planning of technology. With the new modes of technological forecasting, my fourth criterion, the post-industrial societies may be able to reach a new dimension of societal change, the planning and control of technological growth.

Modern industrial economies became possible when societies were able to create new institutional mechanisms to build up savings (through banks, insurance companies, equity capital through the stock market, and government levies, i.e. loans or taxes) and to use this money for investment. The ability consistently to re-invest annually at least 10 percent of GNP became the basis of what W. W. Rostow has called the "take-off" point for economic growth. But a modern society, in order to avoid stagnation or "maturity" (however that vague word is defined), has had to open up new technological frontiers in order to maintain productivity and higher standards of living. If societies become more dependent on technology and new innovation, then a hazardous "indeterminacy" is introduced into the system. (Marx argued that a capitalist economy had to expand or die. Later Marxists, such as Lenin or Rosa Luxemburg, assumed that such expansion necessarily had to be geographical; hence the theory of imperialism. But the greater measure of expansion has been capital-intensive or technological.) Without new technology, how can growth be maintained? The development of new forecasting and "mapping techniques" makes possible a novel phase in economic history—the conscious, planned advance of technological change, and therefore the reduction of indeterminacy about the economic future. (Whether this can actually be done is a pregnant question, discussed in Chapter 3.)

But technological advance, as we have learned, has deleterious side effects, with second-order and third-order consequences that are often overlooked and certainly unintended. The increasing use of cheap fertilizers was one of the elements that created the revolution in agricultural productivity, but the run-off of nitrates into the rivers has been one of the worst sources of pollution. The introduction of DDT as a pesticide saved many crops, but also destroyed wildlife and birds. In automobiles, the gasoline engine was more effective than steam, but it has smogged the air. The point is that the introduction of technology was uncontrolled, and its initiators were interested only in single-order effects.

Yet none of this has to be. The mechanisms of control are available as well. As a number of studies by a panel of the National Academy of Science has shown, if these technologies had been "assessed" before they were introduced, alternative technologies or arrangements could have been considered. As the study group reported:

> The panel believes that in some cases an injection of the broadened criteria urged here might have led, or might in the future lead, to the selection or encouragement of different technologies or at least modified ones—functional alternatives with lower "social costs" (though not necessarily lower total costs). For example, bioenvironmental rather than primarily chemical devices might have been used to control agricultural pests, or there might have been design alternatives to the purely chemical means of enhancing engine efficiency, or mass transit alternatives to further reliance upon the private automobile.[16]

Technology assessment is feasible. What it requires is a political mechanism that will allow such studies to be made and set up criteria for the regulation of new technologies.[17]

The rise of a new intellectual technology. "The greatest invention of the nineteenth century," Alfred North Whitehead wrote, "was the invention of the method of invention. A new method entered into life. In order to understand our epoch, we can neglect all the details of change, such as railways, telegraphs, radios, spinning machines, synthetic dyes. We must concentrate on the method itself; that is the real novelty, which has broken up the foundations of the old civilization."[18]

In the same spirit, one can say that the methodological promise of the second half of the twentieth century is the management of organized complexity (the complexity of large organizations and systems, the complexity of theory with a large number of variables), the identification and implementation of strategies for rational choice in games against nature and games between persons, and the development of a new intellectual technology which, by the end of the

---

[16]*Technology: Processes of Assessment and Choice,* Report of the National Academy of Sciences, U.S. House of Representatives, Committee on Science and Astronautics, July 1969.

[17]To further the idea of technology assessment, the National Academy of Engineering undertook three studies in developing fields, that of computer-assisted instruction and instructional television; subsonic aircraft noise; and multiphasic screening in health diagnosis. The study concluded that technology assessment was feasible, and outlined the costs and scope of the necessary studies. In the case of technological teaching aids, the study considered eighteen different impacts they might have. In the case of noise, they examined the costs and consequences of five alternative strategies, from relocating airports or soundproofing nearby homes to modifying the airplanes or their flight patterns. See *A Study of Technology Assessment,* Report of the Committee on Public Engineering Policy, National Academy of Engineering, July 1969.

The idea of "technology assessment" grew largely out of studies made by the House Science and Astronautics Committee, and in 1967 a bill was introduced in the House by Congressman Daddario for a Technology Assessment Board. The bill was passed in 1972 and the Congress, not the Executive, is charged with setting up a Technology Assessment Office.

[18]*Science and the Modern World,* p. 141.

century, may be as salient in human affairs as machine technology has been for the past century and a half.

In the eighteenth and nineteenth centuries, scientists learned how to handle two-variable problems: the relationship of force to distance in objects, of pressure and volume in gases, of current versus voltage in electricity. With some minor extensions to three or four variables, these are the bedrock for most modern technology. Such *objects* as telephones, radio, automobile, airplane, and turbine are, as Warren Weaver puts it, problems of "complex simplicity."[19] Most of the models of nineteenth- and early-twentieth-century social science paralleled these simple interdependencies: capital and labor (as fixed and variable capital in the Marxist system; as production functions in neo-classical economics), supply and demand, balance of power, balance of trade. As closed, opposed systems, to use Albert Wohlstetter's formulation, they are analytically most attractive, and they simplify a complex world.

In the progression of science, the next problems dealt with were not those of a small number of interdependent variables, but the ordering of gross numbers: the motion of molecules in statistical mechanics, the rates of life expectancies in actuarial tables, the distribution of heredities in population genetics. In the social sciences, these became the problems of the "average man"—the distributions of intelligence, the rates of social mobility, and the like. These are, in Warren Weaver's term, problems of "disorganized complexity," but their solutions were made possible by notable advances in probability theory and statistics which could specify the results in chance terms.

The major intellectual and sociological problems of the post-industrial society are, to continue Weaver's metaphor, those of "organized complexity"— the management of large-scale systems, with large numbers of interacting variables, which have to be coordinated to achieve specific goals. It is the *hubris* of the modern systems theorist that the techniques for managing these systems are now available.

Since 1940, there has been a remarkable efflorescence of new fields whose results apply to problems of organized complexity: information theory, cybernetics, decision theory, game theory, utility theory, stochastic processes. From these have come specific techniques, such as linear programming, statistical decision theory, Markov chain applications, Monte Carlo randomizing, and minimax solutions, which are used to predict alternative optimal outcomes of different choices in strategy situations. Behind all this is the development in mathematics of what Jagit Singh calls "comprehensive numeracy."[20] Average properties, linear relationships, and no feedback, are simplifications used earlier to make mathematics manually tractable. The calculus is superbly suited to problems of a few variables and rates of change. But the problems of organized complexity have to be described in probabilities—the calculable consequences of alternative choices, which introduce constraints

---

[19]Warren Weaver, "Science and Complexity," in *The Scientists Speak,* ed. Warren Weaver (New York, 1947). I am indebted to a former special student at Columbia, Norman Lee, for this citation and for a number of other suggestions in this section.
[20]Jagit Singh, *Great Ideas of Operations Research* (New York, 1968).

either of conflict or cooperation—and to solve them one must go beyond classical mathematics. Since 1940, the advances in probability theory (once intuitive and now rigorous and axiomatic), sophisticated set theory, and game and decision theory have made further advances in application theoretically possible.

I have called the applications of these new developments "intellectual technology" for two reasons. Technology, as Harvey Brooks defines it, "is the use of scientific knowledge to specify ways of doing things in a *reproducible* manner."[21] In this sense, the organization of a hospital or an international trade system is a *social* technology, as the automobile or a numerically controlled tool is a *machine* technology. An *intellectual* technology is the substitution of algorithms (problem-solving rules) for intuitive judgments. These algorithms may be embodied in an automatic machine or a computer program or a set of instructions based on some statistical or mathematical formula; the statistical and logical techniques that are used in dealing with "organized complexity" are efforts to formalize a set of decision rules. The second reason is that without the computer, the new mathematical tools would have been primarily of intellectual interest, or used, in Anatol Rappoport's phrase, with "very low resolving power." The chain of multiple calculations that can be readily made, the multivariate analyses that keep track of the detailed interactions of many variables, the simultaneous solution of several hundred equations—these feats which are the foundation of comprehensive numeracy—are possible only with a tool of intellectual *technology,* the computer.

What is distinctive about the new intellectual technology is its effort to define rational action and to identify the means of achieving it. All situations involve constraints (costs, for example) and contrasting alternatives. And all action takes place under conditions of certainty, risk, or uncertainty. Certainty exists when the constraints are fixed and known. Risk means that a set of possible outcomes is known and the probabilities for each outcome can be stated. Uncertainty is the case when the set of possible outcomes can be stipulated, but the probabilities are completely unknown. Further, situations can be defined as "games against nature," in which the constraints are environmental, or "games between persons," in which each person's course of action is necessarily shaped by the reciprocal judgments of the others' intentions.[22] In all these situations, the desirable action is a strategy that leads to the optimal or

---

[21]Harvey Brooks, "Technology and the Ecological Crisis," lecture given at Amherst, May 9, 1971, p. 13 from unpublished text, emphasis added. For an application of these views, see the reports of two committees chaired by Professor Brooks, *Technology, Processes of Assessment and Choice,* Report of the National Academy of Sciences, published by the Committee on Science and Astronautics, U.S. House of Representatives, July 1969; and, *Science Growth and Society,* OECD (Paris, 1971).

[22]Most of the day-to-day problems in economics and management involve decision-making under conditions of certainty; i.e. the constraints are known. These are such problems as proportions of product mixes under known assumptions of cost and price, production scheduling by size, network paths, and the like. Since the objectives are clear (the most efficient routing, or the best profit yield from a product mix), the problems are largely mathematical and can be solved by such techniques as linear programming. The theory of linear programming derives

"best" solution; i.e. one which either maximizes the outcome or, depending upon the assessment of the risks and uncertainties, tries to minimize the losses. Rationality can be defined as judging, between two alternatives, which one is capable of yielding that preferred outcome.[23]

Intellectual technology makes its most ambitious claims in systems analysis. A system, in this sense, is any set of reciprocal relationships in which a variation in the character (or numerical value) of one of the elements will have determinate—and possibly measurable—consequences for all the others in the system. A human organism is a determinate system; a work-group whose members are engaged in specialized tasks for a common objective is a goal-setting system; a pattern of bombers and bases forms a variable system; the economy as a whole is a loose system.

The problem of the number of variables has been a crucial factor in the burgeoning fields of systems analysis for military or business decisions. In the design of an airplane, say, a single performance parameter (speed, or distance, or capacity) cannot be the measure of the intrinsic worth of a design, since these are all interrelated. Charles J. Hitch has used this to illustrate the problems of systems analysis for bombers. "Suppose we ruthlessly simplify aircraft characteristics to three—speed, range, altitude. What else do we have

---

from a 1937 paper by John von Neumann on the general equilibrium of a uniformly expanding closed economy. Many of the computational procedures were developed by the Soviet economist L. V. Kantorovich, whose work was ignored by the regime until Stalin's death. Similar techniques were devised in the late 1940s by the Rand mathematician G. B. Dantzig, in his simplex method. The practical application of linear programming had to await the development of the electronic computer and its ability (in some transportation problems, for example) to handle 3200 equations and 600,000 variables in sequence. Robert Dorfman has applied linear programming to the theory of the firm, and Dorfman, Samuelson and Solow used it in 1958 in an inter-industry model of the economy to allow for substitutability of supply and a criterion function that allows a choice of solutions for different objectives within a specified sector of final demand.

Criteria for decision-making under conditions of uncertainty were introduced by the Columbia mathematical statistician Abraham Wald in 1939. It specifies a "maximin" criterion in which one *is* guided by an expectation of the worst outcome. Leonid Hurwicz and L. J. Savage have developed other strategies, such as Savage's charmingly named "criteria of regret," whose subjective probabilities may cause one to increase or decrease a risk.

Game theory has a long history but the decisive turn occurred in a 1928 paper of John von Neumann which provided a mathematical proof of a general minimax strategy for a two-person game. The 1944 book by von Neumann and Morgenstern, *Theory of Games and Economic Behavior* (Princeton), extended the theory of games with more than two persons and applied the theorem to economic behavior. The strategy proposed by von Neumann and Morgenstern—that of minimax, or the minimization of maximum loss—is defined as the rational course under conditions of uncertainty.

Games-and-decision theory was given an enormous boost during World War II, when its use was called "operations research." There was, for example, the "duel" between the airplane and the submarine. The former had to figure out the "best" search pattern for air patrol of a given area; the other had to find the best escape pattern when under surveillance. Mathematicians in the Anti-Submarine Warfare Operations Research Group, using a 1928 paper of von Neumann, figured out a tactical answer.

The game-theory idea has been widely applied—sometimes as metaphor, sometimes to specify numerical values for possible outcomes—in bargaining and conflict situations. See Thomas C. Schelling, *The Strategy of Conflict* (Cambridge, Mass., 1960).

[23]R. Duncan Luce and Howard Raiffa, *Games and Decisions* (New York, 1957). My discussion of rationality is adapted from the definition on p. 50; that of risk, certainty, and uncertainty from p. 13.

to consider in measuring the effectiveness of the bombers of 1965? At least the following: the formation they will use, their flight path to target, the base system, the target system, the bombs, and the enemy defenses. This may not sound like many parameters (in fact, it is far fewer than would be necessary) but if we go no higher than ten, and if we let each parameter take only two alternative values, we already have 2^{10} cases to calculate and compare (2^{10} 1000). If we let each parameter take four alternative values we have 4^{10} cases (4^{10} 1,000,000)."[24] The choice of a new kind of bomber system was thus not simply a question one could leave to the "old" air force generals. It had to be computed in terms of cost-effectiveness on the weighing of these many variables.

The crucial point is the argument of Jay Forrester and others, that the nature of complex systems is "counterintuitive." A complex system, they insist, involves the interaction of too many variables for the mind to hold in correct order simultaneously. Or, as Forrester also suggests, intuitive judgments respond to immediate cause-and-effect relations which are characteristic of simpler systems, whereas in complex systems the actual causes may be deeply hidden or remote in time or, more often, may lie in the very structure (i.e. pattern) of the system itself, which is not immediately recognizable. For this reason, one has to use algorithms, rather than intuitive judgments, in making decisions.[25]

The cause-and-effect deception is illustrated in Forrester's computer simulation model of how a central city first grows, then stagnates and decays. The model is composed of three major sectors, each containing three elements. The business sector has new, mature, and declining industries; the housing sector has premium, worker, and underemployed housing; and the population sector holds managerial-professionals, laborers, and underemployed. These nine elements are linked first with twenty-two modes of interaction (e.g. different kinds of migrations) and then with the outside world through multiplier functions. The whole, however, is a closed, dynamic system which models the life-history of the city. At first the vacant land fills up, different elements readjust, an equilibrium is attained, then stagnation develops as industries die and taxes increase. The sequence runs over a period of 250 years.

From this model, Forrester has drawn a number of policy conclusions. He argues that increased low-income housing in the central city has the negative effects of bringing in more low-income people, decreasing the tax base, and discouraging new industry. Job-training programs have the undesirable consequence of taking trained workers out of the city. None of this surprises Forrester because, as he points out, the direct approach is to say that if there is a need for more homes, build more housing, whereas the more difficult and complex approach would be to try to change the job patterns and population

---

[24]See Charles J. Hitch, "Analysis for Air Force Decisions," in *Analysis for Military Decisions: the Rand Lectures on Systems Analysis,* ed. E. S. Quade (Chicago, 1964). His illustration is conjectural. A more relevant but much more complicated illustration is Quade's case history, in the same volume, on the selection and use of strategic air bases.

[25]Jay W. Forrester, *Urban Dynamics* (Cambridge, Mass., 1969), pp. 10–11.

balances. In this sense, the policies which are wrong are the immediate cause-and-effect judgments, whereas the better policies would be the "counter-intuitive ones."

The decision-making logic which follows systems analysis is clear. In the case of Rand and the Air Force, it led to the installation of technocrats in the Defense Department, the creation of the Program Planning Budget Systems (PPBS), which was responsible in large measure for the realignment of strategic and tactical programs, and the imposition of cost-effectiveness criteria in the choice of weapons systems. In Forrester's illustration, it would lead to the substitution of economic rather than political judgments in the crucial policy decisions of city life.

The goal of the new intellectual technology is, neither more nor less, to realize a social alchemist's dream: the dream of "ordering" the mass society. In this society today, millions of persons daily make billions of decisions about what to buy, how many children to have, whom to vote for, what job to take, and the like. Any single choice may be as unpredictable as the quantum atom responding erratically to the measuring instrument, yet the aggregate patterns could be charted as neatly as the geometer triangulates the height and the horizon. If the computer is the tool, then decision theory is its master. Just as Pascal sought to play dice with God, and the physiocrats attempted to draw an economic grid that would array all exchanges among men, so the decision theorists seek their own *tableau entier*—the compass of rationality, the "best" solution to the choices perplexing men.

*   *   *

4

Techniques and Human Life

First written in 1954, *Technological Society* represents Jacques Ellul's profound dissatisfaction with the standards that he feels dominate advanced industrial societies. Ellul's basic argument is that today the means determine the ends; our unquestioning devotion to reason and efficiency produces societies dominated by a host of dehumanizing "techniques," which he defines as "the totality of means, rationally arrived at, and having absolute efficiency in every aspect of human life." Taken together, these techniques (e.g., science, bureaucracy, systems analysis, advertising, war games, sex manuals) constitute a value system that is closed to any but the most practical and business life concerns. The only serious questions in *Technological Society* are: Will it work? Is it scientifically feasible? Can it be done? When?

In order to judge Ellul's hopeless prophecy, we must first question the validity of his argument, and ask to what extent advanced industrial societies *are* dominated by techniques. I think Ellul exaggerates their power, but he still points to many of our most important assumptions. Equally important, to the extent means *do* rule ends, tomorrow is out of control, and people are only the captives of their own dehumanizing creations—techniques.

From The Technological Society
—Jacques Ellul

No social, human, or spiritual fact is so important as the fact of technique in the modern world. And yet no subject is so little understood. Let us try to set up some guideposts to situate the technical phenomenon.

SITUATING THE TECHNICAL PHENOMENON

Machines and Technique. Whenever we see the word *technology* or *technique,* we automatically think of machines. Indeed, we commonly think of our world as a world of machines. This notion—which is in fact an error—is found, for example, in the works of Oldham and Pierre Ducassé. It arises from the fact that the machine is the most obvious, massive, and impressive example of technique, and historically the first. What is called the history of technique usually amounts to no more than a history of the machine; this very formulation is an example of the habit of intellectuals of regarding forms of the present as identical with those of the past.

Technique certainly began with the machine. It is quite true that all the rest developed out of mechanics; it is quite true also that without the machine the world of technique would not exist. But to explain the situation in this way does not at all legitimatize it. It is a mistake to continue with this confusion of terms, the more so because it leads to the idea that, because the machine is at the origin and center of the technical problem, one is dealing with the whole problem when one deals with the machine. And that is a greater mistake still. Technique has now become almost completely independent of the machine, which has lagged far behind its offspring.

It must be emphasized that, at present, technique is applied outside industrial life. The growth of its power today has no relation to the growing use of the machine. The balance seems rather to have shifted to the other side. It is the machine which is now entirely dependent upon technique, and the machine represents only a small part of technique. If we were to characterize the relations between technique and the machine today, we could say not only that the machine is the result of a certain technique, but also that its social and economic applications are made possible by other technical advances. The machine is now not even the most important aspect of technique (though it is perhaps the most spectacular); technique has taken over all of man's activities, not just his productive activity.

From another point of view, however, the machine is deeply symptomatic: it represents the ideal toward which technique strives. The machine is solely, exclusively, technique; it is pure technique, one might say. For, wherever a technical factor exists, it results, almost inevitably, in mechanization: technique transforms everything it touches into a machine.

Another relationship exists between technique and the machine, and this relationship penetrates to the very core of the problem of our civilization. It is said (and everyone agrees) that the machine has created an inhuman atmosphere. The machine, so characteristic of the nineteenth century, made an abrupt entrance into a society which, from the political, institutional, and human points of view, was not made to receive it; and man has had to put up with it as best he can. Men now live in conditions that are less than human. Consider the concentration of our great cities, the slums, the lack of space, of air, of time, the gloomy streets and the sallow lights that confuse night and day. Think of our dehumanized factories, our unsatisfied senses, our working women, our estrangement from nature. Life in such an environment has no meaning. Consider our public transportation, in which man is less important than a parcel; our hospitals, in which he is only a number. Yet we call this progress. . . . And the noise, that monster boring into us at every hour of the night without respite.

It is useless to rail against capitalism. Capitalism did not create our world; the machine did. Painstaking studies designed to prove the contrary have buried the obvious beneath tons of print. And, if we do not wish to play the demagogue, we must point out the guilty party. "The machine is antisocial," says Lewis Mumford. "It tends, by reason of its progressive character, to the most acute forms of human exploitation." The machine took its place in a social milieu that was not made for it, and for that reason created the inhuman society in which we live. Capitalism was therefore only one aspect of the deep disorder of the nineteenth century. To restore order, it was necessary to question all the bases of that society—its social and political structures, its art and its way of life, its commercial system.

But let the machine have its head, and it topples everything that cannot support its enormous weight. Thus everything had to be reconsidered in terms of the machine. And that is precisely the role technique plays. In all fields it made an inventory of what it could use, of everything that could be brought into line with the machine. The machine could not integrate itself into nineteenth-century society; technique integrated it. Old houses that were not suited to the workers were torn down; and the new world technique required was built in their place. Technique has enough of the mechanical in its nature to enable it to cope with the machine, but it surpasses and transcends the machine because it remains in close touch with the human order. The metal monster could not go on forever torturing mankind. It found in technique a rule as hard and inflexible as itself.

Technique integrates the machine into society. It constructs the kind of world the machine needs and introduces order where the incoherent banging of machinery heaped up ruins. It clarifies, arranges, and rationalizes; it does in the domain of the abstract what the machine did in the domain of labor. It is efficient and brings efficiency to everything. Moreover, technique is sparing in the use of the machine, which has traditionally been exploited to conceal defects of organization. "Machines sanctioned social inefficiency," says Mumford. Technique, on the other hand, leads to a more rational and less indiscriminate use of machines. It places machines exactly where they ought to be and requires of them just what they ought to do.

This brings us to two contrasting forms of social growth. Henri Guitton says: "Social growth was formerly reflexive or instinctive, that is to say, unconscious. But new circumstances (the machine) now compel us to recognize a kind of social development that is rational, intelligent, and conscious. We may ask ourselves whether this is the beginning not only of the era of a spatially finite world but also of the era of a conscious world." All-embracing technique is in fact the consciousness of the mechanized world.

Technique integrates everything. It avoids shock and sensational events. Man is not adapted to a world of steel; technique adapts him to it. It changes the arrangement of this blind world so that man can be a part of it without colliding with its rough edges, without the anguish of being delivered up to the inhuman. Technique thus provides a model; it specifies attitudes that are valid once and for all. The anxiety aroused in man by the turbulence of the machine is soothed by the consoling hum of a unified society.

As long as technique was represented exclusively by the machine, it was possible to speak of "man *and* the machine." The machine remained an external object, and man (though significantly influenced by it in his professional, private, and psychic life) remained none the less independent. He was in a position to assert himself apart from the machine; he was able to adopt a position with respect to it.

But when technique enters into every area of life, including the human, it ceases to be external to man and becomes his very substance. It is no longer face to face with man but is integrated with him, and it progressively absorbs him. In this respect, technique is radically different from the machine. This transformation, so obvious in modern society, is the result of the fact that technique has become autonomous.

When I state that technique leads to mechanization, I am not referring to the simple fact of human adaptation to the machine. Of course, such a process of adaptation exists, but it is caused by the action of the machine. What we are concerned with here, however, is a kind of mechanization in itself. If we may ascribe to the machine a superior form of "know-how," the mechanization which results from technique is the application of this higher form to *all* domains hitherto foreign to the machine; we can even say that technique is characteristic of precisely that realm in which the machine itself can play no role. It is a radical error to think of technique and machine as interchangeable; from the very beginning we must be on guard against this misconception.

*   *   *

Technical Operation and Technical Phenomenon. With the use of these few guideposts, we can now try to formulate, if not a full definition, at least an approximate definition of technique. But we must keep this in mind: we are not concerned with the different individual techniques. Everyone practices a particular technique, and it is difficult to come to know them all. Yet in this great diversity we can find certain points in common, certain tendencies and principles shared by them all. It is clumsy to call these common features Technique with a capital T; no one would recognize his particular technique behind this terminology. Nevertheless, it takes account of a reality—the technical phenomenon—which is worldwide today.

If we recognize that the method each person employs to attain a result is in fact, his particular technique, the problem of means is raised. In fact, technique is nothing more than *means* and the *ensemble of means*. This, of course, does not lessen the importance of the problem. Our civilization is first and foremost a civilization of means; in the reality of modern life, the means, it would seem, are more important than the ends. Any other assessment of the situation is mere idealism.

Techniques considered as methods of operation present certain common characteristics and certain general tendencies, but we cannot devote ourselves exclusively to them. To do this would lead to a more specialized study than I have in mind. The technical phenomenon is much more complex than any synthesis of characteristics common to individual techniques. If we desire to come closer to a definition of technique, we must in fact differentiate between the technical operation and the technical phenomenon.

The technical operation includes every operation carried out in accordance with a certain method in order to attain a particular end. It can be as rudimentary as splintering a flint or as complicated as programming an electronic brain. In every case, it is the method which characterizes the operation. It may be more or less effective or more or less complex, but its nature is always the same. It is this which leads us to think that there is a continuity in technical operations and that only the great refinement resulting from scientific progress differentiates the modern technical operation from the primitive one.

Every operation obviously entails a certain technique, even the gathering of fruit among primitive peoples—climbing the tree, picking the fruit as quickly and with as little effort as possible, distinguishing between the ripe and the unripe fruit, and so on. However, what characterizes technical action within a particular activity is the search for greater efficiency. Completely natural and spontaneous effort is replaced by a complex of acts designed to improve, say, the yield. It is this which prompts the creation of technical forms, starting from simple forms of activity. These technical forms are not necessarily more complicated than the spontaneous ones, but they are more efficient and better adapted.

Thus, technique creates means, but the technical operation still occurs on the same level as that of the worker who does the work. The skilled worker, like the primitive huntsman, remains a technical operator; their attitudes differ only to a small degree.

But two factors enter into the extensive field of technical operation: consciousness and judgment. This double intervention produces what I call the technical phenomenon. What characterizes this double intervention? Essentially, it takes what was previously tentative, unconscious, and spontaneous and brings it into the realm of clear, voluntary, and reasoned concepts.

When André Leroi-Gourhan tabulates the efficiency of Zulu swords and arrows in terms of the most up-to-date knowledge of weaponry, he is doing work that is obviously different from that of the swordsmith of Bechuanaland who created the form of the sword. The swordsmith's choice of form was unconscious and spontaneous; although it can now be justified by numerical calculations, such calculations had no place whatever in the technical operation he performed. But reason did, inevitably, enter into the process because man spontaneously imitates nature in his activities. Accomplishments that merely copy nature, however, have no future (for instance, the imitation of birds' wings from Icarus to Ader). Reason makes it possible to produce objects in terms of certain features, certain abstract requirements; and this in turn leads, not to the imitation of nature, but to the ways of technique.

The intervention of rational judgment in the technical operation has important consequences. Man becomes aware that it is possible to find new and different means. Reason upsets pragmatic traditions and creates new operational methods and new tools; it examines rationally the possibilities of more extensive and less rigid experimentation. Reason in these ways multiplies technical operations to a high degree of diversity. But it also operates in the opposite direction: it considers results and takes account of the fixed end of technique—efficiency. It notes what every means devised is capable of accomplishing and selects from the various means at its disposal with a view to securing the ones that are the most efficient, the best adapted to the desired end. Thus the multiplicity of means is reduced to one: the most efficient. And here reason appears clearly in the guise of technique.

In addition, there is the intervention of consciousness. Consciousness shows clearly, and to everybody, the advantages of technique and what it can accomplish. The technician takes stock of alternative possibilities. The immediate result is that he seeks to apply the new methods in fields which traditionally had been left to chance, pragmatism, and instinct. The intervention of consciousness causes a rapid and far-flung extension of technique.

The twofold intervention of reason and consciousness in the technical world, which produces the technical phenomenon, can be described as the quest of the one best means in every field. And this "one best means" is, in fact, the technical means. It is the aggregate of these means that produces technical civilization.

The technical phenomenon is the main preoccupation of our time; in every field men seek to find the most efficient method. But our investigations have reached a limit. It is no longer the best relative means which counts, as compared to other means also in use. The choice is less and less a subjective one among several means which are potentially applicable. It is really a question of finding the best means in the absolute sense, on the basis of numerical calculation.

It is, then, the specialist who chooses the means; he is able to carry out the calculations that demonstrate the superiority of the means chosen over all others. Thus a science of means comes into being—a science of techniques, progressively elaborated.

This science extends to greatly diverse areas; it ranges from the act of shaving to the act of organizing the landing in Normandy, or to cremating thousands of deportees. Today no human activity escapes this technical imperative. There is a technique of organization (the great fact of organization described by Toynbee fits very well into this conception of the technical phenomenon), just as there is a technique of friendship and a technique of swimming. Under the circumstances, it is easy to see how far we are from confusing technique and machine. And, if we examine the broader areas where this search for means is taking place, we find three principal subdivisions of modern technique, in addition to the mechanical (which is the most conspicuous but which I shall not discuss because it is so well known) and to the forms of intellectual technique (card indices, libraries, and so on).

1) *Economic technique* is almost entirely subordinated to production, and ranges from the organization of labor to economic planning. This technique differs from the others in its object and goal. But its problems are the same as those of all other technical activities.

2) *The technique of organization* concerns the great masses and applies not only to commercial or industrial affairs of magnitude (coming, consequently, under the jurisdiction of the economic) but also to states and to administration and police power. This organizational technique is also applied to warfare and insures the power of an army at least as much as its weapons. Everything in the legal field also depends on organizational technique.

3) *Human technique* takes various forms, ranging all the way from medicine and genetics to propaganda (pedagogical techniques, vocational guidance, publicity, etc.). Here man himself becomes the object of technique.

We observe, in the case of each of these subdivisions, that the subordinate techniques may be very different in kind and not necessarily similar one to another as techniques. They have the same goal and preoccupation, however, and are thus related. The three subdivisions show the wide extent of the technical phenomenon. In fact, nothing at all escapes technique today. There is no field where technique is not dominant—this is easy to say and is scarcely surprising. We are so habituated to machines that there seems to be nothing left to discover.

Has the fact of technique no intrinsic importance? Does it spring merely from the march of time? Or does it represent a problem peculiar to our times? Our discussion of the biology of technique will bring us face to face with this question. But first we must survey in detail the vast field which the technical phenomenon covers, in order to become fully cognizant of what it signifies.

*   *   *

A Look at the Year 2000. In 1960 the weekly *l'Express* of Paris published a series of extracts from texts by American and Russian scientists concerning society in the year 2000. As long as such visions were purely a literary concern of science-fiction writers and sensational journalists, it was possible to smile at them.[1] Now we have like works from Nobel Prize winners, members of the Academy of Sciences of Moscow, and other scientific notables whose qualifications are beyond dispute. The visions of these gentlemen put science fiction in the shade. By the year 2000, voyages to the moon will be commonplace; so will inhabited artificial satellites. All food will be completely synthetic. The world's population will have increased fourfold but will have been stabilized. Sea water and ordinary rocks will yield all the necessary metals. Disease, as well as famine, will have been eliminated; and there will be universal hygienic inspection and control. The problems of energy production will have been completely resolved. Serious scientists, it must be repeated, are the source of these predictions, which hitherto were found only in philosophic utopias.

---

[1] Some excellent works, such as Robert Jungk's *Le Futur a déjà commencé*, were included in this classification.

The most remarkable predictions concern the transformation of educational methods and the problem of human reproduction. Knowledge will be accumulated in "electronic banks" and transmitted directly to the human nervous system by means of coded electronic messages. There will no longer be any need of reading or learning mountains of useless information; everything will be received and registered according to the needs of the moment. There will be no need of attention or effort. What is needed will pass directly from the machine to the brain without going through consciousness.

In the domain of genetics, natural reproduction will be forbidden. A stable population will be necessary, and it will consist of the highest human types. Artificial insemination will be employed. This, according to Muller, will "permit the introduction into a carrier uterus of an ovum fertilized *in vitro, ovum and sperm* . . . having been taken from persons representing the masculine ideal and the feminine ideal, respectively. The reproductive cells in question will preferably be those of persons dead long enough that a true perspective of their lives and works, free of all personal prejudice, can be seen. Such cells will be taken from cell banks and will represent the most precious genetic heritage of humanity . . . The method will have to be applied universally. If the people of a single country were to apply it intelligently and intensively . . . they would quickly attain a practically invincible level of superiority . . . " Here is a future Huxley never dreamed of.

Perhaps, instead of marveling or being shocked, we ought to reflect a little. A question no one ever asks when confronted with the scientific wonders of the future concerns the interim period. Consider, for example, the problems of automation, which will become acute in a very short time. How, socially, politically, morally, and humanly, shall we contrive to get there? How are the prodigious economic problems, for example, of unemployment, to be solved? And, in Muller's more distant utopia, how shall we force humanity to refrain from begetting children naturally? How shall we force them to submit to constant and rigorous hygienic controls? How shall man be persuaded to accept a radical transformation of his traditional modes of nutrition? How and where shall we relocate a billion and a half persons who today make their livings from agriculture and who, in the promised ultrarapid conversion of the next forty years, will become completely useless as cultivators of the soil? How shall we distribute such numbers of people equably over the surface of the earth, particularly if the promised fourfold increase in population materializes? How will we handle the control and occupation of outer space in order to provide a stable *modus vivendi?* How shall national boundaries be made to disappear? (One of the last two would be a necessity.) There are many other "hows," but they are conveniently left unformulated. When we reflect on the serious although relatively minor problems that were provoked by the industrial exploitation of coal and electricity, when we reflect that after a hundred and fifty years these problems are still not satisfactorily resolved, we are entitled to ask whether there are any solutions to the infinitely more complex "hows" of the next forty years. In fact, there is one and only one means to their solution, a world-wide totalitarian dictatorship which will allow technique its full scope and at the same time resolve the concomitant difficulties. It is not difficult to understand why the scientists and worshippers of technology prefer not to dwell on this solution, but rather to leap nimbly across the dull and uninteresting intermediary period and land squarely in the golden age. We might indeed ask ourselves if we will succeed in getting through the transition period at all, or if the blood and the suffering required are not perhaps too high a price to pay for this golden age.

If we take a hard, unromantic look at the golden age itself, we are struck with the incredible naïveté of these scientists. They say, for example, that they will be able to shape and reshape at will human emotions, desires, and thoughts and arrive scientifically at certain efficient, pre-established collective decisions. They claim they will be in a position to develop certain collective desires, to constitute certain homogeneous social units out of aggregates of individuals, to forbid men to raise their children, and even to persuade them to renounce having any. At the same time, they speak of assuring the triumph of freedom and of the necessity of avoiding dictatorship at any price.[2] They seem incapable of grasping the contradiction involved, or of understanding that what they are proposing, even after the intermediary period, is in fact the harshest of dictatorships. In comparison, Hitler's was a trifling affair. That it is to be a dictatorship of test tubes rather than of hobnailed boots will not make it any less a dictatorship.

When our savants characterize their golden age in any but scientific terms, they emit a quantity of down-at-the-heel platitudes that would gladden the heart of the pettiest politician. Let's take a few samples. "To render human nature nobler, more beautiful, and more harmonious." What on earth can this mean? What criteria, what content, do they propose? Not many, I fear, would be able to reply. "To assure the triumph of peace, liberty, and reason." Fine words with no substance behind them. "To eliminate cultural lag." What culture? And would the culture they have in mind be able to subsist in this harsh social organization? "To conquer outer space." For what purpose? The conquest of space seems to be an end in itself, which dispenses with any need for reflection.

We are forced to conclude that our scientists are incapable of any but the emptiest platitudes when they stray from their specialties. It makes one think back on the collection of mediocrities accumulated by Einstein when he spoke of God, the state, peace, and the meaning of life. It is clear that Einstein, extraordinary mathematical genius that he was, was no Pascal; he knew nothing of political or human reality, or, in fact, anything at all outside his mathematical reach. The banality of Einstein's remarks in matters outside his specialty is as astonishing as his genius within it. It seems as though the specialized application of all one's faculties in a particular area inhibits the consideration of things in general. Even J. Robert Oppenheimer, who seems receptive to a general culture, is not outside this judgment. His political and social declarations, for example, scarcely go beyond the level of those of the man in the

---

[2]The material here and below is cited from actual texts.

street. And the opinions of the scientists quoted by *l'Express* are not even on the level of Einstein or Oppenheimer. Their pomposities, in fact, do not rise to the level of the average. They are vague generalities inherited from the nineteenth century, and the fact that they represent the furthest limits of thought of our scientific worthies must be symptomatic of arrested development or of a mental block. Particularly disquieting is the gap between the enormous power they wield and their critical ability, which must be estimated as null. To wield power well entails a certain faculty of criticism, discrimination, judgment, and option. It is impossible to have confidence in men who apparently lack these faculties. Yet it is apparently our fate to be facing a "golden age" in the power of sorcerers who are totally blind to the meaning of the human adventure. When they speak of preserving the seed of outstanding men, whom, pray, do they mean to be the judges. It is clear, alas, that they propose to sit in judgment themselves. It is hardly likely that they will deem a Rimbaud or a Nietszche worthy of posterity. When they announce that they will conserve the genetic mutations which appear to them most favorable, and that they propose to modify the very germ cells in order to produce such and such traits; and when we consider the mediocrity of the scientists themselves outside the confines of their specialties, we can only shudder at the thought of what they will esteem most "favorable."

None of our wise men ever pose the question of the end of all their marvels. The "wherefore" is resolutely passed by. The response which would occur to our contemporaries is: for the sake of happiness. Unfortunately, there is no longer any question of that. One of our best-known specialists in diseases of the nervous system writes: "We will be able to modify man's emotions, desires and thoughts, as we have already done in a rudimentary way with tranquillizers." It will be possible, says our specialist to produce a conviction or an impression of happiness without any real basis for it. Our man of the golden age, therefore, will be capable of "happiness" amid the worst privations. Why, then, promise us extraordinary comforts, hygiene, knowledge, and nourishment if, by simply manipulating our nervous systems, we can be happy without them? The last meager motive we could possibly ascribe to the technical adventure thus vanishes into thin air through the very existence of technique itself.

But what good is it to pose questions of motives? of Why? All that must be the work of some miserable intellectual who balks at technical progress. The attitude of the scientists, at any rate, is clear. Technique exists because it is technique. The golden age will be because it will be. Any other answer is superfluous.

5

Science and Human Value

For Theodore Roszak, the main problem of modern society is "the mind-scape" created by science. Rational to the core, and valuing objectivity above all else, science views reality in a light that changes people's "transcendent aspirations" into purely secular—even profane—equivalents. In effect, science argues that if you strip the irrational from reality, a better life is both possible and probable.

Roszak thinks this is nonsense. In his view, even the good-hearted humanists have no chance to radically change society. Themselves prisoners of the scientific world view, humanists also seek rational explanations for everything. This is an error, suggests Roszak, because explaining everything empties the human heart. In order to join together in a new vision of life, people must *feel* similarly, which means that radical change is possible only if we reopen the metaphysical issues closed now by science and sound logic. The new politics Roszak envisions must be a religious politics. Only religion, which he defines as a vision born of transcendent knowledge, can move people to make the changes necessary for a radically different tomorrow.

Although Roszak neglects the benefits of science, I believe his criticisms are generally valid. However, I question his conclusion that religion is the only way to a hopeful tomorrow. Can people so firmly rooted in the value of reason ever again turn to a vision born of transcendent knowledge? I doubt it.

However, whether new beliefs, values, and practices are established via religion, or through such "scientific" approaches as humanism, remember that criticizing science is not the same as rejecting it. Roszak's insight is that modern society's emphasis on objectivity is itself an important value of that society. My own point is that it can be inhuman to emphasize a value that considers other values, such as the significance of human life, to be no more than subjective intrusions.

From Where the Wasteland Ends
—Theodore Roszak

. . . Until our own time, alienation has always stood in the shadow of salvation; it has been the falling rhythm of the soul's full cycle. It carried with it implications of transcendence. Ours is the first culture so totally secularized that we descend into the nihilist state without the conviction, without the experienced awareness that any other exists. I am not close enough to the churches to say how far beyond the level of Sunday school platitudes the clergy and their flocks press the discussion of Christian eschatology. But if that discussion goes more than skin-deep, it is abundantly clear from the character of social and cultural life throughout the west that it has been well quarantined within the congregations. Where public affairs begin, the church-going millions are at one with the atheist existentialist few: in body, mind, and deed they live the conviction that salvation will be found nowhere but in the collective, historical process—in making, doing, and improving. That is where their effort and attention go. Time and matter have trapped their vital energy; secular enterprise consumes it totally. Christian faith—the willful belief of the unbelievable—was never better than a poor substitute for sacramental experience; but even dutiful belief in a transcendent dimension of life has long since degenerated into mere opinion, socially irrelevant, even if privately engaging.

But it is not simply that transcendence has faded from our awareness. For many committed intellectuals and radical activists—those who have spearheaded the struggle for liberal and social democracy—it has been imperiously crowded out by the demands of conscience. In the moral conviction of these crusaders without a god, a science-based humanism and the left-wing anti-clerical legacy have combined to make religion an intolerable distraction from social responsibility. And how the religious, who come to the cause so late in the day, have learned to blush and cringe before the moral fire of militant humanism! At least since the days of Danton and Saint-Just, it has gone without question among increasing numbers of politically engaged people that only the struggle for progress, the struggle for justice are *real;* they must have *all.* To yield to the transcendent longings is selfish indulgence. "If God existed," said Bakunin, "we should have to abolish him." In brief, our ethics is at war with religion. Ours is a culture alienated in fact and *on principle.*

That is unique—terrifyingly unique. Never before have those who would speak for the transcendent ends of life had so little cultural purchase. In times past, the saints and sages have had to suffer the hypocrisy of the world, and its neglect; but their vision was never denied its validity or righteously eclipsed. They have never had to apologize for their knowledge of God or hide it away like a guilty secret.

But what choice does urban-industrial culture leave to a genuine religious sensibility if it wishes to avoid the lunatic fringe on the one hand, and self-serving bourgeois mediocrity on the other? Nothing but to immerse itself in the social gospel, to exhaust itself in a secular ethics. Wherever in the world today religion bids for intellectual reputability, it is by reducing itself to a dense residue of passionate ethical exhortation. That was the course the Deists chose in the age of Newton, relinquishing to the New Philosophy all knowledge of reality beyond the moral impulse; it remains the strategy of every embarrassed clergyman scrambling for "relevance" in the modern world and the acceptance of proudly alienated culture makers.

Granted, moral action is more becoming to the religious life than endless, arid theological nit-picking—the peculiar vice of Christianity; better too than sinking to the level of a middle-class social club or a Billy Graham theater piece. But *none* of these is religion; all are expressions of alienated consciousness, the social gospel no less than the rest. So Blake recognized in taking up his "mental fight" with the Deists. As the brave ally of Tom Paine and the revolutionary forces of his time, Blake took second place to none in his hostility toward aristocratic privilege and capitalist oppression. But whom did he mark out as the prime antagonists of Poetic Genius and the Divine Vision? Not obvious villains and godless scoundrels—Blake wastes little time on easy targets. But Bacon, Newton, Locke, Voltaire, Rousseau, Gibbon . . . the noblest spirits of Enlightenment and natural religion. It is with such giants that Blake tangles. Why? Because it is with them that the denaturing of visionary imagination begins. With them, alienation initiates its climb to supreme virtue. In the name of Reason, Progress, Humanity—the total secularization of mind and energy.

That is why Blake called Deism "the Religion of Satan." Not because it was the faith of wicked men. On the contrary, the very purpose of natural religion was to salvage Christian ethics within Newtonian nature. It was indeed the first step toward that intrepid secular humanism which boasts so proud a history of reform and revolution, and from which the social gospel has taken its inspiration as the minimally religious alternative to the godless ideologies. Yet beneath the ethical cover of Deism, humanism, and the social gospel, single vision has worked its way deep into the bloodstream of modern culture. Hence Blake's titanic effort to integrate radical politics with the Old Gnosis. He knew intuitively that in the long evolution of human consciousness, ethical principle has grown up out of a religious soil, that human fellowship is the moral aspect of that transcendent Oneness whose root meaning is known only by visionary experience. And Blake would not part the soil from the fruit, lest in time the fruit wither. That is what makes his political intelligence (like that of Tolstoy, Gandhi, Buber) so much keener than that of Marx and the secular ideologues. Knowing what horrors follow when the discipline of the sacred has been lost, Blake could discern "the spirit of evil in things heavenly"—bomb physics and the human guinea pigs of Buchenwald emerging from the worldview of Newton and Pasteur, the behavioral reductionism of

Watson and Skinner springing from the humane aspirations of Bacon and Locke, the Frankensteinian nightmares of modern science and technics arising from Promethean dreams of glory.

This is a cultural lineage that even now few humanist intellectuals are prepared to recognize as part of their tradition. Instead, they forcibly ignore it, like a respectable family struggling to conceal a streak of criminal insanity in the blood. They insist that our science and technics need only recover a proper sense of "social responsibility," and all will be well. They argue that by measures of institutional and professional reform—or perhaps by moral exhortation alone—urban-industrial society can yet be "humanized." For obviously it cannot be humanism itself that requires critical examination; it is simply that society is not yet humanistic enough. So they produce eloquent pleas and ingenious schemes for a "humanistic" psychology and psychotherapy, a "humanistic" sociology, a "humanistic" economics, linguistics, literary scholarship, anthropology, technology, city planning, social welfare, medical science; and on the far left, a "humanistic" Marxism. Year after year—and for how many years already!—these bold proposals sound across the pages of the best journals like clarions of a new dawn. Volumes of hotly dissenting humanist opinion pile up on the bookshelf, brilliant critiques of reductionism, mechanism, behaviorism, structural-functionalism: daring revisions that finally break through, with great self-congratulations, to some minor human truth that Shakespeare or Sophocles long ago salted away in a casual epigram and would never have imagined needing to document or defend. Strange, is it not, how we now have whole libraries of heavy research in the humanities and social sciences—including the work of our humanist scholars— that add up to less wisdom, less living insight than many of our youth can find in the words of illiterate primitives like Black Elk or Carlos Casteneda's Don Juan, and surely less than any of us would find in a single dialogue of Plato, a single essay of Montaigne, a single Buddhist sutra?

Can one help concluding that there is something more radically corrupted than humanist intellectuals suspect about a standard of intellect which requires a lifetime of professional study and strenuous debate, much ornate methodology and close research to produce at last a meager grain of human understanding, cautiously phrased and nearly drowning in its own supporting evidence? That people are very likely not machines . . . that love is rather important to healthy growth . . . that "peak experiences" are probably of some personal and cultural significance . . . that living things have "goal-oriented needs" . . . that human beings have an emotional inside and are apt to resent being treated like statistical ciphers or mere objects . . . that participating in things is more rewarding than passively watching or being bossed about . . . how many books do I take up each year and abandon in anguished boredom after the first two chapters, because here once again is some poor soul offering me a ton of data and argument to demonstrate what ought to be the axioms of daily human experience? If our paleolithic ancestors were presented with these "controversial new findings," surely far from applauding our deep-minded humanism, they would only wonder "where along the line did these people become so stupid that they now must prove to themselves from scratch that $2 + 2 = 4$?"

In a recent essay, the humanistic psychologist Sigmund Koch confesses to being plain *tired of* the bone-wearying struggle he has had to wage in his profession against the behaviorist counterfeiters, and must still wage. "Yes, still. . . . I have given half a career as a psychologist," he laments, "to the detailed registration of scholarly error over the phenomenon—and strange time course—of behaviorism. It has been a tiresome role . . . " No doubt. And yet reductionist intellect, like Dr. Frankenstein's monster, refuses to die; it stalks on across the landscape trouncing everything in its path. Why is it the humanists cannot deal the monster its death blow? Is it perhaps because they know that their own life's blood—*their* tradition, *their* dearest values— courses through the monster's body, and therefore they dare not strike? Professor Koch comes close to the heart of the beast when he asks, "What does behaviorism mean? I mean in a human way."

> Really very simple: behaviorism is the strongest possible wish that the organism and, *entre nous,* the person may not exist—a vast, many-voiced, poignant lament that anything so refractory to the assumptions and methods of eighteenth-century science should clutter up the world-scape.

For where, after all, do the humanists think the behaviorist's debased, manipulative caricature of human nature and society springs from? Where do they think the dehumanizing forces originate which corrupt the academic and intellectual traditions they now must strain to rehumanize? Where do they think the strange idea comes from that knowledge can legitimately be detached from wisdom, that specialized research can be a suitable substitute for integral and participative experience? Above all, where do they think the reductionist scholars and scientists draw the influence and conviction which allows them to brush aside humanist moralizing so effortlessly?

The answer is that intellect in urban-industrial society—*including humanist intellect*—is the captive of single vision; and the heart of single vision is that very science of nature from which humanism historically and still today takes inspiration for its project of secularizing value and culture. Humanism, for all its ethical protest, will not and cannot shift the quality of consciousness in our society; *it has not the necessary psychic leverage.* Indeed, it stands full square upon the stone that must be overturned. After all, the reductionists who see nature as a machine and the human being as a robot are not apt to regard moral indignation as anything more than a queer quirk in the robot's electro-bio-psycho-chemico-physical feedback apparatus. And who are the humanists to talk to them of the reality of soul or spirit?

Burdened as they are by single vision, the secular humanists simply do not see the crucial links that bind them to reductionist intellect. They cannot trace alienation back to its germ in the objectified worldview of natural science. They cannot see how the blight that lays waste our life and our culture takes its course from the physics of Newton, Einstein, and Bohr, from the biology of Darwin, Crick, and Watson. They cannot see how the deadly chill of Pavlov's psychology is able to shelter within the high moral flame of "scientific socialism." They do not know that when nature dies beneath Urizen's scalpel, the human soul dies with it. For between mankind and nature there is no conveniently dichotomizing line the humanists can hold against the reductionist advance. Finally and inevitably, the picture we accept as a valid depiction of the molecules and galaxies will be our own self-portrait.

"The spirit of evil in things heavenly . . . " But within the last few generations, as alienation has come to be recognized as a chronic condition of urban-industrial life—a state of sick normality—many intellectuals and artists, with the trendier critics and slick journalists not far behind, have become almost chummy with that "spirit of evil." There has developed a bizarre virtuosity in the varieties of nihilism; whole schools of art and literature now specialize in its iconography and modish nuances, lending it the dignity of being "our twentieth-century way of life." Accordingly, clever, highly literate people now toy with the latest fashions in alienated living. They watch keenly for crisp, new analyses and elaborations and insights; and if these are not forthcoming, they grow bored with the scene and insist that we go on to the *next* subject of discussion. It is rather like getting so used to living with death camps and political terrorism that it all becomes too tiresome to talk about. Already our novelists, painters, playwrights, and film makers must resort to apocalyptic extremes to express in some arrestingly novel way the ingrained death-in-life of normal middle-class society. A madhouse imagery of mass murder, cannibalism, necrophilia, bestiality, Grand Guignol fills their work. They waste their talent in a worthless competition to be the first with the most extreme. Worst of all, they forget that art has any other function than to mirror the horrors. Within the last several years, most of the experimental little theater productions I have seen have been so routinely taken up with breakdown-of-communication, dehumanized encounters, casual sadism, sexual mayhem that I begin to wonder if perhaps these young writers and actors and directors do not too much relish the decay they deal in. They have become so greedy-eager to work out all the permutations of the horrible. And then, "Ah yes," say the connoisseurs, "that was a strong statement . . . though perhaps with a bit too much theater of cruelty in the second act—and Artaud was *last* year."

When I was at college (the middle fifties) I learned the death of God like a data point in freshman survey courses. I took exams on "contrasting concepts of the absurd—time limit twenty minutes." I was taught to admire the latest refinements Beckett and Ionesco had wrought upon the existential vacuum. Modern man, I dutifully noted, is in search of a soul, and the age is an age of longing. But sophisticated minds must know better than to expect that search and that longing to find gratification. There might be private strategies of consolation (like Santayana's cultivation of an aesthetic religiosity), but the first fact of public life was alienation—and alienation was here to stay. Except perhaps in economic affairs. There a strong left-wing commitment permitted one to speak of eliminating the worker's "alienation" from the means and fruits of production—a much reduced Marxist usage of the term, which, of course, had nothing to do with the spiritual life. Of the needs of the spirit one simply did not speak; the very word was without a negotiable meaning in educated company. This, I rapidly learned, was the most intellectually intolerable aspect of personality and accordingly the most repressed. One might discourse in luscious detail about one's sex life in fact and fantasy; but how gauche, how offensive to introduce anything even vaguely religious into serious conversation—unless with a fastidious scholarly detachment . . . as a point of fact . . . about other people . . . in other times and places.

But what was all this clever confabulation with the alienated life but the cultural expression of urban-industrial social necessity? For the sake of the artificial environment, the soul *had* to die. The transcendent impulse that cried out in me for life and a dignified space in the world *had* to stay jailed up in my head as personal fantasy. Either that or be gunned down on sight for subversive activity. God—any god who was more than a presidential platitude—had become an enemy of the new industrial state. This was why secular humanism had become the orthodox intellectual style of the age; why Marxism had become the orthodox radicalism. Neither took issue with science or technics or the psychological mode they demand. Neither broke with the artificial environment. Both served the needs of technocratic politics.

How long could this principled repression of the visionary energies go on? How long before there came a generation which realized that a wasteland is no place to make one's home?

No doubt there are ways and means to ameliorate, at least temporarily, the most dangerous excesses of urban-industrialism and the technocratic politics it breeds. But for the disease of single vision there can be no ad hoc reform, no quick technological fix. And it is single vision that underlies the despair, the anomie, the irresponsible drift, the resignation to genocide, the weakness for totalitarian solutions, which make radical, enduring change in our society impossible. Until we find our way once more to the experience of transcendence, until we feel the life within us and the nature about us as sacred, there will seem to us no "realistic" future other than more of the same: single vision and the artificial environment forever and ever, amen.

That is why the politics of our time must reopen the metaphysical issues which science and sound logic have for the last two centuries been pleased to regard as closed. For to expound upon social priorities or the quality of life without confronting those issues is the very folly of alienation. It is, once again, the half person prescribing the whole person's needs. But it is *experience* that must reopen those issues, not academic discourse. We must learn once more to discriminate experientially between realities, telling the greater from the lesser. If there is to be a next politics, it will be a religious politics. Not the religion of the churches—God help us! not the religion of the churches—but religion in the oldest, most universal sense: which is vision born of transcendent knowledge.

6

Two Possible Futures

Richard Falk adds a political dimension to our analysis by focusing on international relations. The main premise of his article is that "the sovereign state cannot solve the characteristic problems of our time. . . . " He looks upon population, pollution, war, biological research, multinational corporations as international problems that can be solved only if we reevaluate our beliefs about such concepts as nationalism and sovereignty. "The point is to convince as many people as possible that we are in the midst of an emergency, that the traditional priorities, aims, and conflicts need to be subordinated and that there is a way out, but it involves change, sacrifice, and danger for all societies." Phrased differently, we either begin the process of meaningful international organization and cooperation, or we embrace a future whose end is "catastrophe."

When reading Falk's article, keep in mind his argument that although "some sort of global federalism is eventually desirable as a substitute for the sovereign state system, it cannot (and perhaps should not) be brought into being until a period of transition and preparation has transpired." Falk sees the intimate relationship between what I referred to in the Preface as ideological change and institutional change. In planning for tomorrow we seek both simultaneously, but ideological change is the more fundamental of the two. If a meaningful global federalism is to materialize, people must first reevaluate and change their values. Otherwise, there is danger that rhetoric will proliferate, but, because no basic ideological change will occur, the new organizations that spring from the rhetoric will not be very different from the organizations they replace.

So Falk stresses that changes in beliefs and values will and *should* take time. In his view the seventies are (or could be) "the decade of awareness"; the eighties, "the decade of mobilization"; the nineties, "the decade of transformation."

From This Endangered Planet
—Richard Falk

THE FUTURE AS PROJECTED FROM THE PRESENT

We suppose in this first exercise of the imagination that nothing very startling happens to reverse the present course of disintegrating developments. The attentions of governments continue to concentrate upon competitive rivalry in world affairs and economic growth and civil order in domestic affairs. The big states maintain current levels of arms spending and smaller states gradually acquire the capability to wage mass war in the nuclear age. Pollution and population issues are often discussed in the more industrialized societies and larger efforts at abatement and birth control are made. Alarmist predictions about the future are made by a variety of specialists and are carried along with other news of the day. Great strides forward are reported in space exploits, biomedical research, deep-sea exploration, synthetic food production, and computer sciences. The technetronic age is upon us with cold efficiency, central data banks of constricting knowledge, and the disappearance of privacy.

Poorer countries continue with their efforts to modernize their societies, which includes becoming better and better equipped to fight modern wars of mass destruction. Civil strife is present in widely separated parts of the globe. Technological and ecological disasters occur with greater frequency but continue to be reported as unfortunate accidents and isolated disasters: A half-million-ton oil tanker splits open in mid-ocean, a smog attack causes sharp jumps in urban death rates, famine and epidemic reports from the crowded countries of Asia are given prominence from time to time, some radioactive waste leaks from its underground burial place into a subterranean water system that seeps into a major river system, several countries are suspected of developing nuclear weapons in secret and several more are stockpiling nerve gas and bacteriological weapons.

The same political structures as we know today persist as do the basic forms of political conflict. Governments continue to be preoccupied with the ambitions of their rivals, with building up their own GNP, and with stamping out fires of discontent wherever they flare up. The race will continue between the bureaucratic capacities of repressive governments and the insurrectionist capacities of revolutionary groups. Political energy will be directed toward maintaining control over man-in-society by managing the dynamics of power within the nation and in the relations among nations.

Such an emphasis will resist information about the deteriorating character of the international environment. Various kinds of pollution will cross thresholds of irretrievable disaster, causing the disappearance of many species of marine and wildlife. Urban growth will press upon the open spaces and crowd still further the already heavily settled parts of the world. All kinds of ingenious proposals for alleviating environmental pressure will be advanced, but numbers will keep increasing, as will per capita demands.

The human spirit will be worn down even if no cataclysmic event such as a nuclear war or a drastic change of earth temperature, oxygen supply, or ocean level occurs. The regimentation in large societies and the inability of governments to secure a decent quality of life for their populations will lead to widespread human despair. The loss of man's confidence to shape his destiny will become almost total with the appearance of robots and hominoids, making it virtually impossible to distinguish between people and artificially created centers of "intelligent" action.

Against this tableau we expect a tense world system that moves from crisis to crisis and is unable to organize a coherent response to the underlying hazards and decay of the whole experience of mankind. Each national society will shift blame to the machinations of others and concentrate upon upholding "its interests" in a world of impending doom. In terms of sequence, we might expect the following course of events.

The 1970's—The Politics of Despair. In the 1970's there will arise a deepening sense of the inability of major governments to solve the central problems before their societies. The rich countries will continue to build new expensive weapons systems to secure, if possible, a competitive edge over their rivals and a dominant position in relation to their potential challengers. The poorer countries will continue to base their hopes upon small annual increases in their GNP, but population expansion and military spending will eliminate most of the improvement in the standard of living that might otherwise have taken place. Large-scale misery will persist.

The pressure of rising populations will everywhere push back the remaining preserves of nature. Urban sprawls will be the breeding ground of disease, distress, crime, and revolution. Electronic techniques of surveillance and propaganda will try to immobilize internal opposition groups. The struggles of government to survive will overshadow all other concerns and will inhibit the search for solutions to more underlying problems. People will be led to submit or revolt.

Poorer countries will grow more receptive to romantic schemes for the improvement of their position in the world: Threats to develop nuclear weapons, military buildups, and a variety of attacks on the citadels of affluence will send tremors across world society. Radical energies will continue to pin human hope on seizing power from oppressors. More and more, the strategy of seizure will acquire an international dimension. The poor societies will perceive themselves as sharing a condition of oppression and privation, and will challenge the propriety of the world power structure.

In advanced countries many individuals will grow dispirited with politics altogether. The old political concerns will lose their relevance to the imagination of the most enlightened members of a society. Alienation on a massive scale is likely to ensue, leading to severe symptoms of withdrawal and nervous disorder. Politics will lead men of thought and feeling to despair: not caring, not doing. There will be no reason to suppose a better future, just more of the same. *People will increasingly doubt whether life is worth living.* Religions will become a weaker source of comfort and guidance as people in smaller and more backward communities grow more able to act on their unbelief.

Nothing much is likely to change during the decade. Some achievements will be hailed, some disasters will be lamented; there will be more people, more noise, more garbage, more weapons possessed by more governments, more violence of all kinds threatened and proposed, worse accidents, and fewer trees, less wilderness, fewer usable resources. The world scene may be more or less in turmoil, but there will be a continuous effort to ward off catastrophe by monitoring dangerous conditions. Hotlines will interconnect most capitals of the world. Sovereign states will persist as the exclusive centers of political power, but will enjoy less automatic loyalty from their populations and will relinquish to multinational corporations much of their former control over economic activity. The UN will still be there, but its utterances will not matter much more than today, nor will its prestige be much enhanced whether or not, by then, China participates in its activities. National governments will remain entrapped by the values and constraints of the national setting, and no major institutional changes are likely to occur, although a small underground world government movement may be identified in various parts of the world. Some of its leaders may be put in jail as "subversives" or "detained" for long periods. The more prescient members of the various *anciens régimes* of the world will sense hard times ahead and make subtle proposals for thought control and moral conformity. There will everywhere be a drift toward the centralization of power accompanied by greater reliance on police methods and more regulation of dissent. Some concentration camps will be used, many more will be built. TV and newspapers will be increasingly subject to governmental control.

The 1980's—The Politics of Desperation. C. P. Snow asserts that "Despair is a sin. Or, if you talk in secular terms as I do, it prevents one taking such an action as one might, however small it is. I have to say that I have been nearer to despair this year, 1968, than ever in my life." Those men of goodwill who have been concerned with working carefully and peacefully for reform will gradually drop out of sight, mainly victims of despair. Governments will come to realize their own inability to solve the principal problems of man-in-society. The pressure upon the environment will grow even more intense, strains and dislocations will occur with more frequency, on a larger scale, and will arouse greater alarm. Only drastic change will seem capable of doing anything about the situation, but "establishments" everywhere will resist pleas for drastic change, as the dynamics of change would appear to threaten prevailing social structures and produce sudden and massive transfers of wealth and status. Those that have, do not voluntarily give up their privileges to those that have not, but organize defensive efforts.

But not everyone will succumb to the politics of despair. There will be everywhere some who believe in the need for drastic change and are willing to accept the risks of working for it. The espousal of such an outlook will begin to threaten those with power, especially if a prospect for a large change-oriented constituency begins to emerge. The politics of desperation breeds the attitudes, tactics, and reactions of revolution and counterrevolution. Under modern circumstances the technology of government can effectively eliminate a potentiality for resistance and revolution. We already know that totalitarian regimes, if backed up by secret police, media control, propaganda, control over child education, can keep their populations at bay for long periods of time without even having to kill anyone. Such forms of repressive government will be likely to proliferate in the 1980's. The objective of government would be to depoliticize the mass, discourage and punish dissent, and hunt down deviant revolutionary personalities and groups. Such a pattern is to be expected, especially in the most powerful countries, where mass disaffection is likely to result from the inability of government to halt the decline in the quality of life for most of the population. The methods of repression may grow very sophisticated, relying upon subliminal manipulation and a system of perpetual, but nonintrusive, surveillance. Electronic censors might, for instance, be able to monitor all movements of political suspects, record their utterances, and photo-transmit their action. Knowledge alone of such a capability by government would intimidate all but the bravest individuals, and make the entire enterprise of political opposition seem self-destructive and futile. A revolution can take shape only if there are opportunities to persuade and organize, places to hide while building a movement, and sanctuaries for retreat during early stages of struggle. If these open political spaces disappear, then governments will succeed in maintaining regimes of law and order in the 1980's, and will be able to ignore the grievances and disaffection of despairing masses of men and women.

Perhaps the objective situation of impending environmental catastrophe will move members of the establishment to consider or even stage ''inside'' coups. Deteriorating world conditions may prompt a new, hitherto unknown kind and form of domestic revolution that might catch the establishment off guard, as if the radar was pointing toward the probable enemy, but the air attack came from a friendly quadrant of the skies. Such surprise had caught Arab air defenses off guard, even in a period of high tension, when Israeli planes attacked on June 5, 1967, initiating the Six-Day War. The point is that we will find a loss of confidence in traditional modes of political actions, and a sense of desperation will be felt by opponents and a mingled sense of anxiety and impotence by power-wielders. Such a setting is likely to generate a politics of desperation, if it does not induce the disappearance of politics altogether.

In the poorer countries the same kinds of developments are likely to occur, but the hold of the central government over its population is likely to be less secure and less complete during the 1980's. Misery will persist, despair and desperation will ensue. As such, we can project a continuation of cycles of turmoil, strife and repression throughout the Third World.

But an increasing portion of Third World energy will be turned outward in the form of hostility toward those actors in the world that are doing well, at least in an economic sense. Such hostility may turn to rage if the debris of a space flight falls on an Asian inhabited community or if sickness and disease are traced to the effluents of the rich industrial societies. Governments in these countries may also grow convinced (or think it expedient to explain) that their own failures are an outgrowth of a rigid system of international stratification that exploits the poor for the sake of the rich. As such, one can imagine governments in groups or singly pursuing the politics of desperation, by acquiring the capability to destroy or disrupt any society in the world. The strategy of the have-not nations could well move toward adopting a real military strike capability as the essential preliminary to hard bargaining for a new deal in international society. One might recall the sardonic wisdom of the English nineteenth-century literary personality, Rev. Sydney Smith: "From what motive but fear, I should like to know, have all the improvements in our constitution proceeded? I question if any justice has ever been done to large masses of mankind from any other motive. . . . "

Such an arousal of tensions in world affairs might lead to a frenzied realignment of powers that would decisively end the ideological dispute that produced the Soviet-American conflict in the years after World War II. Concessions in the terms of international trade, in capital loans, in economic assistance might be offered by the rich countries, but to no avail. Once the politics of desperation takes root it will not be cajoled into moderation. The man who sees himself mutilated by another and is prepared to die fighting for a new order is not likely to settle for a 2 to 5 percent rate of readjustment, but this is the fastest pace of voluntary adjustment that can be imagined. A rate of 20 to 50 percent is deemed minimal to the extent that bargaining can go forward at all. The politics of desperation may involve a gigantic North-South buildup in preparation for World War III. Surely, the rich, challenged power-wielders would resist the demands for drastic reform as excessive and impractical. The technological gaps may have grown so large by the late 1980's that the superstates will be in a position to disarm and recolonize the poor, populous countries at small risk to themselves. There may be a movement to do this in the interest of world peace and to safeguard the international economy.

In fact, it would not be implausible to discover that a new civilizing mission in the rich countries is engendered by the urgencies of man-in-nature. The powerful governments may convince themselves that their own welfare and the future of the planet depend on imposing population and pollution curbs in Asian, African, and Latin American countries. Trusted advisers to the Soviet and American governments may conclude that the poorer countries of Asia and Africa have no capacity to provide for the welfare of their own populations or to ease up the pressure on the world system. Such a perception is especially likely if population growth continues in the 1980's at a rate of 1 percent or more and if food and environmental resources become scarce in quantity and degenerate in quality. This perception will be reinforced by demands from these troubled lands for freedom to migrate to less populated countries and for the receipt of a fixed proportion of GNP from the richer societies. Perhaps desperate strategies will be initiated by the rich countries to depopulate Asia, Africa, and Latin America to relieve the overall pressure of man upon the environment and to assure the maintenance of an ample flow of raw materials and primary commodities. We may not yet have heard the end of "the white man's burden," or perhaps, of "the yellow man's burden."

Whatever its form, the 1980's are likely to end on some note of desperation in a world fraught with tension and fear. We would still expect no changes in world structure. Sovereign states will continue to act as autonomous agents for national gain, being both abetted and impeded by a very powerful network of multinational corporations; the growth of regional institutions and special functional regimes is likely to remain marginal to mainstream world political concerns, as is the still extant, still enfeebled United Nations Organization.

The 1990's—The Politics of Catastrophe. As we retreat further into the future our political moorings are likely to grow more and more insecure. Our purpose is to identify the probable political impacts of those unchecked trends toward disintegration that have earlier been summarized as the essence of an endangered planet. The gloomy prognosis rests on the conviction that prevailing political perceptions and institutions will prove unable to cope with the challenges of the future, that these inabilities will induce a dominant mood of despair in the 1970's and a dominant mood of desperation in the 1980's, and that this dismal sequence of development will eventuate in catastrophe in the 1990's. This pattern of expectation about the future is an interpretation of emerging rhythms of action and reaction; our schedule may be too slow or too rapid, it may also be too confined by the boundaries of present awareness. We are projecting outward from our current sense of the situation. The world has been vulnerable to catastrophe since the beginning of the nuclear age and certainly since both the United States and the Soviet Union possessed deliverable high megatonnages of nuclear warheads targeted at each other's centers of population and industry. Where something of this sort is possible, it may happen. The risks cannot be calculated, but there is a finite risk of general nuclear war at any time, that appears raised to higher levels during periods of superpower crisis and confrontation, most spectacularly, one supposes, during the Cuban Missile Crisis of 1962. Therefore, throughout the period of the future there will exist at every moment some risk of catastrophe, perhaps gradually increased by the steady buildup of a danger of ecological collapse. There are also other kinds of risks of catastrophe ranging from man-initiated large-scale weather modification and from induced earthquakes to large-scale pollution of oceans, rivers, forests, and skies. The risk of disaster will rise continually in the years ahead, and barring some colossal human intervention, a disaster of catastrophic proportions is likely to occur in the 1990's. In any event, people attuned to their world will anticipate catastrophe in the closing decade of the century.

If there should be some recolonization of the poor portions of the world, then it is possible that the sense of impending catastrophe would recede from political consciousness, especially if the new colonizers were motivated by a large-scale effort to relieve pressure on the environment and reorganize the entire world system along ecologically sound lines. But basement H-bombs and the like will make it quite likely that in some weakly governed societies subnational or resistance groups will gain access to formidable military capabilities. The hypermodern state will grow ever more dependent on an interlinked network of controls and flows, and will become highly sensitive to intended and accidental disruption. The government will devote great energy and resources to prevent disruptive breakdowns and expend much ingenuity on the development of quick-detection and recovery procedures. Such a prospect of imminent breakdown will make ruling groups exceedingly nervous and encourage the deployment of surveillance and repressive technology to enable early warning, detection, and neutralization of disruptive behavior. The rising influence and expanding mission of the police will be justified, if justifications are needed, as essential vigilance given the vulnerability of technology to disruption and the presence of political unrest in the system.

Nevertheless, the mounting pressure on the environment is likely to interact with the politics of catastrophe to bring about the downfall of the world system as we have known it. The depth of the catastrophe, its character, and the prospects for rehabilitation will influence the reaction to it. In its aftermath proposals for sweeping world-order reforms that were earlier dismissed as "impractical" are likely to be studied and considered with solemn seriousness. The occurrence of a global catastrophe is likely to bring an end to the long reign of the sovereign state as the basic organizing unit of human life. What world system will be put in its place will almost certainly proceed from the premise of the wholeness of the planet and work out the ramifications of this premise in light of the dominant goals, values, and points of convergence that take shape in the bargaining and negotiating process. Obviously, it will be one kind of post-sovereign world if only the Afro-Asian societies are left intact, another if only the Euro-American societies survive, and still another if there is a more-or-less uniform impact throughout the world. The outcome will depend greatly on whether the organizing initiative is compulsory or voluntary and whether the dominant human forces are despotic or enlightened in political persuasion.

The Twenty-First Century—An Era of Annihilation. Let us suppose that the organized life of mankind is not permanently disrupted by the politics of catastrophe projected for the 1990's. Perhaps the police techniques of control and the propaganda techniques of manipulation will indeed keep dissident groups under control. Perhaps the dominant states will be able to maintain their control over the activities of secondary states. Perhaps pollution abatement will become a major undertaking of principal governments and manage to keep the air we breathe clear enough and the food we eat pure enough. Perhaps an S-curve effect will lead to a reduced rate of population growth, so that the oxygen supply will not be seriously depleted, or the temperature of the earth rise so much as to produce drastic polar melting or disruptive weather change. Perhaps no Hitlers or Napoleons will take over the administration of a major government, no major leakage of radioactive waste will occur, no major war will break out, no major subversive plot will succeed. Perhaps, in other words, the worst will not happen, despite a context of continuing disintegration and extraordinary danger. Then what?

We would expect no major adaptation in terms of value-change or institutional innovation. Sovereign states would still run the political affairs of mankind, military power would still be the basis of national security, economic growth would still be the primary measure of social progress, and the gap between the rich countries and the poor countries would still be expanding.

How can such an outmoded world-order system hope to endure? Would it not seem certain that it would either be subverted from within, perhaps by a sect of super-robots who are instructed to take over the world for the sake of man, or crash down toward some cataclysmic end? By the next century the tensions will be so taut, the pressures and dangers so great, the lack of space so evident, the interdependencies so critical, the conflicts of interest so profound that the capacity for spontaneous adjustment is likely to be minimal, if not negative. It seems almost certain that the compulsions of the power-wielders will lead to a surge of repressive political energy reinforced by the super-technologies that lie ahead. Such a system cannot be peacefully transformed: It is taken over or it crashes down in ruin, leaving the entire system in disarray, perhaps irretrievably so. For this reason, we would suppose that the twenty-first century will inaugurate the Era of Annihilation.

THE FUTURE—AS A RESPONSE TO THE ENDANGERED PLANET

The positive line of potential development is even less predictable than its negative shadow because the stress is placed on institutional innovation and value change. Success requires a rapid erosion of national constraints on thought and action, perhaps through a quiet initial buildup at first, supplemented later on by more frontal assaults. The political premise that informs our analysis of the future is that the sovereign state cannot solve the characteristic problems of our time, and the sub-premise is that although some kind of global federalism is eventually desirable as a substitute for the sovereign state system it cannot (and perhaps should not) be brought into being until a period of transition and preparation has transpired.

To penetrate the political consciousness of governmental elites is the first task. There are frequent verbal acknowledgments at this time that problems of population pressure, the arms race, and the environment are matters of serious concern. But the acknowledgements tend to be fragmentary and to stop short of drawing appropriate economic and political conclusions. The population problem tends to be *dissociated* from other pressures on the world political and life-support systems, and the proposed solution tends to call for a little more attention, resources, and technology, but nothing more fundamental is deemed necessary. Such views are totally misleading, induce complacency, and do not encourage solution-oriented proposals. There is no way to remove the fourfold threat to mankind within the present structures of attitude, value, and institutional design. Robert McNamara, more sensitive than most eminent men of the day to the emerging crisis, himself split off population pressure from other interrelated matters as he called upon people to become responsible actors: "A rational, responsible, moral solution to the population problem must be found. You and I—all of us—share the responsibility to find and apply that solution. If we shirk that responsibility, we will have committed the crime. But it will be those who come after us who will pay the undeserved . . . and the unspeakable . . . penalties." It is questionable, at least for today's young, whether it will only be those who come after us that will suffer these penalties. Mr. McNamara, despite the ardor of his rhetoric, the depth of his concern, still seems to be a captive of the engineering mentality. The distinctive character of the endangered-planet crisis is that it emphasizes the need for *new political systems* and the inability of the present system, even if attentive to the crisis, to bring about a restored equilibrium between man and his environment. Mr. McNamara's statement by its limited responsiveness helps locate the present highwater mark of enlightenment among the most intelligent members of the power-wielding groups. Such power-wielders tend to keep the authority framework rigid in their prescriptions for the future. This authority framework is part of the obsolete machinery of our present system of world order. As such, it points up the need for a crash program in reality-testing, learning theory, and general education so that a more coherent response can be formed in a pre-catastrophe mood.

We turn now to consider a decade-by-decade account of a positive future for the earth, based on building a new system of world order.

The 1970's—The Decade of Awareness. The first task is to get a real fix on the situation presented by the fourfold threat to planetary welfare and to work toward a model for response. It will be essential to begin monitoring the critical trends immediately to avoid great hazards or points of no return. But the main effort should be to achieve a dissemination of concern by overt and covert forms of transmission throughout the entire world. The United Nations can perform useful roles by involving other countries in the discussion of the endangered-planet agenda.

The point is to convince as many people as possible that we are in the midst of an emergency, that the traditional priorities, aims, and conflicts need to be subordinated, and that there is a way out, but it involves change, sacrifice, and danger for all societies. The vested elites of the various power structures can be expected to fight back, more violently and ruthlessly as the consequences of the endangered-planet argument become more widely understood. Political leaders will resort to many forms of mystification, including giving their endorsement to the endangered-planet analysis accompanied by false assurances that the situation is not so dangerous as is contended or that it can be brought under control or that it is being exaggerated by enemies of the state.

The 1980's—The Decade of Mobilization. A general aroused awareness will produce a number of constituencies around the world demanding change. Proposals for new world-order systems will begin to be taken seriously in various political arenas and will be discussed within all major types of societies. Since the trend-lines appear quite clear there is likely to emerge a strong consensus as to the character of the endangered-planet crisis and the direction, at least, of political response. Sharp disagreements can be expected as to how to resolve the world-order crisis, by what tactics, with what priorities, toward what goals. The locus of jeopardy will be shifted in the direction of other actors, so that the rich and powerful will want their privileges mainly to survive transition, whereas the poor and weak will demand that the transition also emphasize equalization policies.

Transnational elites will play an increasingly important bargaining role in crystallizing a positive consensus upon which action can be taken. In some countries those who are committed to the old system will try to suppress this kind of world political movement, but at some point the momentum generated by the crisis-awareness will become overwhelming. The excitement caused by this mobilization process is likely to produce converging perspectives on action-proposals as well as a wave of confident expectation about a new world community that eliminates war and poverty and works to achieve harmony between man and nature. A new kind of optimism and energy will become evident at many points. New songs, symbols, heroes, movements, and myths will celebrate the transition process, heralding the new order for mankind that is being born.

Unpredictable alliances and antagonisms will reflect the decay of traditional politics in both national and international arenas.

The 1990's—The Decade of Transformation. Of course, as awareness crystallizes and as mobilization proceeds, the transformation of world order will begin to occur. But two decades, more or less, are needed to permit a favorable psychopolitical buildup to take place. At that point, a new definition of political acceptability will prevail in great portions of the world, ideas of sovereign prerogative will be muted or abandoned, and the work of community- and institution-building at a global level will begin to be the dominant political activity of the times.

A new kind of political ethos will have enlarged the idea of politics to include man-and-nature, as well as man-and-society. Several forms of ecological humanism will have arisen to replace earlier ideologies. Each principal cultural and regional setting will have stimulated at least one main ecologically grounded ideology by the 1990's. The separation of man from the rest of nature will seem less defensible than in earlier times. The capacities of supercomputers will deflate the pride of man in his own uniqueness whereas man's sense of dependence on a fragile environment will encourage a more conservative and humble view of man-in-nature. In high places we will find it standard to reflect an ecological outlook of the sort that today we associate with exceptional and nonpolitical men, such an outlook as is possessed by such a poetically inclined naturalist as John Hay:

> There is a chance, in this newly defined arena of darkness and light, a chance to live and let live, a chance, paradoxically enough, to get rid of that terrible, isolating concept of man as the lord of creation. . . . We have a great deal of exploring to do in order to find the place where we share our lives with other lives, where we breathe and reproduce, employ our sight, and join the breadth of chances not as separate, unique entities with doomsday on our docket but as vessels for universal experience.

We will be working toward a stable population that recycles its wastes so as to assure future generations an ample resource base. We will be working toward mass consumption of needs and the provision of satisfactions that are consistent with preserving the strength of diverse forms of life that do not imperil men or other animal species. A new political man will emerge from such a climate of opinion and change. The planet will be governed as a system that needs to guard against relapse and reversion, and regards the diversities within itself as a source of vitality and vigor. Procedures and institutions will be needed to balance the need for unity and uniformity against the claims for autonomy and pluralism. There will be conflicts, disaffections, reactions, movements to go back to the earlier period of international history. The strength of ecological humanism, however, will be too great; its satisfactions will give man a new sense of awe and of magic about the experience of life, and a will to guard this new stage of human evolution against forces that would drag man back to the war-torn, sovereignty-ridden world of the 1970's and 1980's.

The 21st Century—The Era of World Harmony. By the end of the century the institutions and attitudes appropriate for the ideology of ecological humanism will be firmly established among men. Population levels will be falling toward optimum levels. There will be debates about the level and composition of the global optimum, its allocational shares, and the system of incentives attached to its maintenance. The dangers of pollution will be managed by a central international agency working in conjunction with regional and local institutions. Resource use will also be governed by a strict set of standards and responsibilities fixed for recycling. Pollution will have been largely controlled, streams will be pure, air will be clean even in and around large cities. There will, of course, be no reliance at all, or virtually none, on the internal combustion engine for private transportation. Great energy will be concentrated upon community activity, local crafts will flourish, and pride in work and affection will be much more visible.

The applications of science and other branches of knowledge will be guided by service to the maintenance of harmony on the planet. A less homocentric scale of values will underlie political decision. The welfare of plants, animals, and machines will all be considered benevolent in this kind of humanism. It is a humanism only because the whole process is conceived of and worked out by man, as if man were hired as an architect to rehabilitate the ecosphere inhabited by all that exists on earth.

These two visions of the future correspond with "the newly defined arena of darkness and light" that infiltrates the mind. These are the two poles of our political imagination that illumine the choice confronting each of us. This choice will be made knowingly or by default throughout the globe in the years ahead. The prospects for the welfare and survival of the planet will undoubtedly reflect how lucidly and effectively this choice will be made in the critical places at the crucial hours. We improve the prospects to the extent we inform ourselves about "the facts" so as to be in a position to reject or act upon the endangered-planet appraisal.

7

The Counterculture and Social Change

In *The Greening of America,* Charles Reich is full of hope. Today may be horrible, he suggests, but new, more humane cultural principles (such as the primacy of the individual over the machine) are rapidly developing and will soon dominate modern thought. What will be the result? Reich argues that to ask that question "is to fail to see that the great error of our times has been the belief in structural or institutional solutions. . . . For the present *all that is necessary to describe the new society is to describe a new way of life.* When we have outlined a new way of life, we have said all that we can meaningfully say about the future."

I believe that Reich's critique of modern life touches upon the underlying principles of our society. But I am doubtful that change will emerge from the mere description of the new way of life. Refusal to participate in the Corporate State may not be enough.

Others present convincing arguments in opposition to Reich's theory. Some observe that those who flock to the commune are also those who, because of educational opportunities or class position, would have assumed power in the Corporate State. When those positions of power are left open, they will be filled by children of blue collar workers. These young people respect the Corporate State and all its products, and instead of turning America green, will very likely maintain the status quo.

So, although Reich asks and answers important questions, I believe his solution is too simple. While waiting for others to follow their example, counterculturists could see their communes destroyed by nuclear weapons, pollution, or highway construction.

From The Greening of America
—Charles Reich

. . . What happened to the American people? In a word, powerlessness. We lost the ability to control our lives or our society because we had placed ourselves excessively under the domination of the market and technology. Finally we totally abandoned ourselves to the Corporate State, cutting ourselves off from our sources and our consciousness to such an extent that we were threatened with destruction as a species. This history makes clear that the great and urgent need of these times is transcendence. To survive, to regain power over our own lives, we must transcend the machine. We must recapture the ultimate sovereign right to choose values for ourselves. Many philosophers and poets over the last century have called for a return to non-machine values. But by seeming to preach a regression to the past they have caused us to miss the real point. Reality is not served by trying to ignore the machine. Our history shows that what we must do is assert domination over the machine, to guide it so that it works for the values of our choice. The last two hundred years have fundamentally and irrevocably altered the terms of man's existence. The price of survival is an appropriate consciousness and social order to go along with the revolution of science and technology that has already occurred. The chaos we are now experiencing is the inevitable and predictable consequence of our failure to rise to this necessity. Consciousness I and Consciousness II have proven inadequate to guide our society any longer. What is called for is a higher logic and a higher reason. The creation of a new consciousness is the most urgent of America's real needs.

Once we recognize this need, we can see what is evolving in the form we have called Consciousness III. Consciousness III is an attempt to gain transcendence. This becomes apparent when we compare Consciousness III to Consciousness I and II. I and II are more alike than they are different. They both represent the underlying form of consciousness appropriate to the age of industrial development and the market economy, beginning in the eighteenth century. Both subordinate man's nature to his role in the economic system; Consciousness I on the basis of economic individualism, II on the basis of participation in organization. Both approve the domination of environment by technology. Both subordinate man to the state, Consciousness I by the theory of the unseen hand, II by the doctrine of the public interest. Both see man as basically antagonistic to his fellow man; neither has any theory of a human community except in terms of consent to law, government and force. Both deny the individual's responsibility for the actions of society. Both define man's existence in material terms, and define progress similarly. Both define thought in terms of the premises of science. Consciousness II differs from I mainly in that II is adjusted to the realities of a larger scale of organization, economic planning and a greater degree of political administration.

The new consciousness is utterly different. It seeks restoration of the non-material elements of man's existence, the elements like the natural environment and the spiritual that were passed by in the rush of material development. It seeks to transcend science and technology, to restore them to their proper place as tools of man rather than as the determinants of man's existence. It is by no means anti-technological, it does not want to break machines, but it does not want machines to run men. It makes the wholly rational assertion that machines should do the bidding of man, of man who knows and respects his own nature and the natural order of which he is a part. The new consciousness seeks new ways to live in light of what technology has made both possible and desirable. Since machines can produce enough food and shelter for all, why should not man end the antagonism derived from scarcity and base his society on love for his fellow man? If machines can take care of our material wants, why should not man develop the aesthetic and spiritual side of his nature? Prophets and philosophers have proposed these ways of life before, but only today's technology has made them possible. *Consciousness III could only have come into existence given today's technology. And only Consciousness III can make possible the continued survival of man as a species in this age of technology.*

Each of the characteristics of Consciousness III that we have described is a specific illustration of an underlying logic. The logic is obscure if we do not see the assumptions upon which it is based, and these assumptions are rarely articulated. But when the assumptions are recognized the seemingly irrational disappears and a realistic logic appears instead. Reasoning that starts from self is necessary because the prior consciousness forgot self in an obsessive fixation upon organizations and the State. The self and its sources in nature are real; machines alone cannot create real values. The preservation of the self against the State is not anti-social, it is of great and vital importance to the human community. Protection of nature and man from the machine is logical because of the power of the machine to dominate nature. (It is no surprise to the new generation that we can land on the moon.) A personal moral code that transcends law is necessary where law has ceased to express a balanced set of values. A flexible and personal approach to career is necessary because technology itself is rapidly changing and because technology will dictate to man unless he preserves the power to choose his own work. Participatory democracy is necessary because the comprehensive planning that technology requires is incapable of taking into account all significant factors unless many people participate in the process. A powerful new music is necessary to help lift people's minds out of the seductive logic of machinery so that they can have vision beyond the machine and thus escape its domination. Adaptable clothes are necessary because man's rigid compartmentalization into roles has prevented him from enjoying the freedom that technology makes possible. It is perfectly possible to work in an office for a few hours and then ride out on the road on a motorcycle, but formal clothes deny the individual's adaptability. Authority and hierarchy are rejected because they represent the subjection of human values to the requirements of organization. An intense feeling of community is necessary because technology has rendered all men interdependent. Competition, rivalry or personal flights of ego and power have become socially destructive. Given an abundance of material goods, the possibilities of a human community are finally made real, for it is now possible to believe in the goodness of man.

In light of what we have said, we can now see the true significance of the central fact about Consciousness III—its assertion of the power to *choose* a way of life. The people who came to this country chose a life-style; it was for that freedom of choice that they left their native countries. But when the machine took over, men lost the power of choice, and their lives were molded to fit the domination of the machine. The machine slavery, extending upward to the white-collar and professional ranks, became the key reality of twentieth-century existence. The power of choice, the power to transcend, is exactly what has been missing in America for so long. That is why a new life-style is capable of dismantling the Corporate State, when both liberal reform and radical tactics are powerless. The elements of that life may vary and change; the supreme act is the act of choice. For the choice of a life-style is an act of transcendence of the machine, an act of independence, a declaration of independence. We are entering a new age of man.

In pre-industrial times, man's life was integrated with his community and with nature. God dwelt in each man, in growing things and in the sky. Communal life was governed by tribal authority and by tradition. Existence was harsh, dull, limited and virtually static from generation to generation. Religion and ethics expressed the realities man knew.

The industrial age represented man's enormously successful attempt to raise his level of existence by dominating life through reason and science. Man drove himself to ever-higher achievements by isolating each individual and forcing him into the competitive struggle. Work and culture were uprooted from the communal setting and required to serve the industrial machine. Life was regulated by a political system designed to control and regulate man's war against his fellow man. Economic power was heavily concentrated, although Marx and others began a movement toward equality and social ownership of the means of production. Religion, divorced from the realities of life, offered an ethical system to minimize the harm of the competitive and functional basis of existence, but without actually challenging that basis. Man harnessed himself to the machine.

Beyond the industrial era lies a new age of man. The essence of that age must be the end of the subjugation of man, the end of his subordination to the machine and the beginning of the subjugation of the machine—the use of technology to create a still higher level of life but one based upon values beyond the machine. The politics of controlling man become unimportant, the politics of controlling machines and organizations become the new concern of government. Economic equality and social ownership of the means of production are assumed, but they are now only a means to an end beyond. Man's religion and ethics will once again express the true realities of his way of life: solidarity with his fellow man, a genuine community representing a balanced moral-aesthetic order and a continuing expansion of man's inner capacities.

Surely this new age is not a repudiation of, but a fulfillment of, the American dream. What were the machines for, unless to give a new freedom to choose how he would live? What were they for, unless to expand individual freedom, and the range of human possibility? What is the central idea of America, unless each man's ability to create his own life? The dream was deferred for many generations in order to create a technology that could raise life to a higher level. It need be, it can be, delayed no longer.

If we are correct so far, then we can respond to the question of whether Consciousness III is practical and realistic, whether its way of life can really work. That question should, in the first instance, be addressed to our present way of life. It is our present society that does not work. It is the machine-dominated world that represents a fantastic distortion of reality. In seeing our present society without the distortions of false consciousness, in declaring that the choice of values is our greatest need, Consciousness III is more realistic than anything we have known in America for a century. Nor is it bent upon destroying anything that is realistically essential to our life. It does not propose to abolish work or excellence, it proposes to abolish irrational and involuntary servitude. It does not propose to abolish law, organization, or government, it asks instead that they serve rational, human ends. Consciousness III is neither lazy, defenseless nor incompetent. It does not reject technique, it rejects domination by technique. Consciousness III is practical in the most profound sense, because the historic time for man's transcendence over the machine has come.

What social order does Consciousness III propose? To ask this question is to fail to see the basic thing that is wrong with the Corporate State. The great error of our times has been the belief in structural or institutional solutions. The enemy is within each of us; so long as that is true, one structure is as bad as another. Consciousness I and II believed that, to design or describe a society adequately, it was only necessary to refer to its structures and institutions. Consciousness III says, for the present, *all that is necessary to describe the new society is to describe a new way of life*. When we have outlined a different way of life, we have said all that we can meaningfully say about the future. This is not avoiding the hard questions. The hard questions—if by that is meant political and economic organization—are insignificant, even irrelevant.

Once a new way of life is established, structural and institutional questions may again become worthy of discussion. The form of society will once again influence how men live. But existing forms have become so irrational and irrelevant that all that is needed to begin a new way of life can happen without reference to them. We repeat: to describe a new way of life is to describe fully the society that is coming. For the *locus* of that society is not in politics or economics, but in how and for what ends we live.

If this is true, then it is also true that a new way of life does not have to wait for a new world, it can be built out of the elements now available. Pop art illustrates this process. The artifacts of modern life, such as neon signs, juke boxes, Campbell's soup cans, present dominating images of sterility, forming man's life in a sterile pattern. But the pop artist regains power over his environment by using these elements in his own creations, thereby taking responsibility for their ultimate form. He has selected and chosen what he wants, and thereby transcended the artifacts. Likewise the new music chooses from many elements of earlier music, and from many forms of technology, to produce the form it wants.

Tom Wolfe recognized this process in his preface to *The Kandy-Kolored Tangerine-Flake Streamline Baby* (1965). He was writing about subcultures such as stock-car racing or surfing. He came to see that affluence had made it possible for various groups to 'build monuments' to their own life-styles. By implication, this meant that various groups were getting to a position where they could choose a way of life. The life-styles they chose, which Wolfe described, were not very meaningful, and they were still closely tied to the machine. But the element of creativity, of artistry, was unmistakably there. Using such artifacts of the Corporate State as the 1955 Chevrolet, the hamburger drive-in, the technology of neon, groups were able to create something of their own. To do this with a job, to do it with an institution, to do it under all the pressure and burdens of the present society will take much more. It will require imagination, strategy, cunning. But it will be the cunning of art, for it is art when we make something of our own out of the elements of the existing world. It only requires that we not lose sight of what we are doing: creating a way of life that is better for human beings. . . .

. . . In the new society, the existence of technology means that man's great goal must be consciousness, for all the reasons we have already given. And consciousness is a very different thing than material goods or their equivalents, honor and status. These are by their nature in short supply. But consciousness, or, to use an old expression, wisdom, is not a substance that is subject to upward limit. In seeking wisdom, men's interests are not antagonistic. No person's gain in wisdom is diminished by anyone else's gain. Wisdom is the one commodity that is unlimited in supply.

Indeed, each man, his experiences, his personality, his uniqueness, becomes an asset to other men when their object is to gain in wisdom. Each person, by practicing his own skills, pursuing his own interests, and having his own experiences becomes of increasing value to others. In a society that pursues honor and status as goals, each person's deviation from the norm is likely to be mocked and subject to group disapproval. But where people seek wisdom, the 'deviance' and 'absurdity' of others is respected, for each person is like a novelist, seeking knowledge of all the varieties of life, and, like a pilgrim, reverencing all that he sees. The more unique each person is, the more he contributes to the wisdom of others. Such a community makes possible and fosters that ultimate quest for wisdom—the search for self. Each person is respected for his own absolute human worth. No such luxury was possible during most of man's history. It is wealth and technology that have now made community and self possible.

In a community devoted to the search for wisdom, the true relationship between people is that all are students and all are teachers. Teaching in this sense consists of helping each person with his own personal search for experience and his own goals. Although the goals are individual, it is apparent that the search for self cannot take place in isolation, that self must be realized in a community, and therefore the community enhances each person no matter what his particular endeavor.

Consciousness III therefore rejects the idea that man's relation to man is to be governed primarily by law or politics, and instead posits an extended family in the spirit of the Woodstock festival, without individual ego trips or power trips. But it is a complete misconception to suppose that this community is not governed by law, or that it tolerates no individuality and instead demands submergence in a group. On the contrary, the community of Consciousness III has a far more genuine concept of law than exists in the Corporate State, and an infinitely greater respect for individuality.

The basis of a Consciousness III community must be agreement on major values. The oppressiveness of the Corporate State is due in large part to the lack of such values; destruction of environment, inequality, exploitation of individuals, even mass killing are permitted if they serve 'the public interest', i.e., the interest of the State. Life is a struggle for power and advantage because no agreement exists to respect any value or any person. That is not the way of Consciousness III. The V-signal, the recognition of strangers as friends, the intense feeling of community, all bespeak shared values. They all bespeak a community that does have law, in the sense of standards that are universally respected.

We have already described those basic laws upon which the Consciousness III community rests. Respect for each individual, for his uniqueness and for his privacy. Abstention from coercion or violence against any individual, abstention from killing or war. Respect for the natural environment. Respect for beauty in all its forms. Honesty in all personal relations. Equality of status between all individuals, so that no one is 'superior' or 'inferior'. Genuine democracy in the making of decisions, freedom of expression and conscience. If this is not a community of law, what is? This is law in the true sense, not in the perverted sense of mere coercion that we know today. This is a community bound together by moral-aesthetic standards such as prevailed before the Industrial Revolution. At the Woodstock festival hundreds of thousands of people were crowded together without violence or disorder of any kind. That was a community of law, in the sense we mean here; it could only have happened among people who shared a basic set of values.

The values we describe must be accepted democratically by a whole people, as our Bill of Rights was once accepted, and they may of course be changed from time to time. What matters is the concept: the Corporate State tramples all values and ignores all laws, as is recorded indelibly in Vietnam; a true human community is based upon a balanced order that includes land, self, equality, beauty and openness to change, and thus makes freedom possible.

Individuality is protected because the Consciousness III community is based on organic principles, not on identity. Nature is an organic community; its different elements and inhabitants do not resemble each other, they carry out very different functions and they rarely communicate, yet they all contribute to each other and depend upon each other; the squirrel needs the acorn and the acorn needs the squirrel. And each needs the other in all its uncompromising individuality; nature does not ask the squirrel to be like an oak, or an oak like a squirrel. In an organic community, the craftsman, the engineer, the artist are related whether or not they speak to each other, whether or not they are alike in any way.

The Consciousness III community is also based upon a sense of species solidarity, a feeling that is expressed by the word 'together'. Love is not given by one person to another as a sovereign act; love is discovered, it is generated, it is in the community, and not merely the product of each individual's will. People gain strength and warmth and energy from the species community; it multiplies whatever is inside of each of them. It shares a common task—the task of creating lives that are composed of the kind of education, work and culture that we have described, the task of transcending and using technology, the task of creating a life that is philosophic, artistic and heroic.

Ultimately, as the film *Alice's Restaurant* clearly shows, intimate communities will have to be based on something more than love or a common 'trip'. The most successful communes today seem to be the rock groups that live and work together. When liberated individuals are able to achieve excellence in work of their own choosing, it is possible that such common interests will form a more solid basis for the 'extended family'. And at that point, these 'families' will not necessarily want to live in places far removed from the rest of society, but rather in the heart of it, where their work lies, retaining a link to farm or seashore. Eventually they should be able to bring back with them into society the ways of life cultivated in the earlier communes located in remote areas. Such integration promises more than the Brook Farm experiment that failed even in Hawthorne's day. In the long run, a communal family will surely need shared interests, shared conversation, shared standards and aspirations.

It seems likely that the Consciousness III community, and particularly the concept of 'together', represent an effort to recover one of man's deepest needs and experiences. Man may not be a herd animal, but he is a gregarious, tribal animal and before the Industrial Revolution he usually lived within the circle of affection of an extended family, and his work in the fields or at a trade was shared and done side by side. The peasants of a medieval manor, or the anonymous craftsmen who worked on a great cathedral, must have had a feeling akin to 'together'. It seems doubtful that they felt a need for our society's individual egocentric recognition and separation of individual work from that of the group. Art and workmanship came out of a cultural tradition, not an act of individual genius. The Consciousness III community transcends the technological state by restoring some of the wordless security and sharing of tribal man, the ineffable meaning of experience that is shared. It is no accident that marijuana joints are always passed around from hand to hand and mouth to mouth, and never smoked separately when people are in the same room; or that a single pizza or a single Coke is passed from person to person in the same room; the group is sharing its bread and wine.

The spirit inherent in the Consciousness III idea of community, combining the feeling of together, an organic relationship, a shared set of laws or values, and a shared quest for experience and wisdom, is just now beginning to be visible. One of the few places to observe man partially free of the forces of competition and antagonism that are the norms of our social system is in a college dining hall where many of the students are Consciousness III people. A college dining hall has always been a happy spot, because of youth, high spirits, lack of care, and of course, the all-important presence of food. It is a far different place from a restaurant, where people are stiff and formal, carefully playing out roles, or the cafeteria of some large organization, where shirtsleeved employees sit, reduced to pettiness and docility, or a Consciousness II dinner party with everyone untouchably separated from everyone else. A college dining hall has a music of its own, the buzz of different conversations, some professorial and serious, some joking, some intensely intellectual. But in a college dining hall of today there is something more: unguarded smiles, uncalculated gestures of openness, an atmosphere whose dominant mood is affection. It is the atmosphere of breaking bread together; of communion. In dining halls of earlier years the smiles were given cautiously, measured after some thought, after assurances that they would be received and returned; people were afraid of being vulnerable. But with some of that fear gone, with much of the sense of competition gone, with many individuals no longer thinking of their places in some outside hierarchy, students show the naturalness of caring for each other.

In the summer of 1967, when Consciousness III was just beginning and the forces of repression had not yet moved in to create an atmosphere of tension and hatred, one could see the new community in the streets and shops of Berkeley, near the University of California. For just a few months at the very beginning of Consciousness III there was a flowering of music, hippie clothes, hand-painted vehicles, and sheer joy to match nature itself. It seemed to be everywhere, but perhaps one could see it best of all in a vast, modern co-op supermarket in Berkeley, open late at night, almost a community center with a self-service laundry, a snack bar with sweet fresh doughnuts, a highly intellectual selection of books, and a community bulletin board. It possessed an amazing variety of goods—Polynesian frozen foods, San Francisco sour rye, local underground newspapers and guides to the Sierras, dry Italian sausage, the glories of California vegetable farming, frozen Chinese snow peas—a veritable one world of foods—and genuine, old-fashioned, unhomogenized peanut butter, the very symbol of the world that has enjoyed technology and transcended it. If the foods gave the supermarket its sense of gleaming opulence and richness, the people gave it the sense of community. There were hippies looking like Indians, with headbands and proud, striking features; ordinary middle-class families doing their shopping late at night; Hell's Angels of California, in their black leather jackets; frat men with block letters; very young couples in some stage of transitory housekeeping; threesomes, foursomes, fivesomes, all possible varieties of housekeeping, in fact; people going on camping trips and returning from trips; and the checkout clerks, very much a part of it all, joining with smiles in the general scene. For the atmosphere was one of mutual respect and affection—visible and, even more, felt in the vibrations that a casual visitor received. Somehow, all these people were together. The checkout lines, with beards, old ladies, mothers with perambulators, and hippies whose purchase was a single carrot or turnip, resembled nothing so much as a peace march where all kinds of people are joined by a common cause. The scene as a whole, though, was not a march but a kingdom—the peaceable kingdom of those old American paintings that show all manner of beasts lying down together in harmony and love.

What we have said about education, work, culture, and community shows how technology may provide a new basis for generating and guiding the energies of man. Instead of summoning man's energies by the lash of hunger, competition and perpetual dissatisfaction, man can find his souces of energy in the variety, stimulation and hope that technology can provide. Satisfaction can be a greater stimulant than deprivation. Technology need not sap our energy; it can augment it, amplify it, multiply it, as it has done already with music. And the community that technology makes possible can be a still greater source of energy—the energy of group effort and of Eros. When man is reunited with self and with the larger community of nature, all of the cosmos will add to his own sources.

Thus the new age of man can take the best from the ages which preceded it. From the pre-industrial age it can take the integration and balance of life, the sense of God in everything. From the industrial era it can take technology and the steady rise to a higher level of life. From its own age it can take the control and use of technology, and the way of life of satisfaction, community and love, a way of life that aspires higher and higher, without forgetting its human source. In *Eros and Civilization* Marcuse spoke of releasing man's instincts, but the new age will do more; it will not only release but augment and inspire, and make that the chief end of society. And it will do so within a society that makes the Judeo-Christian ethic not merely an ignored command, but a realistic way of life.

This, then, is the plan for a new society, a workable way of life, a realistic approach to the 1970s and beyond. Many will deny that it is a plan at all, but they are looking for a plan where it can no longer be found. Or it may be called utopian, in the sense that it hopes for what never can be. But man, who could build the machines of today, and could learn to live *for* them, can also learn to live *with* them. If human nature can teach itself to serve a lifetime in a factory or office, then it can also teach itself the far more rewarding service of self and community that we have described. Some may say we are unduly optimistic; the only answer we can give is that the new way of life is better for man—has been found better by those who have tried it, and will be found better by those who try it hereafter.

What we have said concerning consciousness, technology, the search for wisdom, and community—about the dining halls and the supermarket—is that man must create his own fictions and live by them. Consciousness takes the elements it finds and arranges them to make a life and a society that reflect man's needs and hopes. In Kesey's *Sometimes a Great Notion,* in Vonnegut's *Cat's Cradle,* in Wallace Stevens's poetry, in psychedelic music, man seeks to create for himself an order by which he can live. Vonnegut says, 'Live by the *foma* [harmless untruths] that make you brave and kind and healthy and happy.'

To call this order 'fiction' is just a way of saying that the only reality man has is the one he makes. The Corporate State cuts man off from his inner sources of meaning and attempts to impose on him an order derived from the state or from the abstract, rational universe. But this imposed order is a fiction too, and it is one that is bad for man. The dining hall and the supermarket, the concept of work as play and of life as a search for wisdom, are fictions that are good for man.

For underlying the higher reason of Consciousness III, its search for meaning, for community, for liberation, is an exalted vision of man. Man, it says, is not part of a machine, not a robot, not a being meant to starve, or be killed in war, or driven like a beast, not an enemy to his own kind and to all other kinds, not a creature to be controlled, regulated, administered, trained, clipped, coated, anesthetized. His true nature is expressed in loving and trusting his own kind, being a part of nature and his own nature, developing, growing, living as fully as he can, using to the full his unique gift, perhaps unique in the universe, of conscious life.

Of all the many ways of life known to history, Consciousness III seems the closest to valuing life for its own sake. Almost always, men have lived subject to rigid custom, to religion, to an economic theory or political ideology. Consciousness III seeks freedom from all of these. It declares that *life* is prior to all of them. It does not try to reduce or simplify man's complexity, or the complexity of nature. It values the present, not the past, the future, or some abstract doctrine of mythical heaven. It says that what is meaningful, what endures, is no more nor less than the total experience of life.

8

Feminism and the Prospects for Change

Many people think the women's movement is about equal rights and opportunities, but Mary Daly disagrees. She is interested in women's rights, but primarily she seeks a "transvaluation of values"—"an awakening process in which layer upon layer of society's deceptiveness (about the two sexes) is ripped away." Ms. Daly provides only an outline, not once and for all solutions. She recognizes that a feminist ethic is still developing, and in the meantime she is willing to "confront ambiguity." She prefers even ambiguity to established beliefs that now subordinate one-half of the human race.

When reading this selection, remember Ms. Daly's (and my) argument that "feminism has a unique potential for providing the insight needed to undercut the prevailing moral ideology." If our social problems are rooted in our most basic assumptions about ourselves, doesn't it make sense to focus on what may well be the most basic of those assumptions—our beliefs about men, women, and their roles in society?

From Beyond God the Father
—*Mary Daly*

If the first woman God ever made was strong enough to turn the world upside down, all alone —these together ought to be able to turn it back and get it rightside up again: and they is asking to do it. The men better let 'em.

—SOJOURNER TRUTH (1851)

See
That no matter what you have done
I am still here.
And it has made me dangerous, and wise.
And brother,
You cannot whore, perfume, and suppress
  me anymore.
I have my own business in this skin
And on this planet.
                    —*GAIL MURRAY (1970)*

A transvaluation of values can only be accomplished when there is a
tension of new needs, and a new set of needy people who feel all old
values as painful—although they are not conscious of what is wrong.
                    —*FRIEDRICH NIETZSCHE*

In order to understand the potential impact of radical feminism upon phallo-centric morality it is important to see the problem of structures of alienation on a wide social scale. Some contemporary social critics of course have seen a need for deep psychic change. Herbert Marcuse, for example, encourages the building of a society in which a new type of human being emerges. He recognizes that unless this transformation takes place, the transition from capitalism to socialism would only mean replacing one form of domination by another. The human being of the future envisaged by Marcuse would have a new sensibility and sensitivity, and would be physiologically incapable of tolerating an ugly, noisy, and polluted universe.[1] Norman O. Brown, recognizing that the problem of human oppression is deeply linked with the prevalence of the phallic personality, quotes King James who in 1603 said: "I am the husband and the whole island is my lawful wife."[2] The statement calls to mind the traditional insistence of ecclesiastics that the church is "the bride of Christ." For Theodore Roszak, such imagery poses a dilemma:

> Does social privilege generate the erotic symbolism? Does the erotic symbolism generate social privilege? . . . Politically, it poses the question of how our liberation is to be achieved. How shall we rid ourselves of the king or his dominating surrogates?[3]

The point is not missed by any of these authors that the desired psychic change is related to overcoming sexual alienation. What is lacking is adequate recognition of the key role of women's becoming in the process of human liberation. When this crucial role is understood and experienced, it can be seen that there are ways of grappling with the problems of psychic/social change that are concrete and real. As distinct from the speculations of Marcuse, Brown, and other social philosophers, the analysis developing out of feminism has a compelling power deriving from its concreteness and spec-

---

[1] Herbert Marcuse, "Marxism and the New Humanity: An Unfinished Revolution," *Marxism and Radical Religion,* edited by John C. Raines and Thomas Dean (Philadelphia: Temple University Press, 1970), pp. 7–9.
[2] Norman Brown, *Love's Body* (New York: Random House, 1966), pp. 132–33.
[3] Theodore Roszak, *The Making of a Counter Culture* (New York: Doubleday, 1969). p. 86.

ificity. It speaks precisely out of and to the experience of the sexually oppressed and has an awakening force that is emotional, intellectual, and moral.
It changes the fabric of lives, affecting also the consciousness of the men
related to the women whose consciousness it is changing.

The dynamics of the psychic/social revolution of feminism involve a twofold rejection of patriarchal society's assumptions about "women's role."
First, there is a basic rejection of what Alice Rossi calls the pluralist model
of sex roles, which involves a rigid "equal but different" ideology and socialization of the sexes.[4] The assumption of such "pluralism" is that there is and
should be "complementarity," based not upon individual differences but
upon sex stereotyping. Feminists universally see through the fallaciousness
and oppressiveness of the "complementarity" theme at least to some degree.
However, there are "levels and levels" of perception of this, and permitting
oneself to have deep insight is threatening to the self. Thus, it is possible to
stop at a rather surface level of denying this stereotypic pluralism, by reducing
the problem to one of "equal pay for equal work," or (in the past) acquisition
of the right to vote, or passage of the Equal Rights Amendment. In the present
wave of feminism, a second and deeper rejection of patriarchal assumptions
is widespread. This is rejection of what Rossi calls the "assimilation model."
Radical feminists know that "50/50 equality" within patriarchal space is an
absurd notion, neither possible nor desirable. The values perpetuated within
such space are seen as questionable. When the myth of the eternal feminine
is seen through, then the brutalization implied in the eternal masculine also
becomes evident. Just as "unveiling" the eternal feminine logically entails
revealing the true face of the eternal masculine, the whole process, if carried
through to its logical conclusion, involves refusal of uncritical assimilation
into structures that depend upon this polarization. The notion of a fifty percent
female army, for example, is alien to the basic insights of radical feminism.

Intrinsic to the re-creative potential of the women's movement, then, is a
new naming of values as these have been incarnated in society's laws, customs, and arrangements. This means that there will be a renaming of morality
which has been false because phallocentric, denying half the species the possibility not only of naming but even of *hearing* our own experience with our
own ears.

HYPOCRISY OF THE TRADITIONAL MORALITY

Much of traditional morality in our society appears to be the product of
reactions on the part of men—perhaps guilty reactions—to the behavioral
excesses of the stereotypic male.[5] There has been a *theoretical* one-sided
emphasis upon charity, meekness, obedience, humility, self-abnegation,
sacrifice, service. Part of the problem with this moral ideology is that it became
accepted not by men but by women, who hardly have been helped by an ethic

---

[4]Alice Rossi, "Sex Equality: The Beginning of Ideology," *Masculine/Feminine,* edited by
Betty Roszak and Theodore Roszak, Harper Colophon Books (New York: Harper and Row,
1969), pp. 173–86.
[5]See Valerie Saiving Goldstein, "The Human Situation: A Feminine View-Point," *Journal of
Religion* XL (April 1960), pp. 100–12.

which reinforces the abject female situation. Of course, oppressed males are forced to act out these qualities in the presence of their "superiors." However, in the presence of females of the oppressed racial or economic class, the mask is dropped. Basically, then, the traditional morality of our culture has been "feminine" in the sense of hypocritically idealizing some of the qualities imposed upon the oppressed.

A basic irony in the phenomenon of this "feminine" ethic of selflessness and sacrificial love is the fact that the qualities that are *really* lived out and valued by those in dominant roles, and esteemed by those in subservient roles, are not overtly held up as values but rather are acted out under pretense of doing something else. Ambitious prelates who have achieved ecclesiastical power have been praised not for their ambition but for "humility." Avaricious and ruthless politicians often speak unctuously of sacrifice, service, and dedication. Not uncommonly such pronouncements are "sincere," for self-deceit is encouraged by a common assumption that the simple fact of having an office proves that the incumbent truly means it. The Judeo-Christian ethic has tended to support rather than challenge this self-legitimating facticity, by its obsession with obedience and respect for authority. Since the general effect of Christian morality has been to distort the real motivations and values operative in society, it hinders confrontation with the problems of unjust acquisition and use of power and the destructive effects of social conditioning. Since it fails to develop an understanding and respect for the aggressive and creative virtues, it offers no alternative to the hypocrisy-condoning situation fostered by its one-sided and unrealistic ethic.

A mark of the duplicity of this situation is the fact that women, who according to the fables of our culture (the favorable ones, as opposed to those that stress the "evil" side of the stereotype) should be living embodiments of the virtues it extols, are rarely admitted to positions of leadership. It is perhaps partial insight into the inconsistency of this situation that has prompted Christian theologians to justify it not only by the myth of feminine evil but also by finding a kind of tragic flaw in women's natural equipment. Commonly this flaw has been seen as an inherent feebleness of the reasoning power, linked, of course, to emotional instability. Typically, Thomas Aquinas argued that women should be subject to men because "in man the discretion of reason predominates."[6] This denial of rationality in women by Christian theologians has been a basic tactic for confining them to the condition of moral imbecility. Inconsistently, women have been blamed for most of the evil in the world, while at the same time full capacity for moral responsibility has been denied to females.

FEMINISM VERSUS THE "FEMININE" ETHIC

While Christian morality has tended to deny responsibility and self-actualization to women by definition, it has also stifled honesty in men. I

---

[6]Thomas Aquinas, *Summa theologiae* I, q. 92, a. 1, ad 2. For Aquinas, this inferiority was so inherent in female nature that women even would have been in a state of subjection before the Fall, which he understood as a historical event in the past.

have pointed out that the pseudo-feminine ethic—which I will also call the passive ethic—conceals the motivations and values that are actually operative in society. While it is true that there has been an emphasis upon some of the aspects of the masculine stereotype, for example, control of emotions by "reason" and the practice of courage in defense of the prevailing political structure or of a powerful ideology (the courage of soldiers and martyrs), these have been tailored to serve mechanisms that oppress, rather than to liberate the self. The passive ethic, then, whether stressing the so-called feminine qualities or the so-called masculine qualities does not challenge exploitativeness but supports it. This kind of morality lowers consciousness so that "sin" is basically equated with an offense against those in power, and the structures of oppression are not recognized as evil.

Feminism has a unique potential for providing the insight needed to undercut the prevailing moral ideology. Striving for freedom involves an awakening process in which layer upon layer of society's deceptiveness is ripped away. The process has its own dynamics: after one piece of deception is seen through the pattern can be recognized elsewhere, again and again. What is equally important, women build up a refusal of self-deception. The support group, which is the cognitive minority going through the same process, gains in its power to correlate information and refute opposing arguments. Nietzsche, the prophet whose prophecy was short-circuited by his own misogynism, wanted to transvaluate Judeo-Christian morality, but in fact it is women who will confront patriarchal morality *as patriarchal*. It is radical feminism that can unveil the "feminine" ethic, revealing it to be a phallic ethic.

*   *   *

ABORTION AND THE POWERLESSNESS OF WOMEN

In panels and discussions on religion and abortion I have frequently cited the following set of statistics: one hundred percent of the bishops who oppose the repeal of anti-abortion laws are men and one hundred percent of the people who have abortions are women. These thoroughly researched "statistics" have the double advantage of being both irrefutable and entertaining, thereby placing the speaker in an enviable situation vis-a-vis the audience. More important than this, however, is the fact that this simple juxtaposition of data suggests something of the context in which positions and arguments concerning the morality of abortion and the repeal of anti-abortion laws should be understood. To be comprehended adequately, they must be seen within the context of sexually hierarchical society. It is less than realistic, for example, to ignore the evidence suggesting that within Roman Catholicism the "official" opposition to the repeal of anti-abortion laws is profoundly interconnected—on the level of motivations, basic assumptions, and style of argumentation—with positions on other issues. Such interconnected issues include birth control, divorce, the subordination of women in marriage and in convents, and the exclusion of women from the ranks of the clergy. The fact that all of the major ethical studies of the abortion problem, both Catholic and Protestant, have been done by men is itself symptomatic of women's oppressed condition.

Since the condition of sexual caste has been camouflaged so successfully by sex-role segregation, it has been difficult to perceive anti-abortion laws and anti-abortion ethical arguments within this context. Yet it is only by perceiving them within this total environment of patriarchal bias that it is possible to assess realistically how they function in society. If, for example, one-sided arguments using such loaded terminology as "the *murder* of the unborn *child*" are viewed as independent units of thought unrelated to the kind of society in which they were formulated, then they may well appear plausible and cogent. However, once the fact of sexual caste and its implications have been unveiled, such arguments and the laws they attempt to justify can be recognized as consistent with the rationalizations of a system that oppresses women but incongruous with the experience and needs of women.

A number of male-authored essays on abortion that have appeared recently in liberal publications have been praised for their "clarity" and "objectivity." Yet in many cases, I suggest, such articles give the illusion of clarity precisely because they concentrate upon some selected facts or data while leaving out of consideration the assumptions, attitudes, stereotypes, customs, and arrangements which make up the fabric of the world in which the problem of abortion arises. Moreover, upon closer examination, their "objectivity" can be seen as the detachment of an external judge who first, does not share or comprehend the experience of the women whose lives are deeply involved and second, has by reason of his privileged situation within the sexual caste system a built-in vested interest opposed to the interest of those most immediately concerned.

Illustrative of this problem is an article by Professor George Huntston Williams of Harvard, in which he proposes as model for the politics of abortion a "sacred condominium" in which the progenitors and the body politic "share sovereignty in varying degrees and in varying circumstances." As he develops his thesis, it becomes evident that the woman's judgment is submerged in the condominium, and that the theory's pretentions to offer reasonable solutions are belied by the realities of sexual politics in the society in which we actually live. Basically, Professor Williams' theory ignores the fact that since men and women are not social equals, the representatives of the male-dominated "body politic" cannot be assumed to judge without bias. It also overlooks the fact that the "progenitors" do not have equal roles in the entire reproductive process, since it is obviously the woman who has the burden of pregnancy and since under prevailing social conditions the task of upbringing is left chiefly and sometimes solely to the woman. It disregards the fact that the male sometimes deserts his wife or companion (or threatens desertion) in a situation of unwanted pregnancy.

The inadequacies of Professor Williams' approach are evident in his treatment of the problem of abortion in the case of rape. He writes:

Society's role . . . would be limited to ascertaining the validity of the charge of rape. Here the principals in the condominium could be at odds in assessing the case and require specialized arbitration. If this were the case, the medical and legal professions could be called upon together with that of social work. But *even if rape is demonstrable* [emphasis mine] the mother may surely assent to the continuance of the misplaced life within her. . . .[7]

What is left out in this eloquent, multisyllabic, and seemingly rational discussion? First, it does not take into consideration the bias of a society which is male-controlled and serves male interests. Second (and implied in the first point), it leaves out the fact that it is very difficult to prove rape. In New York State, for example, for many years corroborating evidence has been required to convict a man of rape. In some states, if the man accused of rape was known previously by the woman, this fact can be used in his defense. According to the laws of many states, it is impossible for a man to rape his wife. Moreover, women who have been raped and who have attempted to report the crime to the police frequently have reported that the police treated them with ridicule and contempt, insinuating that they must have worn provocative clothing or invited the attack in some way. Little or no attention is given to the fact that rapists often force their victims into disgusting and perverted acts, under threat of death. The whole mechanism of "blaming the victim" thus works against women, adding to the trauma and suffering already endured. Nor are the police alone in taking this view of the situation. Their judgment reflects the same basic attitude of sexist society which is given physical expression in the rapist's act.[8]

The kind of spiritual counseling that women frequently receive within the "sacred condominium" is exemplified in an article by Fr. Bernard Häring. Writing of the woman who has been raped, he says:

We must, however, *try to motivate her* [emphasis his] to consider the child with love because of its subjective innocence, and to bear it in suffering through to birth, whereupon she may consider her *enforced maternal* obligation fulfilled [emphasis mine] and may give over the child to a religious or governmental agency, after which she would try to resume her life with the sanctity that she will undoubtedly have achieved through the great sacrifice and suffering.[9]

Fr. Häring adds that if she has already "yielded to the violent temptation" to rid herself of the effects of her experience, "we can leave the judgment of the degree of her sin to a merciful God." Those who are familiar with "spiritual counseling" have some idea of what could be implied in the expression "try to motivate her." Despite Fr. Häring's intention to be compassionate, his solution is not adequate. The paternalistic and intimidating

---

[7]George Huntston Williams, "The Sacred Condominium," *The Morality of Abortion: Legal and Historical Perspectives,* edited by John T. Noonan, Jr. (Cambridge: Harvard University Press, 1970), p. 164. All of the essays in this book are by male authors.
[8]See Debbie Margolin and Ann Sheldon, "Rape," *Women: A Journal of Liberation* III, No. 1 (p. 18–23).
[9]Bernard Häring, "A Theological Evaluation," in *The Morality of Abortion,* edited by Noonan, p. 141.

atmosphere of "spiritual counseling" is not generally conducive to free and responsible decision-making, and can indeed result in "enforced maternal obligation." The author does not perceive the irony of his argument, which is visible only when one sees the environment of the woman's predicament. She lives in a world in which not only the rapist but frequently also the priest view her as an object to be manipulated—in one case physically, and in the other case psychologically. *Machismo* religion, in which only men do spiritual counseling, asks her to endure a double violation, adding the rape of her mind to that of her body. As Mrs. Robinson of the once popular hit song knew: "Every way you look at it, you lose."

Feminist ethics—yet to be developed because women have yet to be free enough to think out our *own* experience—will differ from all of this in that it will refuse to give attention merely to the isolated physical act involved in abortion, and will insist upon seeing this within its social context. Christian moralists generally have paid attention to context when dealing with such problems as killing in self-defense and in war. They have found it possible to admit the existence of a "just war" within which the concept of "murder" generally does not apply, and have permitted killing in self-defense and in the case of capital punishment. They have allowed to pass unheeded the fact that by social indifference a large proportion of the earth's population is left to die of starvation in childhood. All of these situations are viewed as at least more complex than murder. Yet when the question of abortion is raised, frequently it is only the isolated material act that is brought into focus. The traditional maxim that circumstances affect the morality of an action is all but forgotten or else rendered nonoperative through a myopic view of the circumstances. Feminists perceive the fact of exceptional reasoning in the case of abortion as related to the general situation. They ask the obviously significant (but frequently overlooked) question: Just *who* is doing the reasoning and *who* is forced to bear unwanted children?

Feminist ethics will see a different and more complex human meaning in the act of abortion. Rather than judging universally in fixed categories of "right" and "wrong" it will be inclined to make graded evaluations of choices in such complex situations as those in which the question of abortion concretely arises. It will attempt to help women to orchestrate the various elements that come into play in the situation, including the needs of the woman as a person, the rights of women as an oppressed class, the requirements of the species in adapting to changing conditions, such as over-population, the positive obligations of the woman as the mother of other children or as a professional, the negative aspects of her situation in a society which rewards the production of unwanted children with shame and poverty. It will take into consideration the fact that since the completely safe and adequate means of birth control does not yet exist, women are at the mercy of our reproductive systems.

At this moment in history the abortion issue has become a focal point for dramatic conflict between the ethic of patriarchal authoritarianism and the ethic of courage to confront ambiguity. When concrete decisions have to be made concerning whether or not to have an abortion, a complex web of circumstances demands consideration. There are no adequate textbook answers. Essentially women are saying that because there is ambiguity surrounding the whole question and because sexually hierarchical society is stacked against women, abortion is not appropriately a matter of criminal law. In our society as it is, no laws can cover the situation justly. Abortion "reform" generally works out in a discriminatory way and is not an effective deterrent to illegal abortions. Thousands of women who have felt desperate enough to resort to criminal abortions have been subjected to psychological and physical barbarities, sometimes resulting in death. The emerging feminist ethic has as its primary emphasis not self-abnegation but self-affirmation in community with others. The kind of suffering that it values is that which is endured in acting to overcome an oppressive situation rather than that which accompanies abject submission to such a situation.

Some of the essentially unjust mechanisms operative in the arguments of phallic ethicists on abortion have already been illustrated in the passages from Williams and Häring. These include arguing out of the hidden false assumptions that women and men have equal roles in the entire reproductive process, that women and men have an equal voice in the "body politic," that women have completely free choice in the matter of sexual behavior and its consequences, that women have an adequately safe means of birth control, and that passive acceptance of suffering in the victim's role is the better choice.

There are also other devices. Among these is the domino theory or "wedge argument": If the fetus can be destroyed, who will be the next victim? Professor Ralph Potter writes:

When a fetus is aborted no one asks for whom the bell tolls. No bell is tolled. But do not feel indifferent and secure. The fetus symbolizes you and me and our tenuous hold upon a future here at the mercy of our fellow men.[10]

To this argument Jean MacRae has appropriately responded that if no bell tolls for the fetus perhaps this is because the death of the fetus is significantly different from that of a more actualized human being. She also makes another observation that is very much to the point, namely that the question of abortion has to do with a *unique* struggle between two living beings, for it is only in the case of unwanted pregnancy that the *body* and the whole well-being of a person is controlled by another being.[11]

Yet another device is what we might call "the unanswerable argument." This consists in posing such a question as: "When does human life begin?" Since no unanimous response is forthcoming, the conclusion drawn is that women with unwanted pregnancies must passively submit to the situation until they can produce the impossible answer. Still another tactic is that employed by John Noonan in asserting that the moral condemnation of abortion has been an almost absolute value in history.[12] The question that is unasked

---

[10]Ralph Potter, "The Abortion Debate," *The Religious Situation: 1968,* edited by Donald R. Cutler (Boston: Beacon Press, 1968), p. 157.
[11]Jean MacRae, "A Feminist View of Abortion," *Women and Religion,* 1972, pp. 107–117.
[12]John Noonan, "An Almost Absolute Value in History," in *The Morality of Abortion,* edited by Noonan, pp. 1–59.

is: Whose history? The fact that history written by men has ignored the historical experience of women is not taken into account. Indeed it is clear that even within Christian societies multitudes of women have by their actions repudiated the assumption that the life of the fetus is an absolute value. The argument that all or most of these women have suffered great guilt feelings is first of all false as an alleged statement of fact, and second it is dishonest in not recognizing that even if such guilt feelings exist in some cases, they may be explained by social conditioning.[13] Moreover, there are societies in which abortion is accepted without question by both women and men.[14]

As the movement for the repeal of anti-abortion laws began to gain momentum in the United States it became evident that a situation of open warfare was developing between the upholders of religious and civil patriarchal power and feminism in this country. This has a tragic aspect, since fixation upon the abortion issue represents neither the epitome of *feminist consciousness* nor the peak of *religious consciousness*.

As for *feminist consciousness:* abortion is hardly the "final triumph" envisaged by all or the final stage of the revolution. There are deep questions beneath and beyond this, such as: Why should women be in situations of unwanted pregnancy at all? Some women see abortion as a necessary measure for themselves but no one sees it as the fulfillment of her greatest dreams. Many would see abortion as a humiliating procedure. Even the abortifacient pills, when perfected, can be seen as a protective measure, a means to an end, but hardly as the total embodiment of liberation. Few if any feminists are deceived in this matter, although male proponents of the repeal of abortion laws tend often to be shortsighted in this respect, confusing the feminist revolution with the sexual revolution.[15]

In regard to *religious consciousness,* surely lobbying to prevent the repeal of unjust laws cannot be its highest manifestation. A community that is the expression of authentic spiritual consciousness, that is, a living, healing,

---

[13]See Daniel Callahan, *Abortion: Law, Choice, and Morality* (New York: Macmillan, 1970), pp. 67–75. Callahan's study is a most useful source. The author makes every attempt to be objective. His "objectivity" about women's liberation, however, at times manifests itself as noncomprehension. The deficiencies as well as the advantages of this sort of "objectivity" are evident in a more recent article: Callahan, "Abortion: Thinking and Experiencing," in *Christianity and Crisis* XXXII (January 8, 1973), pp. 295–98. Here the author uses the familiar method of "balancing" supposed extremes, a method which leads him to make some insensitive remarks. Sample: "No evidence has ever been offered that women freed by abortion from unwanted pregnancies are profoundly more liberated than those who haven't been" (p. 295). Perhaps persons freed by medicine from crippling diseases are not "profoundly" more liberated than those who haven't been, but the relevance of such a remark is hard to discover. Callahan is troubled by a "reconstruction of history . . . creating a highly charged mythology of male repression, or religious persecution, or puritanical fanaticism" (p. 297). The loaded words "reconstruction" and "mythology" reveal something of the author's noncomprehension of feminism.

[14]See Lawrence Lader, *Abortion* (Indianapolis: Bobbs-Merrill Co., 1966; Boston: Beacon Press, 1967 [paperback]), p. 23.

[15]This confusion is sometimes evident in Lawrence Lader's writings, even though they are very helpful in other ways. In *Abortion II: Making the Revolution* (Boston: Beacon Press, 1973), Lader conveys the impression that he actually thinks the legalization of abortion is the final step in women's liberation.

prophetic religious community, would not cut off the possibility for women to make free and courageous decisions, either by lobbying to prevent the repeal of anti-abortion laws or by psychological manipulation. It would try to *hear* what women are saying and to support demands for the repeal of unjust laws. Women did not arbitrarily choose abortion as part of the feminist platform. It has arisen out of the realities of the situation. On its deepest level, the issue is not as different from the issue of birth control as many, particularly liberal Catholics, would make it appear. There are deep questions involved which touch the very meaning of human existence. Are we going to let "nature" take its course or take the decision into our own hands? In the latter case, who will decide? What the women's movement is saying is that decisions will be made affecting the processes of "nature," and that women as individuals will make the decisions in matters most intimately concerning ourselves. I think that this, on the deepest level, is what authoritarian religion fears. Surely its greatest fear is not the destruction of life, as its record on other issues reveals.

As Lawrence Lader has shown, the lobbying power employed by the Catholic church against abortion has been tremendous. It has available vast economic resources—untaxed funds used for propagandizing, despite the illegality of using tax-free money for campaigning. Lader refers to it as the most powerful tax-deductible lobby in history. It has used the Catholic school system and such organizations as the Knights of Columbus to channel opposition against abortion law repeal. Lader points out that it has made political alliances— pointing specifically to the alliance between Richard Nixon and Cardinal Cooke of New York on the issue. Among the instruments used by the church in this religious war has been language. There has been a planned and concerted tactic on the part of the hierarchy to use inflammatory language such as "murder" rather than "abortion," and "child" rather than "fetus," and to make the sort of odious comparisons that call to mind the massacre of the Jews by the Nazis.[16] A predictable effect of such activity, when it is seen in combination with other sexist policies, is a relocation of women's spiritual energy outside the domain of hierarchical established religion.

If by a kind of reductionism one could imagine the essential goal of feminism to be the repeal of anti-abortion laws, the struggle might be simplified to the dimensions of women's liberation versus the official Catholic church. Then it might appear that liberal Protestantism would offer an alternative channel for female religious activity. However, since feminism cannot be reduced to an isolated "issue," and since the very issue of abortion is revelatory of the fact that feminism is not merely an issue but rather a new mode of being, it is becoming more and more clear to feminist consciousness that the faded authoritarianism of the liberal churches is hardly more acceptable to free women than the pomp and power of the more obvious enemy. For a community really expressive of authentic religious consciousness would coincide with the women's movement in pointing beyond abortion to more fundamental solutions, working toward the development of a social context in which the

---

[16]*Ibid.* There are scattered references throughout the book.

problem of abortion would be unlikely to arise. As catalyst for social change, it would foster research into adequate and safe means of birth control. As educative force, it would make available information about the better means now in existence, for example, vasectomy. Most fundamentally, as a prophetic and healing community it would work to eradicate sex role socialization and the sexual caste system itself, which in many ways works toward the entrapment of women in situations of being burdened with unwanted pregnancies. I think it should be clear that authentic religion would point beyond abortion, not by instilling fear and guilt, but by inspiring the kind of personal, social, and technological creativity that can, in the long run, make abortion a nonproblem.

Patriarchal power structures, whether civil or ecclesiastical, of course do not operate in this humanizing way. The blindness induced by them is revealed in the incongruous and biased statements of those who serve them—many of whom are in highly responsible positions and are "well-educated." A Massachusetts legislator argued that "those who play must pay." Richard Nixon stated:

> Further, unrestricted abortion policies, or abortion on demand, I cannot square with my personal belief in the sanctity of human life—including the life of the yet unborn.[17]

Writing in the Boston *Globe,* a physician made comparisons between abortion and the German mass murders of Jews.[18] Similar comparisons have been made by Brent Bozell of the Catholic *Triumph* magazine. A poignant response to this comparison was made by Regina Barshak, a Jewish woman who as a teenager was incarcerated in Auschwitz and then became the sole survivor of a large, mass-murdered family. Ms. Barshak wrote of the "callous exploitation of these ignoble events." In temperate terms she reminded readers of the differences between "a safe medical procedure on fertilized zygotes and, on the other hand, the deliberate sadism performed upon fully formed bodies and souls of active, fully conscious, loving human beings." She pointed out that the voices of the prestigious Vatican leaders were not heard "on behalf of these tortured lives."[19] . . .

. . . The church has harnessed (but not succeeded in destroying) [the] power of diversity, irregularity, and exceptionality by standardizing it into its bland and monolithic image of Mary. It has captured this power of diversity and imprisoned it in a symbol. The real diversity and *insight* into diversity is in existing rebellious women, whose awareness of power of being is emerging in refusal to be cast into a mold. The primordial experiencers of powerlessness and victims of phallic injustice, fixed in the role of practitioners of servile and impotent "love," having been aroused from our numbness, have something

---

[17]Statement released in conjunction with a presidential order reversing liberalized abortion policies at military hospitals, April 3, 1971. Cited in *Ms.* I (November 1972), p. 109.
[18]Dr. Joseph Stanton, M.D., Letter to the Editor, the Boston *Globe,* March 9, 1972.
[19]Regina Barshak, Letter to the Editor, the Boston *Globe,* March 18, 1972.

to say about the Most Holy and Whole Trinity of Power, Justice, and Love.[20] Grounded in ontological unity this Trinity can overcome Rape, Genocide, and their offspring, the Unholy Spirit of War, which together they spirate in mutual hate.

Women are beginning to be able to say this because of our conspiracy—our breathing together. It is being said with individuality and diversity, in the manner of *outlaws*—which is exactly what radical feminists are. It is being said in the diverse words of our lives, which are just now being spoken.

---

[20]For a clear, accurate treatment of feminism and justice see Elizabeth Farians, "Justice: The Hard Line," *Andover Newton Quarterly* XII (March 1972), pp. 191–200. Dr. Farians has written and compiled a packet of useful articles under the general title *The Double Cross: Writings on Women and Religion*. She has also compiled a *Selected Bibliography on Women and Religion, 1965–72*. These are available from the Ecumenical Task Force on Women and Religion, of the National Organization for Women. They have also been reprinted by KNOW, Inc.

Part II

SPECIFIC PROBLEMS

Introduction

Since the future is in the realm of probability, it is impossible to know with any certainty if the specific problems discussed in Part Two are the only ones that will make the future our major social problem. Perhaps other difficulties will appear. Or perhaps scientists will miraculously discover a way to feed rapidly increasing populations.

No one knows for sure. But we do know that if present trends continue—for example, in population or pollution—the probability is disaster. This is not inevitable, and in hopeful moods it is possible to dream of how things could be. However, hope is a commodity in increasingly short supply, for our problems are so numerous and complex that, like a series of dark clouds hiding the sun, they forecast a gloomy future.

But the probable is not the inevitable. Only our failure to make changes will turn one into the other.

When reading Part Two, remember that distinctions between problems are often arbitrary. For example, even if we provide enough food for growing populations, many writers argue that with unchecked population growth, pollution will overwhelm us. Or, if we seek to spread out our cities, how will we travel? With the rapid exhaustion of fossil fuels, cars and highways seem to make less sense every day.

As we have seen before, our problems are always interrelated in the most varied and complex ways. Solutions in one area often lead to greater problems in another so that it becomes impossible to isolate one problem for study. Two or three problem areas together such as population, pollution, and industrialization demand solutions that are both comprehensive and basic.

We begin with politics. In Chapter 9 Emmet Hughes analyzes the concentration of political power in the hands of the national state, especially in the American Presidency. Now the presidency is important for at least two reasons. First, if we transcend our ties to nationalism and create meaningful international bodies, we must try to decentralize power as much as possible; otherwise we get the dangers of the presidency. Second, whether in America or the world, the concentration of so much power, in such a complex world, makes leaders dependent on a host of experts. And that raises the question of who actually makes the decisions: the people, the president, or the experts?

Herbert Gans' essay, "The New Egalitarianism," points up that many groups today are asking the state to assume even greater power and responsibility. Indians, Chicanos, women, and blacks all want the state to step in and correct long-standing abuses and inequities. So, the need for international organization plus the demands of various groups for equality may contribute to the concentration of unprecedented power in the hands of political leaders in the future.

Our problem, then, is to create world and local institutions that solve problems, respect the need for personal freedoms, and eliminate the inequities between different groups and countries. All told this is probably an impossible task, but we must try. Some suggestions follow.

We must recognize and try to avoid the self-righteousness that often accompanies the centralization of power. This attitude often leads to death for dissenters, and it creates political states that forbid the open debate needed to accomplish a thorough yet peaceful reevaluation of our present values. Also, our institutions must include safeguards against the abuse of power. What James Madison said in *The Federalist Papers* is still true: ". . . power is of an encroaching nature and it ought to be effectually restrained from passing the limits assigned to it."

We must assign priorities. We cannot be both totally free and totally equal. For example, in order to redistribute wealth, we must give up the freedom to do as we please with our money and property. How much equality can political freedom tolerate? How much is necessary to ensure our survival?

We must also try to check the power of expertise. Inevitably, experts will be required if we are to solve many of our more technical problems. However, our ideological goal must be to create a future in which technical reports outlining what is useful, efficient, or possible are subordinate to our ethics. To paraphrase Jacques Ellul, we cannot allow means to shape ends.

The chapter on economics begins with Geoffrey Baraclough's article, "The Oil Crisis." Baraclough stresses that the exhaustion of fossil fuels is occurring in many countries that have done little to develop alternate energy sources. Conceivably, this crisis may turn into an opportunity for us to reexamine the overwhelming value we place on industrialization.

John Kenneth Galbraith's reading calls for a new socialism. Nationalism of various industries appears to Galbraith the only way to resolve the unequal development of the American economy. But can socialism alone eliminate the problems discussed by Ellul or Heilbroner? Will nationalization of industry be able to reduce the stress on efficiency, impersonality, and bureaucratization? And if we must reexamine the need to limit the amount of industrial growth, will traditional socialism deal with this issue?

Probably not. I contend that in order to reduce economic inequalities, as well as avoid the impersonal rule of the expert, we must combine public ownership with a decided stress on decentralization of power and authority. And if the future must see less industrialization, then one sure means of reducing inequalities is to redistribute wealth. But on this, see Willard Johnson's article, "Should the Poor Buy No Growth" (Chapter 17).

Last in economics is Christopher Tugenhat's analysis of the problems created by multinational corporations. If we rethink our ties to the machine these may lessen, but in the meantime, this economic problem is eminently political. Seemingly, the only way to control a multinational corporation is via an international organization. And that brings us right back to the issues of nationalism, sovereignty, and power.

In Chapter 11 on the family, William Goode suggests that one of the consequences of industrialization will be a worldwide trend toward the development of the nuclear family as opposed to the traditional and more widespread extended family. However, even if the pace of industrialization slows down, Goode doubts that this would affect the trend toward increasing nuclear families. The nuclear family's appeal, particularly for women, is due partly to the freedom from the domination of in-laws and men. And as the growth of the women's movement continues, increased freedom is likely to remain a major objective.

Richard Farson, in *Why Good Marriages Fail,* theorizes that many good marriages fail because success makes the partners expect too much; the resulting disappointment leads to searches for new partners. Consider the relationship between Farson's article and Reich's focus (Chapter 7) on self-realization. I believe that the counterculture places an unreasonable burden on life—by stressing life's highs, counterculturists hide its inevitable lows. For example, a person can gain only so much satisfaction from changing soiled diapers, but the job still must be done at least six times a day.

The section on the military begins with General Giap's discussion of the Vietnamese guerilla war. Although he presents some interesting points, I question the General's status as a revolutionary. His philosophy seems to lead us backward toward a socialism that self-righteously centralizes power in the hands of a few, and toward a view of war that is a carbon copy of the capitalistic imperialists' view he denounces.

My article, "Obliteration Bombing," tries to outline the evolution of twentieth century military strategy. I try to show how the mass bombing of civilians symbolizes a change in cultural values, and I stress that this change is linked to our allegiance to science and technology. We often seem unable to believe that just because something is possible, say nuclear weapons, we cannot avoid producing or using it.

Closing out Chapter 12, Roger Williams' article provides an outline of future weapons. The prospect is for "progress" on all fronts. For with endless government spending, science and technology will significantly improve our ability to destroy one another.

In Chapter 13, Catherine Wurster lays out four possible paths for future cities, while David Owen's article on Latin American cities stresses the crisis atmosphere in which city planning so often takes place. For example, Owen suggests that we reexamine our premises before making any decisions. But is such a reexamination possible until we first decide to slow down the pace of change, and in the underdeveloped nations, slow down the rate of population growth?

In Chapter 14, Jim Hoagland's analysis of South Africa suggests that since blacks are rapidly changing their views of self and world, whites must also change—or fight. Unfortunately, Hoagland feels that whites will fight. Unwilling to change, whites will maintain control in the near future, but the long-range prospect is for war between white and black.

Willard Johnson's article, "Should the Poor Buy No Growth," shows that the gap between rich and poor, both in America and worldwide, is steadily widening. And he suggests that a redistribution of wealth is one good way to eliminate inequalities, help reduce population growth, and avoid the terrible consequences of unimpeded industrial growth.

Chapter 15 discusses the "advances" being made in the area of biological research. In analyzing the potential for disaster this research holds, we must return to the issues raised by Theodore Roszak. I do not believe that head grafting will be controlled, much less stopped, until we change our beliefs about science and the value of objectivity. Naturally, the power of control must be vested in some public institution, but can meaningful laws be created and enforced unless we first reexamine the position of science on modern society's hierarchy of values?

Although the articles on pollution and population appear at the end of Part Two, they are probably our most pressing problems. They end the volume because their solution is intimately linked to the issues already discussed.

For instance, the articles on pollution do not assert that doom is inevitable. They do demonstrate that if we are to avoid the probable, we must change now. However, such change requires the formation of international bodies and it also demands strict—and strictly enforced—laws for the control of pollution both at home and abroad. I see no way to peacefully gain the political momentum needed to form international bodies or to enforce laws until we lessen our commitments to nationalism and industrialization.

Rapid population growth is an equally crucial problem. In "Some Consequences of Rapid Population Growth," the authors show that the problems created by too many people are numerous, worldwide, and interrelated. For example, although Baraclough's article demonstrates that everyone can be fed, the pollution articles suggest that feeding everyone via rapid industrialization risks unbearable pollution. So, while modernizing agriculture we must avoid getting trapped by pollution, and if that means less industrialization then one way to reduce population growth is to redistribute wealth. But redistributing wealth would undoubtedly lower standards of living in the advanced industrial societies, and lower standards of living will not be accepted with ease.

Baraclough also shows that one major reason underdeveloped nations have great trouble feeding themselves is that land ownership is concentrated in the hands of a few. So, any change in agriculture also represents radical political change, which immediately raises the prospect of even more civil and international conflict in the underdeveloped nations.

It is easy to go on listing problems. My point is that in order to check population growth, there is no way to avoid a wide variety of other issues. Only if all countries recognize the many interrelated problems and help one another through international bodies, can we hope to escape the terrible consequences of rapid population growth—consequences such as the pollution of everyone's environment or the possibility that underdeveloped nations such as India will attempt the nuclear blackmail of developed nations like the United States.

9
Politics

Emmet Hughes stresses the great powers of the presidency. From "Guardian of National Security," to "Protector of National Prosperity," to "Maker of World Peace," the presidency is so powerful that it makes America unique. Is there another republic in the world "where one national party, year after year, may commandingly control the legislature—but not the Executive—and be known quite simply as the party *out* of power?"

In thinking about the presidency's power, we should ask another question: Do presidents actually make decisions, or do they only ratify the decisions made by experts? For example, in deciding economic policy, a president relies more or less heavily on the Council of Economic Advisers. Composed of professional economists, the Council often presents the president with a list of alternative strategies and solutions. Does the president actually decide which solutions are feasible? And, in a world where expertise reigns supreme, does a nonprofessional such as the president dare risk disagreeing with the experts?

Questions like these bring us back to the debate between Bell and Ellul in Part One. Can we have a new tomorrow if we continue to follow the political pattern of the last seventy years? Or must we heed Ellul's warning and revolt against the concentration of power in the hands of a national state, and especially a presidency?

Ellul obviously has a point. So much concentrated power is dangerous, and rule by experts is often dehumanizing. However, we must remember that in order to solve some of our problems—such as the pollution of the oceans we discussed in the Introduction to Part One—we must be willing to concentrate power in the hands of international organizations. So perhaps we should use the presidency as a standard for future concentrations of power. In building new organizations we should decentralize power as much as possible and continually try to make expertise take a back seat to ethical and moral values and beliefs.

From The Living Presidency
—Emmet Hughes

The greatest difficulty lies in this: you must enable the government to control the governed; and in the next place oblige it to control itself.[1]

—JAMES MADISON

The year 1832 and the state of South Carolina confronted the seventh President, Andrew Jackson, with an ugly sort of challenge. The "fire-and-brimstone eaters" leading the local zealots of states' rights had summoned and dominated a state convention in Charleston to denounce an obnoxious tariff act, passed by the Congress in Washington, as "null, void, and no law." When the President replied with a proclamation reminding the citizenry that the Constitution "forms a government, not a league," the South Carolina legislature shouted its defiance of "King Andrew" and summoned volunteers to repel any federal "invasion." Raising the uproar to a new pitch, the governor of Virginia wrote the President to warn that any national troops dispatched to the South would have to march over his dead body. Although both Washington and Charleston managed to make some mutual concessions to blur for a spell the fateful issue of nullification, this truce was not reached before the President had made vividly clear his response to the threat of the Virginia governor. "If it becomes necessary for the United States troops to go to South Carolina," Andrew Jackson was said to have avowed, "I, as Commander-in-Chief of the army, will be at their head. I will march them by the shortest route. They may pass through Virginia. But if the Governor makes it necessary to pass over his dead body, it will be found that I have previously taken off both ears."[2]

There was more than the humor of the frontiersman in these possibly legendary words—and more, too, than the omen of a sundered national union. There was the gruff reminder that any President often will, occasionally must—and almost always can—effectively assert his powers in ways nowhere to be read in the articles of the Constitution or the debates of its authors. Whether the ghosts of the Founding Fathers shuddered or cheered over the militance of Jackson, they had only themselves to thank for such Presidential performances, since they had bequeathed a charter of power no more indisputably explicit about the nullification of national laws than about the mutilation of state governors. They had seemed to share, it is true, a general intuition that the integrity of the Union was intimately related to the authority of the Presidency. But the truth of this was left to be proved in real life by the very few men in the White House as resolute as a Lincoln.

Thanks to these slack terms, the nation-leading and nation-saving powers of the President have proved no more constant than clear. The President—*any* President—has some power to do almost anything, absolute power to

Reprinted by permission of Coward, McCann & Geoghegan, Inc. from *The Living Presidency* by Emmet Hughes. Copyright © 1973 by Emmet J. Hughes.
[1]*The Federalist*, p. 337.
[2]Cited by Leon A. Harris, *The Fine Art of Political Wit* (New York, E. P. Dutton, 1964), pp. 63–64.

do a few things, but never full power to do all things. From these obvious facts, there have followed some less obvious anomalies. In any political season, the President—*any* President—may discover that he can make a hostile nation politically tremble, while he can make a hostile Senator merely sneer. He may find his relations with American industry more exasperating than his relations with the Soviet Politburo. He might even launch a foreign war with more success than a party purge. And all through the span of his Presidential life—even as he brandishes his powers to appoint justices, assign ambassadors, veto laws, dispatch armies, lower tariffs, raise taxes, test bombs, or bully colleagues—he may feel most distraught in his ceaseless search for the secret to the trust of the ordinary, sovereign citizen, with no fame but one vote.

The Founding Fathers matched their reluctance to grant the Chief Executive many absolute prerogatives, of course, with their refusal to shackle him with many absolute restraints. For this reason, a Woodrow Wilson could plausibly talk of the President as enjoying "liberty" to be "as big a man as he can." The Presidential charter could be read, in fact, as even more sweeping: so far as constitutional writ is concerned, a President can be—short of treason or "other high Crimes"—not only the size, but also the character and manner of man he chooses to be. Rudely stated, he possesses the freedom to be "as big" a deceiver or demagogue, aggrandizer or sloth as the politics of the times may tolerate.

Yet for all the concern and caution of the men of 1787, the dynamic growth of the Republic has allowed no holding of a nice or near balance between frustration and freedom in the Presidency. Relentlessly, the authority of the office has come to swell with an array of resources quite beyond the more fearful imaginings of a Madison or a Jefferson. Even a Hamilton might grimace at some modern ways which Presidents have chosen to prove their "energy" and "despatch." And yet all the actions of even the most assertive and ambitious Presidents have had less to do with the final result than a few historical forces, beyond the cunning or control of any man.

The most decisive of these impersonal forces have been four in number.

First: the emergence of the once-small Republic as a world giant did not merely transform the range of Presidential power in quantitative terms. It almost redefined the office by compelling the man in the White House to accept as his supreme roles the Guardian of National Security and Maker of World Peace. And this radical change has largely come to pass because the very nature of modern warfare bears so little resemblance to any military concepts envisioned by the Founding Fathers.

From the Constitutional Convention to the First World War—and except for the convulsion of the Civil War—the habit of both the Republic's scholars and its leaders was to conceive of war as an enterprise of governments specifically, not of citizens generally. When the contributors to *The Federalist* wrote about Presidential authority over "the common defense," they were thinking about executive or administrative command of armed forces that consisted of volunteers or mercenaries and fought in an arena quite remote from the marketplace or the public forum. The modern experience of "total" or "general" war was wholly unknown, of course, and its complex challenges and dilemmas did not have to be faced until the year 1917, when all the *nation* truly went to war. This confrontation with the unprecedented was met—as so often it would be—by new delegation of extraordinary power to the President. The endowment was conveyed, following the declaration of war, by a series of sweeping enactments that included the Lever Fuel and Fuel Control Act, the Selective Service Act, the Espionage Act, the Priority Shipment Act, and the Trading with the Enemy Act. These statutes spelled out the swift and general assumption that the President was the only citizen who could lead "a citizens' war." Accordingly, he was armed with powers broad and varied enough to regulate manufacturing and mining; or requisition foods and fuels; or take over factories or rail, water, telephone, or telegraph systems; or raise an army or control exports; or fix wheat prices or reorganize executive agencies; or license trade or censor mail or control enemy aliens or regulate the foreign-language press.

These were the first stark signs of what the advent of modern war meant for the modern Presidency. After the Second World War, the successive tricks and duels with Communist powers made this meaning ever more plain. Even without the pressures and passions of total war, the President came to be accepted—ever more unquestioningly—as the sovereign sage to define the nation's role in the world, to determine troop levels and weapons systems, to discern danger and to proclaim crisis, and—in the awesome process—to set peacetime defense spending at levels that made annual expenditures of $70 billion or $80 billion come to seem commonplace. So profoundly did all this ramify through America's society and economy that the general-President, Dwight Eisenhower, devoted his final Presidential address in 1960 to a grave warning against the insistent growth and threat of what he christened "the military-industrial complex"—whose final master must be, of course, the modern Commander in Chief.*

Second: the evolution of the Republic's original thirteen states into the world's industrial marvel has decreed the role of the President as the ultimate Protector of National Prosperity. From the first years of the New Deal, the guardian against Aggression has been no less expected to be the savior from Depression. Such grand expectation undoubtedly burdens and complicates modern Presidential life. Nonetheless, the unavoidable responsibilities have brought with them unparalleled powers. These have been legislatively enshrined in such statutes as the Emergency Banking Act of 1933 and the Securities Exchange Act of 1934, whose sum of powers was accurately assessed by Clinton Rossiter as a call upon the President to prevent any future economic

---

*The historian Henry Steele Commager has brought this long history up to date with this biting summation: "We had written into our Constitution the principle of the supremacy of the civilian over the military authority. The constitutional provision still stands, but has been in large part circumvented by the willing acquiescence of two successive commanders-in-chief [i.e., Lyndon Johnson and Richard Nixon] in the exercise of independent authority of the Pentagon and the CIA. . . . Much of the emergence of military power has been the consequence of drift rather than of calculation. When Washington became President, the United States Army consisted of fewer than 1,000 men and officers. Now ours is the largest and most powerful military establishment in the world. . . . We delude ourselves if we think the principle [of civilian supremacy] means what the Founding Fathers supposed it to mean." (*The New York Review,* October 5, 1972, p. 7.)

collapse "by declaring a state of financial martial law."[3] Lest this not suffice, the Employment Act of 1946 defined the Presidential role in the economic arena with memorable clarity and breadth:

> The Congress hereby declares that it is the continuing policy and responsibility of the Federal Government to use all practicable means . . . to coordinate and utilize all its plans, functions, and resources for the purpose of creating and maintaining in a manner calculated to foster and promote free competitive enterprise and the general welfare, conditions under which there will be afforded useful employment opportunities, including self-employment, for those able and willing to seek work, and to promote maximum employment, production, and purchasing power.

Throughout this statute, the President was expressly designated the key federal officer "to avoid economic fluctuations" and to promote prosperous times for all. He not only was called upon to make annual economic reports but also was provided with a Council of Economic Advisers—to give a uniquely authoritative ring to any of his economic pronouncements.

The steady movement of these powers toward the White House, moreover, has been a process that has cut across partisan and ideological lines. Thus, the Taft-Hartley Act of 1947, dedicated to fostering a "sound and stable industrial peace," came out of a Congress dominated by Republican leaders, notably the House's Joseph W. Martin and the Senate's Robert A. Taft. This was a legislature eager to curtail rather than enlarge Presidential power. Yet the only *method* that the law's authors could find to achieve their ends was to endow the *President* with new authority to move against major strikes. While Harry Truman deplored the law's intent, he went on to invoke its powers no less than ten times.[4] When a Republican President next came to office— with a clear commitment to restrain federal trespassing on the private sector— he turned out to be Dwight Eisenhower. He was an economic conservative, indeed. But he was also the Presidential author of a message to Congress that accompanied his 1953 Economic Report and conveyed these assurances:

> The arsenal of weapons at the disposal of Government for maintaining economic stability is formidable. It includes credit controls administered by the Federal Reserve System; the debt-management policies of the Treasury; authority of the President to vary the terms of mortgages carrying Federal insurance; flexibility in administration of the budget; agricultural supports; modification of the tax structure; and public works. We shall not hesitate to use any or all of these weapons as the situation may require.

Third: a couple of events in the early part of the twentieth century contrived a fiscal revolution which—again, by no one's design or desire—made the old White House a new sort of citadel.

---

[3]Rossiter, *op. cit.*, p. 33.
[4]*Ibid.*, p. 83.

In the year 1913, the passage of the Sixteenth Amendment allowed Congress to institute a graduated income tax. This would prove to be the most lucrative source of revenue known to modern democratic government. Rather ironically, the innovation had not been pressed upon Congress by venturesome Presidents like Theodore Roosevelt or Woodrow Wilson but by the circumspect William Howard Taft—as unaware as any member of Congress of the amendment's ultimate political impact. The first such tax imposed, during the Wilson years, amounted to a meager 1 percent of net income up to $20,000. But the principle was established and ready for lavish use by future Presidents to meet future needs or crises. And without such a reservoir of funds, there hardly could have followed any grand dreams of Presidential programs in the realms of welfare, education, health, housing, and transport.

Eight years later the Congress passed the Budget and Accounting Act of 1921. Far from being any attempt to enlarge the powers of the Presidency, this had evolved merely from a long-overdue Congressional effort to bring order to chaotic fiscal procedures. As an earlier House committee study had made clear, the traditional budgetary procedures were so haphazard that expenditures were not rationally geared to revenues, the requests of agencies and departments of the executive branch were not subjected to coherent review, and the constellation of Congressional committees could not possibly bring discipline to a process so vagrant. Accordingly, the 1921 act established a new agency, the Bureau of the Budget—directly responsible to the President—with the power "to assemble, correlate, revise, reduce, or increase the estimates of the several departments or establishments." The principal *purpose* of this act was an uncontroversial quest for "efficiency and economy" in federal fiscal planning. The principal *effect* of it, however, was wholly different. It offered a Congressional confession of inability to assume responsibility for preparing a national budget, and it assigned this task to the Presidency, thereby arming the office with new and commanding power for both its struggle with Congress and its control over executive departments and agencies.

With the passage of a little time, the consequences of such events as these reached even further. The familiar balances within the federal system, throughout the fifty states, were upset. More and more, the governments of states and of major cities found the demands upon their services—from schools and police to garbage and transport—far exceeding their sources of revenue. As these sources were drawn off by the federal government, the search for local solvency almost inevitably had to turn toward some scheme of federal revenue sharing. And once more, all political paths pointed toward the White House—without anyone having intended any such thing.

Fourth: there may have unfolded no sequence of developments to change the Presidency so effectively as the politically neutral—and relentless—force of modern technology. And of this force, there appear three major examples.

The character of *nuclear weaponry* drastically recast the nature of the Republic's strategic planning and decision. Even as this sophisticated armament made a President dependent on the expertise of scientists and soldiers, it also made the Congress and the nation singularly dependent on *him* and *his* final judgment. Accordingly, the age of atomic weaponry was inaugurated in 1945 by President Harry Truman's decision to let the atomic bombs fall on Hiroshima and Nagasaki, and his right to make such a wartime decision met virtually no immediate challenge. The following year brought peace, along with the Atomic Energy Act of 1946—and its laconic words outlining a new and awesome Presidential power:

> The President from time to time may direct the Commission (1) to deliver such quantities of fissionable materials or weapons to the armed forces for such use as he deems necessary in the interest of the national defense or (2) to authorize the armed forces to manufacture, produce, or acquire any equipment or device utilizing fissionable material or atomic energy as a military weapon.

Against the background of such events and laws, there remained few citizens—by 1950—ready to question whether it should be the President's prerogative alone to order forthwith the development of the hydrogen bomb. For as it could most plausibly be asked: where else in the constitutional system might such a decision be weighed and made—reflectively, discreetly, and swiftly?

The modern network of *mass media* has given the Presidency an almost revolutionary opportunity to create, to control, to distort, or to suppress the news. As the cases of Lyndon Johnson and Richard Nixon have shown, a President's manipulative use of television by no means can guarantee his personal popularity or credibility. But there was no earlier time in the Republic's history when a President could stage for all the nation such a drama as Richard Nixon's pilgrimage to Peking—with more than 120 television correspondents, producers, technicians, and engineers enlisted to report to the citizenry every Presidential act or word, frown or smile. And still more awesome is the *kind* of Presidential power underlying and provoking such an impassioned indictment of the Nixon Presidency as these words of Henry Steele Commager:

> Even more dangerous than secrecy and deception . . . is the deliberate effort of the Administration to intimidate the press and the television networks. . . . Never before in our history has government employed so many methods for manipulating and distorting the truth as during the past decade, not even during the First and Second World Wars. . . . No other administration in our history has practiced deception . . . as has the Nixon Administration. Where totalitarian regimes invented the technique of the Big Lie, this Administration has developed a more effective technique, that of lies so innumerable that no one can keep up with them.[5]

Whether or not this particular indictment of one Presidency be wholly true or fair, the critical fact is that it *could* be true of *any* Presidency—precisely because of the nature and power of the national media. Such a network of communications, so rich in facilities for the widest circulation of "innumerable lies," alone makes possible any Presidential "technique" for massive misleading. Such a network—precisely because of its own vaunted power and its own vested interests—must also be sensitive and vulnerable to the variety of attacks that any administration may launch: through public critiques of its professionalism or through private threats to its employees, through antitrust actions against television networks or through statutory control over their licenses to exist. And quite possibly there can never be a man in the White House certain to reject at all times any temptation to bring such weapons into play.

The advent of *jet transport,* finally, has done more to enlarge life—and excite ego—in the Presidency than in any other office in the land. It was not until 1960 that a Presidential candidate could campaign on the nation's Atlantic coast *and* its Pacific coast—on the same day. With this, there came the ease of even longer flights that any President could take to distant governments and peoples, on all continents and for any motives. On such occasions, all the White House may seem airborne to attend the Chief Executive: Cabinet members and personal staff, counselors and cooks, generals and secretaries, Secret Service and press corps. At his will and call, he may fly around the globe on a path quite his own: first to the helicopter outside his doors on the White House lawn, next to the military base where Air Force One waits, then into the air lanes cleared for his flight, and onward to the meeting with the statesman—or the throng—of his choice who await his arrival, his waving arms, and his resolving words. In such a world, what President any longer greatly needs a Department of State—or its far-flung ambassadors and ministers—for the supreme moments of negotiation or exhortation? These moments become *his.* For it is both expedient and exhilarating for *him* to play the heroic role in the historic act.

There has been another set of twists and turns in the Republic's life to help a President appear "as big a man" as he can. These have been matters of historical luck. For they amount to the various reasons why the other two branches of the federal government—for all their own imposing and separate powers—so often have *not* challenged or restrained the Presidency.

The case of the Supreme Court approaches something of a study in institutional timidity. There have been occasional confrontations with the modern Presidency, to be sure, when the Justices have known moments of bravura—as when they enraged Franklin Roosevelt, by striking down early New Deal statutes, or when they dismayed Dwight Eisenhower, by striking down school traditions of segregation. But these have been rare exceptions to what one student of the Presidency has called a "lesson of history"—namely:

> Where exercises of extraordinary power are involved, the Court restrains itself and not the President. . . . The Court's primary function in checking a strong President is to act as a symbol of restraint, a moral force, and a constant reminder of established principle—a function which is by no means unimportant—but with regard to executive power, Article II of the Constitution is what the President, and not what the Court, says it is.[6]

---

[6]Hirschfield, *op. cit.,* p. 246.

The proofs of this have appeared in a couple of ways. In the first place, the pertinent decisions of the Supreme Court, over the generations, have tended to enlarge rather than to narrow the range of Presidential power. Among the more notable of these have been the Prize Cases (1863), approving Lincoln's blockage of the Southern states; *Myers v. U.S.* (1926), assuring full Presidential removal power over the executive branch; and *U.S. v. Curtiss-Wright Export Corp.* (1936), emphasizing Presidential authority in foreign relations. In the second place, the Court has shied, almost embarrassingly, from any serious challenge to the wartime powers of the Commander in Chief, whether brandished by Abraham Lincoln or Woodrow Wilson or Franklin Roosevelt. It is probably not too harsh to say that the judiciary's retreats have been most abject precisely when the Executive's actions have been most arrogant—from Lincoln's suspension of habeas corpus to Roosevelt's consignment of more than 110,000 Japanese-Americans to their "relocation centers" during World War II. Or as Professor Edward S. Corwin unhappily concluded: "It is the lesson of these cases that in the war crucible the more general principles of constitutional law and theory . . . become highly malleable, and that even the more specific provisions of the Bill of Rights take on an unaccustomed flexibility."[7]

As with the principles of law, so also with the practices of Congress: they have proved, quite often, unpredictable and unreliable as constraints upon Presidential initiative and power. If the Republic's highest court has left even the Bill of Rights to operate sometimes with "an unaccustomed flexibility," the Senate and the House have displayed what might be called an unusual perversity in asserting themselves most slackly when they might have been expected to act most sternly.

This has been the case with even the venerable Congressional power of the purse. From the first—indeed, from the earliest of Hamilton's polemics—this authority was conceived to be critical and irresistible. It should "be regarded," as Hamilton wrote in *The Federalist*, to be "the most complete and effectual weapon with which any constitution can arm the immediate representatives of the people. . . . "[8] But it has proved to be no such thing. Instead, there have arisen remarkably few occasions since the year 1789 when a stubborn denial of funds by Congress has frustrated a major program or purpose urgently pressed by any President.

The historical pattern has been that the times of internal or international stress—which are also those times when some check upon frantic spending has most been needed—generally have found Congress racing the President to spend a little faster to resolve the crisis a little sooner. In terms of the national economy, as the federal responsibility has steadily grown, the prevailing Congressional habit has been not so much to limit the full sum of public largesse as to assure each Congressman's own constituency a fair share in the general dispensation. In terms of international commitments and military

---

[7]Corwin, *op. cit.,* p. 236.
[8]Cf. Rossiter, *op. cit.,* p. 48.

budgets, the House of Representatives, especially after the Second World War, has been ready, more often than not, to inflate rather than reduce appropriations sought by the Executive. Any programs plausibly related to "national security" or "national prestige" have found the House almost eagerly responsive—as befitting its rural and conservative political temper, with its preoccupation with the virtues of patriotism and the vices of Communism.

The Senate also has shown a capacity for a sort of discreet subservience, whenever its withholding of money might thwart Presidential policy. In the case of the Vietnam War, the upper House almost classically demonstrated its preference for disputing Presidential policy with rhetoric rather than action. In 1967 an Associated Press survey reported forty out of eighty-four responding Senators opposed to President Lyndon Johnson's Southeast Asia policy, but the same year found only three of these Senators actually voting against a $12 billion supplemental appropriation to carry on the war in Vietnam.[9] As one Washington reporter of Senate ways observed:

> While opposition to any other legislation is within the rights of a senator, voting against any defense bills is like civil disobedience, a congressional version of not paying taxes. . . . It is part of the whole confusion between President as Executive and as Commander-In-Chief that has resulted in the logic that even if a war was started wrongly, it is unpatriotic to force a President to stop it before he is ready.[10]

Such surrender of "the power of the purse," moreover, marks nothing new in the ways of the legislature. During the Second World War, the Congress appropriated billions of dollars for a wholly unknown project, which turned out to be the development of the atomic bomb. Almost a half century earlier, it had found itself acquiescing in underwriting the famous dispatch by Theodore Roosevelt of the Great White Fleet on its journey around the world. And still another half century before, Lincoln had spent some $2,000,000 of public funds, as the Civil War began, wholly without prior Congressional authority or subsequent reproach.[11]*

The failure of "the power of the purse" to prove reliably effective has been only one of several of the Founding Fathers' expectations about Congress that went awry. The whole Senate had been envisioned, for example,

---

[9]John Rothchild, "Cooling Down the War: The Senate's Lame Doves," *The Washington Monthly* (September, 1971), pp. 7–8.

[10]*Ibid.*, p. 13.

[11]Cf. Hirschfield, *op. cit.*, p. 248.

*Over the generations, the Presidency also has helped further to blur "the power of the purse" by the simple refusal to spend certain funds appropriated by the Congress. This practice has dated at least from Thomas Jefferson's refusal to spend money authorized for Mississippi River gunboats at the turn of the nineteenth century. Of the modern Presidents, almost all have impounded or frozen a percentage of his annual budget. By the end of the thirty-seventh President's first term, however, Richard Nixon had pressed this strategy to unprecedented lengths, with the impounding of sums estimated to exceed $12 billion. Despite much predictable outrage on Capitol Hill, the White House insisted, through its Director of Management and Budget, that the authority to withhold funds amounted to "an absolutely essential right for every President to have." (New York *Times,* January 22, 1973.)

as a kind of Presidential council of wise men in the general formulation and direction of foreign policy. As one of the authors of the Constitution, Rufus King, assured the Senate itself, some thirty years after the Philadelphia convention: "The Senate are the Constitutional and the only responsible counsellors of the President. And in this capacity the Senate may, and ought to, look into and watch over every branch of the foreign affairs of the nation."[12] But long before these sentiments were sounded, they had realistically been overrun by events—not least among them, the simple growth in the Senate's size. Just from 1789 to 1795, the Senate membership had risen from twenty-two to thirty-two, an increase already sufficient to make unworkable any notion of the body serving as a confidential and coherent council. Meanwhile, the same years had seen the genesis of what would be known as a "Cabinet"— a logical usurper of the special place earlier planned for a small Senate. Eventually, the growing population of the upper house made more and more impracticable its sharing in the substantive development of foreign policy, so that its role in treaty-making became essentially not a creative power but a veto power, with the President left largely free to negotiate as he wished with other nations. At the same time, the whole of the Congress tended to dilute specifically Senatorial authority in another way: by substituting for treaty ratification the looser process of Congressional resolution. In 1845, Texas was formally annexed by such a simple resolution (after the Senate had rejected a treaty drafted to the same end). And in 1921, after the bitter struggle over the Treaty of Versailles and the League of Nations, it was not a Senate action but a Congressional resolution that officially terminated the First World War.[13]

Both the size of the Senate and its devotion to unreined oratory help somewhat to explain its frequent failure to dispute or rebuff a President, much less anticipate him. With respect to the Vietnam War, again, it could be said that—while the Senate almost surely would not have started this war—its hundred members proved equally incapable of forcing an end to it. The hazy character of any effort to do so once was rather sadly suggested by an aide to one of the war's more vocal critics, Senator Edward Kennedy, who summarized Senatorial striving thus: "The best way is to *persuade* the President. We don't make executive decisions; it is not the nature of the legislative branch. The Senate never does anything clear-cut or definitive."[14] In the light of such philosophizing, it becomes easy to understand how Lyndon Johnson could tease one of the three Senators actually challenging funds for the Vietnam War, by saying to a Senator from Alaska, Ernest Gruening: "I don't care what kind of speeches you make as long as you don't vote against the appropriations."[15]

Whatever its institutional reasons, the recurrently reticent temperament of Congress—always more apparent when problems look more awkward— can encourage any President to seize the chance to set his own course in

---

[12]Cited by Corwin, *op. cit.*, p. 208.
[13]Cf. *ibid.*, pp. 211 and 216–17.
[14]Rothchild, *op. cit.*, p. 11.
[15]*Ibid.*, p. 13.

most spheres of policy. One aspect of this accommodating spirit in the legislature was summed up in 1972 by the Senate's Democratic majority leader, Mike Mansfield: "There are members of Congress who are called 'the President's men.' In their view, everything a President recommends is right. Everything a President does is right."[16] This allusion to "the President's men" on Capitol Hill was not confined to members of the President's own party, for there always are Senators and Representatives of both parties sensitive to the pleasures of knowing a President's favor—be it personal, social, or political. At the same time, the Senate's own grave and courtly regard for itself, as a group and as an institution, can serve to muffle the kind of debate that might too rudely challenge a President or his apologists within the chamber. Thus, even during the sometimes passionate discussion of the Vietnam War, the fraternal amenities commonly prevailed over the ideological differences—as when Oregon's Senator Mark Hatfield could punctuate a speech, on behalf of his amendment to end the Indochina war, with his tribute to one of the amendment's most dedicated opponents, Mississippi's Senator John Stennis:

> Mr. President, I have listened carefully to the comments and the presentation made by the Senator from Mississippi, the chairman of our Armed Services Committee. I am grateful for the relationship that we have here as colleagues on this floor. . . . Often, people from outside the Senate organization cannot understand how men can deeply, vociferously, and intensely differ on issues and still maintain mutual respect and personal friendship. I think of all the men and one lady with whom I have served in this body, this is always one of my most reiterated thoughts as it relates to my personal relationship with the Senator from Mississippi.[17]

When the voices of Senate critics rise no more "vociferously" than this, the Presidents at the far end of Pennsylvania Avenue have no cause to quake at the sound of forensic thunder on Capitol Hill.

The sum of all these habits of Congress—as it braces or bows before the force of any Presidency—points toward a concluding paradox. There is no doubt that the members of this Senate and House belong to a body whose leaders can exercise, indeed, more political influence than those of any other legislature in the world. But there also is probably no other Republic in the world where one national party, year after year, may commandingly control the legislature—but not the Executive—and be known quite simply as the party *out* of power.

Contemporary preoccupation with equality among people is the subject of Herbert Gans' article. Citing the increasing demands of such groups as women, Blacks, and Chicanos for a politics that will offer them a more equitable share of the nation's wealth and opportunities, he notes that this tendency is a new

---

[16]*Time* (May 22, 1972), p. 18.
[17]Rothchild, *op. cit.*, p. 11.

one. "Traditionally, Americans have been more interested in life, liberty, and the pursuit of happiness than in the pursuit of equality."

In making this observation, Gans implicitly calls attention to the conflict between freedom and equality; for example, if children are bussed to equalize educational opportunities, then some people will lose the freedom to send their children to the school of their choice. Or, if property and wealth are nationalized in order to redistribute the wealth, then some people will lose the freedom to own and earn as they choose.

Clearly, freedom and equality often travel on different roads; in order for some to be more equal, others must be less free. And political struggle is likely to occur when the new stress on equality meets the old stresses on freedom, individualism, and survival of the fittest.

Finally, we must consider that, historically, the equalization of social conditions has necessitated placing the power of enforcement in a centralized authority. In order to gain equality, we must also give up authority and power; as always, our problems are interrelated in the most varied and complex ways.

From The New Egalitarianism
—*Herbert J. Gans*

Although the fundamental idea of the Declaration of Independence is that "all men are created equal," Americans traditionally have been more interested in life, liberty, and the pursuit of happiness than in the pursuit of equality. In the last decade, however, their interests have begun to shift, and equality may be on its way to becoming as significant as liberty in the hierarchy of American goals.

The shift began approximately on the day in 1955 when Mrs. Rosa Parks of Montgomery, Alabama, decided that she was no longer willing to sit in the rear of a bus. Much has been written about the ensuing political and social unrest, but few observers have emphasized that the revolts of the blacks, the young, and others have a common theme: the demand for greater equality by the less than equal. Blacks have agitated for racial equality through black power; students, in high schools as well as in colleges, have demanded more power on the campus; teen-agers have begun to claim the sexual freedom now available to young adults, and in less public ways they—and even younger children—have sought more equality within the family. And, of course, many women are now demanding equality with men, and homosexuals with heterosexuals. Similar developments have been occurring in the economy and the polity. Wage workers have begun to demand guaranteed annual incomes and the other privileges that salaried workers enjoy. Public employees have struck for wage equity with workers in private industry. Assembly-line workers have sought better working conditions and more control over the operation of the line. Enlistedmen have called for reductions in the power of officers.

In politics the 1960s saw the emergence of the drive for community control—attempts by urban residents to obtain more power over their neighborhoods. Subsequently, community control broadened into a movement to reduce the power of bureaucracies at all levels of government and of professionals over their clients; for example, of doctors over patients, teachers over parents, and planners over home owners. Consumers have called for more control over what goods are to be produced and sold, environmentalists over how they are to be produced. Stockholders have demanded a greater role in the decisions taken by management. Few of these demands have been explicitly phrased in terms of equality; most of those making the demands have spoken of autonomy and democracy. Many have actually asked for more liberty. Still, if all of these demands are put together, they mean more income for some and higher costs for others, more power for some and less for others. If the demands were heeded, the eventual outcome would be greater overall equality.

No one can accurately predict whether or not these demands will be heeded, but egalitarian ideas are cropping up with increased frequency among politicians and in the media. Senator Fred Harris's populist presidential campaign, which called for some income redistribution, was short-lived, but Senator George McGovern has proposed a comprehensive tax reform program along the same lines, and Governor George Wallace occasionally injects egalitarian notions into his campaign speeches. Widely read journalists, such as Tom Wicker, Jack Newfield, and *New Republic*'s TRB, have talked and written about the need for equality. Last March [1972] an article entitled "Equality" appeared in *Fortune*; it sought, rather gingerly, to prepare the business community for a more egalitarian future.

The current interest in equality cannot be explained away as the plaints of discontented minorities and newly radicalized public figures. It stems from the fact that America's is, and always has been, a very unequal society. Take the distribution of income. The poorest fifth of the U.S. population receives only 4 per cent of the nation's annual income, and the next poorest fifth, only 11 per cent, while the richest fifth gets about 45 per cent, and the 5 per cent at the top, over 20 per cent. Inequality of assets is even greater: 1 per cent of the people control more than one-third of the country's wealth. Although many Americans now own some stocks, 2 per cent of all individual stockholders own about two-thirds of stocks held by individuals.

The same inequality exists in the business world. Of the almost two million corporations in America, one-tenth of 1 per cent controls 55 per cent of the total corporate assets; 1.1 per cent controls 82 per cent. At the other end of the spectrum, 94 per cent of the corporations own only 9 per cent of the total assets. Even the public economy is unequal, for the poor pay a larger share of their incomes for taxes than other groups; people earning less than $2,000 pay fully half of their incomes in direct and indirect taxes as compared with only 45 per cent paid by those earning $50,000 or more. Moderate income groups are not much better off; people earning $8,000–$10,000 a year pay only 4 per cent less of their income than those making $25,000–$50,000.

Of course, the poor get something back from the government through welfare and other subsidies, but then so do the affluent, especially through indirect subsidies in the guise of tax policies, such as the oil-depletion allowance, crop supports, and tax exemptions granted to municipal-bond purchasers. Philip Stern, author of *The Great Treasury Raid* and himself a multimillionaire, recently described these subsidies as "a welfare program that reverses the usual pattern and gives huge welfare payments to the superrich but only pennies to the very poor." Stern estimated that the annual subsidies came to $720,000 per family for people with million-dollar incomes, $650 per family for the $10,000–$15,000 middle-income group, and $16 per family for the under-$3,000 poor.

Political inequality is also rampant. For example, since about 13 per cent of the population is poor in terms of the official poverty line, an egalitarian political system would require that almost fifty congressmen and thirteen senators be representatives of the poor. This is not the case, however, even though big business, big labor, and even less numerous sectors of the population have their unofficial representatives in both houses of Congress. While Supreme Court action has finally brought about the one-man, one-vote principle in electing these representatives, the seniority system maintains the traditional pattern of inequality, and so a handful of congressmen and senators, many from rural districts, still hold much of the real power on Capitol Hill. Affluent individuals and well-organized interest groups in effect have more than one vote per man because they have far greater access to their elected representatives than the ordinary citizen and because they can afford to hire lobbyists who watch out for their interests and even help to write legislation.

These patterns of inequality are not new; although America has sometimes been described as a nation of equals and as a classless society, these are simply myths. To be sure, America never had the well-defined classes or estates that existed in Europe, but from its beginning it has nevertheless been a nation of unequals. For example, in 1774, among the minority of Philadelphians affluent enough to pay taxes, 10 per cent owned fully 89 per cent of the taxable property. Over the last 200 years the degree of economic inequality has been reduced somewhat, but in the last sixty years—since reliable statistics on income distribution have become available—that distribution has changed little.

Although the ideal of a nation of equals has existed in American life from the beginning, it has, in fact, never been pursued very energetically in either the economy or the polity. Even the ideal that every boy could be President of the United States or chairman of the board of General Motors has rarely been achieved; most of our presidents have been rich, and studies of the origins of American businessmen show that in the nineteenth century, as now, the large majority have themselves been sons of businessmen.

Nevertheless, over the last 200 years most Americans seem to have put up quietly with the prevailing inequality. Today, however, the traditional patience with inequality has disappeared, and for three reasons. First, many Americans are now beginning to realize that the frontier, by which I mean the opportunity to strike out on one's own and perhaps to strike it rich, is closing down. The literal frontier in the West was closed before the turn of the century, but until recently, other frontiers were still thought to be open. Rural people hoped that they could become independent by saving up for a farm; factory workers, by going into business, perhaps opening a gas station or small workshop; and middle-class people, by entering the independent professions.

Today these hopes have begun to disappear, for the family farm is economically obsolete, the small store cannot compete with the chain, and the independent professions now consist more and more of salaried employees. Of course, there are still exceptions, and every year a few well-publicized individuals strike it rich, but their small number only proves the rule. Most Americans now realize that they will spend their working lives as employees and that they can best improve their fortunes by making demands on their employers and, because the government's role in the economy is rapidly increasing, on their political representatives.

Second, as people have voiced more political demands, they have also become less patient with political inequality, particularly with their increasing powerlessness as bureaucracies and corporations continue to get bigger. Indeed, many of the demands for change that sprung up during the 1960s were fledgling attempts to fight powerlessness and to redress the political imbalance.

Third, the affluence of the post-World War II era has enabled many Americans to raise their incomes to a point where they are no longer preoccupied solely with making ends meet. As a result, new expectations have emerged, not only for a higher standard of living but also for improvements in the quality of life and for greater power to control one's destiny. And, more than ever before, people believe that the economy and the government should help them achieve their new expectations.

What people demand is not necessarily what they will get, as the lingering recession of the last few years and the continuation of the war in Vietnam have persuasively demonstrated. Still, the demands associated with the equality revolution will not recede, and if America is to have any chance of becoming a more stable society, it must also become a more egalitarian society.

Once upon a time inequality helped to make America great. The country was built out of the energy of restless entrepreneurs, the labor supplied by the unequal, and the capital generated from both. Today, however, inequality is a major source of social instability and unrest and is even a cause of the rising rates of crime, delinquency, and social pathology—alcoholism, drug addition, and mental illness, for example. The conventional wisdom maintains that crime and pathology are caused largely by poverty, but during the 1960s poverty declined while crime and pathology increased. In these same years, however, inequality did not decrease; by some estimates, it actually grew worse.

One conventional measure of inequality is the number of people who earn less than half of a country's median family income. In the U.S. between 1960 and 1970, when this median rose from $5,620 to $9,870, the number earning half the median dropped only 1 per cent—from 20 to 19. One can also define inequality by measuring how far the poor are from the median income. In 1960 income at the poverty line, earned only by the richest of the poor, came to 50 per cent of the median: by 1970 it came to only 40 per cent. In other words, during the decade the poverty line rose far more slowly than the median income, and the inequality gap between the poor and the median earners actually widened by a full 20 per cent.

This gap is not just economic, however; it also produces social and emotional consequences. Inequality gives rise to feelings of inferiority, which in turn generate inadequacy and self-hate or anger. Feelings of inadequacy and self-hate, more than poverty, account for the high rates of pathology; anger results in crime, delinquency, senseless violence—and, of course, in political protest as well. But inequality also has less dramatic consequences. For example, because they cannot afford to dress their children properly, some poor mothers refuse to send them to school; shabby clothes may protect a youngster from the elements—a flour sack made into a suit or dress will do that—but shabby clothes also mark the child as unequal, and mothers want to protect their children from this label even at the cost of depriving them of schooling.

The social and emotional consequences of inequality are also felt by moderate-income people, especially the almost 40 per cent of Americans who earn above the poverty line but below the median income. For example, many young factory workers now realize, as their fathers could not afford to realize, that they hold unpleasant jobs without much chance of advancement or escape, and that much blue-collar work is inferior to white-collar jobs, which are now the norm in the American economy. In fact, the pathology and the protest normally associated with the poor are beginning to develop among factory workers as well. Hard drugs are now showing up in blue-collar neighborhoods, and strikes over working conditions, such as the recent one at the General Motors plant in Lordstown, Ohio, are increasing in number and intensity.

Indeed, if the most serious inequalities in American life are not corrected, people who feel themselves to be most unequal are likely to find new ways of getting even with America. New kinds of school, factory, and office disturbances, ghetto unrest, and dropping out of the system can be expected, and more crime in middle-class urban neighborhoods and suburbs is likely, for crime has always been a way by which at least some poor people can obtain a primitive kind of income redistribution when society pays no heed to their inequality. Inequality does not harm only the unequal; it hurts the entire society. The last ten years have demonstrated the fragility of the American political fabric, but the social fabric is also weak. Old sources of stability have disappeared, as has much of the traditional American culture that once provided satisfactions even under inegalitarian conditions. The small towns and rural areas that gave people a sense of rootedness, which compensated them for their poverty, are being depleted by out-migration. In the cities the ethnic groups, which maintained the peasants' necessary resignation to European inequality and provided group cohesion and a close-knit family life as compensation, are now Americanized. (Although a revival of ethnic identity may be taking place currently, the old cultures are not being resuscitated, for the new ethnic identity is political and actually calls for more equality for ethnics.) Increasingly, Americans today are members of a single mainstream culture, partly urban, partly suburban, and distinguished primarily by differences in income and education. The mainstream culture pursues values long identified with the American way of life, mainly individual and familial comforts, security, and self-improvement, but it strives for ever higher levels of these, and with ever rising expectations that they will be achieved. As a result, mainstream culture rejects traditional rural, ethnic, and other values that call for modest expectations of comfort, security, and self-improvement and that thus accept the prevailing inequality.

The continued rise in expectations makes it likely that America will enter a period of greater economic and political conflict, for, when almost everyone has higher expectations, there must inevitably be conflict over how these expectations are to be met and just whose expectations are to be met first and foremost.

America has always endured conflict, of course; after all, economic competition is itself a form of conflict. But conflict can tear society apart unless it can be resolved constructively. This is possible only if the participants in the conflict have, and feel they have, a chance to get what they want or, when this is not feasible, to get about as much as everyone else—if, in other words, the conflict ends in a compromise that meets everyone's needs as fairly as possible. But if the participants in the conflict are unequal, those with power and wealth will almost always get what they want, whether from government or from the economy.

Conflicts can best be compromised fairly if the society is more egalitarian, if differences of self-interest that result from sharp inequality of income and power can be reduced. The more egalitarian a society, the greater the similarity of interests among its citizens, and the greater the likelihood that disagreements between them can be settled through fair compromise. Also, only in a more egalitarian society is it possible to develop policies that are truly in the public interest, for only in such a society do enough citizens share enough interests so that these policies can be considered to be truly public ones.

Consequently, the time has come to start thinking about a more egalitarian America and to develop a model of equality that combines the traditional emphasis on the pursuit of liberty with the newly emerging need to reduce inequality. As Daniel Patrick Moynihan put it in the famous "Moynihan Report" of 1965, Equality of Opportunity must be transformed into Equality of Results. Equality of Opportunity simply enables people with more income and better education to win out over the less fortunate, even when the competition itself is equitable. Equality of Results means that people begin the competition more equal in these resources; therefore, the outcome is likely to be more equitable. Equality of Results does not mean absolute equality, however, either of income or of any other resource. It does mean sufficient reductions in present inequities to erase any insurmountable handicaps in the competition.

Models or methods for achieving equality have generally been *collectivist;* they call for replacing private institutions with public agencies that will take over the allocation of resources, typically through a nationalization of industry. This approach assumes that all resources belong equally to all people and that public ownership will bring about equality. When all the people own everything, however, they really do not own anything, enabling the officials who govern in the name of the people to make themselves more than equal politically and to restrict others' political liberties. This seems to be an almost inevitable outcome of collectivist policies, at least in poor countries, even though these policies have also reduced overall economic inequality.

An American equality model must be *individualist;* it must achieve enough equality to allow the pursuit of liberty to continue but not restrict equal access to liberty for others. An individualistic model of equality begins with these assumptions: that people are not ready to stop competing for material or nonmaterial gain or self-improvement; that they will not, for the sake of equality, become altruists who repress their ego-needs for the public good; and that they are not ready to surrender control over their own lives to a government, however democratic, that doles out liberty and equality through collective ownership of all resources. Consequently, an individualist model would aim for greater economic equality, not by nationalizing industry but by distributing stock ownership to larger numbers of people, as Louis Kelso, among others, has suggested.

Similarly, the model would not provide the same public or private goods and services to everyone; rather, it would attempt to equalize income and then let people decide to spend that income on goods and services of their own choosing. Nor would everyone have the same income. Instead, the model would enable people to maximize their earnings through their own efforts; it would create more equality through tax and subsidy policies, as in Sweden and Great Britain, for example. Greater equalization of incomes after taxes should not significantly reduce incentive, for even now rich people continue trying to make more money although most of the additional earnings goes to the tax collectors.

The reconciling of equality and liberty is not simple, and only a great deal of public debate can determine how it ought to be done. It is not simply a matter of giving up a little liberty for a little equality. There are many kinds of equality—economic, social, political, and sexual, among others. Which kinds are most important, how much equality is needed, and which resources, powers, rights, and privileges need to be equalized and which need to be allocated on libertarian principles must be debated.

Nevertheless, some of the basic requirements of a more egalitarian society can be outlined. The American political-bureaucratic complex must be restructured so that it will attend to the demands of average citizens rather than of those best organized to apply maximal political pressure or the largest campaign contributions. The right combination of centralization and citizen control has to be found to make this complex both effective and democratic, responsive to majority rule as well as to the rights of minorities, at state and inferior levels as well as at the federal level. Some basic services, such as health, education, legal aid, and housing, should be available to everyone at a decent level of quality, so that, for example, the poor would not be confined to slums or public housing projects but could choose from the same kind of housing as everyone else. They would obtain rent subsidies to help pay for it.

The economy must also be democratized; corporations need to become more accountable to consumers and the general public, and they must be required to shoulder the social and other indirect costs of their activities. Stock ownership has to be dispersed, taxes must be made progressive, and subsidies should be used extensively for egalitarian purposes. Unemployment and underemployment have to be eliminated and the poverty line raised so that the gaps between those at the bottom, middle, and top are reduced and so that eventually no one will earn less than 75 per cent of the median income: $7,500 by today's income figures. Whether a ceiling on top incomes is economically necessary remains to be seen, although it may well be socially desirable. Even now there is considerable uproar over millionaires who pay no taxes. Nevertheless, more income equality cannot be achieved solely by redistributing some of the great wealth of the superrich; redirecting the benefits of future economic growth to the now less-than-equal and imposing higher taxes on the corporations and the top fifth of the population would also be necessary. Still, greater income equality can be brought about without excessive soaking of the rich; S. M. Miller has estimated that if only 10 per cent of the after-tax incomes of families earning more than $15,000 were shifted to those earning less than $4,000, the income of persons earning less than $4,000 would increase by more than half. America is today sufficiently affluent to afford more income equality without great sacrifice by anyone. The Gross National Product is currently so high that if it were divided equally among all Americans, a family of four would receive $19,000. Part of the GNP must be used for investment, of course, but if what economists call Total Personal Income were divided up, a family of four would still receive $15,600, fully half as much again as the current median family income.

A more egalitarian America is thus economically feasible, but it would not be politically achievable without considerable political struggle. The more-than-equal would fight any inroads on their privileges, but even the less-than-equal might at first be unenthusiastic, fearful that promises would not be kept and that, as has so often happened in the past, high-sounding policy proposals would continue to result in legislation benefiting the wealthy and powerful. The less-than-equal would soon rally to genuinely egalitarian legislation, but the affluent would still have to be persuaded that money and privilege alone cannot buy happiness in a conflict-ridden society and that the current American malaise, from which they suffer as much as others, will disappear only with greater equality. Indeed, I am convinced that what Daniel Bell has called the postindustrial society cannot be held together unless private and public resources are shared sufficiently to give every American a fair chance in the pursuit of liberty. That is why equality is likely to become an increasingly insistent item on the agenda of American politics.

10

Economics

Although Geoffrey Baraclough's article focuses on the oil crisis, he sees that crisis as a symptom of the overall failure of "neocapitalism." Western countries have squandered oil for decades and "nothing was done to plan for alternatives to meet a contingency [i.e., the exhaustion of fossil fuels] which everyone knew was bound to arise." So, because nothing was done, and because fuels can no longer be squandered—even if we should find four times the oil we now think lies in the ground, the current growth of consumption could be maintained for only fifteen years longer—Baraclough feels we have no choice but to make radical changes in an economy that now rests on the use of extraordinarily large amounts of fossil fuels.

I believe Baraclough's predictions are accurate, but I also see the crisis of neocapitalism as an opportunity to voluntarily reevaluate our assumptions about energy and industry.

From The Oil Crisis
—Geoffrey Baraclough

When the history of the approaching depression comes to be written—a depression likely, on present showing, to be even more severe and more world-shaking than the depression of 1929–1940—the second half of 1974 will appear as the time when an unwilling world, preoccupied with inflation and mounting unemployment, was suddenly brought face to face with the twin issues of food and energy.

Ever since Watergate passed into history we have heard of little else. On the radio, on television, on the front pages of the daily newspapers and on the covers of weekly magazines, the food and energy crisis has become head-line news, the subject of endless conferences, study groups, projects, and reports.

When I began writing this review in mid-November, the World Food Conference, attended by representatives of some 130 nations, was meeting in Rome. My desk is littered with reports, all reciting the same facts and proposing much the same remedies. Predictably enough, the annual reports of the World Bank and the International Monetary Fund were dominated by oil and food, and almost simultaneously came the elaborate study commissioned by the Ford Foundation, at a cost of $4 million, on "America's Energy Future."

In addition, a whole array of private institutes have sprung into action, all protesting their independent status and therefore, presumably, their disinterestedness: the Trilateral Commission ("A Private North American-European-Japanese Initiative on Matters of Common Concern"),[1] the Management Institute for National Development,[2] the Transnational Institute ("a community of scholars from different countries dedicated to the study of problems that can no longer be studied within the confines of any single country"), the Institute on Man and Science,[3] to say nothing of old established organizations such as the Brookings Institution.[4]

The result is an impressive volume of information, but a multiplicity of voices. The trouble for the ordinary man and woman—for you, in fact, and for me—is that the gathering crisis has so many facets, so many interlocking ramifications, each reacting upon the other, until in the end we seem to be trapped in a deteriorating situation with no obvious solution in sight.

Merely to list the problems is to see their complexity, the crisscrossing web of unresolved issues in which the world has suddenly become entangled. On the one hand, there is the fourfold increase in the price of oil since the Arab-Israeli war of October, 1973; on the other, the inexorable approach of the end of the hydrocarbon age, the drying up—hard even now to visualize, but by all accounts not more than fifty years away—of the main source of energy on which the industrial world has come to depend. Then, the short-term famine conditions arising from the droughts of 1972 and 1973, the desperate plight of 800 million people in Asia and Africa, as well as the long-term problem of providing adequate feeding for a growing world population.

Add to these the problems of mounting inflation and growing unemployment, the instability of the Middle East and the shaky future of the Western alliance, the effects of a vastly increased fuel bill on the economies of the

---

[1]John C. Campbell, Guy de Carmoy, and Shinichi Kondo, *Energy: The Imperative for a Trilateral Approach* (Triangle Papers, no. 5, The Trilateral Commission, 345 East 46th Street, New York, 1974, 35 pages).
[2]*World Food Supply: A Global Development Case Study,* prepared by J. Carlisle Spivey (Management Institute for National Development, 230 Park Avenue, New York, 1974, 62 pages).
[3]*The World Food and Energy Crises,* a report by Richard N. Gardner, co-sponsored by the Institute on Man and Science, Rensselaerville, NY, the Aspen Institute for Humanistic Studies, the Overseas Development Council, and the Charles F. Kettering Foundation, November, 1974, 76 pages.
[4]*Cooperative Approaches to World Energy Problems* (Brookings Institution, Washington, DC, June, 1974, 51 pages, $1.00).

United States's European trading partners and of Japan, and the difficulties of the underdeveloped countries of Asia and Africa, unable to pay for the necessary imports of oil, fertilizers, and foodstuffs, and it is easy to understand the fears and premonitions of ordinary people, in America and in Europe. Suddenly their whole future has become precarious.

So far, as *The Washington Post* observed last September, people are confronting the crisis "without visible signs of anger and despair."[5] But the gnawing fear that the good times are past, that even modest expectations are unlikely to be fulfilled, that the industrial West, with its high standards of living, is passing into an age in which shortages are the norm and not the exception, is a traumatic experience, and like all traumatic experiences its consequences are incalculable. That is why it is necessary to analyze what has happened coolly and dispassionately. Economic strain breeds desperate remedies, and economic strain is building up inexorably, nationally and worldwide.

The orthodox view of the crisis, as seen in the West, received its most authoritative formulation some three months ago in *The New York Times*.[6] Analyzing what it called "the real economic threat"—a threat which, if left unchecked, would lead to a "world economic catastrophe as fraught with danger to political stability and peace as was the Great Depression"—the *Times* found it in the operations of "the international oil cartel" and the "skyrocketing of oil prices." This, it affirmed, was the "major source of inflation and balance-of-payments instability"; this was what was driving "nations with weak economies . . . into insolvency." Through the "sudden and massive transfers of income, wealth and power to the small group of oil-exporting countries," the world was faced by a "breakdown in trade and payments" and "the double threat of world inflation and world depression."

The *Times* article was intended as a call to action, a challenge to "the United States and its allies" to demonstrate "that they mean business." And yet the assumptions upon which the whole argument rests are not as self-evident as the authoritative tone of the article suggests. No one will deny that increased oil prices have contributed to the inflationary spiral—though their exact share is not easy to quantify—but the approaching economic downturn was clearly apparent, for those who wished to see it, even before the first sharp rise in oil prices in 1971. As one of the Trilateral Commission reports correctly states, the war of October, 1973, the embargoes, cutbacks in oil production, and rises in prices did not create the energy problem; they merely "speeded up trends already visible."[7]

To lay the blame for current economic dislocations on "the international oil cartel" is, in fact, a gross simplification. "Even before the recent sequence of events," the secretary-general of the United Nations has pointed out, "it was clear that the world monetary system was suffering from malfunction-

---

[5]"Bad Times," by Haynes Johnson and Noel Epstein, *Washington Post,* September 22, 1974.
[6]"The Real Economic Threat," *The New York Times,* September 22, 1974.
[7]*Energy: The Imperative for a Trilateral Approach,* p. 9.

ings'';[8] and the International Monetary Fund states in its 1974 report that ''it is only in the past few years that rising costs of primary commodities and fuels have become significant elements in the inflationary trend.'' Moreover, ''a slowing down of economic expansion in most industrial countries was already in process in the course of 1973, prior to the sudden emergence of energy problems later in the year.''[9]

It is possible, of course, to argue that, while these facts may be true, the actions of the oil cartel have changed the whole situation, transforming what was at worst a controllable secondary recession, comparable to the recession of 1957–1958, into a global economic crisis which threatens, through an uncontrollable chain reaction, to trigger off a world depression. That, I suspect, is the position of *The New York Times*. If so, it is a partial and inadequate interpretation. Neither the oil crisis nor the food crisis is a chance happening. On the contrary, they are the outcome of policies which have been pursued with unswerving tenacity and disregard for consequences for a quarter of a century. What confronts us, in short, is the crisis of neocapitalism, and it is sometimes tempting to wonder whether the barrage of propaganda to which we have been subjected during the last six months may not have the hidden purpose of diverting attention from that unpalatable fact.

The problems of food and energy are not, after all, sudden afflictions which descended upon us out of a blue sky in 1973. Millions were starving to death in Bangladesh and India long before the droughts and crop failures of 1972. For twenty years at least scientists like Harrison Brown have been warning us of the disastrous consequences that will ensue if we continue to use up the limited world reserves of fossil fuels at the present spendthrift rate. It would be encouraging to think that the plight of the so-called Fourth World—the underdeveloped countries of Asia and Africa with per capita incomes less than $200 a year—has at last stirred the conscience of mankind. But the impression one gets, as one reads through the pronouncements of politicians and the inspired comments of journalists, is different. What worries *The New York Times* is not the specter of world poverty and rampant starvation but the leverage which the ''shift of wealth'' will give to ''the oil-producing states of the Middle East,'' their ''growing influence'' over ''business and government establishments,'' and their ability ''to acquire vast holdings of industrial and real estate properties in the West.''

The same preoccupation characterizes the much-heralded ''five-point energy plan'' announced by Henry Kissinger on November 14.[10] Here, if anywhere, what the secretary-general of the United Nations calls the ''cold reality'' of the situation is exposed to view, and the cold reality is that the developed nations get the lion's share. For the rich, if the plan goes through,

---

[8]*The World Food and Energy Crises*, p. 2.
[9]International Monetary Fund, *Annual Report*, pp. 5, 7.
[10]''Energy Crisis: Strategy for Cooperative Action,'' address by Henry A. Kissinger, Chicago, Illinois, November 14, 1974 (Department of State, Washington, DC).

there is to be a $25 billion "international lending facility" for "recycling, at commercial interest rates, funds flowing back to the industrial world from the oil producers"; for the poor, a nebulous "trust fund" of indeterminate size, managed not by the countries of the developing world, but by the International Monetary Fund, in which the United States and the United Kingdom between them control more than 30 percent of the votes.

I do not for one moment wish to suggest that this concern with the problems of the industrialized world is illegitimate. Here also, after all, are millions of ordinary people—clerks, schoolteachers, shop assistants—whose modest aspirations and even their livelihood are imperiled through no fault of their own. But this does not alter the fact that the key to the present clamor is not the plight of the starving peoples of Asia and Africa but (as one commentator puts it) the "devastating impact" that the "siphoning of billions of dollars from the business market and into OPEC accounts" is having on "the shaky economies of Italy, Britain, and France" and the repercussions that may ensue for the United States.[11]

There is, of course, an impressive body of economic doctrine which justifies this priority, arguing that the hub of the world economy is the industrialized West, and that the first necessity—upon which all else, including the welfare of the poor nations, depends—is to set the industrial world, like Humpty-Dumpty, back on its feet again. How far, if at all, this hoary argument is true in present-day conditions is a question I shall come back to. For the moment, it is sufficient to say that it is more likely to commend itself to Western governments than to the great majority of the world's population. I do not mean that the concern of people like Robert McNamara for the starving millions of Asia and Africa is not genuine. But what is driving Western politicians to despair is not the plight of the poor nations but the plight of the wealthy nations, and above all else the dislocation of the economic system which has made the wealthy nations wealthy. This preoccupation is natural enough; but we should be very foolish if we expected the rest of the world necessarily to take the same view or endorse the same priorities.

If we are to understand what is portentously called the "food and energy crisis"—but what, in reality, is a crisis of prices and money—and if, still more, we are to understand the current political uncertainties and the very real possibility that they may spark off the Third (and last) World War, it is essential to look beyond the immediate issue of Middle East oil and try to place the events of the last twelve months in a wider context. What we are experiencing, in other words, is not a short-term emergency but a last desperate attempt by industrial society, as we have known it since 1950, to climb out of a crisis of its own making. The actions of the oil-producing countries may have been the last straw, but they were not the cause of the problems confronting us today.

No one better expressed the underlying realities of the situation than Giscard d'Estaing when he said that the present crisis is an "enduring crisis" involving

[11] "Investing Arab Oil Profits," by Eliot Marshall, *New Republic*, October 12, 1974, p. 8.

a redistribution of the world's resources. It is the result of many different factors, of which oil is only one, and is "no passing perturbation." What we are witnessing, he concluded, is "the revenge on Europe for the nineteenth century."[12] He might have added (though he did not) that it is also the revenge on the United States for Vietnam and the dislocations it caused.

As the crisis of neo-capitalism comes to a head, nothing would be more self-defeating—unless we wish, like Hitler, to bring the whole world down with us into catastrophe—than to suppose that we can wriggle out of it by "pressures on the oil-exporting countries," or that all would be well if the price of oil could be reduced to its 1970 level. The real issue, as Ronald Segal says,[13] is not the price of oil but "the mounting incapacity of the system in general and of the United States in particular to provide the functioning and resources" necessary to make neo-capitalism work. It is only necessary to look at the long, tangled, and sometimes sordid history of oil to see what has gone wrong, and why.

When we turn to the so-called "energy crisis," the essential point to remember—for so accustomed to it have we become that a real effort is required to recall it to mind—is how recent a phenomenon the dependence of industrial society on oil and oil products really is. If, as Lenin is reputed to have said, communism equals Soviet power plus electrification, neo-capitalism equals American power plus oil.

The basic facts about the oil situation are set out briefly and judiciously in Tad Szulc's new book [*The Energy Crisis*], and more elaborately in the Ford Foundation report, and there is no need to recapitulate them here. What is evident is that the onward march of postwar neo-capitalism and the ever more prodigal use of oil went hand in hand; they are two sides of the same medal, and without the latter the former would have been almost inconceivable.

In the United States alone oil consumption rose from 2.37 to 6.3 billion barrels a year between 1950 and 1973, and in other industrial countries the rate of increase was more spectacular still. Under 1.5 million barrels a day in 1950, Western European oil imports reached over 15 million barrels in 1973; in Japan, during the same period, they rose from around 100,000 to almost 6 million.

The result, as the Ford Foundation report puts it, was that "the world oil market" became the "artery of Western European, Japanese and American prosperity." Put more crudely—but not, I think, less correctly—the virtually continuous economic growth among the industrial nations of the West since the early 1950s was subsidized, and probably made possible, by the oil-producing countries. The power that drove the machine was an abundant flow of cheap oil, controlled by an immensely powerful consortium of international oil companies, which shared out the market between them, with the backing of the American and British governments.

---

[12]*The New York Times*, October 25, 1974.
[13]Ronald Segal, *The Decline and Fall of the American Dollar* (Bantam Books, 1974, 199 pages, $1.95), p. 11.

The predominance of oil is something entirely new—as new and as fragile as the economic system built upon it. Fifty years ago oil contributed only 14 percent to America's energy needs, and substantially less elsewhere. Even in 1950 solid fuels accounted for approximately two-thirds of energy consumption; and it was only then, as the postwar economy got into its stride, that the ratio was reversed, until by 1970 petroleum and natural gas supplied more than 60 percent of the vastly inflated total.[14]

The reason, of course, was its cheapness and the ease with which the vast Middle East deposits could be extracted. I am no great admirer of the Shah of Persia, but he was surely right when he said that it was "twenty-two years of cheap fuel," from 1947 to 1969, "that made Europe what it is" and "made Japan what it is."[15] He might have added that it made the US what it is, as well; for in 1973 it was the US, with only 6 percent of the world's population, that was consuming one-third of the world's total energy output, at a cost of only 4 percent of its gross national product.

Buoyed by the apparently inexhaustible supply of cheap and abundant oil flowing from Middle East wells, the industrialized world took off like a runaway horse with the bit between its teeth. It was now that the belief took hold that the cycle of boom and depression had been conquered, together with the heady vision of an era of continuous self-sustaining growth, and steadily increasing affluence. It was always a mirage, but while it lasted it did irreparable harm. There is no need to go into the details of the story. The essential point is that there was energy to waste, and everything conceivable was done to ensure that it should be wasted, provided only that the oil-fired industrial machine could be kept going at full speed ahead.

It is not only, as everyone knows, that in fuel consumption the American automobile is the most inefficient in the world, or that millions of dollars are wasted annually, at the expense of the hard-pressed consumer, through inefficient space-heating in homes, stores, schools, and offices. As Tad Szulc points out, it would only be necessary to improve the performance of American cars to European or Japanese standards to save practically 40 percent of American oil consumption and wipe out the need for imports. But these much-publicized inefficiencies are only illustrative, and far more fundamental is the distortion which the entire economy has undergone.

Two striking examples illustrate its nature. The first is the sabotaging (no other word is adequate) of the railroads and public transport systems, although for shifting freight, as the investigations of the Ford Foundation show, "rail transport is four times as efficient as truck transport and sixty-three times as efficient as air transport." The second, more significant still, is the running down of the coal industry, for this means that the United States's richest source of energy is being grossly underused.

The shift from coal is dramatic. In 1920 it supplied 78 percent of American energy needs; by 1973 its share was down to 18 percent. Utilities, in particular,

---

[14]*The World Food and Energy Crises*, p. 41.
[15]His "shrewd comments" are cited in *A Time to Choose*, p. 158.

switched from coal to oil. As Szulc points out, in the New York City metropolitan area—"and the same thing was happening all over the country"—the utilities, which used only 22 percent ten years earlier, were by 1970 "relying on oil for 80 percent of their electric output." As 70 percent of the energy content of the original fuel is lost in the production of electricity, and as electricity accounts for about 54 percent of total energy consumption, it is not difficult to see that this (in Szulc's words) is "one of the most important elements in the energy crisis of the 1970s."

Meanwhile, millions of dollars were spent by oil companies, utilities, electrical appliance manufacturers, and the automobile industry to persuade the consumer to squander energy, and the government aided and abetted the waste "through promotional pricing, tax advantages, and other forms of subsidies." There was nothing necessary or inevitable about these developments. Energy was wasted because, so long as oil was cheap, there was no incentive to save. In the industrial sector—by far the biggest user, accounting for 40 percent of total consumption—managers simply did not bother to economize because, as the Ford Foundation report remarks, energy "accounted for only about 5 percent of value added."

Two points are commonly made in defense. The first is that, at least until 1973, the energy industries were remarkably successful in keeping prices low. The second is that growth in energy usage and growth in the economy are inextricably linked.

Like most such statements, both are half-truths. No one would deny the simple proposition that, throughout history, the substitution of nonhuman and nonanimal for human and animal energy has been a major factor in economic growth. But this does not mean that the more the energy consumed, the greater the rate of growth will be. On the contrary, as the Ford Foundation report points out, whereas between 1870 and 1950 GNP per capita rose sixfold for a mere doubling of per capita energy use, between 1950 and 1973 energy growth per capita actually exceeded the per capita growth in production.

The abundance of cheap energy, in other words, was detrimental to technological improvement and innovation and probably held back economic progress. Nor was the constantly increasing use of energy necessary. Other industrialized nations achieved enviably high standards of living with a far lower per capita energy consumption than the United States. Switzerland, for example, consumed only one-third and West Germany less than one-half as much. The United States level of energy consumption—six times as high per capita as the world average—to a considerable extent represented sheer waste.

As for the argument that the oil industry and the utilities contributed to economic prosperity by keeping prices low, it may be true that in real terms (i.e., discounting inflation) energy prices decreased between 1950 and 1970, but everyone knows there is another side to the story. I do not wish to discuss the alleged abuses of the oil combines: the extortionate profits which have given rise to such violent denunciation, the widely publicized contributions to Nixon's election campaigns, the charge heard at every gas station a year ago of artificially withholding supplies to boost prices and wipe out competitors. They are not irrelevant, but they can easily obscure the real issues if they persuade people—as frequently they do—that all will be well if the oil industry is brought under firmer control. Nothing could be further from the truth. The problem is not how the oil industry is run but how neo-capitalist society is run.

Nevertheless, it is perfectly true that the flow of oil has been manipulated for twenty years in ways which, to say the least, do not always coincide with the public, to say nothing of the consumer's, interest. Apart from depletion allowances, estimated to cost the US taxpayer $3.5 billion a year, and other fiscal advantages, it is notorious that consumers paid about $5 billion more for oil products in 1969 than they would have done if trade had not been restricted by quotas. At a time when the extraction of Middle East oil cost sixteen cents a barrel, the price was set by the oil companies at the American cost of production, i.e., $1.75 a barrel. Not surprisingly, American production was run down, and in 1971, with a rising demand, output fell below the 1970 level. After 1956, according to Szulc, "the number of newly completed wells began to drop catastrophically" and "not a single new refinery was built along the East Coast between 1961 and 1973."

It would be easy, but it is unnecessary, to add to this catalogue. The basic fact, as Tad Szulc says, is that, given the cheapness of Middle East oil, "investments in overseas ventures were infinitely more profitable." As far back as 1950 domestic oil production was lagging over 10 percent behind consumption; by 1973 the gap rose to over 35 percent, and the difference was made up by imports from abroad.

In itself, according to all current theories of foreign trade, this situation was unexceptionable; but the reality of everyday life was different. As the United States's need for oil imports grew, it found itself competing with industrialized Western Europe and Japan, both dependent on the Middle East and North Africa for around 80 percent of their oil. The result was predictable. Oil, as late as 1969 a glut on the market, became a sought-after commodity, and the way was open for the Organization of Petroleum Exporting Countries (OPEC) to intervene effectively.

Leaving aside for the moment the use of the oil embargo as a weapon in the Yom Kippur war, the aims of OPEC were two. The first and almost certainly the main objective—achieved either by nationalization or by participation in foreign consortia—was to ensure control over their own resources. It was, as the Trilateral Commission concedes, a perfectly "legitimate desire," and though the oil companies reacted (in Tad Szulc's words) "as if they had been robbed in broad daylight," it caused, after the first shock, comparatively little excitement in the West. The second aim was to secure a larger share—in fact, the lion's share—in the profits which had been flowing so freely to the oil companies, and this called down a torrent of abuse. Kissinger spoke of "blackmail" and *The New York Times* of "extortion," and both were echoed far and wide.

How justified these charges are is a matter of dispute. As Lester Brown observes, the Arabs are certainly not the first or only country to use their control of natural resources as a political weapon. So far as the increase in and redistribution of profits is concerned, the Arab contention—as expressed, for example, by Abderrahman Khene, the secretary general of the petroleum exporting countries—is that it could have been carried through without so steep a rise in oil prices. When the OPEC countries decided on October 16, 1973, to increase the "take" of the producing governments to $3.40, this still left the oil companies with a profit margin of $.70 a barrel. But instead of absorbing the extra cost, the companies passed it on to the consumer, in the United States and throughout the world, and this—at least according to Abderrahman Khene—was one justification for increasing the "take" to $7.00 or $7.50 a barrel. Szulc even maintains that it can be argued that the companies "welcome the higher payments they must make . . . because it balloons their profits." But whatever the rights and wrongs of the argument, one fact is clear and that is that the companies have not suffered. According to Szulc, "the majors' profit in Middle East operations early in 1974 increased on the average from $.30 to over $1 a barrel" and in the case of Aramco, the biggest of all producing companies, "from $.80 early in 1973 to $4.50 a barrel in March 1974."[16]

The truth, of course, is that the price of oil has always been artificial, based not on cost of production or the market mechanism, but on monopoly power and international politics. All that has happened is that monopoly power has changed hands. Unfortunately, it has not yet shifted to the poorer and more populated countries of the world, and even in the oil-rich countries the poor have not noticeably benefited. In Teheran two-thirds of all families have an income of less than $200 per person a year and their living conditions are at least as bad as this figure indicates.

Ironically, the factor immediately responsible for this transformation was the action of the oil companies themselves in cutting production so as to maintain prices and thus creating a shortage the oil producing countries could exploit. But the change was overdue and would have occurred sooner or later as a result of the profound shift in world political relationships following the Suez War of 1956 and the deterioration in the international position of the United States as a result of Vietnam. "The old international economic order," as the Institute on Man and Science puts it, "was characterized by unacceptable inequality in the distribution and management of the world's wealth," and could not last.

If, as Szulc rightly says, the crisis of October, 1973, had "been in the making for a long time," what remains to be explained is why it took the

---

[16]Abderrahman Khene's statement is reported in *The World Food and Energy Crises,* page 21; Szulc, *The Energy Crisis,* pp. 101–105, explains the involved process by which the companies' profits were inflated. He appears (p. 105) to concur with the Shah of Iran when, even after the original increase in October, 1973, he said that "there is at least one dollar in the price that for no reason at all goes to the oil companies."

world by surprise. The easy answer is to blame the international oil combines, and they certainly were not innocent. But if we look more deeply, we shall be more likely to place the responsibility on the Western governments, particularly the United States and British governments, which backed the companies (in Iran, for example, in 1953, or in Peru in 1966), not merely, as is often alleged, because of political pressure from the ''oil lobby,'' but, more fundamentally, because the prosperity and even the working of the economic system were geared to the flow of cheap oil.

For this reason they were prepared to condone and tolerate the vast profits and fiscal privileges of the companies, and it is only in the last few months—roughly since the disappearance of Nixon, who defended them to the last—that the US government, fitfully and ineffectively, has shown signs of turning against them. The reason, quite simply, is that they are no longer providing the cheap oil on which the economic system depends. If the oil companies got away with murder in the past, it was because nothing succeeds like success; if now their days are numbered, it is because nothing fails like failure.

Nevertheless the consequences are irreparable. It is often said that, in absolute terms, there is no immediate shortage of crude oil in the world. That is true enough, if we are prepared to drain the world dry of oil for immediate advantage, and there is little doubt that, given the chance, the oil companies would have exploited the Middle East oil fields to the last drop, with no thought to the future, leaving the Arab and Persian populations not much better off than they found them. But it is also true that the age of fossil fuels is drawing rapidly to a close, and the real charge against government is that, so long as cheap Middle East oil was there for the asking, nothing was done to plan for alternatives to meet a contingency which everyone knew was bound to arise.

This is the fundamental failure of neo-capitalist society over the last quarter of a century, and it is bound to take its revenge. In any realistic view—except the realism of politicians who can't see beyond the ends of their noses—the fuel crisis confronting us today has little to do with Middle East oil prices and a great deal to do with the depletion of expendable but irreplaceable energy reserves.

Even if Arabs, Persians, Libyans, and other oil-producers can be forced to toe the line—even, in other words, if the immediate crisis is solved—we are still faced with the fact that, at the present galloping rate of fuel consumption, industry is destined to grind to a halt in the first half, at latest, of the twenty-first century, and with it industrial society as we know it in the West. As the victims will be our children born today or yesterday, who will be living, or starving, through the crisis, this is not a prospect most people will regard with the detachment they feel when confronted by harrowing pictures of starving babies in Bangladesh. It cannot be fobbed off with a tax-deductible donation to Oxfam.

Something, of course, can be achieved by strict policies of conservation. That is the burden of the message conveyed in the Ford Foundation report. The danger of this approach is that it may delude people into thinking that conservation is enough. Nothing could be further from the truth. Conservation may buy time, but it leaves untouched the problem of the exhaustion of the current sources of energy.

What is needed, in other words, is a planned policy for the development not only of coal and shale but of basically new resources: solar energy, geothermal power, breeder reactors, controlled nuclear fusion, and hydrogen. Considering the rapid approach of the year 2000 AD and the long "time lead" (from a minimum of ten to an average of twenty-five years) before the initial research can be expected to produce practical results, this is the most urgent question confronting the world today. For the future of industrial societies, such as the United States, it is absolutely vital.

Nevertheless, for twenty-five years it has been brushed aside as a remote, hypothetical contingency which can be left to the future. Given the character and motivations of neo-capitalism, it could hardly have been otherwise. Although the exhaustion of fossil-fuel reserves and the end of the hydrocarbon age could easily be foreseen, the only non-fossil source of energy to which any attention was paid—and that not very successfully for industrial purposes—was nuclear fission, and this, of course, was because of its military potential, and not on account of any peaceful side uses it might have.

In other cases, development was deliberately stifled. Methyl alcohol ("methanol") is described by the Swedish International Peace Research Institute as "an especially attractive alternative fuel to gasoline"; but production has been suppressed, as the institute discreetly says, for "politico-economic" reasons, or in reality for fear lest it would compete with petroleum.[17] The only conclusion that can be drawn—a conclusion to which we shall return—is that the real energy crisis, which is not identical with the "crisis" arising from increased oil prices, can only be solved by a radical change in the whole existing economic system.

The future of mankind, to put it bluntly, can no longer be left to what the Ford Foundation report calls "the so-called marketplace." And since nothing less than the future of mankind is at stake, and no government anywhere is going to stand aside and watch its people starve, we can be sure that, as the crisis comes to a head, fundamental changes will take place. They may not be what you or I would wish; but the days of neo-capitalism are numbered. An economic system based, as Ronald Segal puts it, on "the control of society by the relationships of money, rather than the control of money relationships by society," can only, in today's circumstances, lead to disaster.

In the introduction to *Economics and the Public Purpose,* John Kenneth Galbraith claims that he is not a revolutionary, but a reformer. To summarize his plan for reform, he seeks to solve what he sees as the central problem of the modern economy—"unequal development"—by nationalizing those

[17]*Oil and Security* (Stockholm International Peace Research Institute: Stockholm, Almquist and Wiksell, Sw. Kr, 42.00; New York: Humanities Press, $12.50), pp. 102–103.

industries unable to compete with the larger and more technologically advanced corporations. In Galbraith's estimation, the only way to increase both the fairness and efficiency of economic factors like housing, transportation, and medicine is to place them under state ownership and control.

I doubt that the kind of reforms which Galbraith demands will be adequate to alter the future envisioned by Ellul or Heilbroner (Part One). If we seek to avoid concentrating power in offices like the presidency (Chapter 9), public ownership must be linked to a decentralization of power and, above all, we must decide how much industrialization the world can tolerate. In short, the problem of eliminating inequalities cannot be separated from equally important questions about centralization of power in the hands of the national state, impersonal rule by experts, and the limits of industrial growth.

From Economics and the Public Purpose —*John Kenneth Galbraith*

. . . No design for social reform is so completely excluded from reputable discussion as socialism in the United States. Its disavowal by the major political parties is assumed. Even the most radical candidate for office, if serious, follows suit: ''I am certainly not advocating socialism.'' Frequently he explains that the measures he proposes, by their very radicalism, are designed to save the country from socialism. Free enterprise must be protected from the ill will that results from its own deficiency, excess or aberration.

More than economics is involved. There is also an association between free enterprise and personal freedom. Those who decry socialism are defending more than their power, property and pecuniary return. As also with the barons at Runnymede, personal interest is reinforced by higher moral purpose. So high is this moral purpose that men of exceptional zeal do not hesitate to urge that advocacy, even discussion, of socialism be outlawed in order that freedom may be preserved.

The position in other developed countries is different in form but not greatly in consequence.[1] In Western Europe and Japan socialism is an evocative, not an evil word. The American result has there been accomplished by divorcing the word from its established meaning and even more completely from any implication of practical action. An Englishman, Frenchman or German can be an ardent socialist. But however ardent he is also practical. So he will not seriously propose that banks, insurance companies, automobile plants, chemical works or, with exceptions, steel mills be taken into public ownership. And certainly if elected to public office he will not press legislation to such end. However much he favors such action in principle, he will not be for it in practice.

The reasons for placing socialism under such stern interdict will, by now, be comprehensible. Socialism is not something that commends itself to the

From *Economics and the Public Purpose* by John Kenneth Galbraith. Copyright © 1973 by John Kenneth Galbraith. Reprinted by permission of Houghton Mifflin Co.
[1]One not unimportant difference will be noted presently.

technostructure; the latter, having won autonomy from the owners, does not invite subordination to the state. Its protective purposes argue strongly to the contrary. The technostructure, as an autonomous entity, enjoys freedom in shaping its own organization, in designing, pricing and selling its products, in bringing its persuasion and therewith its power to bear on the community and the state and in compensating and promoting its own members. Instinct warns that this autonomy would be threatened were the technostructure an arm of the state. Then decisions on where to locate a new plant, on what executives are paid, on standards of promotion would be public business. As such they would legitimately be the subject of public comment and review and perhaps of public action. Thus the desire to protect the present fiction, which is that these are matters of no legitimate public concern; they are as the market makes them—purely private business.

But it would be wrong to associate the decline of interest in socialism exclusively with the needs of the technostructure and the beliefs thus induced—important as this influence may be. Democratic socialism (and revolutionary socialism, for that matter) has for long been in accord with classical and neoclassical economics in identifying and locating the central fault in economic society. That exists where there is monopoly power. Where there is monopoly, the public is exploited by smaller output than would be possible, at higher prices than are necessary. Given the power of the employer in the labor market, workers are paid less than could be afforded and is their due. They too are exploited. As in neoclassical economics the most pejorative term is monopoly, so in socialism it is monopoly capitalism.

The reader will see why the old passion for socialism has disappeared—or survives only in oratory and nostalgia. The monopoly behavior which was its original raison d'être does not exist, even though a tradition in socialist criticism requires that any such suggestion be condemned as an exercise in capitalist apologetics. The central problem of the modern economy is unequal development. The least development is where there is the least monopoly and market power; the greatest development is where there is the most. The more highly developed the firm and technostructure, the stronger, in general, its commitment to growth. A firm that is cozening its customers in order to expand sales cannot at the same time be exploiting them in the manner of a classical monopoly. This the public knows or senses. Only if one is deeply educated can one overlook the reality and be guided by the doctrine. The doctrine guides the deeply committed socialist, in the curious companionship of the neoclassical economist, to the wrong part of the economy.

Workers have deserted socialism for the same reason that consumers have. Workers, we have seen, are exploited—or they exploit themselves. But the exploitation occurs in the market system. In the planning system workers are defended by unions and the state and favored by the market power of the employing corporation which allows it to pass the cost of wage settlements along to the public. Workers in this part of the economy are, relative to those in the market system, a favored caste. The socialist guides attention to workers who are employed in industries of great economic power. These are the industries—steel, automobiles, chemicals, oil—where power is used, in effect, to meet the major demands of workers. Like the public the workers do not march. The American trade unionist disavows socialism. His European counterpart hears it advocated, applauds, but wants no action.

A final factor which this analysis also illuminates has weakened the traditional appeal of socialism. The modern corporate enterprise, as we have sufficiently seen, is highly organized—highly bureaucratic. So is, or will be, the publicly owned firm. When the choice was between private monopoly power and public bureaucracy, the case for the latter could seem strong. The public bureaucracy might not be responsive, but it was not exploitative and thus malign. The choice between a private bureaucracy and a public bureaucracy is a good deal less clear. A very great difference in substance has been reduced, seemingly at least, to a much smaller difference in form. Added to this has been the discovery that the larger and more technical of the public bureaucracies—the Air Force, Navy, Atomic Energy Commission—have purposes of their own which can be quite as intransigently pursued as those of General Motors or Exxon. Private bureaucracies rule in their own interest. But so do public bureaucracies. Why exchange one bureaucracy for another? As elsewhere noted, the declining appeal of the Soviet Union to the modern radical is here also explained. Why exchange one bureaucratic society for another? China and Cuba seem much more appealing models. Some of their appeal, alas, is the result of their lower level of development with, and for this reason, less elaborate organization—a defect they are strenuously anxious to correct.

Yet for those who hold the fortress against inconvenient ideas life is never simple. The same circumstances which have been reducing the appeal of the traditional socialism in the positions of power have been making a new socialism urgent and even indispensable elsewhere in the economy. The word indispensable must be stressed. The older socialism allowed of ideology. There could be capitalism with its advantages and disadvantages; there could be public ownership of the means of production with its possibilities and disabilities. There could be a choice between the two. The choice turned on belief—on ideas. Thus it was ideological. The new socialism allows of no acceptable alternatives; it cannot be escaped except at the price of grave discomfort, considerable social disorder and, on occasion, lethal damage to health and well-being. The new socialism is not ideological; it is compelled by circumstance.

The compelling circumstance, as the reader will have suspected, is the retarded development of the market system. There are industries here which require technical competence, related organization and market power and related command over resource use if they are to render minimally adequate service. Being and remaining in the market system, these they do not have. So they stay in a limbo of nondevelopment or primitive development, and, as development goes forward elsewhere, their contrasting backwardness becomes increasingly dramatic.

Adding forcefully to the drama (and the distress of those who would resist all thought of socialism) is the fact that certain of the retarded industries are of peculiar importance not alone for comfort, well-being, tranquillity and happiness but also for continued existence. They provide shelter, health services and local transportation of people. Housing in a cold climate, medical attention when one is sick and the ability to reach one's place of employment are remarkably unfrivolous needs. One can readily detect the hand of a perverse Providence in the selection of the retarded industries. He is clearly bent on bothering the truly pious free-enterpriser.

The failure of these industries to pass into the planning system has diverse causes. Housing construction and medical services are geographically dispersed. As with all services this militates against the development of a comprehensive organization and specialization at any particular point. Such division of labor as may be possible is accomplished with manifest inefficiency. The time of carpenters, plumbers and electricians or, in the case of medical services, specialized surgical practitioners, physicians or technicians cannot be so scheduled as to avoid long intervals of ineffective use or idleness.

Unions have also played a retarding role. They are not uniquely strong in these industries. But employers have been uniquely weak as in the case of the construction industry, compliant as in the case of the transportation industry or members of the union itself as in the case of the American Medical Association. Thus the unions have had a free hand in regulating or prohibiting technical innovation or (as in the case of the AMA for a long time) organization that would have allowed of more effective economic development. Finally, in construction and transportation, public regulation, often inspired by employees or unions, has acted to inhibit technical innovation and the associated organization.

There is only one solution. These industries cannot function in the market system. They do not develop in the planning system. They are indispensable as people now view their need for means to move about and for protection from disease and the weather. With economic development the contrast between the houses in which the masses of people live, the medical and hospital services they can afford and the conveyances into which they are jammed and the other and more frivolous components of their living standard—automobiles, television, cosmetics, intoxicants—becomes first striking and then obscene.

The impact of unequal development in the case of health and medical services is especially bizarre. Virtually *all* of the increase in modern health hazards is the result of increased consumption. Obesity and associated disorders are the result of increased food consumption; cirrhosis and accidents are the result of increased alcohol consumption; lung cancer, heart disease, emphysema and numerous other disabilities are the result of increased tobacco consumption; accidents and resulting mortality and morbidity are caused by increased automobile use; hepatitis and numerous disabling assaults are often caused by increased drug consumption; nervous disorders and mental illness follow from efforts to increase income, observation of the greater success of others in increasing income, the fear of loss of income or the fear of the various foregoing physical consequences of high consumption. At the same time medical and hospital care is not part of the development which induces these disorders. It lags systemically behind—for a large part of the population, including many who are relatively affluent, its availability is uncertain and its cost alarming or prohibitive. Again the hand of a perverse Providence.

The only answer for these industries is full organization under public ownership. This is the new socialism which searches not for the positions of power in the economy but for the positions of weakness. And again we remark that most reliable of tendencies—and the best of tests of the validity of social diagnosis—which is that circumstance is forcing the pace. In all the developed countries governments have been forced to concern themselves extensively with housing, health and transportation. Everywhere they are already, in large measure, socialized. This is true in the United States as elsewhere. Local and commuter transportation has passed extensively into public ownership. So, with the arrival of Amtrak, has intercity rail travel. In the United States the old, who combine exceptional medical need with inferior ability to pay—for whom, in other words, the market operates with peculiar inadequacy—are provided with medical and hospital care. There is a bewildering variety of public medical assistance to other individuals and groups. In the housing industry there is an even more intricate complex of publicly sponsored construction, publicly aided construction, publicly financed construction, public subsidies to private occupancy and public control of rents. These functions, in turn, are divided among federal, state and local levels of government in such fashion that it is doubtful if any single official in any major American city knows all of the public sources of support to housing in his community.

This is, however, a highly unsatisfactory form of socialism. The term itself is scrupulously avoided.[2] And the resulting action is not undertaken affirmatively and proudly with the requisite means, the best available organization and with a view to the full accomplishment of the needed task. Rather it is viewed as exceptional and aberrant. It requires apology. The most desirable organization is never that which is best but that which seems least to interfere with private enterprise; the test of result is not the full accomplishment of the task but what is sufficient to get by.

Only as socialism is seen as a necessary and wholly *normal* feature of the system will this situation change. Then there will be public demand for high performance, and there will be public pride in the action. This is not vacuous and untested optimism; proof is to be found in Europe and Japan. There, as noted, the word socialism is evocative, not pejorative. And while socialists

---

[2]The term socialized medicine was, until recent times, highly pejorative. It has now, one judges, ceased to be so. Unsocialized medicine is for so many so unsatisfactory and expensive that alternatives can no longer be condemned by adverse terms. Socialism, too many people suspect, might be better.

in other developed countries are attracted theologically by the positions of power, they are not repelled by the need for public action elsewhere in the economy. This means that they can act pridefully in the market system. This has produced a radically superior result in the areas of weakness where socialism is compelled. Although there is much variation as between countries, urban land has been taken extensively into public ownership; a large part of all urban housing has been built under full public auspices and continued with full public ownership and management. Similarly hospitals are full public enterprises; doctors and other medical attendants are well-paid employees of the state. And it is, of course, taken for granted that public corporations will run the railroads and urban transportation. The performance of all of these industries in Britain, Scandinavia, Germany and Holland is categorically superior to that in the United States. In other countries—France, Italy, Japan, Switzerland—the enterprises that have been fully socialized, notably rail and urban transport, are superior. Only those that have not been socialized are deficient. The difference between Americans and Europeans is not that Americans have a peculiar ineptitude for operating public enterprises. The difference is that Americans have been guided by a doctrine that accords a second-rate and apologetic status to such effort.

In the past the case for public ownership was conceded where, because of the importance of the service, as in the case of education or the national defense, or the difficulty in pricing it to a particular user, as in the case of road building or street cleaning, it could not be left to the market. Or public ownership was pressed where, as in the case of public utilities, there was an inevitable monopoly and thus a danger of public exploitation. With the rise of the market and the planning systems, and the consequent inequality in development, the case for public ownership becomes much more general. It is not that the market, though generally satisfactory, fails in particular cases. It is rather that the market system is generally deficient in relation to the planning system. Accordingly there is a presumption in favor of public intervention anywhere in the market system.

The point applies particularly to the arts. Unlike poor development in housing, health or transportation poor development of the arts does not inflict physical discomfort. But these enjoyments are in the market system; without special public sponsorship and support there must be a presumption of underdevelopment. People are denied pleasure and happiness that, with relatively greater development of music, theater, painting, would be theirs. Given the power, including the persuasive power of the planning system on behalf of its products and its development in general, a society where there is no public intervention on behalf of the arts and humane studies will be grievously unbalanced. It will have great wealth. And as compared with earlier periods when patronage of the arts was more generous its artistic achievements will be much less.

In the last decade or so the notion that the arts require special support in the modern industrial society has achieved a measure of recognition. And limited, even primitive, steps have been taken by way of public development of facilities and public sponsorship of work. Instinct as to the public need has again run ahead of the underlying theory. The present analysis shows an extensive and expanding sponsorship and support of the arts to be not only a normal but an essential function of the modern state.

Public intervention on behalf of agriculture—socialization of agricultural technology, support to agricultural prices to encourage and protect investment, cooperative procurement of fertilizer, petroleum and equipment, cooperative or public supply of electricity, subsidy in support of new techniques— is also essential for a balanced development. In the absence of such social action the supply of food and fiber would be insufficient and unreliable, the cost (like that of housing and medical care) very high. Here, however, the instinct which leads to action in conflict with approved principle but in keeping with the realities of economic life has been very strongly manifested. And the approval of farmers, if not of economists, has been sufficiently strong so that these tasks have been undertaken not with apology but with pride. Largely in consequence of such public action agricultural development has, at least until now, been relatively satisfactory in the industrial countries. Had agriculture been free from such public interference—had orthodox principle been controlling—the performance would unquestionably have been deficient and perhaps by now dangerously so. And agriculture would now be exhibiting, in incipient fashion, the weaknesses elsewhere associated with the market system.

Circumstances, it is evident, are not kind to those who see themselves as the guardians of the market economy, the enemies of socialism. And because it is circumstance and not ideological preference that is forcing the pace, there is little that can be done about it. Not even the epithet "socialist" can rewardingly be hurled at the individual who merely describes what must be done. Such is the case with the socialism so far described.

But the story is not yet complete. The case for socialism is imperative in the weakest areas of the economy. It is also paradoxically compelling in the parts of exceptional strength. It is here the answer, or part of the answer, to the power of the planning system that derives from bureaucratic symbiosis.

Where the technostructure of the corporation is in peculiarly close relationship with the public bureaucracy, each, we have seen, draws power from its support by the other. The large weapons firms—Lockheed, General Dynamics, Grumman, the aerospace subsidiaries of Textron and Ling-Temco-Vought —propose to the Pentagon the weapons systems they would find it advantageous to develop and build. The Department of Defense proposes to them the systems the Services would like to have. The resulting decisions are then justified either by the need to keep up with the Soviets or the need to remain ahead of the Soviets.[3] One or the other of these justifications is bound to succeed. As previously noted, not even the most devout defender of orthodox

---

[3] For a brief period in the late sixties the Chinese were employed in this role. This usage appears to have been discontinued as unduly implausible.

models risks his reputation for minimal percipience by arguing that the resulting output is in response to public will as expressed through the Congress.

Two bureaucracies, one public and one nominally private, are stronger than one. The public bureaucracy, in citing the need for new weapons, can seem to be speaking out of a disinterested concern for the public security. Its control over intelligence allows it, as necessary, to exploit public and congressional fears as to what the Soviets are doing or might be doing. Commonplace procedure requires that any proposed new weapon be preceded by a flood of alarming information on what the Russians are up to. The private bureaucracy has freedom and financial resources not available to the public bureaucracy for making strategic political contributions, for mobilizing union and community support, for lobbying, for advertising and for public and press relations.

The combined power of the two bureaucracies would be usefully reduced by converting the large specialized weapons firms into full public corporations along lines mentioned in the last chapter. The government would acquire their stock at recently prevailing stock market valuation. Thereafter the boards of directors and senior management would be appointed by the Federal Government. Salaries and other emolument would henceforth be regulated by the government in general relation to public levels; profits would accrue to the government; so also would losses as is now the case. Political activity, lobbying and community persuasion would be subject to such constraints as a public bureaucracy must abide.

This change is one of form rather than substance. For the large, specialized weapons firms the cloak of private enterprise is already perilously, and even indecently, thin. General Dynamics and Lockheed, the two largest specialized defense contractors, do virtually all of their business with the government. Their working capital is supplied, by means of progress payments on their contracts, by the government. A not inconsiderable portion of their plant and equipment[4] is owned by the government. Losses are abosrbed by the government, and the firms are subject to financial rescue in the event of misfortune. Their technostructures are the upward extension of the hierarchy of the public bureaucracy; generals, admirals, subordinate officers and civil servants, on completing their careers in the public bureaucracy, proceed automatically and at higher pay to the corporate bureaucracy. The corporate bureaucracy, in return, lends its personnel to the upper civilian levels of the Department of Defense. The large weapons firms are already socialized except in name; what is here proposed only affirms the reality. As a rough rule a corporation (or conglomerate subsidiary) doing more than half of its business with the government should be converted into a full public corporation as here proposed.[5]

---

[4]Information on such ownership is in Hearing before the Subcommittee on Economy in Government of the Joint Economic Committee, 90th Congress, 2d Session, November 12, 1968, Pt. 1, p. 134. It was furnished (at my behest) by some of the companies with notable reluctance.

[5]I've discussed this proposal at more length in "The Big Defense Firms are Really Public Firms and Should Be Nationalized," *The New York Times Magazine,* November 16, 1969.

For unduly weak industries and unduly strong ones—as a remedy for an area of gross underdevelopment and as a control on gross overdevelopment—the word socialism is one we can no longer suppress. The socialism already exists. Performance as well as candor would be served by admitting to the fact as well as to the need. And in doing so we would be showing that the planning system cannot always make disreputable that of which it disapproves.

Sales of General Motors products are five times greater than the Gross National Product of Ireland and twice as great as Greece's GNP. It is true that Standard Oil's sales are slightly behind the GNP of Switzerland, but Standard is ahead of Denmark, Austria, Norway, Finland, Greece, and Ireland.

Multinationals are big, big business that create problems on at least three levels. One level is political. Many nations resent the power foreign companies have to allocate markets, invest where they choose, and "move vast sums of money between different countries and currencies." In his article, Christopher Tugendhat cautiously outlines some of the problems this resentment is likely to generate. For example, if the nations of the world remain committed to nationalism, it is unlikely that they will react favorably to the realization of the following prediction: "By 1980 foreign owned internationals will account for about half the total exports of many Western European nations, and locally owned internationals for the rest."

In addition to political problems, the growth of multinationals promises to increase the power and significance of what Jacques Ellul refers to as "techniques" (Chapter 4), and to the extent nations react to multinationals with political solutions, the gigantic firms should contribute to an even greater concentration of power in the hands of national states.

Finally, and most important, there are problems that concern humanity on a very basic level. Since the investment goal of the multinational corporations is profit, developing nations will continue to go hungry if, for example, Costa Ricans increase meat production by ninety-two percent and then send the meat to the McDonalds and Burger Kings of America.* Another important question of values concerns the allocation of resources and talent: Is it really important for General Motors to sell cars and refrigerators in Asia, or should governments insist that resources and talent be used to solve problems like starvation and pollution?

In short, we once again return to the problems of nationalism, power, industrialization, and the impersonal rule of the expert. For if industrial growth is to be limited, some form of international control will be required. And if we are seeking to prevent the problem we have today from recurring in our future, that form of control must attempt both to decentralize power and to avoid rule by technique. At any time and under any circumstances, that would be a formidable task. Today it is ours.

*See Richard Barnet and Ronald Müeller, *Global Reach* (New York: Simon and Schuster, 1975).

From The Multinationals
—Christopher Tugendhat

We are now at the half-way stage between the end of the war and the end of the century. The years behind us saw the establishment of the foundations and superstructure of the contemporary international business system. The years ahead will see its completion. Important changes will also take place in the nature of the nation state, and in the relationship between states. But at this stage it seems highly unlikely that national political systems or international political federations will develop at the same pace. The central feature of our politico-social system will remain the nation state, to which people look for the management of the economy, the constant improvement of their standard of living, defence against internal disorder and external attack, and the solution of political and social problems. His country and his sense of nationality will remain the focal points of a man's loyalty, while international companies, as a group, become an ever-increasing source of industrial power and influence. It is in the interests of both companies and governments to appreciate the realities of the situation. Only then can they hope to be successful at finding ways to reconcile their respective aspirations and interests in order that they may work together as harmoniously and effectively as possible.

In some quarters it is suggested that the rate at which the companies' power and influence is increasing will accelerate dramatically, and that we are rapidly moving into an era of super-giant firms. A leading exponent of this theory, whose ideas have widespread support among industrial leaders, is Professor Howard V. Perlmutter. He believes that by 1985 world industry will be dominated by 200 or 300 very large international companies responsible for the greater part of industrial output.[1] There will still be small companies, he suggests, exploiting new inventions, providing special services, and carving out niches of their own. But the middle-sized group will virtually disappear.

It is difficult to believe that the reality will be quite so startling. Enormous agglomerations of power always call forth countervailing social and political forces. In international business these[2] will probably have the support of governments, which already tend to create or support national enterprises whenever they fear that an important or strategic industry will otherwise fall into completely foreign hands.

However, the trend is clear. The leading multinationals have for some time been increasing their production and sales faster than most countries can

---

[1]'Super-giant Firms in the Future' by Howard V. Perlmutter, *Wharton Quarterly,* Winter 1968; and numerous other writings.
[2]For an interesting discussion of this point see 'Big Business in the late 20th century' by Andrew Shonfield, *Daedalus,* Winter 1969.

expand their gross national products. Each year new companies join the international ranks. The value of goods produced by international companies outside their home countries is rising more rapidly than the value of world trade. A growing proportion of the imports and exports of all industrialized countries is accounted for by the internal transactions of international companies, and the same applies to the movement of funds through the world currency markets. There is no doubt that in absolute terms these companies will account for a much larger share of world production and trade in 1985 than today.

In some industries this trend will be accomplished by a sharp reduction in the number of competing companies. The large multinationals will grow even larger, while their rivals merge so that a small group of mammoth companies is left to carve up world markets. Fiat's chairman, Giovanni Agnelli, believes that this will happen in the European motor industry. 'Eventually,' he says, 'there will be the three American companies, and one British. The rest will wind up together—as one or two companies.'[3] In view of the fact that only three companies account for almost the entire U.S. car production, Agnelli's vision is not unreasonable. His company has indeed started to work towards its fulfilment through its partial acquisition of the French Citroen. But as it presupposes the ultimate merger or disappearance of about a dozen companies in Italy, Germany, France, Sweden, and Holland, it is still pretty dramatic. Another industry where equally far-reaching moves towards concentration are expected is chemicals. N. G. S. Champion, who is in charge of planning at B P Chemicals, suggests[4] that over the next few years the eighty or ninety leading European chemical companies could be whittled down to ten. In computers too there are signs that the various European companies are moving towards the conclusion that the most effective way of competing against I B M is to pool their efforts. At the same time they are putting out feelers to the smaller U.S. companies engaged on the same difficult task.

Mergers and attempted mergers always attract a good deal of publicity, and there is a tendency to assume that when a number of industries are being concentrated into fewer units, the same thing will happen everywhere. This is not the case. In some important industries there is a clear trend the other way, towards greater competition. Oil, for instance, was dominated from 1945 until the late 1950s by the so-called seven sisters—Standard Oil (New Jersey), Shell, Texaco, Mobil, Gulf, Standard Oil of California, and British Petroleum. According to much contemporary business theory they should have spent the 1960s forming themselves into three or four vast all-embracing groups accounting for virtually the whole international industry. Instead, they not only remained apart, but throughout the decade saw their percentage share of production, refining, and sales diminish as newcomers from the U.S., France, Italy, and Germany, as well as the producer countries, elbowed their way in.

---

[3]*Fortune*, 15 September 1968.
[4]*Daily Telegraph*, 30 January 1970.

Oil is the longest-established international industry, and its experience is therefore relevant to all others. It demonstrates that such an industry need not be dominated by an oligopoly, and that when an oligopoly has been formed it can be broken. But it is significant that the successful challengers were themselves either extremely large in their domestic market before they expanded abroad, or enjoyed access to government funds and the support which went with it. U.S. 'independents', such as Continental and Phillips, fall into the first category, and the Italian E N I and French E R A P into the second. Both groups realized that if they were to hold their own against the multinational giants at home, they had to compete everywhere.

In the long run oil rather than motors, chemicals, or computers is likely to provide the best guide to the future. This is partly because governments will not wish to see their whole industrial structure controlled by foreign-owned firms, and will support national enterprises that fight back. To have any chance of success these enterprises, like the newcomers in oil, will have to be prepared to compete across the world.

Another reason is that purchasers of every sort of industrial raw materal and manufactured product never want to be dependent on a very small group of suppliers. They know that the smaller the group the more likely are price rings and other restrictive practices, and the more vulnerable they are to having their supplies disrupted by strikes and stoppages. So regardless of their own status and ambitions, they try to encourage competition in those industries that supply them. The car companies, for example, have learned from bitter experience that dependence on a small group of component manufacturers invariably leads to production holdups as a result of strikes in strategic factories. Consequently Volkswagen is increasing the proportion of its components bought outside Germany, and the badly hit British Leyland is buying more from the continent. Sometimes large buyers positively encourage their suppliers to go international, as happened with the U.S.-owned Eaton Yale and Towne, whose president says it expanded abroad, 'because our major automotive customers rather strongly suggested that we establish manufacturing facilities in the various countries where they proposed to build trucks and cars'. This kind of thing will happen much more in the future.

Regardless of the way in which their own industry may develop, the extent to which all international companies integrate their activities across frontiers will increase. The necessity to secure the greatest economies of scale will drive them to concentrate production of particular products in a small number of plants designed to serve several national markets. In some cases the eventual finished product, such as a car or computer, will be the culmination of work carried out in up to half-a-dozen different countries. In others, each national subsidiary will produce one or two complete items in the company's product line for international distribution, and rely on its affiliates to provide it with the rest for its own home market. Some companies already operate on these lines, of course. By 1980 it will be the rule rather than the exception.

The integration of national economies through the activities of international companies will also be increased by the spread of central purchasing of supplies by a head office or regional office on behalf of several of its subsidiaries. Again the oil industry provides an indication of the shape of things to come. For many years it has been customary for the companies to offer a comprehensive bunkering service throughout the world to substantial customers. After one set of negotiations the price and terms of delivery to an individual shipping line at every major port, or airport for an airline, can be arranged. The terms of the contracts vary from line to line, but for each line they are based on the same agreement the world over. The possibility of this principle being extended to other products and commodities is very real. For some time the British Steel Corporation has believed that in due course steel will be purchased in this way by the major users. The car companies have talked about negotiating for the purchase of some components for their European subsidiaries on a centralized basis with the individual suppliers. In practice this would mean that the head office or European office of, say, Ford, would deal direct with S K F for bearings, and negotiate a contract for the terms by which S K F would supply all their factories. The purchaser might stipulate where each subsidiary's supplies should come from and in what proportion, or it might leave that to the seller to decide. But either way the freedom of action of the various national subsidiaries of both the buyer and the seller would be further reduced.

In this context the relationship between international companies and their professional advisers also has important implications. Just as companies like Eaton Yale and Towne expanded abroad in order to provide a world-wide service to their big domestic customers, so have banks, advertising agencies, accountants, and numerous other providers of professional and specialist services. The advance of the multinationals can be likened to that of an army with a large band of camp followers. When the company settles in a new market it likes to have familiar faces around it, and to seek advice from the local subsidiaries of the same firms who provide it at home. Thus the Chrysler and Gulf Oil subsidiaries in Britain, for instance, employ the U.S.-owned Young and Rubicam for much of their advertising and public relations, and Young and Rubicam in turn has an account with the London branch of the First National City Bank of New York.

International companies do not, of course, confine their patronage to banks and advertising agencies from their home country. For a variety of reasons they often employ local ones as well. They want to integrate themselves into the local community, and to maintain a wide range of choice. Sometimes they find that a local concern is simply better or more suitable in a given situation than any other. But the final choice of whom a subsidiary employs either lies with head office or must be acceptable to it. Banks, advertising agencies, and the rest find that this means they must secure the confidence of the companies' head offices, which can only be effectively accomplished by establishing themselves in the countries concerned. So the spread of international companies affects those who service them in two respects. In the first place it forces them to internationalize, either from the head office country to the subsidiaries, or vice-versa. Secondly it leads to the gradual evolution of a common mode of behaviour and set of practices.

As the role and influence of international companies increases, their tensions with governments will become worse. Some will arise from the scale of their operations, the flexibility inherent in their position, and the difficulties faced by governments when trying to maintain a check on them. Others will result from the companies acceding to the wishes, laws, or policies of some governments, and thereby offending others. The companies themselves will in general continue to try to be good citizens everywhere. But their cverriding commitment to their own profits and self-interests on the one hand, and their need to choose between the conflicting demands and aspirations of several governments on the other will create inevitable problems.

The first category of tensions stemming from the nature of the companies has three potentially explosive aspects. These are the companies' power to allocate markets, their freedom of choice about where to invest, and their ability to move vast sums of money between different countries and currencies.

Even the most tolerant and liberal governments are becoming resentful of the international companies' ability to allocate markets. They feel that it is wrong that a subsidiary occupying a prominent place in the domestic economy should be barred from attempting to export to certain markets just because its parent has decided that they should be served by another affiliate. The subsidiary in question may justifiably claim that despite the restriction it has a good export record, but this leaves it open to the riposte that if it was a free agent it could do better still. If the export record is bad the government is likely to blame the parent company's restrictions, even if the fault really lies with its own economic and industrial policies, low productivity, or persistent strikes. Governments also dislike seeing the subsidiaries of international companies being forced by their head offices to import components that could be purchased locally. Sometimes the subsidiaries can answer that the imports are cheaper than comparable local products, with the result that their own finished products are cheaper and more competitive than would otherwise be the case. But governments are often reluctant to accept this, especially if they see that the subsidiary in question happens to be spending more on imports than it earns in exports. As the integration of international companies' activities across frontiers increases, and the practice of giving each subsidiary a specific and limited role in the total operation spreads, the problem will get worse. It will be intensified by the growing dependence of many industrialized countries on international companies for the bulk of their exports. By 1980 foreign-owned internationals will account for about half the total exports of many Western European countries, and locally-owned internationals for much of the rest.

The allocation of markets is closely linked with the question of investment, since a decision to build a new plant or to reorganize existing ones usually precedes export planning. . . . governments are beginning to compete with each other to attract the investment favours of international companies. This is a contest which once begun will be difficult to stop. Although governments may recognize that it is bound in the long run to lead to diminishing returns, its short-term attractions are enormous. A company like Shell now announces investment plans of £200m. at a single stroke, which is enough to make a sizeable impact on any Western European country's annual level of industrial investment, and creates orders that flow throughout the economy. Moreover, the country which can secure the largest share of an international company's new investment is well situated to pick up its best export markets. The successful countries in these situations are bound not to want to do anything to deter the goose with the golden eggs. But the less successful are equally bound to become resentful. If a government finds that not only is its country's level of industrial investment lagging behind those of its neighbours, but that a sizeable proportion of its total and of its neighbours' is provided by the same group of companies, this resentment could reach formidable proportions. This will be so even if much of the fault lies with the government's own policies, as would probably be the case.

Moreover, investments which have been 'purchased' at a high price in terms of tax concessions have a habit of creating political difficulties. The Irish experience with Gulf Oil provides an illustration of what can happen. At first when the company decided to take advantage of the tremendous concessions and inducements offered by the government to build its massive crude oil trans-shipment facilities in Bantry Bay instead of elsewhere in Europe, the Irish public was delighted. But later when it became apparent that the company was operating on more favourable terms than it could have secured in other countries, criticisms developed. The government was accused of having been outsmarted, and the company of having taken advantage of a small country's ignorance. The upshot was that the government began to look for ways of squeezing more money or other benefits out of the company.

The importance of the international companies' ability to move money between different countries and currencies is closely linked to the scale of their activities. As these increase, the influence of their financial operations grows. By the time they are accounting for the greater part of the western industrialized countries' trade in manufactured goods and for much of the investment it will be considerable. If for some reason they should lose confidence in a particular currency, and simultaneously set out to drain their subsidiaries in the country concerned, the effects would be far-reaching. The subsidiaries' outward dividend payments would be increased, and their royalty payments brought forward. They would have to settle their liabilities quickly, while money due to them from their parents and affiliates would be delayed. As the process gathered momentum the unfortunate country's reserves would rapidly diminish and confidence in its currency would drain away. A vicious spiral would have been set in motion that is very difficult to stop. Alternatively, if the companies believed that a currency was in line for revaluation they would run down their other balances, and buy it on a large scale. Much of the money that flowed into Deutsche Marks in the autumn of 1969 when the German government was pressured into revaluing against its will was generated in this way. In both sets of circumstances the companies are not responsible for creating the situation in which their actions take place, but the weight of their money is so great that they can drive it to extremes.

The existence of the Eurodollar market helps to make this possible. Its main purpose is to enable the companies to raise and invest money with which to carry on their business. By mid-1970 it was estimated to be employing funds equivalent to well over half the stock of international currency reserves. Its size, flexibility, and freedom from controls have enabled the companies to expand rapidly, but these same factors also mean that it acts as a sort of lung, sucking in money from some currencies, and pumping it out into others. When companies want to speculate against a currency they sell it to buy Eurodollars, and when they want to speculate in its favour they sell the Eurodollars in order to buy it. The speculation would take place in any case, and used to do so before the Eurodollar market was invented, but its existence makes the process much quicker and more efficient than would otherwise be the case.

The second category of tensions are those stemming from the companies acceding to the wishes, laws, or policies of some governments and thereby offending others. The most potentially explosive crises in this area are likely to arise over attempts by a government to limit trade with another country. In the past the most obvious example of this has been the U.S. boycott of China. There are innumerable examples of U.S.-owned subsidiaries in Western Europe and Canada refusing to trade with China in direct contradiction to the wishes of their local host government for fear of contravening U.S. laws. Sometimes, too, non-U.S. companies have preferred to follow the U.S. line on this issue rather than risk the possibility of action being taken against their U.S. interests. China is not an isolated example. In 1966 the U.S. Government prevented Control Data from exporting two computers to France for use in a French nuclear weapons laboratory. These computers were to have been shipped from the U.S., but there is little doubt that the U.S. Government would have at least attempted to prevent their sale even if they had been manufactured by one of Control Data's foreign subsidiaries. In the 1970s several governments, notably the Swedish, but possibly the U.S. and British as well, may decide to impose a limited trade boycott on South Africa. Once this principle is accepted there will always be suggestions that it should be employed in other situations, and the more moral issues are brought into political and commercial policies the greater will be the danger of this practice spreading.

Anti-trust and competition policies are another fruitful source of disagreement between companies and governments. Again the long arm of the U.S. is the likeliest source of trouble. The Americans claim universal jurisdiction in these matters over companies that operate in their market. Consequently any company with U.S. interests, even if it is not American-owned, may be inhibited from a merger or trading practice in another part of the world for fear of falling foul of U.S. law. In doing so it runs the risk of countervailing action being taken by the local government to offset the U.S. claims. This problem has been a constant irritant in Canadian–U.S. relations. With the growth of U.S.-owned companies in Europe and of European investment in the U.S. there are fears that it could spread across the Atlantic.

11

The Family

William Goode's argument is that industrialization pushes societies away from the concept of the extended family and toward some form of the nuclear family. Inevitably, societal demands for geographical mobility, increased education, or occupational specialization are increasing the independence of children and undermining the ideological and practical importance of the extended family.

Goode's thesis is based primarily on the continuing industrialization of the developed and underdeveloped nations. Should the pace of industrialization slow down, the pressures on the extended family might decrease. But Goode also points out that, despite pressures of industrialization, people still assent to the nuclear pattern because it promises greater freedom—especially to women dominated by tyrannical in-laws. So, even if the rate of industrialization were to diminish, the pressure for freedom in the family probably would not. Although this pressure alone could conceivably lead to the establishment of some form of the nuclear family as the norm, the reevaluation of traditional sex roles sought by feminists like Mary Daly (see Chapter 8) introduces a major doubt. Such a reexamination, based on the assumption that greater freedom should be coupled with greater equality, might result in entirely new family forms.

Finally, we should examine our prospects if industrialization and the women's movement both proceed apace. Could the social structure favor one kind of family form while many members of the society favor another?

From World Revolution and Family Patterns
—William Goode

There are some commentators who claim that a revolution in family behavior is taking place. We believe this is a correct judgment. On the other hand, those who experience the events of any given decade often claim that change is going on at a rapid rate. We suppose that if we could interview the English of seven centuries ago, they would tell us that "things are not the same as in our fathers' day." At the time of the colonial period in the United States, our Pilgrim Fathers asserted that the family was changing rapidly, that the children insisted upon choosing their own spouses, and that parents were losing control over children.

It is almost certainly incorrect to assume that both society and family were relatively static prior to industrialization and that the recent changes have occurred only because the modern world has begun to share in a new technology. We shall never know the details of earlier social structures, especially family relations in many regions, but whenever we are able to obtain concrete historical reports about adjacent periods of a specific culture, such as the tenth and eleventh centuries in Europe, it is quite clear that substantial changes in social relations have sometimes occurred in the past. An example may be found in Stone's study of the expansion of the marriage market and the changes in dowry relationships among the English nobility during the sixteenth and seventeenth centuries.[1]

In the modern era, many commentators have remarked on the increasing power of the wife in family relationships, but it is at least arguable that from the fourteenth to fifteenth centuries the European wife experienced an equal change in the opposite direction: She *lost* authority. A wife once had the right of assuming her husband's authority when he was absent or insane, but in France, by the sixteenth century, she was legally incapable of an independent act.[2] Although the Consulate and the Empire were short lived in France, important changes in family patterns were at least initiated under the banner of egalitarianism. The major family systems have not remained static for centuries, nor did they begin to change only with industrialization. Neither can we assume that where Western powers have ruled a region, as in the Arab world or India, all the changes came solely from the West. Indigenous changes are also important. We noted earlier, for example, the decline of the traditional marriage system among the Nayar. The English, believing that system to be immoral, did not approve of it, but their disapproval cannot be assumed to be the cause of change; they made no great campaign against it, and other family patterns persisted that they disliked. Changes that occurred under Western powers deserve specific attention, but we cannot assume *a priori* that it was the Western world that created them.

It is clear, however, that at the present time a somewhat similar set of influences is affecting all world cultures. All of them are moving toward

Reprinted with permission of Macmillan Publishing Co., Inc. from *World Revolution and Family Patterns* by William Goode. Copyright © 1963 by The Free Press of Glencoe, a Division of The Macmillan Company.
[1]Lawrence Stone, "Marriage Among the English Nobility in the 16th and 17th Centuries," *Comparative Studies in Society and History,* 3 (January, 1961), 182–206; see also my "Comment" in *loc. cit.,* 207–214.
[2]See Pierre Petot, "La Famille en France Sous l'Ancienne Regime," *Sociologie Comparée de la Famille Contemporaine* (Paris: Editions du Centre Nationale de la recherche scientifique, 1955), 9–18.

industrialization, although at varying speeds and from different points. Their family systems are also approaching some variant of the conjugal system. We have stated as an initial point of view, validated throughout by data, that the *direction of change* for each characteristic of the family might be very different from one culture to another even though the pattern of movement for the system as a whole is toward a variant of the conjugal type. For example, the divorce rate has dropped in Japan during the past half-century, whereas it has risen in the Western world; in both instances the move is toward a conjugal pattern. The illegitimacy rate has increased in urbanizing and industrializing Africa, but it has been dropping in the Western world.

Even though all systems are more or less under the impact of industrializing and urbanizing forces, we have not assumed that the amount of change is a simple function of one or the other, or even of combinations of both. On the contrary, we have asserted that we do not believe that the theoretical relations between a developing industrial system and the conjugal family system are entirely clear. On the empirical side we suggest that the changes that have taken place have been far more rapid than could be supposed or predicted from the degree of industrialization alone. We have insisted, instead, on the independent power of ideological variables. Everywhere the ideology of the conjugal family is spreading, even though a majority does not accept it. It appeals to the disadvantaged, to the young, to women, and to the educated. It promises freedom and new alternatives as against the rigidities and controls of traditional systems. It is as effective as the appeal of freedom or land redistribution or an attack on the existing stratification system. It is radical, and is arousing support in many areas where the rate of industrialization is very slight. Yet, the ideology of the conjugal system would have only a minimal effect if each newly emerging system did not furnish some independent base for implementing the new choices implicit in the ideology. We believe that the crucial points of pressure from industrialization on the traditional family structure are the following:

1. It calls for physical movement from one locality to another, thus decreasing the frequency and intimacy of contact among members of a kin network—although at the stage of full industrialization this is partly counteracted by greater ease of contact at a distance (telephone, letter, etc.).

2. Industrialization creates class-differential mobility. That is, among siblings or kindred, one or more persons may move rapidly upward while the others do not, thus creating discrepancies in styles of life, taste, income, etc., and making contact somewhat less easy and pleasant.

3. Urban and industrial systems of agencies, facilities, procedures, and organizations have undermined large corporate kin groupings since they now handle the problems that were solved within the kin network before industrialization: political protection, pooling funds to educate bright youngsters, defending a locality, lending money, etc.

4. Industrialization creates a value structure that recognizes achievement more than birth; consequently, the kin have less to offer an individual in exchange for his submission. He has to make his *own* way; at best his kin can give him an opportunity to show his talent. Without rewards, control is

not possible. The success of the Japanese family in keeping the kin group intact proves the rule more effectively, since some family control over jobs has been maintained. On the other hand, as industrialization has moved forward, the individual is more likely to be able to make his own way without his kin so that he need not consult them in important decisions. Note too that such a change brings new attitudes as well: Kin are less *willing* to call upon one another for such help because they would be embarrassed; they too accept the values of achievement.

5. Because of specialization, by which thousands of new jobs are created, it is statistically less likely that an individual can obtain a job for his kinsman. He may not be in a suitable sector of the occupational sphere, or at a level where his influence is useful.

[There is an] apparent theoretical harmony between the conjugal family system and the modern world and the modern industrial pattern, but [there are also] some disharmonies. . . . though the conjugal system serves the needs of the industrial system, it is not at all clear that the latter serves the needs of the *family* pattern. The creation of a new family structure in China, which would further reduce the kinship ties that are part of the conjugal system, might well be more effective in industrialization; but it also has its costs.

To point to another theoretical and empirical obscurity—contemporary theory asserts that a society based on achievement is likely to have a conjugal system, but we suggest that various periods of the past—such as the twelfth and thirteenth centuries in Europe, or the beginnings of the four major Chinese dynasties prior to the 1911 Revolution—were to a considerable extent based on achievement, with no measurable trend toward a conjugal system.

Perhaps equally important, . . . although some type of conjugal pattern and the ideology that often precedes it begins to emerge along with industrialization, we cannot suppose that only the industrializing elements are causally important. We must also entertain the hypothesis that the changes in the family itself may facilitate the process of industrialization. . . . For example, . . . earlier changes in the Western family system, beginning perhaps with the seventeenth century, may have made that transition to industrialization easier than in other cultures. That is, the family variables are themselves independent and have an impact on the total social structure. The mere fact of their resistance suggests some independent power but we believe that in addition they may facilitate or retard the acceptance of industrialization. It is perhaps at this point that the ideology of the family plays an important role by opening the way to the new family behavior as well as to the industrial role pattern.

. . . The conjugal family system is not equivalent to a "nuclear family" composed only of parents and children. . . . The conjugal family has far more kinship ties and correlatively is under far more kinship control than is sometimes supposed by Western observers or non-Western analysts. It seems impossible to cut down the size of the effective conjugal family to its nuclear core only, either in the West or in any other society, without some type of political or coercive force. The additional kin who are included are there because of a direct emotional tie with some members of the nuclear core, a tie supported by the institutional structure: Siblings are necessarily involved with their siblings-in-law; husbands and wives are tied to their parents-in-law; grandparents are emotionally attached to their grandchildren and vice versa. The ties among these kin may be traced through some member of the nuclear core and it is impossible to eliminate these additional kin ties without disrupting the nuclear family itself. Thus, the corporate kindred or lineage may lose most of its functions under urbanization and industrialization, but these extensions of kin ties continue to remain alive and important in social control, through reciprocal gifts and exchanges, visits, and continual contacts.

But although we must not commit the error of *minimizing* the extension of kin in a conjugal family system, we must also avoid *exaggerating* the ties of the extended family which preceded the modern conjugal family. It seems empirically clear that prior to the modern era in the Western world, and in all of the cultures we have been examining, several generations of one family did not live under the same roof, and did not carry on all of their productive activities there. If only because of the brute facts of mortality and the necessity of gaining a living on small plots of land, this was true for both urban and rural strata. On the other hand, the extended kin played a substantial role in non-Western cultures even when they did not live together, and the *ideal* remained that of a common household. When an individual attained sufficient wealth and social standing, he succeeded in creating and maintaining a large assemblage of kin under his leadership.

Even when an extended family was created, as we suggested for India and the Arab world, this was often a *phase* in the development of a single family between the initial fission by which a man established a conjugal unit separated from his father's household and the next generation of fission when the man's grown married siblings began to break off from their father, or from the household after their father died. This was undoubtedly a common historical process in the past, and the present merely accentuates and intensifies it, since now there are more and earlier opportunities for the younger generation to break off and set up independent households.

With reference to the question of *how* the impact of industrialization occurs on the family, we have suggested that the primary process hinges on the control by elders of the new opportunities under industrialization. That is, do *they* create the new jobs and can *they* hand them out to the younger generation or to their women? A crucial difference between upper- and lower-class elders lies in the fact that the new opportunities are typically created and developed by upper-class elders, who can thus control their own sons or women and thus maintain their lines of authority long after these have begun to disintegrate among lower-strata families. Elders in lower-strata families cannot generate these opportunities. Consequently, they have little to offer the younger generation to counteract their normal tendency to independence. As a result, even in the modern Western world, upper-strata families maintain a far larger extension of kin and far greater control over their own young than do lower-strata families.

This central variable is qualified somewhat by the factor of ideology. Those who hold power cannot keep it unless they believe in the *rightness* of their authority. It is especially difficult to hold to that belief in the face-to-face relations of the family, because of the inherent love and affectional ties among its members. When that faith weakens under the impact of the new ideology, the normal push of the disadvantaged, the young, and women may become sufficiently strong to change family relations if new opportunities are available through which these younger people can obtain an independent social and economic base.

This same evidence of a role bargaining process may be found in the radically changing position of women in all of the cultures under examination. The fundamental transformation of woman's estate is sometimes overlooked, because in certain past epochs women had a considerable amount of *personal* freedom. The modern industrial world is the first cultural system, however, to permit women to occupy independent jobs. They have become independent of members of their family. They obtain their work by themselves, and also control the money they earn. This has meant an enormous increase in the economic productivity of populations that have made use of their women in this fashion. At the same time, it has changed the bargaining position of women within the family system. Needless to say, this is a reciprocal process. It is by virtue of a change in the general evaluation of women and their position in the large society that the permission is granted to work independently; but once women begin to take these positions in the large society, then they are better able to assert their own rights and wishes within the family. This process need not be, and probably rarely is, rational or even conscious.

Class differences remain, and so do their inherent paradoxes. Toward the lower strata, in all of these cultures, it is evident that the woman actually has had somewhat more authority. The sheer lack of funds and services at these levels has given the woman a key position within the family. This has been especially so in areas and places where she has held independent or semi-independent jobs: Japanese women divers in the coastal or forestry villages are an illustration of this pattern. Toward the upper strata, men have had less need of a particular wife, and could obtain almost any service a wife could perform by using alternative women as concubines, servants, housekeepers, and so on. The funds were available to seclude or protect the wife more, and the discrepancy between the man's economic and social power and her own was much greater.

Ideological *differences* in the modern world run in the opposite direction. Toward the upper strata, men who are better educated and more strongly affected by the new philosophy of the family are somewhat more willing on a philosophical level to concede rights, and women are somewhat more eager to demand them, although their behavior may in fact be less free than toward the lower strata. Men in the lower strata, by contrast, are much more traditional-minded than their counterparts in the upper strata, and are less willing to concede the new rights being demanded; but they have to do so because of the increased bargaining power of their women.

Thus, in the age-old war between the sexes and between generations, the entrance of a new ideology of the family plays a crucial role. It validates and speeds the emergence of some minority patterns into majority patterns; but it slows others down. It strengthens and gives bargaining power to some kinship positions, and weakens still others. It does this not only because of the demands on the part of those who seek new rights, or because of the values of those who resist the concession of the new rights, but also and perhaps centrally, because the third parties, that is, other people involved in their role network, may support the recalcitrants or weaken the innovators.

However, we do not believe that any family system now in operation, or likely to emerge in the next generation, will grant full equality to women, although throughout the world the general position of women will improve greatly. The revolutionary philosophies which have accompanied the shifts in power in Communist countries or in the Israel *kibbutzim* have asserted equality, and a significant stream of philosophic thought in the West has asserted the right to equality, but no society has yet granted it. Nor does the movement in Western countries, including the Communist countries, suggest that the future will be greatly different. We believe that it is possible to develop a society in which this would happen, but not without a radical reorganization of the social structure. The family base upon which all societies rest at present requires that much of the daily work of the house and children be handed over to women. Doubtless, men can do this nearly as well, but they have shown no eagerness to assume these tasks, and families continue to rear their daughters to take only a modest degree of interest in full-time careers in which they would have equal responsibilities with men.

A subsidiary thesis in our analysis has been that different relations within the family, and between the family and the larger society, are under a differential tension even in the *traditional* system. Some relations are well-buttressed, while others contain great strains which are overborne by the dominant social patterns. When new elements enter, however, such as a new ideology, or differential opportunities, then the relations under greatest strain are likely to give way first. Still, many relations may continue with undiminished vigor. [It has been] noted, for example, that in China the mother-in-law's domination over the daughter-in-law was a theme for literary and philosophical comment, and that the pattern continued although people deplored it. The new forces at work in China, from the 1911 Revolution on, had undermined the strength of this traditional relationship, and the Communists merely implemented the change further. In the new social system that has been emerging in China and Japan, the mother-in-law is less useful in the new household. Her husband, the father of her son, no longer has the same power over *his* son, and thus can no longer threaten the daughter-in-law to the same degree. The young man is more likely to have become emotionally attached to his wife even before marriage, so that he is less willing to support his mother in a dispute between the two. The young wife is more likely to be working, and thus making a real contribution to the prosperity of the household. At many points, then, the daughter-in-law can resist the mother-in-law more easily, and has been reared to believe that resistance is proper. The mother-in-law, on the other hand, does not feel the same certainty of success. Consequently, this relationship has changed substantially.

Yet, the intense mother-son relationship in the traditional Indian and Arab family systems was not under great strain, and has not been under any ideological attack. The newly emerging family patterns do not seem, therefore, to weaken it at any important point.

Since the world is becoming industrialized and urbanized simultaneously, it may not be possible to isolate these two processes as separate sets of causal factors. . . . A common theoretical error is to treat "urbanization" as a *single variable,* but to include in that variable almost all of the social changes that are now going on. Since these are the changes that are taking place, one cannot treat them as causal variables. Indeed, they are the phenomena to be explained. Or, alternatively, by including under this category almost every conceivable social change, one can say that "urbanization causes everything" simply because urbanization is so loosely defined as to include everything.

Similarly, industrialization cannot be defined as the *impact* upon the "social structure" of the factory system, rapid communication and transportation, a high level of scientific training, and so on. These are all part of the same complex. The former set of phenomena cannot come into being unless the social structure is being transformed somewhat. They are not, strictly speaking, to be viewed as a set of *causal* variables working on a static and passive set of social patterns. Rather, they *are* the changes to be explained. We cannot find cases in which suddenly there is a full industrial complex in interaction with a so-far unchanged social structure. Machines do not make social structures; people with specific social patterns make machines. At present, we see no great clarity emerging from these theoretical arguments, although we have tried to suggest various points at which industrialization may have an impact on the family, and have thereby selected from the total phenomena of industrialization a few of the key variables.

From time immemorial philosophers and observers have noted differences in the social relationships in the city as against those in the country. This observation points to the need to distinguish between two aspects of urbanization, the urbanization of an *individual* or an individual family, and the increase in the *percentage* of people in a society who are urbanized or living in an urban context. The individual family that becomes urbanized is doubtless more likely to utilize the urban agencies of social control, finance, transportation, help, and so on, because these are available and because they may be easier to deal with in the long run than the required reciprocal exchanges with kin. Thus, in the cities the large corporate or kin groups or lineages are reduced in importance. This merely creates an urban-rural difference in family patterns, however.

Cities came to be part of man's heritage about 6 thousand years ago, but urbanized *nations*—nations in which a majority of the population lives in cities—did not emerge until recently. The urbanizing of a nation leads to somewhat different consequences than the mere existence of one or more urban centers in a nation. When a large part of the nation begins to urbanize, there are many new opportunities in the cities for *most* people who move there. People flock to the cities, and thus undergo individually or as a family the social processes by which many older, traditional kin ties or obligations are undermined. The urban patterns begin to be viewed as dominant and proper, even by rural people. The cities expand economically and often industrially, so that those who move are justified by their success. The traditional class composition shifts because of this expansion. People are attracted by the new realms of experience available in the city. The city becomes the carrier of new ideologies, thus giving a moral validation to these alterations in social patterns. Thus, the urban-rural differences begin to *decline,* since the thinking of those who live in rural areas is shaped by the forces that urbanize the nation.

One aspect of the movement to the city ought to be briefly noted. The industrial world is not based on family ownership of land; it has become the first civilization not based upon landholding. Land is no longer the major source of production, and man's relationship to it is no longer correlated with his social position.

Thus, a major change has taken place. The transformation in modern times is that the elders give the young man and woman an education. This is their inheritance, their dower or dowry. Elders are left with only education, maintenance, and love as levers for controlling their young. Love is not a sufficient lever, because in the modern world it is a reciprocal relationship, and the young as well as the older generation can wield the threat of withdrawing love. Education cannot be used so easily, because it is not exclusive, as land is; it can be given to all the siblings equally. Moreover, most people feel that even the worthless child should be educated, because without education he might be still worse. There is no widespread view that such an educational patrimony can be lost, misspent, or wasted as fully as can money or land. There is thus no great social support for withholding an education from the young, and almost no one does. Those who do are criticized by their peers. Less able to control their young by withdrawing social or economic benefits from them, the elders lose some of their ability to maintain the family line itself, as well as the family traditions of the society against which the young of each generation always rebel, if only briefly and with little success.

These factors are causally related to the decline in the control over the marriage choice of the young. With reference now primarily to the upper strata, where control still remains firm in most cultures, the advantages of a family alliance have declined with the lessened importance of land and the increased importance of occupation. The family cannot easily guarantee the young man's future through a job, because his ability and work, over which they have little control, count so much. They can give him an opportunity, but he has to make that opportunity good by his own efforts. Neither side of the family can count on the continuance of the alliance, since the decision lies in the couple's hands: the high rate of divorce in a conjugal system may undo the alliance. Neither, then, is willing to invest so much in a union as they once would. Consequently, the elders have less motivation for making an alliance, and leave it increasingly in the youngsters' hands. They are less willing to bend their efforts toward maintaining it for so precarious a gain, while empirically their actual control has weakened.

Another aspect of this greater freedom may be seen in the greater liberty to remarry. In an earlier work, I suggested the general hypothesis that whenever there is a high divorce rate, there is a high remarriage rate.[3] I have found no reason as yet to change this conclusion. Both Japan under the old system and Islam have had very high rates, coupled with a nearly universal "settling down" to a stable marriage. Very few adults continue to live outside the marriage state in spite of a high rate of marital disruption.

A change in the marriage of widows was also noted in India, where it was formerly forbidden, and in China, where it was strongly opposed. Such opposition had many roots, differing of course from culture to culture. Some were economic: A widow, as contrasted with a divorcee, normally has certain property rights—for example, the money which she brought to the marriage and which may remain hers under some legal definition, the inheritance from her husband, or simply a customary right to receive some support from her husband's family. Since she is now a member of her husband's family, her parental family has little right to arrange a new marriage for her; her husband's family may have a strong material interest in opposing a new marriage which might either alienate some property which they enjoy or confuse the matter of inheritance. She may also have to leave her children behind if she remarries. In addition, of course, remarriage suggests disrespect to the memory of the dead.

In the West, widows may remarry, although it seems safe to say that there always was some feeling against remarriage, partly because of the sentiment (backed by the Church) that a woman properly remains forever married to her first husband, and partly based on the notion that older women ought not to respond to the promptings of sexual feeling. Pitt-Rivers, for example, found the custom of the *vito* in Andalusia, an at least half-serious charivari directed against widow remarriage. He suggests that it can be found as a rather widespread custom here and there in rural areas.

However, when the ideology of the conjugal family begins to assert that each individual, even though a female, has a right to her own life choices, and as the prevalence of joint-family property declines, neither sentiment nor economic interest supports the celibacy of widows. Moreover, the husband's family no longer cares to assume the obligations of support for the widow as she is increasingly able to support herself. As the bride price or groom price becomes less important, neither her family nor his has any interest in hindering her free choice. In industrialized nations, she also becomes somewhat more independent through insurance, pensions, and social security provisions.

Thus a general trend, rapid in some areas and slow in others, is toward an increase in the remarriage of both widows and divorcees where there had

---

[3]William J. Goode, *After Divorce* (New York: The Free Press of Glencoe, 1956), p. 216.

been some opposition in prior generations. Both may now enter the marriage market independently, free from the social stigma which they once had to suffer.

Both freedom of choice and equalitarianism are of importance in another step toward the conjugal family: a reduction in the proportion of the adult population living under concubinage or some form of polygamy. Several factors are at work in this process. Most important, the emotional demands which each spouse can legitimately make on the other preclude the acceptance of polygamous arrangements. Under this system, wives are less inclined to share the emotional intensity of the family with other women, and husbands do not wish to share a single wife with cohusbands. Polygyny itself was generally confined to those men who had considerable wealth or prestige, and under most systems it was expensive. Africa was an exception to some degree, since an additional wife might add economic wealth and sometimes even represented an investment. Wives were acquired by paying out a bride price, but in turn they engaged in agricultural work which brought additional income. Of course the wives of chiefs were in another category, for they represented an investment in prestige.

The female's bargaining position has also improved, since now she has alternative modes of employment. She does not have to accept the "protection" of a male in order to survive.

Concubinage, the acquisition of additional women without the formality of true marriage, is a somewhat more complex matter, although both arguments also apply to it. Youngsters have more sexual freedom in the conjugal system than in most systems prior to the modern era, although certainly they have less than in most primitive societies. But sexual freedom is not necessarily associated with concubinage. The equalitarian ideology that accompanies this system denies an overwhelming importance to class or caste rules, so that it is much less possible now for the male to suggest a concubinal arrangement with the woman whom he claims to love. He is less able to assert that he would "love to marry" a woman but cannot because of social restrictions. Under present conditions in most Western countries, and increasingly in others, this excuse is an empty one.

Perhaps more important, however, is the fact that the relative advantages— including time, attention, and even money—that the modern male of high standing can give to a concubine are far less than once were possible. His rank does not permit him easily to avoid the scorn and criticisms of her friends or class equals. She *can* earn a living alone. He cannot, in the older phrase, "protect her." In addition, the man's legitimate wife objects to such arrangements.

The equalitarianism of the conjugal system applies to the man as well: for although some men may enjoy a feeling of possession when they pay the expenses of a concubine or mistress, others are much less willing to do so because increasingly they feel that *they* are giving as much of themselves as the woman is, and that it is therefore somewhat demeaning for a man to pay her expenses. In China these aspects of equalitarianism are especially important, since the Communists want to draw *everyone* into the productive system regardless of sex, and the concubine is a symbol of the pampered and loose life of the old regime.

In our analyses, we have attempted to bring together as adequate a body of data as possible to test a considerable number of hypotheses about past or present changes in family patterns in the major cultures of the world. At many points, however, it seems clear that the data miss some of the most significant aspects of family life. Structural changes can often be noted by the passing observer. For example, a tiny shift in Japanese family behavior permits the woman to walk alongside her husband in public. What, however, of the tone, the *timbre,* of feelings and emotions that are changing? Most Japanese marriages are still arranged by the parents, but the fact that some are not, and that the new values do not approve of so vigorous a control over mate choices, means that there are more dreams about possible romantic courtships among young adults, which gives a character and a flavor to contemporary Japanese relations between young men and women that is qualitatively different from the recent past. Another example—the elderly Japanese widow is still being taken care of by her sons, but if she was reared in a rural household in which she saw her own mother achieve greater authority with age, ruling as a matriarch behind the public authority of her husband, then the modern widow cannot have the same experience and may experience a lack of fulfillment—but we cannot capture such nuances with the crude measuring instruments at our disposal.

Implicitly, Richard Farson asks us to consider reality. Are we asking too much of marriage and of human life? Can any relationship produce constant highs? Good marriages seem bound to fail, he suggests, because, although two people may make each other happy, neither can make the other constantly ecstatic.

Compare Farson's article to *The Greening of America.* If we place great emphasis on self-realization and self-actualization, we may never be satisfied with anything. If we are always required to grow, grow, grow, we may never be able to resolve the paradox Farson presents: that success in marriage produces high-level but seemingly inevitable discontents.

From Why Good Marriages Fail
—Richard E. Farson

As impossible as it may sound, good marriages probably fail more often than bad ones. What's more, they fail precisely because they are good.

Human experience is full of such paradoxes. People often do just the opposite of what one would expect. For example, researchers have found that revolutions do not break out when conditions are at their worst but when the situation has begun to get better. Once reforms have started, people gain strength and, more importantly, a vision of what their lives might be like—both of which are necessary to energize a revolution. Historians call this the problem of rising expectations.

The same kind of analysis can help us understand why so many good marriages fail. Perhaps if couples could incorporate such paradoxical thinking into their lives, their chances of maintaining a good marriage might improve. At least they might eliminate some of the ugliness of divorce by not depreciating what was, all things considered, a good relationship.

How can a good marriage fail? The easy explanation is that it wasn't basically good. It may have looked good on the outside, but it must have been flawed on the inside. That's the way we usually try to rationalize divorce. But what about marriages that by every conceivable criterion compare favorably with most other marriages? They can fail, too. And because of the heightened expectations present in good marriages, they are often in greater jeopardy than bad ones.

It is not easy to find support for this point of view, because we tend to look at divorces for things that went wrong, not for things that went right. In fact, the best evidence for this argument will have to come from marriages and divorces you know about, perhaps even from your own marriage.

Take, for example, the most recent divorce among your friends. Try to remember what the marriage was like. Chances are you thought of it as being as good as most. You knew of nothing seriously wrong. On the contrary, the couple seemed to enjoy family life, had adequate finances, physical attractiveness, common interests. Even more, they may have had a good deal of respect for each other, perhaps even deep affection.

Yet, they decided to separate. You try to imagine what could have happened. You look for some basic incompatibility, some distinct flaw, some terrible incident. But when you ask them why they are divorcing, they are apt to say something like, "Well, we've simply grown apart," or "I feel trapped in this relationship," or "We just can't communicate," or "He won't let me be me," or "We just felt that surely there must be more to life than we are getting from this marriage."

In all probability, there is no awful hidden truth. Probably there is nothing in their marriage that makes it different from, or worse than, most others.

The common element in all their answers is that they are expressing high-order discontent. Their complaints have nothing to do with the rather low-order justifications for divorce recognized by law—brutality, desertion, adultery, etc. Instead, their complaints reflect an awareness of what the good life should be. Then discontent comes from the difference between what they are actually experiencing in their marriage and what they have come to believe is possible.

The couples who get in the most trouble are those who know enough to see the things that are wrong with their marriage. And, ironically, it takes quite a bit of success in a marriage to make that understanding possible.

So good marriages fail because, by the very fact of being good, they generate discontent. The discontent may come from many sources, some rather unexpected. Here are eight of them:

1. *Discontent arises because the basic needs of the marriage have been satisfied.* Yet, people are never entirely satisfied. Once they have met one set of needs, they simply move on to develop higher-order needs, in an ever-accelerating pattern of demand.

Marriage, after all, was never meant to be as good as it is. It was instituted in the beginning to insure survival, then security, then convenience. Now we take for granted that it will not only meet all those basic needs but much higher needs as well. Marriage is now burdened with the expectations that husbands and wives should enjoy intellectual companionship, warm intimate moments, shared values, deep romantic love, great sexual pleasures. Couples expect to assist and enhance each other in ways never thought of as being part of the marriage contract.

The trouble is that these higher-order needs are more complex, and therefore less easy to satisfy on a continuing basis, than are, say, financial needs. For that reason, they give rise to more frustration and discontent when they are not met.

2. *Discontent arises because mass education and mass media have taught people to expect too much from marriage.* Today almost no one is ignorant of the marvelous possibilities of human relationships. Time was when people modeled their own marriages after their parents' marriage; it was the only model they knew. Now, with much of our population college-educated, saturated with books, recordings, films, and television, just about everyone has some new ideals for his marriage to live up to—and has, consequently, some new sources of dissatisfaction.

The problem is made even worse by the mass media: The romantic vision has been oversimplified, translated into a smoothly functioning, syrupy sweet "nuclear" family and sold to the American public. The perpetuation of this stereotype (two married adults and their own minor children) as the only acceptable marriage model, and the implication that a constant state of affection and unity in family life is actually achievable, give cause to rising dissatisfaction in one's own marriage.

Television is totally devoted to the nuclear family; the only variation ever shown is when one parent is widowed (rarely divorced) and is seeking a return to "normal" family life. Not only is the nuclear family a relatively new invention (never before in history were families formed along these lines), but many authorities now regard this arrangement as entirely too burdensome and difficult to remain workable. Two parents having to serve as all-purpose adults, accomplishing everything by themselves, is anything but easy. TV just makes it look easy.

The simple fact is that more than 60 percent of Americans now do not live in nuclear-family arrangements. They live in some other form of domestic unit—as single adults, for example, or divorced adults with children. But their constant instructions from the mass media are that to be genuinely fulfilled, they must be part of a nuclear family.

3. *Discontent arises because couples succeed in filling their masculine and feminine roles.* One would think that success in meeting society's expectations as men and women should make marriage work better. Shouldn't the woman who is feminine, gentle, tender, aesthetic, childlike, emotional, understanding, and yielding be a perfect companion for a man who is masculine, firm, strong, aggressive, rugged, decisive, rational, and dominant?

The odds are that it works just the other way. These roles are so limiting, and at the same time so demanding, that the result can be truly monstrous. As we are now beginning to see, the oppressive concept of "woman's role" and "woman's place" has led to great rage on the part of many women, rage that has only recently been openly expressed. Similarly, the man's role leads to such strong feelings of pressure, guilt, impotence, and artificiality that he, too, is now demanding relief.

One would think that the strain of such role-demands could be alleviated in the intimacy and protection of the family unit, but for the most part, it is not. Unfortunately, the marriage relationship is not usually a place one can let down. Too often it serves not as a buffer against the impositions of society, but as a reinforcer. Husbands and wives are notorious for forcing these stereotyped roles on one another. The frustration that comes from an inability to deliver on such expectations only makes matters worse, and instead of blaming society for demanding that they perform these roles, they blame themselves and each other.

The various liberation efforts for men and women that are currently underway may eventually offer relief, but in the short run they simply deepen the problem. The stress on marriage that has resulted from women's liberation, for example, has already taken its toll in separation and divorce. No one can say why. It could be because the husband and wife are not being liberated at the same rate, or because they have come to see their marriage as symbolizing their slavery to these oppressive roles, or because their new understandings show their marriage to be so limiting that they can no longer live with the incongruity between what they have and what they feel they *must* have.

4. *Discontent arises because marriage now embraces a new concept of sexual fulfillment.* The deluge of words and images giving us a totally new idea of what human sexuality could be has become inescapable. We are no longer willing to settle for the sexuality of past generations. Married couples now expect sex to be playful, experimental, and greatly permissive. They expect a wide range of sexual performance and are seriously disappointed when the experiments don't succeed. Not only is there a desperate search for orgasm, but more—superorgasm, ecstasy, peak experiences. Not sometimes, but every time; so here again, while the sexual relationship in a marriage may have been quite adequate, it is now expected to be a good deal more than adequate. The better it is, the better it must become.

No one wants to turn back the clock, to deny the new understandings of human sexual potential and return to Victorian prudery. We should be pleased that individuals now demand the right to full sexuality. But we can't ignore the fact that in previous generations these high expectations were not a recognized source of discontent.

5. *Discontent arises because marriage counseling, psychotherapy, and other efforts to improve marriage actually make it more difficult.* It may be that marriage counseling and psychotherapy with married couples tend to create more discontent than they cure. Not because counseling isn't any good, but partly because it *is* good; by helping, it has made the problem worse.

First of all, any effort to improve life—whether by education or religion or philosophy or therapy—seldom makes life simpler. In fact, it makes it more complex. Just as labor-saving devices have caused us more labor and complicated our lives, so counseling has further burdened our marriages by asking us to live up to what we know to be our best. That always turns out to be difficult and painful.

Secondly, counseling provides an example of an intimate relationship that is achievable only under the special circumstances of the psychotherapeutic hour; nevertheless, it makes the client wonder why that level of intimacy and understanding can't exist at home. In comparison to an expert counselor, most marriage partners must seem obtuse indeed.

Third, most psychotherapists continue to endorse, even promote, narrow and outdated ideas, based largely on Freudian concepts of sexuality, male-female roles, and family relationships. They describe a model of marriage that is all but impossible to live up to, and is, in the light of newer understanding, not very desirable anyway. In this area, the psychotherapist is, for the most part, the unwitting enemy of the liberation movements for both men and women. This is especially tragic when you realize that human liberation, the chance to live up to one's potential, is what counseling and psychotherapy are all about.

Fourth, and perhaps most serious, counseling gives a person the feeling—much more than is probably true—that he is in charge of his own life, that his problems are basically of his own making, and that their solutions are within his control. People constantly live with the idea that they are beset with unique and *personal* problems—problems that stem from their own neurotic disorders or from mistakes they have made, conditions that are solvable and correctable by individual action. But more likely, for most people, it is the *situation* in which they find themselves that is the problem. And it is not always a situation that individual initiative can do much about.

Constant attention to our problems as personal rather than as universal (which happens in counseling) has given us a highly distorted picture of what we can do about the problems we find in marriage. We actually have very little control over the major conditions that affect our marriages, and, consequently, marriages change very little as a result of counseling.

Finally, it is rather well known that psychotherapists and marriage counselors themselves have a high incidence of separation and divorce. This is not cited to suggest that, as a way of justifying their own actions, they subconsciously welcome their clients' decisions to separate. Rather, it points out yet another example of how constant attention to marriage, and the consequent high-order expectations about the marriage relationship, can produce casualties in those one would think best able to avoid them.

6. *Discontent arises because marriages suffer from the gains made in the consciousness revolution.* This revolution, thought by some to be the only revolution that is actually changing behavior, stems from the hippie movement—drug culture, new-left politics, rock music, Eastern philosophy, occult phenomena, encounter groups, etc.—all combining to paint pictures of what life might be if we were to reach the human potential.

The alternate life-styles that have grown out of this revolution are now affecting the values of all of us, and, most certainly, they have reshaped our concepts of married life. Consider, for example, the impact of the encounter group and other group efforts to develop awareness and sensitivity to one's self and others. More than six million Americans have now participated in encounter groups of one form or another. As is the case with psychotherapy, the encounter group has given its participants moments with other people that are remarkably beautiful, intimate, and fulfilling. These experiences can't help making a person think that he is going to be able to bring this new awareness and strength into his own marriage. But it seldom works that way. More likely, it has furnished him with a reference point indicating what a relationship *might* be, but which his marriage can never achieve. Not because his marriage isn't good, but because it can't match the freedom of a temporary relationship.

The consciousness revolution works in other ways to make marriage more difficult. For example, the value placed on honest relationships, on complete truthfulness in dealing with others, puts such an excessive strain on marriages that some cannot survive. The idea is, the more honesty the better. Following the teachings of the new-consciousness gurus, husbands and wives have regaled each other with all manner of honest statements in what appear to be efforts to enrich marriage, but in fact make it almost impossible to endure. Most marriages can't take such honesty as sharing fantasies about other people during sexual intercourse, detailing extramarital affairs, etc. Jean Kerr wrote a good line for a wife who has just been told by her husband that he has been cheating, "If you had the decency of a truck driver, you'd keep your lousy affair secret!"

The values of the new consciousness emphasize honesty over loyalty and kindness. Honesty is rarely unadulterated, however, and all too often is used to alleviate guilt and transfer responsibility. It may help to remember that marriage, like any other important institution, needs some myth and mystique to keep it vital.

Above all, the new consciousness has created the expectation of high-level intimacy in marriage, something that is very rare indeed. There is little question that the intimacy of shared feelings that occurs between teen-age friends, for example, far and away transcends that which is possible in most marriages. Perhaps marriage is too important to be burdened with such intimacies. People simply cannot take such risks with a relationship that matters so much to them.

7. *Discontent arises because of fantasies about what other marriages are like*. Just as individuals find it necessary to present a façade in life, married people feel that they must create an image of their marriage that shows only its best side. The truth is that we live in almost total ignorance of what other people's marriages are like. Everyone recognizes that no marriage is perfect, that everyone has fights and difficulties and disillusionments. Yet, many times we undermine our marriages by assuming that other marriages must somehow be better. This fantasy, like a casual flirtation, doesn't have to pass any real tests of real life. And, if we really could know more about other people's marriages, we would see that they are much more similar than different—painfully, hilariously, reassuringly alike.

8. *Discontent arises from comparing the marriage relationship with itself in its better moments*. The memories couples carry of their premarital or early marriage experiences inevitably make their current situation seem less romantic and exciting.

This is particularly true for couples with children. For most people, the major change in life comes not with marriage, but with the birth of the first child. It is at that point that real commitment is required, that major limitations set in, and it is then that the affection and attention of the wife moves from the husband to child. A decrease in sexual activity, and an increase in the complications of family life, as treasured and as beautiful as they may be, are sources of discontent when compared with what went before.

But probably the most important source of discontent is the comparison of the marriage with its own good moments in the present. Not too many marriages have great moments, but the best ones do. These peaks, however, are inevitably followed by valleys. Couples lucky enough to have these moments find themselves unable to sustain them, and, at the same time, unable to settle for ordinary moments. They want life to be a constantly satisfying state. But to be a constant state, to avoid the valleys, it is necessary to eliminate the peaks, which puts the marriage on a narrow band of emotionality and involvement. Good marriages are not like that, but the price they exact in depression and pain is high.

The constant talk today about marriage, whether it's positive or negative, has only led to greater hopes for it, making it more popular and desirable than ever. As someone once remarked, "Marriage is like a besieged city. Everybody that's out wants in, and everybody that's in wants out."

What's difficult to remember is that marriages of all kinds, bad and good, are very fragile, easily wrecked. They can withstand some kinds of difficulty and trauma, but they cannot stand the abuse of unmet expectations. They particularly can't stand comparisons between what they are and what they might be. It is that kind of comparison that leads to separation and divorce. That is why maintaining a good marriage is more difficult than maintaining a bad one.

The calamity of divorce is not in the failure of the relationship; the relationship has probably succeeded fairly well, right to the end. Instead, the calamity comes from the problems of child custody, property, finances, social stigma, unsolved feelings of dependency, responsibility, guilt, and failure—the feelings of having let everyone down.

It's a pity that we must regard the end of a marriage as proof of its failure. In order to justify a separation, we must somehow put down the marriage, negate it, make it less worthy than it has been.

Society won't allow us to celebrate separations, but perhaps that's not such a bad idea. There is some reason to believe that people leave one rich relationship to find a richer one. Sociologist Jessie Bernard's classic study of divorce and remarriage suggests that couples move on to seek and find high-order marriages, sometimes several in a series. Clearly a new concept of evaluating marriage must be brought into being, one that assesses not longevity or satisfaction but the quality and level of the discontent it engenders.

Somehow we have the idea that we can only leave a marriage if it's bad. We simply can't bring ourselves to see that the reason for leaving a marriage may be because of the new vision it permitted us to have of what life could be like. Too bad we can't live with this paradox—that it is because of the *success* of our marriages that we have developed this high-level discontent.

If we could realize that the better the marriage is, the worse we will sometimes feel, then we might prevent the incidents that occur in any marriage from leading to separation and divorce. Such an understanding could give us the insight we need to make one good marriage last a lifetime.

12

The Military

Barring major social changes in the developed nations, the future is virtually certain to be filled with guerrilla wars. In this excerpt, the North Vietnamese General, Vo Nguyen Giap, presents one version of the guerrilla's aims and methods.

Giap says he is a revolutionary but I am not sure. For example, he says that "the people as a whole took part in the armed struggle . . . , but always in pursuance of the one and same line, and the same instructions, those of the Central Committee of the Party and the government." Does Giap challenge the dominance of the state over the lives of the people? What is revolutionary about the political changes he wants?

Finally, we should note the extent to which Giap is dominated by techniques. Do his paragraphs read like a manual on guerrilla warfare? How different are many of Giap's beliefs and values from those of soldiers who write manuals on the art of counter-revolutionary warfare?

From People's War, People's Army
—General Vo Nguyen Giap

Even to this day, bourgeois strategists have not yet overcome their surprise at the outcome of the war in Indochina. How could the Vietnamese nation have defeated an imperialist power such as France which was backed by the United States? They try to explain this extraordinary fact by the correctness of strategy and tactics, by the forms of combat and the heroism of the Vietnam People's Army. Of course all these factors contributed to the happy outcome of the resistance. But if the question is put: "Why were the

Reprinted from *People's War, People's Army: The Viet Cong Insurrection Manual for Underdeveloped Countries,* by General Vo Nguyen Giap, by permission of Frederick A. Praeger, Inc. Copyright © 1962 by Frederick A. Praeger, Inc.

Vietnamese people able to win?'' the most precise and most complete answer must be: ''The Vietnamese people won because their war of liberation was a people's war.''

When the resistance war spread to the whole country, the Indochinese Communist Party emphasized in its instructions that our resistance war must be the work of the entire people. Therein lies the key to victory.

Our resistance war was a people's war, because its political aims were to smash the imperialist yoke in order to win back national independence, to overthrow the feudal landlord class in order to bring land to the peasants; in other words, to radically solve the two fundamental contradictions of Vietnamese society—the contradiction between the nation and imperialism on the one hand, and the contradiction between the people, especially between the peasants and the feudal landlord class, on the other—and to pave the socialist path for the Vietnamese revolution.

Holding firmly to the strategy and tactics of the national democratic revolution, the Party pointed out to the people the aims of the struggle: independence and democracy. It was, however, not enough to have objectives entirely in conformity with the fundamental aspirations of the people. It was also necessary to bring everything into play to enlighten the masses of the people, educate and encourage them, organize them in fighting for national salvation. The Party devoted itself entirely to this work, to the regrouping of all the national forces, and to the broadening and strengthening of a national united front, the Vietminh, and later the Lien Viet which was a magnificent model of the unity of the various strata of the people in the anti-imperialist struggle in a colonial country. In fact, this Front united the patriotic forces of all classes and social strata, even progressive landlords; all nationalities in the country, majority as well as minority; patriotic believers of each and every religion. ''Unity, the great unity, for victory, the great victory''; this slogan launched by President Ho Chi Minh became a reality, a great reality during the long and hard resistance.

We waged a people's war, and that in the framework of a long-since colonized country. Therefore, the national factor was of primary importance. We had to rally all the forces likely to overthrow the imperialists and their lackeys. On the other hand, this war proceeded in a backward agricultural country where the peasants, making up the great majority of the population, constituted the essential force of the revolution and of the resistance war. Consequently, the relation between the national question and the peasant question had to be clearly defined, with the gradual settlement of the agrarian problem, so as to mobilize the broad peasant masses, one of the essential and decisive factors for victory. Always solicitous about the interests of the peasantry, the Party began by advocating reduction of land rent and interest. Later on, as soon as the stabilization of the situation allowed it, the Party carried out with great firmness the mobilization of the masses for land reform in order to bring land to the tillers, thereby to maintain and strengthen the resistance.

During the years of war, various erroneous tendencies appeared. Either we devoted our attention only to the organization and growth of the armed forces while neglecting the mobilization and organization of large strata of the people; or we mobilized the people for the war without heeding seriously their immediate everyday interests; or we thought of satisfying the immediate interests of the people as a whole, without giving due attention to those of the peasants. The Party resolutely fought all these tendencies. To lead the resistance to victory, we had to look after the strengthening of the army, while giving thought to mobilizing and educating the people, broadening and consolidating the National United Front. We had to mobilize the masses for the resistance while trying to satisfy their immediate interest in improving their living conditions, essentially those of the peasantry. A very broad national united front was indispensable, on the basis of the worker-peasant alliance and under the leadership of the Party.

The imperatives of the people's war in Vietnam required the adoption of appropriate strategy and tactics on the basis of the enemy's characteristics and of our own, of the concrete conditions of the battlefields and balance of forces facing each other: in other words, the strategy and tactics of a people's war, in an economically backward, colonial country.

First of all, this strategy must be the *strategy of a long-term war*. It does not mean that all revolutionary wars, all people's wars, must necessarily be long-term wars. If from the outset the conditions are favorable to the people and the balance of forces turn in favor of the revolution, the revolutionary war can end victoriously in a short time. But the war of liberation of the Vietnamese people started in quite different conditions: we had to deal with a much stronger enemy. It was obvious that this balance of forces took away from us the possibility of giving decisive battles from the opening of the hostilities and of checking the aggression from the first landing operations on our soil. In a word, it was impossible for us to defeat the enemy swiftly.

It was only by a long hard resistance that we could wear out the enemy forces little by little while strengthening ours, progressively turn the balance of forces in our favor, and finally win victory. We did not have any other way.

This strategy and slogan of long-term resistance was decided upon by the Indochinese Communist Party from the first days of the war of liberation. It was in this spirit that the Vietnam People's Army, after fierce street battles in the big cities, beat strategic retreats to the countryside on its own initiative in order to maintain its bases and preserve its forces.

The long-term revolutionary war must include several different stages: stage of contention, stage of equilibrium, and stage of counteroffensive. Practical fighting was, of course, more complicated. There had to be many years of more and more intense and generalized guerrilla fighting to realize the equilibrium of forces and develop our war potentiality. When the conjunctures of events at home and abroad allowed it, we went over to counteroffensive first by a series of local operations, then by others on a larger scale which were to lead to the decisive victory of Dien Bien Phu.

The application of this strategy of long-term resistance required a whole system of education, a whole ideological struggle among the people and Party members, a gigantic effort of organization in both military and economic fields, extraordinary sacrifices and heroism from the army as well as from the people, at the front as well as in the rear. Sometimes erroneous tendencies appeared, trying either to bypass the stages to end the war earlier, or to throw important forces into military adventures. The Party rectified them by a stubborn struggle and persevered in the line it had fixed. In the difficult hours, certain hesitations revealed themselves, and the Party faced them with vigor and with determination in the struggle and faith in final victory.

The long-term people's war in Vietnam also called for appropriate forms of fighting: appropriate to the revolutionary nature of the war as well as to the balance of forces which revealed at that time an overwhelming superiority of the enemy over the still very weak material and technical bases of the People's Army. *The adopted form of fighting was guerrilla warfare.* It can be said that the war of liberation of the Vietnamese people was a long and vast guerrilla war proceeding from simple to complex then to mobile war in the last years of the resistance.

Guerrilla war is the war of the broad masses of an economically backward country standing up against a powerfully equipped and well-trained army of aggression. Is the enemy strong? One avoids him. Is he weak? One attacks him. To his modern armament, one opposes a boundless heroism to vanquish either by harassing or by combining military operations with political and economic action; there is no fixed line of demarcation, the front being wherever the enemy is found.

Concentration of troops to realize an overwhelming superiority over the enemy where he is sufficiently exposed in order to destroy his manpower; initiative, flexibility, rapidity, surprise, suddenness in attack and retreat. As long as the strategic balance of forces remains disadvantageous, resolutely to muster troops to obtain absolute superiority in combat in a given place, and at a given time. To exhaust the enemy forces little by little by small victories and at the same time to maintain and increase ours. In these concrete conditions it proves absolutely necessary not to lose sight of the main objective of the fighting, that is, the destruction of the enemy manpower. Therefore, losses must be avoided even at the cost of losing ground. And that for the purpose of recovering, later on, the occupied territories and completely liberating the country.

In the war of liberation in Vietnam, guerrilla activities spread to all the regions temporarily occupied by the enemy. Each inhabitant was a soldier, each village a fortress, each Party cell and each village administrative committee a staff.

The people as a whole took part in the armed struggle, fighting according to the principles of guerrilla warfare, in small packets, but always in pursuance of the one and same line, and the same instructions, those of the Central Committee of the Party and the government.

At variance with numerous other countries which waged revolutionary wars, Vietnam, in the first years of its struggle, did not and could not engage in pitched battles. It had to rest content with guerrilla warfare. At the cost of thousands of difficulties and countless sacrifices, this guerrilla war developed progressively into a form of mobile war that daily increased in scale. While retaining certain characteristics of guerrilla war, it involved regular campaigns with greater attacks on fortified positions. Starting from small operations with the strength of a platoon or a company to annihilate a few men or a group of enemy soldiers, our army went over, later, to more important combats with a battalion or regiment to cut one or several enemy companies to pieces, finally coming to greater campaigns bringing into play many regiments, then many divisions, to end at Dien Bien Phu where the French Expeditionary Corps lost sixteen thousand men of its crack units. It was this process of development that enabled our army to move forward steadily on the road to victory.

People's war, long-term war, guerrilla warfare developing step by step into mobile warfare, such are the most valuable lessons of the war of liberation in Vietnam. It was by following that line that the Party led the resistance to victory. After three thousand days of fighting, difficulties and sacrifices, our people defeated the French imperialists and American interventionists. At present, in the liberated half of our country, sixteen million of our compatriots, by their creative labor, are healing the horrible wounds of war, reconstructing the country and building socialism. In the meantime, the struggle is going on to achieve the democratic national revolution throughout the country and to reunify the fatherland on the basis of independence and democracy.

After this account of the main lines of the war of liberation waged by the Vietnamese people against the French and American imperialists, I shall speak of the Vietnam People's Army.

Being the armed forces of the Vietnamese people, it was born and grew up in the flames of the war of national liberation. Its embryo was the self-defense units created by the Nghe An soviets, which managed to hold power for a few months in the period of revolutionary upsurge in the years 1930–1931. But the creation of revolutionary armed forces was positively considered only at the outset of World War II when the preparation for an armed insurrection came to the forefront of our attention. Our military and paramilitary formations appeared at the Bac Son uprising and in the revolutionary bases in Cao Bang region. Following the setting-up of the first platoon of National Salvation, on December 22, 1944, another platoon-strong unit was created: the Propaganda Unit of the Vietnam Liberation Army. Our war bases organized during our illegality were at the time limited to a few districts in the provinces of Cao Bang, Bac Can, and Lang Son in the jungle of the North. As for the revolutionary armed forces they still consisted of people's units of self-defense and of a few groups and platoons completely free from production work. Their number increased quickly, and there were already several thousands of guerrillas at the beginning of 1945, at the time of the *coup de force* by the Japanese fascists over the French colonialists. After establishing people's power in the rural regions of the six provinces in Viet Bac that were established as a free zone, the existing armed organizations merged to form the Vietnam Liberation Army.

During the August insurrection, side by side with the people and the self-defense units, the Liberation Army took part in the conquest of power. By incorporating the paramilitary forces regrouped in the course of the glorious days of August, it saw its strength increase rapidly. With heterogeneous materiel wrested from the Japanese and their Boa An troops*—rifles alone consisted of sixteen different types including old French patterns and even rifles of the tsarist forces taken by the Japanese—this young and poorly equipped army soon had to face the aggression of the French Expeditionary Corps which had modern armaments. Such antiquated equipment required from the Vietnamese Army and people complete self-sacrifice and superhuman heroism.

Should the enemy attack the regions where our troops were stationed, the latter would give battle. Should he ferret about in the large zones where there were no regular formations, the people would stay his advance with rudimentary weapons: sticks, spears, scimitars, bows, flintlocks. From the first days, there appeared three types of armed forces: paramilitary organizations or guerrilla units, regional troops, and regular units. These formations were, in the area of organization, the expression of the general mobilization of the people in arms. They cooperated closely with one another to annihilate the enemy.

Peasants, workers, and intellectuals crowded into the ranks of the armed forces of the revolution. Leading cadres of the Party and the state apparatus became officers from the first moment. The greatest difficulty to be solved was the equipment problem. Throughout Vietnam there was no factory manufacturing war matériel. For nearly a century, possession and use of arms were strictly forbidden by the colonial administrations. Importation was impossible, the neighboring countries being hostile to the Democratic Republic of Vietnam. The source of supply could only be the battlefront: take the matériel from the enemy and turn it against him. While carrying on the aggression against Vietnam the French Expeditionary Corps fulfilled another task: it became, unwittingly, the supplier of the Vietnam People's Army with French, even United States arms. In spite of their enormous efforts, the arms factories set up later on with makeshift means were far from being able to meet all our needs. A great part of our military materials came from war booty.

As I have stressed, the Vietnam People's Army could at first bring into combat only small units such as platoons or companies. The regular forces were, at a given time, compelled to split up into companies operating separately to promote the extension of guerrilla activities while mobile battalions were maintained for more important actions. After each victorious combat, the people's armed forces marked a new step forward.

Tempered in combat and stimulated by victories, the guerrilla formations created conditions for the growth of the regional troops. And the latter, in their turn, promoted the development of the regular forces. For nine succes-

---

*Local Vietnamese militia units established under the auspices of the Japanese puppet government.

The question is to synthesize past experiences and to analyze well the concrete conditions of our army in organization and equipment, consider our economic structure, the terrain of the country—land of forests and jungles, of plains and fields. The question is to assimilate well the modern military science of the armies of the brother countries. Unceasing efforts are indispensable in the training of troops and the development of cadres.

For many years, the Vietnam People's Army was based on voluntary service: all officers and soldiers voluntarily enlisted for an undetermined period. Its ranks swelled by the affluence of youth always ready to answer the appeal of the fatherland. Since the return of peace, it has become necessary to replace voluntary service by *compulsory military service*. This substitution has met with warm response from the population. A great number of volunteers, after demobilization, returned to fields and factories; others are working in units assigned to production work, thus making an active contribution to the building of socialism. Conscription is enforced on the basis of the strengthening and development of the self-defense organizations in the communes, factories, and schools. The members of these paramilitary organizations are ready not only to rejoin the permanent army, of which they constitute a particularly important reserve, but also to insure the security and defense of their localities.

The People's Army was closely linked with the national liberation war, in the fire of which it was born and grew up. At present, its development should neither be disassociated from the building of socialism in the North, nor from the people's struggle for a reunified independent and democratic Vietnam. Confident of the people's affection and support, in these days of peace as during the war, the People's Army will achieve its tasks: to defend peace and the fatherland.

My article outlines the evolution of grand military strategy in the twentieth century. It traces a major change in cultural values: In 1925 military men said that the systematic bombing of civilian populations was barbaric; in 1942 Western governments adopted a policy of terror bombing; and in the sixties military strategists spoke of fifty million deaths as an acceptable loss in a nuclear war.

I find it impossible to imagine the absence of nuclear weapons until we first return to an ethical system that forbids the killing of noncombatants— no matter what the circumstances. Remember: It is bad history to argue that war always meant the systematic slaughter of noncombatants. Throughout the eighteenth century, war rarely interfered with civilians; for example, after their defeat at Auerstadt in 1806, the supposedly vicious Prussian Army remained cold and hungry rather than take supplies from civilians. It is also false to argue that because the technology exists, it must be used. The weapons at Napoleon's disposal were very similar to those used by his immediate predecessors. The difference is that Napoleon used the weapons against civilians; his predecessors did not.

From Obliteration Bombing*
—Ronald Fernandez

Obliterate means to erase, to destroy, to reduce to an almost imperceptible state. Coupled with bombing, obliteration means the systematic destruction of, e.g., enemy soldiers, enemy military bases, or enemy airfields. But, since obliteration bombing often aims only at undermining *civilian* morale, soldiers frequently escape its terrible effects. Theoretically, the guiding notion is that the erasure of common people and crowded cities promises a quicker victory than battles with soldiers.

Today many believe that obliteration bombing is inevitable. They unthinkingly embrace the doctrine that, in the event of nuclear war, open cities will be the principal targets. Analysts speak of fifty million deaths as acceptable, while the majority of us remain quiet. Indeed, in Vietnam, a limited war, we permitted our leaders to conduct bombing raids specifically aimed at undermining non-combatant morale. Although this went on for over ten years, and hundreds of thousands died as a result of these missions, most of us were not appalled. Apparently, we accept slaughter of civilians as a normal phase of modern warfare. Remember: months before Hiroshima and Nagasaki, close to 100 thousand people were napalmed to death in Tokyo, and the Dresden (Germany) raids killed more than 125 thousand people. Perhaps to us, strategic bombing for the purpose of undermining civilian morale—obliteration bombing—is old hat. Perhaps it is even an assumption of late twentieth century culture.

As recently as 1920, few Americans believed that air bombardment of non-combatants was permissible. Then, many—soldiers included—called it immoral and barbaric. We forget it, but we now conduct our wars in a manner that would shock many of our historical predecessors. Throughout the eighteenth century, for example, European warfare rarely interfered with civilian life. To a remarkable extent, soldiers left civilians and their property alone. Fighting Napoleon, Austrians refused to destroy Belgian farm land; and after their humiliating defeat at Auerstadt in 1806, the supposedly vicious Prussian soldiers went unsheltered and hungry rather than disrupt civilian life. Moreover, in the eighteenth century an army lived off the magazines it accumulated in peace time. This served to limit strategic and tactical flexibility, since reliance on magazines meant that five days was the maximum an army could leave its source of supply. But, to the pre-French revolutionary soldier, keeping war away from civilians was more important than the singleminded pursuit of military efficiency.

The above is a revised version of an article that first appeared in *The Humanist* (March–April, 1973).

*As the terms are used in this article, obliteration bombing is a subdivision of strategic bombing. The latter uses air power—independently—for the purpose of victory in war. The former also aims at victory, but its primary targets are not soldiers, but civilians; not airfields or railways, but centers of population.

Although systematic slaughter of non-combatants was also alien to Napoleon, the roots of today's doctrines lie in the military transformations that accompanied the eighteenth century's political revolutions. For Napoleon and his colleagues did more than reorganize the army; they also changed the goals of warfare. Napoleon consciously desired to completely overthrow his opponents. His military aims were "unlimited" and he was therefore uncommitted to the traditional approach. In fact, in contrast to the French Marshall de Saxe (writing in 1740), who was unable to convince his colleagues to pursue a defeated enemy—"tis contrary to custom," they responded—Napoleon aimed at the complete destruction of the enemy's military forces. Whereas his predecessors thought pursuit "unnecessary cruelty," Napoleon considered it a military necessity.

By far, the most important manifestation of the new military thinking was Karl von Clausewitz's *On War,* first published in 1831. Today Clausewitz is best known for his assertion that "war is nothing but a continuation of politics by other means,"[1] but his immediate military successors were relatively uninterested in the political implications of Clausewitz's thought. They focused instead on his military ideas.

Clausewitz said that all warfare was directed toward one general direction: absolute war. But we mistake him (and his immediate influence) if we equate absolute war with the first and second world wars. The leading principle of war for Clausewitz was the destruction of the enemy's *military* force. War was absolute because it was absurd "to introduce into the philosophy of war a principle of moderation."[2]

So, for Clausewitz, war's object was the enemy's military downfall. Ideally, a society mobilized all the resources at its command and sent its troops into the field with the object of completely defeating the enemy. How was defeat to occur? Clausewitz said that the enemy must be defeated in battle, but in a special type of battle, for "only great and general battles can produce great results."[3] Clausewitz refined this axiom, however, for he argued that *one* great battle should be the "leading means and central point" of military strategy. Naturally, since Clausewitz advocated great battles, large numbers of men were required for the armies. In fact, whereas the average army of the eighteenth century numbered 45,000 men, strategists now talked in terms of hundreds of thousands. And large armies were important in their own right because great size "demanded" a number of organizational changes. The use of conscription (first employed in 1798) is closely linked to the rise of large armies, and so too are adequate staff preparations, mobilization plans, and conversion of parts of the economy to war production. After all, if large armies were to succeed, political and military centralization, rationalization, and bureaucratization were "unavoidable."

---

[1] Karl von Clausewitz, *On War* (1831; reprint ed., Baltimore, Md.: Penguin Books, 1968), p. 119.
[2] von Clausewitz, *On War,* p. 102.
[3] von Clausewitz, *On War,* p. 342.

By 1914, European military thinking was dominated by the principles of *On War*. Indeed, affirmation of Clausewitz allowed World War I military strategists to make a number of assumptions, the most important of which was that future wars would be short. Since great battles inevitably produced great results, a prolonged encounter was relatively inconceivable from a Clausewitzian perspective. Besides, modern societies would never withstand a long war—the economy would soon be undermined, the human destruction would be too great. So, because short wars were envisioned, Richard Challener correctly notes that, "in 1914, mobilization was an event which concerned *only* the armies, and the nation in arms was a concept which referred solely to the utilization of manpower in the military services."[4]

World War I—especially its protracted length—undermined many of Clausewitz's assumptions. After the war, scores of books appeared documenting the mistakes made by military leaders and by Clausewitz. One lesson of the war was that an entire society had to be mobilized for a great war— mere military mobilization was insufficient. Survival demanded that everyone and everything be subordinate to the goal of victory. It also became clear that nations could fight very long wars. So, in *total* wars, conscription was a must, the economy had to be closely supervised by politicians, and the enemy had to be completely overthrown—he might even be forced to surrender unconditionally.

Present day theories of air warfare are a direct consequence of the crisis in military thinking that World War I generated. These theories logically followed the military precedents of the French Revolution, Napoleon, and World War I. As the British strategist Liddell Hart wrote in a volume first published in 1925, *Paris or the Future of War*, warfare could be directed at three general objectives: the military power, the country, and the will of the enemy. Clausewitz's alleged mistake was that he concentrated on military power, and, in modern war, this was useless. As long as the will of the people (civilians) was not undermined, a society could continue to provide men and supplies for an indefinite period. "Put in a nutshell," says Hart, "victory in modern war is obtained by dislocating their [civilians'] normal life to such a degree that they will prefer the lesser evil of surrendering their policy, and by convincing them that any return to normalcy is hopeless unless they do surrender."[5]

Liddell Hart's views were controversial, but not out of the ordinary. An Italian, Guilo Douhet, published a volume on air warfare as early as 1910, and in 1927 he published his influential *The Command of the Air*. In America General Billy Mitchell was persistent if not fanatic about the need for an air force capable of both offense and defense; and in England, where an independent Air Force existed since 1918, Chief of the Air Staff Hugh Montague

---

[4]Richard Challener, *French Theory of the Nation in Arms* (New York: Columbia University Press, 1958), p. 100.
[5]Sir B. H. Liddell Hart, *Paris or The Future of War* (1925; reprint ed., New York: Garland Publishing Company, 1972), pp. 28–29.

Trechard was certain that in the next war the air arm would prove to be the decisive service.

To all these men and their apostles, armies and navies were not necessarily anachronistic, only peripheral. To strategic air power advocates, World War I proved nothing. It was true that citizen morale seemed to increase (rather than decrease) when bombing occurred, and it was also correct that bombing had not destroyed cities; but, after all, the air arm was so restricted that World War I was not even a quiz, much less a real test of air power's effectiveness. Just allow the planes to be used as theory directed, and then, assuredly, theory would prove itself fact.

Just what were these theories? Essentially, theorists argued that the object of modern war was to destroy the enemy's country and undermine his (and her) morale. Rather than attack the enemy's army—as Clausewitz argued—we should destroy his industries. Centers of population far removed from the fighting forces were to receive the brunt of any attack. As General Billy Mitchell proclaimed in 1925: "to gain a lasting victory in war the hostile nation's power to make war must be destroyed—this means the manufactories, the means of communication, the food products, even the farms, the fuel and oil, and the places where people live and carry on their daily lives."[6]

Obviously, General Mitchell perceived few limits to military activity. Others did. In fact, when the above statement was made (at hearings of the President's Aircraft Board in 1925), it aroused a good deal of controversy. Major General C. P. Summerall stated that "I do not understand that in war it is in accordance with the laws or rules of war to bomb cities or areas occupied by non-combatants." His colleague, Captain W. S. Pye, U.S. Navy, went further. He argued that General Mitchell's theories "struck at the root of civilization . . . Is this nation which fought for the preservation of international law and the sacredness of treaties to adopt this theory of ruthlessness . . . Are we to become the 'baby killers' and the 'boches' of the future? The civilized world would stand aghast at any such decision made by the United States of America."

In 1925, no real decision was made, but some did try to resolve the controversy. J. M. Spaight, in his *Air Power and the Cities* (published in London in 1930) clearly recognized the ominous consequences of leaving the question of air bombardment rules unsettled. Noting that existing doctrines of air warfare were "tentative, hesitant, and groping,"[7] Spaight resolved to construct a doctrine that would prove both humane and militarily useful. He argued first that the proposed bombardment of cities had many precedents. To prove his point, Spaight presented a detailed analysis of naval bombardments over the previous century. His conclusion was that air bombardments of cities and industrial concentrations were morally legitimate, with certain limitations: Only military objectives were permissible targets. Moreover,

---

[6]Burke Davis, *The Billy Mitchell Affair* (New York: Random House, 1967), p. 197.
[7]J. M. Spaight, *Air Power and the Cities* (London: Longmans, Green, 1930), p. 14.

since the term "military objective" lent itself to loose translation, Spaight stated that indiscriminate terror bombing of non-combatants must be prohibited, and that military objectives in heavily populated areas could not lawfully be bombed if, because of restricted space or their location in a densely populated area, the probable result of such bombing would be "the widespread and wholly disproportionate loss of non-combatant life throughout the district."[8]

Spaight did try. The problem was that he qualified the above by arguing that his proposed limitations did not prohibit the terror bombing of factory workers in essential industries. He thus opened the door that led, for the British, to a strategic bombing policy that culminated in Dresden. Spaight contended that the terror bombing of factory workers would always be "one of the main purposes of air attack."[9] Such raids were perfectly legitimate, since factories and their inhabitants were military objectives. Granted, some might argue that this view perverted the traditional definition of military objective, but to Spaight, the question apparently never arose. Indeed, he was convinced that missions of this type would be a central feature of air attacks both in any future "private Wars" and in any conflict conducted by leagued states against an aggressor.

In 1930 the doctrine of *Air Power and the Cities* was representative of the British Air Staff. In America, however, General Billy Mitchell had been courtmartialed and and a more moderate stance adopted. In Germany the airplane was a tactical rather than a strategic weapon. Thus, even in military circles, no consensus on the use of air power existed. In 1930, something could have been done to make certain that all non-combatants remained free from attack. After all, since the end of the Thirty Years War in 1648, non-combatants had enjoyed relative immunity from injury. Two hundred and seventy-five years of precedent would be disregarded if air power advocates won out.

But they did win out, and for a number of reasons. Since 1648, the basis—what Whitehead called the "tone"—of Western civilization, had changed. Science and reason had replaced religion and faith. Gradually, efficiency became more important than tradition, the art of war became the science of war, and people realized that the march of science made technological innovation "inevitable." More specifically, since Napoleon, people had become accustomed to the idea that a general war would involve enormous losses in life and treasure: Especially in World War I, people began to sense and accept the belief that in modern war anyone was a legitimate target. So, while the prophecies of destruction were frightening, nothing could be done. The plane existed and the exigencies of war would force people to use it in whatever manner was necessary.

---

[8]Spaight, *Air Power*, p. 201.
[9]Spaight, *Air Power*, p. 219.

Naturally, none of this was necessarily inevitable. Using the same weapons as Napoleon, pre-revolutionary soldiers fought very limited wars. Too few moderns asked: If chemical and biological weapons are prohibited, why not the indiscriminate bombing of non-combatants? Somehow, precedent was relevant for gas, but not for the airplane. Somehow, even in the minds of many soldiers, gas was barbaric but the slaughter of non-combatants— including babies—was not.

Explaining the anomaly is difficult. Perhaps it is best to regard the prohibition of chemical and biological warfare as a welcome affirmation of tradition in a world otherwise dominated by doctrines of "logical ruthlessness." However, no matter how we explain it, when World War II began, air power enthusiasts held positions of power in the Allied and Axis military. With no widely supported prohibitions in existence, it was a good bet that air power would eventually be used in any manner necessary—if only to prove that all the theories were correct.

Britain was the first to begin strategic bombing in World War II. The German use of air power in Rotterdam and Warsaw was tactical; it was in support of the army and subordinate to it. As Spaight wrote in *Bombing Vindicated* (published in London in 1944) "the British idea of an air force as the coequal of the other services and the possible predominant partner in warlike ventures in which they (the other services) would have minor parts to play would have seemed nothing short of heresy to the German higher strategists."[10]

Britain began strategic bombing on May 11, 1940, when a force of eighteen bombers attacked railway communications on the German mainland. The date is important, since it preceded the German strategic bombing of London by some four months. Of course, if strategic bombing had been an integral part of German military thinking, they would have used it. The point is that those who were fighting for "honor" and "morality" and "civilization" against Nazi despotism were also so mesmerized by the potentialities of the new forms of warfare that they failed to see the awful precedents they were setting.

On September 2, 1939, for example, the British and French governments had declared that only "strictly military objectives in the narrowest sense of the word would be bombarded." By March of 1942, however, when the British bombing raids had failed to achieve their objectives, one civilian advisor argued that future bombing be directed at working class homes. The raids on strictly military objectives were insufficient; the way to victory was the terror bombing of factory workers. In fact, the advisor argued that if the British concentrated their efforts, fifty percent of all the houses in German cities with more than half a million people could be destroyed.

The advisor's suggestion was adopted. On March 28, 1942, Lubeck was attacked. The raid proved to be "a first class success." Between 45 to 50

[10]J. M. Spaight, *Bombing Vindicated* (London: Geoffrey Bles, 1944), p. 30.

percent of the city was totally destroyed. Results must have encouraged Allied leaders, for on January 23, 1943, they issued the Casablanca directive, "which called for the destruction and dislocation of the German military industrial and economic system and the undermining of the morale of the German people to the point where their capacity for armed resistance is fatally weakened." As the American General Carl Spaatz put it, "strategic bombing *at last* had the green light; and it possessed a plan of operations of its own, with an approved order of priorities in targets, to achieve the objectives of the Casablanca Directive. That plan called for bombing by night and day, round the clock."[11]

Viewed from this perspective, the Dresden raid, the napalming of Tokyo, and even the use of the atomic bomb cannot surprise us. They are simply conspicuously horrible examples of a doctrine that was then, and is now, taken for granted. Dresden was part of Operation Thunderclap, and an expansion of the now accepted use of terror bombing. Instead of attacks on working class houses, however, the Dresden raid was part of a plan "designed to dislocate the refugee evacuation from the East and to hamper troop movements." Allied leaders were operating in support of the Russian Army's advance. The raid was to demonstrate "solidarity with the Russians" and also to act as a sign of the terrible power the Allies possessed. It succeeded. As noted, estimates are that at least 125 thousand people died in the Dresden raids.

The fire bombing of Japanese cities was part of a "softening up" process for the Allied invasion. But, soldiers said that if they won by strategic bombing alone, there would be no need for an invasion. General Curtis LeMay was the new commander in the Pacific. Investigating the failures of his predecessor, General LeMay recognized that napalm and phosphorous bombs would be the most efficient weapons. After all, Japanese industry was spread out in homes that were made of wood, so incendiaries were the quickest way to get the job done. In his autobiography General LeMay shows that "the physical destruction and loss of life at Tokyo exceeded that at Rome . . . or that of any of the great conflagrations of the Western World—London, 1666 . . . Moscow, 1812 . . . Chicago, 1871 . . . San Francisco, 1906. . . ." Indeed (and the emphasis is the General's) *"no other air attack of the war, either in Japan or Europe, was so destructive of life and property."* [12]

Although one can ask whether such destruction merits pride in achievement, General LeMay is correct. However, if the atomic bombs were not as destructive as the Tokyo raids, they set precedents which haunt us today—and will haunt us tomorrow. Unfortunately, precedents were not a prime concern in the middle of 1945. For President Truman agreed with the overwhelming majority of his advisors: since we had the bomb, we had to use it. It was ter-

---

[11]General Carl Spaatz, "Strategic Air Power," *Foreign Affairs,* 1947, Volume 21, pp. 385–396.

[12]General Curtis LeMay with MacKinley Kantor, *Mission With LeMay* (Garden City, N.Y.: Doubleday and Company, 1965), p. 353.

rible but still the lesser of two evils. For if we did not use it, millions would die in the invasion planned to begin in November of 1945. No doubt thousands of innocent people would die as a result of the bombs, but many less than if they were not used.

Study of the decision to drop the bomb reveals that the OK was given only after careful—if hasty—consideration by serious and thoughtful men. Nevertheless, given their basic assumptions, the decision was a foregone conclusion. As Robert Batchelder points out, it was an "irreversible decision."[13] Time had accustomed people to such slaughter that the bomb was perceived as a variation in degree, rather than a monumental change in kind.

Although the atomic bombs did help end the war, what they did not do was alter the basic axioms regarding the legitimacy of air bombardment. On the contrary, the postwar world demanded that adults accept and children learn, that in the event of major war, cities would be the principal targets. Consider: The Cold War provided the ideological backdrop; the Air Force became a separate institution, more aggressive and powerful than ever before; and the coming of the military industrial complex gave birth to a research network that would argue endlessly over whether it was better to deploy nuclear weapons tactically, strategically, or both. All too few argued that they should not be used at all, and even fewer argued that they were immoral.

Today all proportion seems to have been lost. Conceivably, some might argue that Dresden or Tokyo resulted from a war policy that demanded unconditional surrender—and there is some truth in this argument. But today, even so-called limited wars have given birth to unprecedented amounts of air bombardment. Today, air power is so taken for granted, its use so relatively uncontested, that we fail to realize and/or care about what we are doing. In Vietnam, more than six million tons of bombs were dropped. Large sections of Vietnam are no longer habitable. Furthermore, the use of anti-personnel weapons committed us to a policy that was, to my mind, barbaric. These weapons were specifically designed to inflict peculiar and hard-to-cure injuries. They have, to quote *Aviation Week,* "a separate and distinguishable psychological impact . . . apart from the actual destruction they cause."[14] Since many people are required to care for the victims of anti-personnel weapons, the sufferings of the injured have more of a demoralizing effect on survivors than those who are simply dead.

What is to be done? One thing is to recognize that obliteration bombing is only part of the problem. Undoubtedly, it is the most conspicuous example of modern war's horrors, but it does not by any means stand alone. Search and destroy missions, free fire zones, and the reintroduction of chemical and

---

[13]Robert Batchelder, *The Irreversible Decision* (New York: Free Press, 1961).
[14]"Vietnam Spurs Navy Weapons Advances," *Aviation Week,* March 21, 1966.

biological warfare are also manifestations of today's accepted strategy and tactics. Seemingly, the loss of any restraint in the air has helped produce a similar loss of restraint on the ground. Seemingly, whether non-combatants are systematically slaughtered from the air, or face-to-face, it makes no difference; most of us now take the systematic "erasure" of non-combatants and their property as an unquestioned fact of modern war.

Throughout history, civilians often suffered at the hands of soldiers. And writers correctly stress the evil, such as My Lai, that normally accompanies war. But my point is that today, everyday policy is worse than the aberrations. Focusing on My Lais or torture closes our eyes to taken for granted strategy and tactics. In short, if it was wrong for Lieutenant Calley and his men to murder women and children, why is it right when we permit soldiers to burn them alive from a plane?

Restraint in tomorrow's wars can come from at least two directions. One is a set of "laws" along the line of the Hague and Geneva Conventions. If only to provide an accepted standard of judgement, these would be very helpful. But, unless someone or some group is given the power to enforce the laws, it will be difficult to make countries law-abiding. For while many people obey because they believe in the legitimacy of the laws, many others obey primarily because of the penalties for disobedience.

Another way to begin to restrain modern war is to reevaluate and change the beliefs and values which presently sustain it. Is it true that systematic slaughter of non-combatants is now an automatic assumption of modern culture? Is it true that few of us question a policy that deems fifty million deaths an acceptable loss in a nuclear war? Is it true that we see nothing immoral in the intentional burning alive of children?

To the extent we respond to these questions affirmatively, the need for a total reassessment and change of our values is obvious. After all, unless we subscribe to Freud's notion of a death instinct, consider our situation: We presently endorse concepts that could easily lead to the destruction of the world—and ourselves.

Roger Williams tells us how we can expect to kill, and be killed, in the coming years. He foresees "advances" on almost every front in a future in which conventional weapons are rapidly approaching nuclear bombs in destructive capability.

To some extent new weapons are a result of generals, scientists, and politicians jointly providing for the nation's defense—the attitude that "the U.S. must be the Number One world power." But weapons are also a crucial part of our economy. Since one in ten Americans works for a defense related industry, weapons rank almost as high as cars on a scale of economic significance. What would happen to the economy if we stopped making weapons?

Since few people talk seriously about stopping, we need not worry. Americans, for example, are now solving part of their balance of payments problem by selling arms worldwide, and the French now sell thirty percent of their arms production. Profits go into research and development of new weapons, so France remains a world power.

Change is possible, but its prospects are dim. Underdeveloped nations are closely imitating the big powers (witness India's drive for nuclear weapons), and although our recent economic woes have produced big cuts in health, education, and welfare budgets, the military budget has been increased.

I believe the prospects for change would improve significantly if we re-evaluated our beliefs and values. Williams' essay highlights the extent to which political and military thinking is often dominated by techniques of all sorts. But if we switch from a stress on means to one rooted in ends, we uncover even more basic beliefs and values. For example, in *Peace With Honor* (1932), A. A. Milne made points that are still quite relevant today. Milne noted that political leaders rarely spoke of great nations. They always talked of great powers, and didn't that stress mirror their values—and ours? Weren't the "good" countries as interested in power as the "bad"? And what is the relationship between powerful nations and the idea of and applause for the traditional notion of masculinity?

From Science, Technology, and the Future of Warfare
—*Roger Williams*

The relationship between science and war is so disturbing that there seems every justification for reflecting again and again on the terrible contents of the military Pandora's Box which science has opened up. The discussion which follows therefore deals with 'science' and 'warfare', though both are imprecise terms in this context. Strictly defined, science is a systematic, and typically empirical, explanation of natural phenomena, but in common usage the word 'science' refers not only to this but also to technology, development work and even invention. Similarly, 'warfare' must be construed to cover possibilities as well as actualities, since a chief characteristic of the impact of 'science' on 'warfare' has in fact been the phenomenon of technical obsolescence before operational use. Below, considerations of style have made it necessary to talk of 'progress', 'advances' and 'improvements' in weapons development. It is ironic that no more suitable modes of expression present themselves. The author's belief, shared with most people, that the less war the better, absolves neither him nor them from considering its likely future shape. Indeed, it demands especially that adequate attention be given to any characteristic of the weapons acquisition process which encourages the threat, precipitates the outbreak, or worsens the consequences of war

It is well worth pausing at the outset to remember just where we are so far as the science/warfare interaction is concerned. This is sensible in that

From *War in the Next Decade,* edited by Roger Beaumont and Martin Edmonds. Copyright © 1975 by the University Press of Kentucky and reprinted by permission of the publisher.

it provides the best foundation for talking about the future.[1] As regards military personnel, there is undoubtedly a good deal of truth in the criticism that, at least until recent years, their professional appreciation has generally lagged behind technical development substantially, and in many cases seriously. Nor is the suggestion that this reflects a contrast between the military and the scientific approaches meant as a compliment to the military. Fortunately for them, history demonstrates that other professions, including the scientific one, have often failed to anticipate and adjust to change. Certainly it is change, formerly slow, now frighteningly rapid, which lies at the heart of the science war symbiosis, and the record suggests at least five senses in which the former has contributed to the latter, all five therefore requiring to be considered here.

Three of these senses are mainly specific to weapons systems and relate to fire power, mobility and communications. Science has made the fire power available to modern forces stupendous in historical comparison, and of remarkable accuracy. It has dramatically improved land, sea, and air mobility, and it has fostered spectacular advances in the precision, speed and richness of communication. Independent developments in each of these three dimensions have led both to changes in the others and also constantly altered the military field as a whole. It is with this field as a whole that science has been concerned in a fourth way. The argument here has been that if the complexities continually being introduced into the military environment by modern technology are to be reduced to the point where effective choices and decisions can still be made, then the scientific method itself must be used to ensure this. Variants of, or perhaps approximations to, this method have as a result come to be applied, again primarily during and since the Second World War, to the conduct of most military affairs, from stock control and tactical questions right up to grand strategy. Finally, since science has also transformed the non-military sectors of society, the corresponding economic, demographic, political and technical changes constitute, to the extent that they have military importance, a fifth aspect of the science/war theme. In discussing the future of conflict it is not therefore likely to be sufficient to confine study to the obviously military. The net must be cast much wider than that. Political changes produced in the world as a direct or indirect result of science and technology may in the end prove far more crucial determinants of military

---

[1]It is also salutary in that we are forced to recognize that we may still be at quite an early stage of the process, this century, the Second World War above all, marking the critical take-off phase.* The development of weapons was extremely slow, in the majority of cases the pressures to innovate simply not being felt by those who might have stimulated development. And this in spite of the fact that technical superiority in weaponry had commonly led to victory in war, and was often recognized to have done so. Gradually, a distinct class of military engineers emerged, a status distinction came to be drawn between 'pure' and 'applied' science, and some scientists and engineers began to experience a moral repugnance against any warlike use of science. See, for instance, Bernard and Fawn Brodie, *From Crossbow to H-Bomb* (New York: Dell Publishing Co., 1962).

*Before it, through most of history, one is surprised by the absence of a persisting corpus of knowledge about military equipment, weapons often being used once or twice and then forgotten. The history of science and war is thus in large measure one of invention and war, true science being a feature mainly of the last two or three centuries.

requirements than narrower developments in military or associated technology. After all, we have hardly yet begun to exploit the capacity of science to modify the world at large, and whereas we may hope to reduce the causes of war, we need to be aware constantly of any new tensions we simultaneously create.

With these five categories in mind, what does the future seem to hold in terms of atomic, biological, chemical, conventional and exotic warfare?

Looking first at atomic warfare, here it appears that nature has already been persuaded to give up all the necessary secrets. Technology has made nuclear bombs or warheads available with yields ranging from a fraction of a kiloton to 60 megatons and more. They are capable of delivery at distances from less than a mile up to half way round the earth, or further. They can be constructed as extremely dirty or as relatively clean weapons. We have fission and fusion devices: there is no good reason for supposing that a new explosive process of comparative violence is likely to be discovered. Most possibilities, matter/anti-matter annihilation for example, seem to belong firmly in the realm of science fiction. If they did not, it would be hard to imagine a military requirement for them. What is to be feared is the development of an alternative or uranium fission as a standard fusion trigger. Even though, on current knowledge, the alternative might be expected to be at least as complex to construct as an uranium trigger, it would be prudent not to ignore the dangers of a simpler mechanism eventually becoming available. As it is, with alternatives to gaseous diffusion now being proved for uranium enrichment, obtaining a supply of U235 may in the next decade present few more difficulties than now arise in establishing a plutonium stock. Already enough plutonium is being produced throughout the world to make possible the manufacture of some 1,500 plutonium bombs per annum, and this is predicted as likely to rise to some 15,000 by 1980. Of course, this is almost entirely civil production, but the plain fact remains that it is becoming easier year by year, both technically and economically, for a nation to arm itself with nuclear weapons.[2] Since over the long term the political inducements in favor of going nuclear seem likely, in the case of several countries, despite international agreements, to outweigh the restraints, there would seem to be a high risk of a world with more than the present five nuclear powers. There is a general suspicion that the step to the sixth is the most significant, and that if this occurs it may in fairly quick succession prompt the seventh, eighth, etc. Apart from whether horizontal proliferation of itself automatically decreases international stability—it is sometimes claimed that only possession of nuclear weapons ensures full national responsibility—what is certain is that the nuclear weapons which some powers might choose to develop would be maintained under much less secure safeguards than those instituted by at least four of the present five nuclear countries.

---

[2]See, for instance, United Nations, *Report of the Secretary-General: Effects of the Possible Use of Nuclear Weapons and the Security and Economic Implications for States and the Acquisition and Further Development of these Weapons,* 1968, A/6858.

If horizontal proliferation is the greatest of the nuclear questions, then vertical proliferation and the problem of China are the second and third. Each of the two Superpowers has in recent years perceived the other as presenting a serious and/or growing threat to its strategic deterrent. Partly each to deny the other a position from which it could destroy its opponent's retaliatory capacity in a first strike, and partly for reasons of general defense, both the United States and the Soviet Union have pursued the development of the anti-ballistic missile. There is no doubt that the gross uncertainties associated with the A.B.M., and with its counterparts, the multiple independently-targeted re-entry vehicle, the fractional orbital bomb and other offense-aiding systems, have together already introduced a new element of instability in the balance between the Superpowers.[3] The SALT talks in progress at the time of writing may check this decay; on the evidence of the past it would be unrealistic to expect them to reverse it. Technology is too good at creating uncertainty. In any case, some pretty fundamental assumptions seem certain to receive a major challenge from technology over the next decade or so. For instance, it is acknowledged now that even hardened missile silos may have only a limited lifetime.[4] To quote an American ex-Director of Defense Research and Engineering: ' . . . there is no technical solution to the dilemma of the steady decrease in our national security that has for more than 20 years accompanied the steady increase in our military power.'[5]

The more complex the strategic balance becomes, the greater the scope for misunderstanding of intentions or miscalculation of capability. However, there are no grounds for supposing that the technological nuclear stalemate between the United States and the Soviet Union will really be broken technically in the coming decades, still less for believing that a situation is imminent in which either will again be permitted by the other to establish a first strike capability. The urgent question for both is rather at what level of cost the stalemate is to be held, and this in turn depends to an important degree on American and Soviet interpretations of the motives and policies of China. The advent of a third Superpower, at least in the nuclear sense, has a distressing parallel in the world of mathematics. There, while the equations of motion of a two body system are fully determinate, only approximate solutions are obtainable for a three body system. For a quarter of a century the United States and the Soviet Union have contrived to stay in stable equilibrium with each other, in spite of apparent incompatibilities. It is still to be shown that the dynamics of a three Superpower system will lend themselves to an equally tolerable solution over time.

---

[3]Two of many books on this subject are Abram Chayes and Jerome B. Weisner (eds), *ABM* (London: Macdonald, 1970) and Johan J. Holst and William Schneider Jnr (eds) *Why ABM?* (London: Pergamon Press, 1969).

[4]G. W. Rathjens and G. B. Kistiakowsky, 'The Limitations of Strategic Arms', *Scientific American,* 222 (Jan 1970) p. 26. But see also the letters column in the same periodical for May 1970, p. 6.

[5]Herbert F. York, 'Military Technology and National Security,' *Scientific American,* 221 (Aug 1969) p. 29.

If this is an imponderable, so too, if we are honest, is the true military utility of tactical nuclear weapons. The short-term, long-term and genetic effects of these weapons are well enough known to be taken for granted here. Military formations are naturally expected to be able to operate on a nuclear battlefield, and special training and equipment for this purpose can be provided. The underlying premises here are that the situation does not deteriorate into a strategic exchange, and that, in addition, the use even of battlefield nuclear weapons by both sides is fairly discriminate. Where an essentially continuous spectrum of nuclear weapons is to hand these premises cannot be relied upon to hold. In addition to the appalling destructiveness of even small nuclear weapons, and the absence of an unequivocal firebreak between a tactical and a strategic nuclear exchange, a third risk attends the use of tactical nuclear weapons. This derives from the mystique of nuclear weapons in general and could easily mean that tactical nuclear weapons were called upon to perform a role for which they were very unsuited, thereby inviting local military failure as well as strategic escalation. In fact, nuclear weapons of all kinds, as instruments of indiscriminate annihilation, have no natural place in the evolution of military doctrine. In particular, responsibility for the bee-sting deterrent is an extremely abnormal military function. The human mechanics of it—the personnel in missile silos and Polaris submarines especially—have received much attention from psychologists and others. The human element will presumably demand still further study if, as seems likely, new technology eventually makes necessary yet more stringent standby conditions. At higher levels in the military organization, Kahn *et al.* notwithstanding, those with the decisions to make will be ill-advised to repose confidence in any single calculus of nuclear use.

If the future of nuclear weapons is more politically than technically unpredictable, that of biological (B) and chemical (C) weapons is perhaps both. . . . an extensive range of weapons of both types has now been tested and developed. These weapons also have a major drawback—uncertainty of control and effect. The user has the taxing problem of ensuring that his own defenses are adequate; each substance has its own specific disadvantages; and most troubling of all are the possible long-term effects, perhaps stretching from devastating local pollution with chemical weapons to a major ecological disturbance, or even to a massive human epidemic from biological weapons. Certainly it must be anticipated that continuing research will lead to still more deadly products than those now to hand. For instance, some of the chemical weapons are directed against basic life cycles which tend to be very complicated and delicate, therefore affording plenty of opportunity for fatal interference. The power of these chemical weapons may then be expected to grow not only as a result of direct research, but also as an indirect consequence of the greater understanding of such life cycles, the latter being a legitimate concern of medical science.

Delivery systems for B and C weapons are somewhat less straightforward than those for conventional or nuclear explosives but, while refinements will no doubt continue to be made, the advanced powers have already investigated most of the feasible options very thoroughly, and a large range of munitions for chemical warfare are known to have been manufactured. Aerosol delivery of B weapons has also been greatly improved, if not perfected.

There are several general points about B and C weapons which need emphasizing. First, on grounds of cost and ease of manufacture, non-nuclear countries, the poorer ones particularly, may find them quite irresistible, not only to stockpile but also, in certain circumstances, to use. Second, it is tacitly assumed that the nuclear powers would also resort to them in any general nuclear war. Third, in spite of these two probabilities, B and C weapons seem to have received very little attention from strategic analysts. Fourth, with biological agents the possibility of covert attack must always be borne in mind. Finally, it seems right to regard both B and C weapons as bringing to war only a new style of lethality: the speculation that certain B and C agents could ultimately make possible war without killing can safely be forgotten.

B and C weapons might be employed against civil populations or against military units. Very much more could be done to protect the former were governments to think the effort worthwhile. Nevertheless, it must be confessed that a comprehensive defense of a large population would be prohibitively expensive and would also require constant revision as potential enemies amended their B and C threats. Furthermore, certain countries or regions would continue to manifest a special vulnerability, and all would remain vulnerable to surprise attack. The position with regard to military units is much less hopeless. Here, several programs of defensive measures can usefully be contemplated. Much depends upon adequate detection and warning systems. These problems are much more severe with B than with C attacks, and with B attacks there may be extra difficulties involved in identifying the agent. The first line of defense here in situations of doubt will be the working assumption that a B or C attack has already occurred or is likely soon to occur. A reliable source states that 'the weapons of C.B.W. are the only ones against which protection of a high order can be effected on the battlefield without severe restriction of fighting capabilities; and C.B. defensive equipment is either issued or held in reserve for most of the major armies of the world.'[6] Such equipment will include antidotes, vaccinations, specific antisera, masks, permeable and impermeable protective clothing, protection arrangements such as special shelters or vehicles, and decontamination systems.

The problems of mounting a B.C. defense are complex, and are exacerbated by shortness of time; the problems confronting the attack are scarcely formidable. B.C. weapons may seem to promise exceptionally high utility for certain missions, but the attacker will not be able to predict, except approximately, the effect he will produce in practice. Skilled analyses of atmospheric and meteorological conditions will necessarily precede all but the crudest

[6]Stockholm International Peace Research Institute (SIPRI), *Yearbook of World Armaments and Disarmament 1968/9* (London: Gerald Duckworth and Co. Ltd, 1969) pp. 130–1.

attack, the choice of the most appropriate agent must then be made, and in the end the attacker must properly make only the most pessimistic assumptions. He must also weigh the risk of escalation. In the words of the recent United Nations Report: '[C.B.W.] could open the door to hostilities which could become less controlled, and less controllable, than any war in the past. Uncontrollable hostilities cannot be reconciled with the concept of military security.'[7] B and C weapons are different in principle from nuclear or conventional ones in that conventional wars are fought and nuclear ones are imaginable, but B.C. war seems likely only as an adjunct to one or both of these. It is evidently not very suitable against the dispersed forces of a nuclear battlefield, or against guerrillas where these are indistinguishable from friendly forces or non-combatants. Against concentrated units or cornered insurgents it might be thought an ideal form of attack. Those who reserve a particular abhorrence for B.C. weapons will hope that Dedijer is right:

> . . . if some highly lethal new weapon, such as a nerve gas or an infectious micro-organism, were used effectively against the guerrillas, that local victory of the regular forces would be bought at a price of moral catastrophe which would make political victory utterly impossible.[8]

Bearing in mind the part played in war by expediency, they will perhaps be less sure that Meselson is right: 'The general problem of preventing chemical and biological warfare is to a large extent a psychological one.'[9]

In spite of the brevity of this summary of B.C. weaponry, reference inevitably must be made to Vietnam. The lessons to be drawn from the use of C weapons in the First World War are extremely suspect. Nor is it easy to draw valid conclusions from the occasions between that war and the Vietnam War on which C (and B) weapons were used or were alleged to have been used. In Vietnam, chemical warfare has taken two forms. (The use of napalm is excluded here.) These are (1) the use of harassing and riot control agents, which can kill of course, though rarely; and (2) herbicides, defoliants and anticrop agents. Three and four respectively of these agents are acknowledged as having been used. Although this represents a comparatively mild form of chemical warfare, its political repercussions have been very damaging for the United States in the world at large, and in South Vietnam itself it appears to have promoted resentment and hostility on the part of the population. On the other hand:

> The military is emphatic about the effectiveness of defoliation in reducing American casualties. . . . The demand for the . . . 12th Air Commando Squadron greatly exceeds their ability to supply them . . . military

[7]United Nations, *Report of the Secretary-General on Chemical and Bacteriological (Biological) Weapons and the Effects of their Possible Use*, 1969, A/7575, para. 368.
[8]Vladimir Dedijer, 'The Poor Man's Power', in Nigel Calder (ed.) *Unless Peace Comes* (London: Allen Lane, The Penguin Press, 1968) p. 36.
[9]Mathew S. Meselson, 'Chemical and Biological Weapons', *Scientific American*, 220 (May 1970) p. 25.

experts [generally agree] that defoliation is a potent weapon in guerilla warfare . . . [and] that in any future [limited] wars . . . extensive use will be made of it.[10]

The same authors conclude a competent and notably unbiassed account by observing that in their judgment the ecological consequences of defoliation are severe and extend far beyond actual target areas. The military usefulness of defoliation is naturally challenged by other authors, and the practical utility of harassing agents, except in situations of limited violence, seems to be an open question even within the military.

With regard to atomic, biological and chemical warfare one must theorize almost from the first: since the Second World War, conventional warfare of one kind or another has unfortunately been virtually continuous somewhere in the world. There have been lightning wars, prolonged struggles and guerrilla wars: no doubt other types could be identified. Nor, unhappily, does a change for the better appear in prospect. The business of compromise and adjustment between the United States and the Soviet Union seems far from complete, and the role of China is still almost wholly undefined. Then, quite apart from these major issues, occasions for war persist elsewhere, mainly between and within particular states of the developing world. It seems most useful here to discuss conventional warfare in terms of the refinements in it being sought by the most advanced powers, since the evidence of the past suggests strongly that most, if not all, of the developments these powers accomplish will become available, sooner or later, to countries of the second and other ranks.[11] The advanced countries might well feel in the future that it was in their interests to slow down this transfer, and they might even agree upon ways of doing this, but artificial technology gaps are still best regarded as temporary and unstable.

The quite rapid developments in conventional warfare capabilities which have been obtained in the advanced countries in recent years have derived from two principal sources. These are, first, the military exploitation of the computer and electronic equipment generally, and second, a much more concentrated effort than ever before to ensure that conventional weapons systems fully reflect the current state of technology. According to Sir Zolly Zuckerman:

> . . . computers can take over jobs done at 'middle management' levels which, till now, have been manned by specialist officers . . . of greater interest is the possibility . . . that . . . computers and rapid communications could put distant military operations under immediate central control. . . . It is difficult to see what effect this . . . could have on . . . 'generalship . . .'[12]

[10]Gordon H. Orians and E. W. Pfeiffer, 'Ecological Effects of the War in Vietnam', *Science* 168 (1970) p. 553.
[11]See, for instance, George Thayer, *The War Business* (London: Weidenfeld and Nicolson, 1969) and Lewis A. Frank, *The Arms Trade in International Relations* (London: Praeger, 1969).
[12]Sir Zolly Zuckerman, *Scientists and War* (London: Hamish Hamilton, 1966) pp. 88–90.

We are clearly likely to witness a continuing electronic battle between offensive and defensive systems with respect to land, sea and air fighting, and at any future stage a major war between technically advanced powers, excluding the use of A.B.C. weapons, could only be, in General Beaufre's words, a 'truly enormous experiment'.[13] And, we may add, an extremely grim one.

The upper limits, as presently conceived, on what may be achieved are well indicated in the following quotation from an article written by Leonard Sullivan in 1968 when he headed the special office in the Pentagon set up to expedite research and development (R and D) activities of relevance to the South-East Asia War.

> . . . we can detect anything that perspires, moves, carries metal, makes a noise, or is hotter or colder than its surroundings. . . . Eventually we will be able to tell when anybody shoots, what he is shooting at, and where he was shooting from. You begin to get a 'Year 2000' vision of an electronic map with little lights that flash. . . .[14]

Sullivan added that this kind of development was what was needed for 'porous war', where the friendly and the enemy were mixed together. He felt that R and D had already demonstrated the possibility of providing, with the appropriate instrumentation, real time surveillance of the battlefield round the clock, and had even shown that in the end there would be little difference between fighting at night and during the day, though this he admitted would be the toughest challenge. On the latter point, an authoritative British source is less optimistic:

> Although the prospect of making ground combat fully as efficient by night as by day remains remote, there are now becoming available a wide range of experimental techniques . . . which should go far to remove many of the current limitations.[15]

In fact, the true modernity of modern armies is apparently wide open to argument. In his book, *Machine Age Armies,* John Wheldon makes some penetrating comments on this subject.[16] He believes that modernity in armies should be measured not by comparing their past performances with their present capabilities 'but by comparing the army's degree of sophistication in organization and communication with the best contemporary civil practice.' In particular, he feels that army vehicles compare very badly with civil ones, having evolved too slowly by contrast with developments in the lethal apparatus they carry. 'If fighting ships and aircraft must have mobility far superior to the common norms of the civilian world, why not military land vehicles?' He holds that full integration of air and land activity is a highly significant trend, and he states that 'the first military organization to rationalize this

[13]André Beaufre, 'Battlefields of the 1980s', in *Unless Peace Comes,* p. 20.
[14]Leonard Sullivan Jnr, 'R & D for Vietnam', *Science and Technology* (Oct 1968) p. 38.
[15]E. C. Cornford, 'Technology and the Battlefield', in *The Implications of Military Technology in the 1970s,* Institute for Strategic Studies Adelphi Papers No 46 (London, 1968) p. 52.
[16]John Wheldon, *Machine Age Armies* (London: Abelard-Schuman, 1968), chap. 8.

process, accelerate it, and ruthlessly prune the dead wood from it will place itself in the forefront of military competence.' He would like to see the military cast off what he considers to be an 'obsession with simple destruction', aiming instead at paralyzing resistance through 'swifter reaction and superior mobility'. His conclusions go to the heart of the relationship between societies, their armed forces and technology:

> The modernization . . . of ideas is a task not just for . . . soldiers . . . but for the nation as a whole . . . military concepts are strongly bound to the military social organization, and both . . . are more subject to . . . potentially disastrous collision with new knowledge and . . . artefacts . . . than any other type of human society. . . .

He may be right. Certainly the military susceptibility to change and capacity for innovation receive very little attention from organizational analysts compared with that which they lavish on civil and commercial organizations. In his study of the contribution of science and engineering in the Second World War,[17] Guy Hartcup concludes in a similar vein that technical ingenuity counted for less than did the integration of the military and scientific disciplines.

Whatever the current state of this integration, it is difficult to think of a weapon or aspect of conventional warfare which has not in the last few years been subjected to determined up-dating and improvement. Beginning with espionage, here the specialist aircraft has already been for many purposes superseded by the new spy satellite and, while taking much of the James Bond technology with a pinch of salt, on this front too there are known to have been quite technical advances. In field warfare, Vietnam especially has accelerated the introduction of new conventional weapons and has led to striking increases in the killing power of the old. And killing power naturally remains a chief ingredient of military success. Much more savage anti-personnel bombs and mines have thus come forward and considerable evidence has been gathered about the comparative effectiveness of various types of gun and rifle. At the same time an old lesson has had to be relearned, namely that while the technical frontier moves ever on, not everything it leaves behind becomes obsolete or redundant. To cite an embarrassing example, the best of air launched missiles do not necessarily remove the need for aircraft to be provided with old-fashioned cannon. Too great a commitment to technical advance can easily mean neglect of the more elementary means needed to counter the methods and equipment of less sophisticated forces, e.g. the Israeli's use of the 'obsolete' M–4 Sherman.

It has now been demonstrated unequivocally in Vietnam that engineering development, coupled with operational analysis of battlefield conditions, can steadily raise the kill or casualty-inflicting capacity of a military force, nor has any definite limit to this trend yet revealed itself. Speaking of the gap between conventional and tactical nuclear power, one author points out that 'the gap may never be completely closed, but we already have so-called con-

---

[17]Guy Hartcup, *The Challenge of War* (Newton Abbot: David and Charles, 1970) p. 274.

ventional munitions that are in the same league with nuclear when it comes to killing power'.[18] It might therefore come about that in a standard conventional war between advanced countries battlefield operations could be made prohibitively expensive in terms of material and/or personnel. In the limit, conventional war might even become as 'unthinkable', being almost as devastating as nuclear war, while the upper limit on the destructiveness of conventional war might not be very different from that with which we are already familiar. Continued refinement of equipment and methods might show diminishing returns on the battlefield as the technical demands on the individual, perhaps at low levels in the military hierarchy, began to approach the limits of his abilities. Appalling levels of attrition might even be accepted again as they have so often been in the past. Alternatively, with the battlefield an anachronism, surgical attacks on nerve centers might lead to quite disproportionate success. It is impossible to know and, if one hopes for conventional stalemate, one should still fear conventional attrition. In any case, the argument may never hold for guerrilla wars. . . .

What progress to be looked for in strategic and tactical mobility? The constraints likely on tactical mobility are perhaps the most difficult to foresee. In this category the helicopter (or airmobile) division has claims to being the most striking curiosity. A relatively long time after its introduction an astonishing number of roles have now been discovered for it, as transport, as command post, in reconnaissance, as a weapons platform, and so on. A revelation in Vietnam, General Wheeler has said of them: 'In my judgment, the introduction of the airmobile concepts . . . has put back into the military arsenal a capability which went out with the disappearance of horse cavalry'.[19] In situations similar to those encountered in Vietnam the helicopter can hardly in future be denied an important part, sometimes perhaps even a decisive one. However, the helicopter has an intrinsic vulnerability and against a defense of equal technical competence, provided with specific anti-helicopter weapons, it might well, in at least the most dangerous of its roles, go the way of the horse. Even if that happened, the helicopter would still have to be regarded as having for long exemplified poor appreciation of exploitable potential. Air-portable tanks might conceivably be another example of the same thing.

Other very vulnerable military facilities are airfields and aircraft carriers. The acute problems of defense here have for some time indicated a switch to STOL and VTOL aircraft, each one in the limit capable of sustained independent action. At the same time, the complexity, and therefore cost, of conventional fighters has been forcing a move from special purpose to multi-role aircraft, functions as different as continental air defense and interdiction being demanded of what is basically the same airplane.[20] With so many design compromises having therefore to be made, and made easily, there is a new

---

[18]John S. Tompkins, *The Weapons of World War Three* (London: Robert Hale Ltd, 1967) pp. 112–13.
[19]Ibid. p. 47. General Wheeler was at the time chairman of the U.S. Joint Chiefs of Staff.
[20]See, for instance, Joseph Rees and Arnold Whitaker, 'The Next Generation of Fighter Aircraft', *Science and Technology* (Oct 1968).

high premium on the right choices, a premium measured in terms of development time, cost and value-in-use of the aircraft.

Important strides in strategic mobility seem certain to occur for some time yet. Aircraft larger than the C5A, very high-speed hydrofoil or hovercraft transport ships, and large submarine transports may all one day become realities for the strategic planner. Actions to forestall the outbreak of hostilities have been possible several times since 1945, and enhanced strategic mobility may in the future make this politically desirable option more frequently available.

Given the confusion, richness of technical choice likely to obtain indefinitely across the whole military field, it must be assumed that the scientific analysis of decision-making will expand from its already notable status. In the formulation[21] of the then American assistant secretary for defense, Alain Enthoven, one has: operational analysis for the evaluation of military effectiveness in specific situations; weapons systems analysis for the examination of alternative feasible weapons systems in a range of uncertain applications; force requirement studies to probe the variety of force postures; and strategic studies for the major policy problems involving a military, political, technical and economic mix. Scientists—natural and social—are essential to such studies, but it would be a mistake to assume either that the quality of work in this field is always high, or that analyses are free of aberration or bias. For a long time to come those with real decisions to make will need to examine cautiously the premises, the conduct and the conclusions of any studies of the foregoing type. Such studies are naturally ideal ground for the computer. This can increase the reliability of the results, but can also make sound criticism more difficult for those who lack time, facilities or competence to check the analytical procedures. In the military field as in the civil, we must expect a constant struggle to ensure that the computer remains firmly the servant of its users.

A summary of the state of the art of conventional warfare must note several things. First, the postwar neglect of this art, a neglect noticeable in the United States because of trust in the nuclear deterrent, has now been more than rectified. The art is currently in a state of uncertain flux and the outcome of conventional wars in future will be far less predictable as a result. Thirdly, since modern civilization has become dependent upon modern technology, selective conventional attacks on communication systems, power, supplies and transport facilities could go far towards paralyzing societies—militarily as effective as the crippling use of nuclear weapons. Finally, it is unwise to dismiss conventional wars as somehow safe: even partial conventional defeat may drive a non-nuclear country to develop nuclear arms, and certainly such a defeat gives a nuclear country a pressing temptation to threaten their use.

Turning next to exotic warfare, there are possibilities here, geological and meteorological warfare for instance, discussed by others but which seem too

---

[21]2nd Report from the Select Committee on Science and Technology, Session 1968–9, *Defence Research,* HC 213, Appendix 43.

remote to be worth serious consideration. In such cases the human race does not as yet possess much of the basic science involved and it may never do so. In the meantime, each natural disaster, an earthquake say, brings forth from commentators the natural hope that science will make possible warning and better still, some remedy. However, a remedy at least could only be rendered possible by the kind of understanding and capability which might in other circumstances be used to cause a similar disaster. This deliberately far-fetched example makes that point very well, but it applies no less with more familiar scientific discoveries.

There are more detailed exotic concepts too, laser and acoustical weapons and plastic armor for instance, of which, at this stage, one can again do little more than take note. Under the same 'exotic' heading, there are, however, two new theaters of war which may be about to open up under the challenge of technology, namely the deep sea and seabed and near and planetary space.

True submarine warfare had to await the development of nuclear engines. A naval craft which operated by surface-effect rather than displacement, in consequence relatively small and very fast, would by itself quickly revolutionize surface naval strategy.[22] This apart, there are already strong reasons, both economic and military, for supposing that the conquest of the deep sea is about to begin in earnest, so that the submarine and a deep-ranging counterpart may pose much graver tactical and strategic problems than ever before. In the ocean depths electro-magnetic radiation cannot be used for surveillance and area cover must give way to monitored barrier lines. Such lines will not be cheap to establish or maintain, and away from friendly coasts, at depths and in uncomfortable conditions, might not be possible at all. A long battle between detection measures and evasion counter-measures may lie ahead: at the outset at least, the odds distinctly favor the latter.[23]

In spite of the remarkable steps which have been made in space exploration it is hard to imagine that conflict is about to be exported to near-earth space, still less to interplanetary space. As weapons platforms, the earth and seas are likely to retain distinct advantages for some time to come, and satellites are fundamentally vulnerable craft. On the other hand, satellites have a tremendous value for surveillance/communication, etc. and this could lead by gradual stages to their defensive armament and then to experiments with them as strategic weapons platforms. It seems that it is absence of military need rather than technology which is preventing this. With existing and immediately projected space propulsion systems, and their support hardware, extended contests in interplanetary space are not a real contingency.

Regardless of whether these more *outré* speculations ever materialize, it is apparent that there has been a permanent change in the relationship between the military and the scientists/engineers. In the words of Marshal Malinovsky: 'Tumultuous scientific-technical progress has evoked radical changes in the

---

[22]See, for instance, William A. Nierenberg, 'Toward a Future Navy', *Science and Technology* (Oct 1968).
[23]John P. Craven, 'Ocean Technology and Submarine Warfare', in Adelphi Papers no. 46.

development of military technology. [Soldiers are now confronted] with the task of deep study of technology, to know how to exploit and adapt it.'[24]

There would have been grounds for predicting that the military technology of the last thirty years and the chronic international perils of that period together would have led to a widely mobilized citizenry, though 'the technological military acuteness of every level of the population' could never have been what Major-General Pokrovsky claimed it was for the Soviet Union in 1959,[25] namely 'the undeniable foundation of our national defense and of our preparation against any unexpected events'! Instead, the political natures of the Western democracies now leave no doubt but that they will rely permanently on professional forces. The standards demanded of these forces, and of all others undertaking to confront a technically advanced and determined foe, are already high and show every sign of rising further. They can be simply stated, but that is the only simple thing about them:

A widely disseminated capability to improvise and reach accurate decisions will call for the highest possible educational level throughout; a willingness to take and act upon those decisions will call for a deep commitment to national goals.

Military units will expect to enjoy maximum support from the agencies of psychological and political warfare.

They will possibly need to be equipped and trained for widely different sorts of warfare but, in spite of a nurtured competence to operate fast and flexibly, they will typically meet situations where the soundest tactics may be dangerously uncertain.

The exact configuration of their equipment will be the result of growing friction between the 'pull' of strategy and tactics and the 'push' of technical feasibility, and they will seek to maintain the closest contacts between military planning staff and defense scientists and engineers.

The two Superpowers are now on a relative technological plateau—relative only to the astonishing changes of the last century. Already in the mid-1960s, Erickson, in noting many signs that the military-technical revolution had slowed at the strategic level, pointed out also that it might actually be speeding up in the area of limited warfare.[26] It remains a possibility that a new scientific discovery could lead to a steep change in military thinking, similar in magnitude to that prompted by fission weapons, but the possibility is a remote one. But if the risks of either side producing a surprise ace are very low, the steady development of existing systems is a formidable challenge to both. They must choose ever more wisely from alternatives made mutually exclusive on cost grounds. They must both fear wrong choice. Already both have found their freedom of action restricted by earlier choices between

---

[24]Quoted in Raymond L. Garthoff, *Soviet Military Policy* (London: Faber and Faber, 1966) p. 106.

[25]Major-Gen G. I. Pokrovsky, *Science and Technology in Contemporary War* (London: Stevens and Sons Ltd, 1959) p. 166.

[26]John Erickson (ed.) *The Military-Technical Revolution* (London: Pall Mall Press, 1966) p. 14.

technical options; and in spite of cost benefit analysis, such situations will recur. There are too many technical avenues for even the Superpowers to be able to explore them all. As long as both remain on the technological plateau, or, substituting metaphors, in the shadow of the deterrent, the outcome is more likely to be frustrating than critical. At the same time, the pressures for cooperative R and D between lesser powers will harden, and yet in spite of this they may commonly find themselves in situations for which they are not prepared technically.

But if the Superpowers are capable of ensuring that over-all strategic balance between them remains a dominant feature of the international environment, what happens beneath it? In many areas of the world the local situation resembles the world at large before the advent of nuclear weapons. Since the countries concerned tend to be selectively armed with equipment developed by the major powers, the wars that break out between them must in part resemble the Second World War, being more or less sophisticated depending upon local availability of the most modern conventional weapons, together with the ability to use them effectively. It is a first priority that such local wars be disconnected from the Superpower balance, and a second priority that such local conflicts should not be allowed to bring about the development, deployment and use of A, B and C weapons. In this context one must describe as encouraging the apparent recognition by each Superpower that it cannot with safety act successfully in the back yard of the other. At the same time, it is vital to remember how much of the world falls in the back yard of neither.

It is usually said that the quality of man's politics is much lower than that of his science. As long as war is a characteristic of international behavior, then the application to it of science and engineering seems as politically inevitable as it is technically logical. Thus the process of procuring military systems came to be the most important single pressure for technological development.[27] Our technology, and to a lesser extent our science, are so far predicated upon military demands that were these suddenly removed, we should undoubtedly find that the differentials between and rate of progress within the various technologies altered rapidly from familiar norms. The more our technology mirrors our military wants, the less it mirrors our economic ones. While hard to quantify, it already seems likely that in terms of economic growth, we lose more indirectly because we are not developing the right technologies fast enough than we lose through diverting production resources to military ends. The burden is heavier still because where there are considerations of national security the only tolerable risk is that of being caught with excess capacity.[28] The dove-tailing of military requirements, industrial interests and

---

[27]In the USA, 80 per cent of Federal R & D is concerned with the external challenge—OECD, *Reviews of National Science Policy: United States,* 1968, p. 36. It has often been acknowledged in the Soviet Union that it is only in the 'priority' sectors, essentially those closely connected with defense, that planning has really worked—OECD, *Science Policy in the USSR,* 1969, p. 435.
[28]Lt-Gen. A.W. Betts, then head of the U.S. Army R & D, interviewed in *Science and Technology* (Oct 1968) p. 95. See also in the same number John S. Foster Jnr, the Director of Defense Research and Engineering in the Pentagon, 'The Leading Edge of National Security', p. 18.

technological innovation has led to a serious social concern with 'the scientific-technological elite' and what Eisenhower described in the United States context as 'the military-industrial complex'.

In any event, military systems acquisition is not a normal market activity. The severe uncertainties of both demand and supply associated with military work put a very heavy strain on those R and D programs which increasingly call for ambitious state-of-the-art advances in situations of high military urgency.[29] One corollary of this is that, according to SIPRI, in countries such as Britain, the United States and France, the research input-output ratio is 'at least twelve times greater in the military field than in the civil'.[30] Arms races between advanced powers can now be said to consist of calculated responses to technical challenges that are more qualitative than quantitative. This happens in several ways. First, countries at similar levels in an area of technology can expect to make a particular advance in that technology at about the same time as each other. Then, following the so-called Action-Reaction Phenomenon, two such countries aiming at full security must not only counter the *actual* moves of the other, but because of the long time scale of military R and D, offset any other possible move which the other could make from its initial technical position. Further, so-called Worst Case Analysis requires that each country makes the most pessimistic assessment of its own research, development, deployment and operational efforts and the most pessimistic assumptions about those of its potential adversaries.

Still other complications can occur. For instance, R and D and deployment directed towards strictly defensive ends can, in certain circumstances, increase the actual probability of war. It is easy to see why the momentum and intrinsic instabilities of military technological innovation are seen as a threat to the preservation of the nuclear equation, a danger equal to and perhaps less controllable than premeditated, preemptive or accidental war.[31]

The activity of R and D is now carried on by armies of professionals. Genius is welcome but by no means essential. This, incidentally, diminishes one of the hopes sometimes expressed for disarmament, namely that the scientific community could be self-policing. The extent and density of research is now too vast for monitoring except at the highest levels where administrators need scarcely be aware of what appear to be essentially routine, though in fact extremely sophisticated, development programs. In any case, the scientific community is divided. One observer, confessing himself 'quite baffled by the mentality' of those who do biological warfare research, has reflected: 'How far this is a betrayal and perversion of the aims of science and medicine, probably only scientists and doctors would properly understand.'[32] Another

[29]Merton J. Peck and F. M. Scherer, *The Weapons Acquisition Process: An Economic Analysis* (Cambridge, Mass: Harvard Business School Division of Research, 1962), especially the concluding chapter.

[30]SIPRI Yearbook, p. 94.

[31]See, for instance, Alastair Buchan, *War in Modern Society* (London: Collins, 1966) pp. 154–75.

[32]John Cookson and Judith Nottingham, *A Survey of Chemical and Biological Warfare* (London: Sheed and Ward, 1969) p. 282.

admits disappointment when told by a laboratory, company or university that they did not feel it appropriate for them to participate in R and D for the Vietnam War. He added: 'I also find it personally embarrassing to find this nonconstructive attitude within the engineering and scientific community. . . .'[33] Both are members of the scientific/engineering community, broadly defined. The effort of some members of the community to persuade colleagues of responsibility for the consequences of their work, however commendable, encounters a very harsh political reality. It is, of course, possible still that the net effect of the application of science to warfare will in the long term be beneficial to the human race. It is usually conceded that nuclear weapons may have been largely responsible for the fact that there has been no major world war in the last quarter century. It must be hoped that nuclear war will be permanently eschewed, even though, as noted above, conventional warfare might one day be made to approach nuclear warfare in its lethality and therefore its 'unsuitability'. On the other hand, as McNamara observed, we do sometimes overlook the fact that every future age of man will be a nuclear one.[34] It follows that as long as leaders judge that there are certain international political problems best given over to military solution, then every day brings greater risks. As Konrad Lorenz has said:

> An unprejudiced observer from another planet, looking upon man as he is today, in his hand the atom bomb, the product of his intelligence, in his heart the aggression drive inherited from his anthropological ancestors, which this same intelligence cannot control, would not prophesy long life for the species.

It seems that we must wait to see whether in the case of our species the ethical neutrality of science is in the event a truly genuine one.

---

[33]L. Sullivan, *Science and Technology,* p. 32.
[34]Robert S. McNamara, *The Essence of Security* (London: Hodder and Stoughton Ltd, 1968) · p. 51.

13

Urbanization

The late Catherine Bauer Wurster saw four possibilities for future cities. Although her article takes a general approach, she lays out what appears to be the choices before us, ultimately casting her lot with "a constellation of relatively diversified and integrated cities." In thinking about any of the possibilities, she suggests we cannot forget reality. Concern about the quality of life in our cities and the dangers of pollution must be linked to a recognition of the limits of industrial growth. For example, the rapid exhaustion of fossil fuels seemingly requires future urban complexes to organize transportation in a way that places little emphasis on the automobile or highway.

From Form and Structure of the Future Urban Complex
—*Catherine Bauer Wurster*

TRENDS, COUNTERTRENDS, AND THE POTENTIAL FOR CHANGE

Planning, in Perloff's and Wingo's words, must be related to "the things that matter: the major social movements." I have tried to identify some of "the things that matter" which have a direct influence on urban form and structure because they are the forces behind certain key trends and variables. Two dimensions have been selected: from extreme dispersion (low density and scatteration) to extreme concentration (high density, contiguity, and strong centering); and from large-scale integration (a single metropolitan system with specialized parts) to small-scale subintegration (diversified communities within the region with relatively balanced facilities for most ordinary functions). In these terms, what are the significant current trends and the forces behind them? What are the resulting problems and conflicts which could change the present picture?

Centrifugal forces: the selective push for private space. The dominant trend toward low densities and scatteration in outlying development reflects the demand for private space for certain functions: large areas to permit greater freedom on the site for industrial production and building operations, for shops and schools, and above all for middle- and upper-class family life. Closely related to the latter is the desire for natural amenity at home in private gardens and attractive vistas (and also increasingly in vacation cabins which produce a much wider ring of scattered development). Land speculation enhances the trend but is not the prime cause. In addition to these outward pulls, there is also the push to escape from city conditions—obsolete housing or inadequate schools, racial and cultural diversity, conflict, discomfort, high taxes, and helplessness—into small, safe, homogeneous, self-run communities with middle-class standards and status.

These varied "private" purposes which are related to the qualities of a particular site or small neighborhood area have been brought within reach by the achievement of another kind of private value, *automobility,* which permits individual freedom of circulation in a piece of personal property. Because private autos perform badly in the traditional type of multipurpose urban center, automobility has also contributed to the dispersal of business, cultural, and service facilities. Technology is serving these ends in other ways too: new equipment makes both houses and factories more self-sufficient; large-scale building operations provide most of their own utilities for standardized one-price homes; and rising opportunities for long-distance communications—mail, phone, radio, TV, and travel—make the individual or firm less dependent on immediate physical contacts within the metropolitan area.

These choices are open today, however, only to limited groups and functions: relatively foot-loose industries and businesses; the services that follow resident populations; families able to acquire suburban homes despite high prices, restrictive zoning practices, race discrimination, and rising taxes.

Of course, there is a great deal of medium- and high-density development, old and new. But dispersal has been the dominant trend for several decades, reflecting the conscious choice of multitudes of consumers and entrepreneurs. It has produced unanticipated problems and generated some counterforces, but unless these actually weaken the basic drives for private space they will probably not have much effect. In these terms, is the push for dispersal likely to increase or decline in the future?

The desired life-style of most American families with children still seems to call for the private home with a yard. High marriage and birth rates, and upward mobility with rising incomes and education, will only increase this demand, as will any abatement in race discrimination, or policies to provide cheaper housing in outlying areas.

There are, however, some qualifying factors in the trend toward endless suburban sprawl. Rising land prices and the demand for a wider range of dwelling types to suit varied household types and tastes are producing a greater admixture of multifamily rental units in some localities. Large-scale operations tend to result in patches of contiguous development, sometimes at "city" scale and including rental housing, community facilities, and industry. Public awareness of the costs of scatteration is likewise mounting, due to high taxes for inadequate services on the one hand, and the rising demand to preserve public open space and natural amenity within metropolitan areas, on the other. But measures to insure more compact development, or open space reservation, are not yet generally effective.

The force of purely "escape" motivations can become either stronger or weaker, depending largely on the increase or decline of race and class prejudice for whatever reasons, and the degree to which older cities become more or less ghettoized, or suburbia more mixed.

Accessibility to work is also an ambivalent factor. The business and professional people who continue to work in central cities have been willing to pay a high price for their home environment, in transportation time, trouble, and expense. But as their journey to work increases, or requires both a private car and one or more public conveyances, other solutions may be sought. If the offices move out to accommodate them, this can mean more dispersal. But if they settle for higher density housing, whether in the city or near a mass transit stop, it would have the opposite effect. Similarly, the factories and services which depend on relatively low-paid labor cannot move very far away from the old central districts, so long as the supply of cheap housing is predominantly located there. But if the suburban housing market were broadened, these jobs might become more dispersed.

The number of second homes for leisure-time use will probably increase enormously. This will broaden the extent of scatteration throughout a vast region, but at the same time it might conceivably mean greater acceptance of compact development, with greater convenience to work and other urban facilities, for weekday use.

In any case, centrifugal forces and private values, however dominant in new development, are still countered by some opposing influences, actual or potential.

Centripetal forces: by choice and by compulsion. The revival of sky-scraper office development in many downtown districts reflects the continued demand among certain types of business enterprise for face-to-face contacts and adjacent services within "walking precincts," or merely for the prestige value of a particular location. This is clearly a conscious choice, despite the increased ease of long-distance communication and the increased burden of commuting; and it is therefore a centralizing factor which is likely to endure in some form. However, routine or mechanical office operations are beginning to move out, along with industry and consumer services. Over-all employment is unlikely to increase in most central cities, and business districts may tend to become specialized enclaves, whether they stay downtown or move outside.

In most cities, the old consumer uses of the center for shopping, amusement, and cultural pursuits have either remained static or declined, despite metropolitan growth. Where entertainment does thrive, it seems to owe its existence primarily to "visiting firemen," business travelers, vacationers, and conventiongoers rather than the local suburbanites who, as a matter of fact, may be more likely to patronize a central theatre or restaurant when visiting in some other city.

In general the choice of central locations for business and leisure use still appears to be strongest in cities with traditionally strong centers, like New York and San Francisco, and weakest in cities which have always been more or less dispersed, such as Detroit and Los Angeles.

The other major use of central cities is both more universal and much more involuntary: lower-income and minority households are forced to concentrate there, by and large, because old districts provide the only major source of cheap or unrestricted housing—whether in obsolete structures or new subsidized projects, and regardless of locational trends in their particular job opportunities. If the rate of upward mobility increases, or if the flow of disadvantaged in-migrants finally begins to dry up, or if the suburban housing market is expanded, this part of the picture might change quite rapidly. The degree to which they would choose suburban living, if they could, is sometimes questioned. The crowded slum enclave offers a semblance of security to the recent arrival and the disadvantaged, as Leonard Duhl points out elsewhere in this volume, and as redevelopers have belatedly discovered. But all our urban history suggests that their aspirations are probably not very different from those of the millions who have moved upward and outward before them.

Some middle- and upper-income white people have stayed in the cities by choice, of course, but increasingly these have been single workers, adult households, Bohemians, and—if the attractions are great enough—wealthy families who put their children in private schools and have second homes in the country.

Those who voluntarily select a tight city environment for homes or business have something in common. They all value private space and the freedom of automobility far less than the attractions of convenience to work, the opportunity for specialized contacts and facilities within a small area, the stimulation of diversity, or the sense of being part of a cosmopolitan community in direct touch with world affairs. These are traditional urban values, and it is quite possible that more would choose them if they could be had without a heavy sacrifice in private living conditions. Yet, the half-worlds of City-and-Suburb rarely offer such a choice.

This is the background situation, but there is a rising push to "save" the central cities which is taking two positive forms: urban renewal programs with federal aid, and efforts to create or improve mass transit systems for commuting. These movements stem primarily from the increasingly desperate desire of economic and political interests in the central cities to protect property values and the tax base, with a variable intermingling of other forces, such as the need to provide better housing for slum-dwellers and the new wave of intellectual concern for urban historical and cultural values, which also tends to be anti-suburbia and anti-automobile.

Redevelopment brings new private and public structures of various types—office buildings and apartments, civic and cultural facilities—usually at increased densities and all subsidized to varying degrees. Expensive apartments predominate, but there are also middle-income ventures and low-rent public housing projects. In addition (often in opposition) conservationist programs are active here and there.

Central city traffic conditions have been worsened by the tremendous expenditures in freeway construction since the war, and it is now widely recognized that large-scale concentration is incompatible with universal dependence on private automobility. Despite the declining use of public transportation, the improvement or creation of metropolitan transit systems is a lively issue with several entirely new schemes either built, approved, or under discussion.

To the extent that these movements fulfill their present aims they will tend to maintain or promote concentration, at least for certain types of residence, work, and leisure-time activity. But these programs are very expensive, in terms of both financial subsidy and such disruptive social costs as forcible dislocation, and the degree to which they can actually offset the predominant trend toward dispersal depends on many imponderables. Will the restrictions of the housing market continue to force most low-income and minority households to live in the old cities, whether in successive blighted areas or in heavily subsidized public housing projects? Will the Negroes use their rising political power for greater integration throughout the metropolitan area or for separatist strength within the central cities? To what extent will middle-class white families and business enterprise favor convenience and city attractions if it means political domination by lower-income and minority voters? Will mass transit mainly facilitate more two-way commuting, instead of more jobs in the city?

The movement to save old cities has been narrowly focused on central problems thus far, with little concern for the pattern of outlying development or the desirable form and structure of the region as a whole. This may change. It is already recognized that transportation is a region-wide problem in its political as well as in its functional aspects. Regional population distribution is likely to become a mounting issue, in terms of housing choice, suburban race and class discrimination, the increasing disparity between residence and job opportunities, and, above all, the tendency of central cities to become ghettoized with all the related implications for tax-base problems and renewal hopes.

These issues are just beginning to be posed, however. Effective measures to deal with the shape and structure of regional development have not yet been devised, and no public image of the appropriate goals has developed. Housing, land use, transportation and renewal policies could be used not only to promote either dispersion or concentration, but also to encourage a wider range of residential choice in both outlying and central areas. This leads into the whole question of "balance" and the level of functional and political integration, which is the second dimension I wish to discuss.

Toward region-wide specialization: a single super-city? The widespread dispersal of certain functions, while others remain highly concentrated, generates a pattern which poses some basic structural issues. In a way it is still the classic form of the modern city, with business in the center, industry on the fringe, and the outward neighborhood succession from poor to rich, only greatly expanded in all its dimensions and administered by hundreds of independent local governments. At the moderate scale of a single municipality, the urban community had problems of slums and services, but the pattern itself posed no great difficulties. For the metropolitan complex, however, communications and integration are critical issues which raise questions about social, economic, and political structure.

Above the neighborhood level with its domestic functions, is the metropolis necessarily a single organic system with highly differentiated parts? Is it essentially one labor and job market, one housing market, one set of leisure-time and service facilities? Is it made up of so many specialized but interdependent activity orbits of varying scale that they can only be integrated at the metropolitan level? If this is true, then the basic problems are likely to be intercommunications and unified regional government.

Or can it be too big to operate sensibly or efficiently as a single system? Could the ordinary activities of the vast majority of people be better cared for within subregional sectors or smaller diversified communities? If so, then basic changes in housing and land use policy are required within a structure of stronger local governments co-operating through some kind of regional federation. There are influences in both directions, and the picture presented here is inevitably over-simplified, but the strongest current trends seem to lean toward specialized sectors and communities rather than subregional integration, with central cities and outlying areas serving quite different but highly interdependent functions. Consider the distribution of resident population, jobs, and leisure-time facilities with some of the resulting disparities.

The social divisions among residents of old cities and newer suburbs are increasingly sharp, by income level, by age group, and, above all, by race. These divisions are largely created by the housing pattern, and strengthened by the limitations of the current housing market, which by and large serves only upper and upper-middle income white families in areas of recent growth. If present trends continue, low-income and minority households will soon predominate in many central cities.

Meanwhile, the locational specialization of employment and business enterprise is following a different pattern, with most new industrial and service jobs outside the cities, and certain types of office and professional work still downtown. As for outdoor recreation, any major open spaces that may yet be saved are likely to be out beyond the fringe, near people who already have private land but far away from the families who live in crowded slums or high-rise projects and who frequently do not have automobiles. For urban leisure-time activities, the old multipurpose centers provide cheap attractions for the poor, and also, to varying degrees, Bohemia for the beatniks and intellectuals, and very expensive entertainment for the rich and the visiting firemen. Equivalent middle-class facilities are likely to be scattered around outside or in specialized suburban "centers" for shopping, culture, or amusement (Disneyland, for example).

This pattern poses obvious problems of extended cross-commuting, of limited housing choice, of accessibility to an adequate choice of leisure-time facilities, and of critical tax-base discrepancies. It is a serious threat to the future of current renewal efforts. These problems may be the inevitable price of the increasing specialization which produced great urban agglomerations in the first place, and their solution may require a strong metropolitan government to insure over-all productive efficiency, equity, and effectiveness of intercommunication. The inherent trends, however, confront us with a paradox: the sharpening class and race divisions along with the tax-base disparities lead to deepening political conflict between central cities and suburbia which makes metropolitan unification ever more difficult, if not impossible, unless it is imposed by direct state or federal intervention.

The potential for subregional integration. The American metropolis has in certain ways been moving toward a vast unitary "city"-type structure with highly specialized interdependent parts, and it cannot be claimed that there is any conscious countermovement to encourage a greater degree of functional balance and self-containment within subregional sectors. Proposals for "satellite communities" keep coming up in metropolitan plans, however, doubtless stimulated by the evidence from Britain and elsewhere that relatively independent new towns can be developed successfully, while renewal programs reflect efforts to create in central areas a better balanced population related to downtown employment opportunities. But the relation of the functional structure of metropolitan areas to the development pattern has received inadequate research attention; we have little practical understanding of how it works now or how its workings might be improved. Obviously it is an overlay of numerous interlocking activity patterns, large and small, including many that extend far beyond the region, and many that are normally circumscribed within a neighborhood. But we do not really know to what degree and for what specific purposes the entire region is necessarily a single system. In question particularly are certain functions which used to be integrated at the city-wide level, such as the special consumer demands which brought people to central districts, and above all the trip between home and work. It is frequently assumed that these activities, with their implied range of choices, can only be encompassed to any significant degree today at the metropolitan-wide scale. But there are trends and pressures which tend to favor some form of subregional integration.

Human activity systems range all the way from the bedroom-bathroom trek to the astronaut's orbit around the moon. Within the metropolitan complex, a great many functions have catchment areas which are normally quite limited: schools, playgrounds, meeting-halls, churches, ordinary shops, services and amusements, even junior colleges, general hospitals, super shopping centers, and little theatres.

The pattern varies tremendously with personal means and tastes. Some people go to any lengths to visit a race track, a symphony concert, an exotic restaurant, or a wilderness park, which others would ignore if they were next door. In between, a growing number of people would enjoy such specialties if they were fairly accessible. By the same token, many of the special "goods" can and should be more numerous and more accessible—in theory at least—because it would take a smaller over-all population to provide the selective demand. Mumford's principle of the cultural "grid," based on the British Museum's decentralized library service, is important for some of the highly refined but mobile resources. And if a tight multipurpose center has the stimulating and universal advantages claimed for it by central city saviors, then a large metropolitan region should probably have several such centers to serve the potential demand.

The critical questions seem to stem from the relations between the spatial systems of residence and employment. We have been acquiring some information about commuting patterns, and there will be more from the 1960 Census, but intensive analysis is also needed: case histories for a sampling of different occupations in different areas, including employment changes, residential changes, and how both jobs and homes were found. From preliminary Census data on commuting patterns as well as from more intensive recent studies it appears that the number of employed people who somehow manage to live and work in the same subregional sector may be surprisingly high, considering the limitations of choice in the housing market. Both home-moves and job-moves within a metropolitan area appear to be frequently influenced by a desire to reduce the journey-to-work, even at the cost of breaking family ties or living in a less desirable home on the one hand, or subordinating economic opportunity to home values on the other. People who make such choices do not see or use the whole region as a single urban community: many of its opportunities might as well be in another area entirely. The lack of convenient jobs may therefore promote residential mobility, neighborhood instability and long-distance commuting, while the restrictions on housing choice can tend to limit economic opportunity, particularly for low-income and minority households. Of course, accessibility is more important than mapped distances, and my rather conservative judgments must be balanced against Webber's revolutionary concepts of metropolitan communications potentials . . . But it seems fairly clear that technology has not yet overcome the friction of space for the metropolitan commuter.

Although the residential pattern is greatly influenced by public actions, these broad locational issues have not yet been seriously posed in American planning or policy. The suburban market for new housing is limited more than ever to upper-income white families, while federal aids for low-cost housing are confined to city renewal and rehousing programs. Most European countries, however, have long assumed that new housing development must accommodate a more or less cross-section population. In the United States strong pressures are building up against suburban racial barriers and for a wider range of housing choice for middle- and lower-income families of all races and household types. The central cities may come to support these pressures, although their political motivations will be mixed. But both state and federal governments will be increasingly involved in the rising metropolitan issues of class and race, of city and suburbs, of tax inequities, transportation costs, and general inefficiency.

Present trends might shift, therefore, toward a somewhat wider balance of population in both outlying areas and the central city, posing the possibility of greater functional integration below the metropolitan level. Strong resistance from existing suburban communities will affect the resulting pattern, however. Will there be a scattering of additional types of one-class enclave, for middle-class Negroes, for the aged, for cheaper homes? Can the present suburban communities, many of which already have industries, be induced to become socially diversified? Will entirely new cities be developed on the remote fringe where a wide range of housing and job choices may be particularly desirable? Can a reasonably healthy social balance be maintained in the central cities?

ALTERNATIVE DIRECTIONS FOR FORM AND STRUCTURE: SOME ROUGH COMPARISONS

The wide range of hypothetical possibility seems to come down to four reasonably practicable alternatives. The dominance of one or the other in a particular situation would depend on the dominant public, private, and individual purposes behind the environment-shaping decisions, the acceptability of the means required to achieve certain purposes, and differing local conditions which might enhance or impede the feasibility of moving in certain directions.

Before considering these alternatives and their implications in more concrete terms, let us try to summarize the conceivable public attitudes that would lead in one direction or another—the various common images of the future metropolis that might be influential. At the same time, certain precedents and prototypes which relate to these different sets of attitudes will be suggested, including Utopian images and practical experience.

COMMON IMAGES AND THEIR PROTOTYPES

1. *"There's nothing serious that can't be solved by better transportation and central improvements."* Seen from this viewpoint, quite prevalent among business and political leaders, it seems that some of the experts are making too much fuss. There's nothing abnormal or seriously wrong about the present metropolitan pattern, they feel. A lot of people like suburban living, and it's fine if they can afford it. The others must naturally live in older districts, but they will gradually move outward into better dwellings as we tear down the worst to make way for new apartments and office buildings. If necessary we can build some public housing. Of course, the metropolitan area is essentially a single community, and there should really be some kind of over-all

government and planning, but local vested interests may be too strong. However, the state and federal governments can help to equalize the tax burdens a bit, to save some open space, and above all to solve the transportation problem. As long as we can get around, whether by automobile or mass transit or both, we'll be all right.

Since this simply assumes the projection of present trends which are visible in most American metropolitan areas, no additional illustrations or prototypes are necessary.

2. *"Let people have what they want: space and mobility."* This attitude, very unfashionable in intellectual and downtown business or government circles today, reflects such powerful popular forces, however inarticulate, that it might win out. The rationale behind it might be put into words as follows:

It is stupid and reactionary to put huge public investments into central redevelopment and mass transit. People don't want to live or travel that way any more, and they won't unless they're forced to. Open up plenty of new land and build plenty of homes on it for all kinds and classes. Even if some of it were subsidized it would be a lot cheaper than current redevelopment and public housing projects. And it would offer the slum dwellers a real choice which many of them would be glad to accept, instead of merely forcing them out of their present homes into something no better. More and more jobs will follow the people, and perhaps commuting could get easier. When the old city is thinned out, it will be simpler and cheaper to fix it up for the few things that really need to be there, which people can then reach by car. Most of the old-time city attractions are better outside where they have more space.

These are the forces that shaped Los Angeles and stimulate its fantastic growth despite the smog and other problems. At the Utopian level, the same values are reflected in Frank Lloyd Wright's "Broadacre City," and in Buckminster Fuller's lifelong effort to develop a completely mobile and self-contained house, free of the utility network. In some ways Melvin Webber's theoretical emphasis on the spatial freedom resulting from communications technology leads to a similar viewpoint.

3. *"The Metropolis is a single Great City: pull it together and urbanize it."* This is the fashionable sophisticated view among the new urbanists, including many critical writers, social scientists, modern architects, central renewal promoters, and certain economic interests. The number of conscious adherents is probably quite small, but the intellectuals have often turned out to be the vanguard of much larger movements, and the potential strength of this view should not be discounted. It has various facets which are oversimplified and perhaps exaggerated in this brief interpretation:

Great concentrated cosmopolitan cities, with their close contacts and stimulating diversity, have always been the source of civilization. The metropolitan community is still essentially a city, no matter how many people there are in it, but it is being disintegrated by the boring sprawl and stupid escapism of suburbia and the automobile. City and country are two entirely different things, while the suburban hybrid has the virtues of neither one nor the other and is

rapidly destroying both. We should put a stop to all scattered fringe development, fill in suburbia with apartment houses, greatly densify and diversify
the old center (although some would like to save its historic flavor), develop
the best possible mass transit system, forbid private cars in cities wherever
possible, and in general promote an exciting and civilized life. Week-ends,
if we want a change, we can go to real country or the wilderness. Nearby
open spaces for everyday recreational use can also be saved, if we stop suburban scatteration in time.

Utopias related to this view range from the technocratic models of Le
Corbusier and the Bauhaus leaders to the nostalgic humanism of Jane Jacobs.
It is also reflected in official planning practices, inevitably somewhat modified,
in many central city renewal programs (with no suburban jurisdiction however),
and in metropolitan planning for Philadelphia, Copenhagen, and (mixed with
the fourth alternative) Stockholm.

4. *"The behemoth is too big to be a single city: guide growth, at least, into
relatively self-contained communities."* This is an old reform movement which
has had many followers and widespread international influence in various
guises. Rather scorned by the current *avant-garde,* it is quite as much an
urbanist, anti-sprawl philosophy as it is anti-Big-City, and still has considerable appeal to a large and varied group of people, roughly in the following
terms:

Instead of scattering houses, factories, shops, offices and services all over
the landscape, we should pull them together into compact cities, with adjacent open space saved for recreation, agriculture and general amenity. There
would be disagreement as to ideal city size, but suitable housing for a cross-
section population should be provided, with more emphasis on row houses
and garden apartments. A variety of employment opportunities should be
encouraged, as well as a bona fide urban center. The cities would be readily
accessible to each other and to the central city; indeed, such a pattern would
favor a mass transit system if it is needed. The central city would normally
provide certain region-wide services, and its population should also become
better balanced. Some kind of regional federation and effective regional planning would be necessary. But local government would in many ways be
strengthened, and democratic citizenship made more meaningful. A balanced
choice of city and nature, privacy and opportunity, would be available to
everyone.

These principles were originally stimulated by the Garden City movement,
which led directly to the postwar British program of New Towns and expanded
old towns. But they also have much broader manifestations: the current reorganization of Greater London into moderate-sized districts with considerable
powers of self-government; Israel with its carefully developed state-wide
system of cities and towns; the great metropolitan circle of old and new cities
in Holland with the center reserved for agriculture and recreation; Stockholm's
arc of satellites within the city limits; and various planning efforts in the
United States, including the Year 2000 scheme for the National Capital
Region and some California proposals.

How would these variant directions tend to work out? Would they fulfill the claims made by their proponents? What local conditions would favor one or the other? Following are some brief personal judgments:

1. Present trends projected. The wider dispersal of certain special classes and functions into outlying areas, with greater concentration of others in central districts, would probably tend to magnify the present problems of accessibility, inadequate choice, social and political schisms, and rising costs, particularly for transportation and housing. This might therefore be an unstable pattern, likely to push eventually toward one of the other alternatives, and there would in any case be an increasing degree of intervention by state and federal governments. The ultimate direction taken in a particular locality would depend in part on present limitations and opportunities in the area, in part on locally determined goals and actions, and in part on federal and state inducements.

2. Toward general dispersion. The underlying popular forces which favor low-density scattered development, particularly the desire for private space and automobility, are still very strong. If they become increasingly dominant, more housing for lower-income and minority households will be made available in outlying areas, with federal and state assistance in new forms. This will hasten the decentralization of industry and even the most specialized consumer services. Some office functions may try to remain downtown where they are now highly centralized, and it would be easier to provide acceptable housing for middle-income and upper-income families in the old centers as they are thinned out and become less dominated by lower-class population. But the expanse of the region would be so enormous in the larger metropolitan areas that even the region-wide functions might tend to be scattered around, in some cases in close but highly specialized groups.

There could be a tendency for homes and work opportunities to be somewhat closer than they would be if present trends were projected. But subregional integration in any clear-cut form is highly unlikely. Instead there would be a complex chain-like system of overlapping catchment areas for daily activities, extending outward indefinitely, as is already more or less visible in southern California. Residential development would probably continue to take the form of socially specialized enclaves, and class and race conflicts would make the creation of large suburban cities even more difficult than it is today. Service costs would be high, due to scatteration. Because there would be no strong reason for new development to be close to existing development, public open spaces and agriculture could be preserved, but this would call for direct state action. Indeed, all the unified powers required to maintain service and communications networks, and equalize tax burdens, would probably have to be exercised by state and federal agencies, either directly or through the creation of a regional government by their initiative.

Some will argue, with Webber, that increasing accessibility plus aspatial communication overcomes distance, with the result that people living at exurban densities can participate effectively in numerous realms, including a strong local community, and enjoy urban values along with their private space and mobility. This is a real issue, worthy of the most intensive study, but I am yet to be convinced. In my perhaps conservative and rather anti-technocratic view, the argument holds up for most of the personally selective and specialized realms of communication and interaction, and of course for one-way mass communication by TV and such, but not for the kind of community which provides contacts and responsibilities that cut across special interests creating common ground and stimulating mutual adjustment and integration. And I suspect that specialization, without an effective framework for integration, may be the basic curse and threat of our times, whether at the local, national, or international level. In our social, civic, and political life we have not learned how to apply the real lesson of the scientific and industrial revolution: the cross-communication and interdependence that make specialization effective in the common interest.

This pattern is hardly possible in regions with highly concentrated populations where metropolitan areas are already beginning to overlap, such as the central section of the Atlantic Coast. To accommodate future growth they will be forced to choose one of the other alternatives. To the extent that these values have universal force, however, the rate of westward migration is likely to be stimulated. On the other hand, the people who have moved to the West are already somewhat self-selected to favor a dispersed pattern of living.

3. Toward a concentrated super-city. This is probably the least likely alternative, except under very special conditions. But if we are at the start of a general swing toward a Manhattan life-style, with supporting policies at all levels of government, programs for high-density redevelopment in central cities will be greatly accelerated for all income groups and for a variety of functions. State and federal action would prevent further sprawl in outlying areas, and a powerful metropolitan government would fill in the scattered spaces between present suburbs (often with industrial development) and rezone them for multiple dwellings. The most advanced technology would be applied to mass transit and high-rise structures, perhaps with coordinated three-dimensional circulation in central districts. Private automobiles would be banned wherever possible, and pedestrian enclaves encouraged.

This pattern would tend, I think, toward a high degree of functional and social specialization in its various sectors. Structures and subareas would have to be carefully designed to fit particular activities, and social conflicts among heterogeneous populations could be aggravated if they were mixed up together in such close quarters.

One problem will be difficult to solve: the enormous demand for week-end homes in secluded locations, with attractive natural surroundings. Perhaps this could be managed by providing air or rail service to many distant centers where family station-wagons would be kept.

Costs would be very high for central reconstruction and transportation, and would be increased by the demand for second homes with automobiles for recreational purposes.

The New York region particularly might tend in this direction because it has limited space, a highly centralized power structure, and a population that is probably more or less self-selected to favor these values.

4. *Toward a constellation of relatively diversified and integrated cities.* If the desire for private space and natural amenity is modified by greater concern for accessibility, diversity, and other traditional urban values, a tendency toward subregional integration could take various forms. Housing for all classes, races, and age-groups would, in any case, be provided in new outlying development, at mixed densities, and related to varied employment opportunities in the same general area. Since these cities would be fairly self-contained, they could be located quite far out on cheap land. This would require strong public and private initiative combined in some new form of agency. It could also be done by stimulating more balanced development in suburban communities already started, but this would encounter considerable resistance and require very ingenious inducements not yet devised. A system of greenbelts or wedges could be preserved, but this would require state or federal initiative at the start, when it would be most needed, pending the formation of a regional federation of cities with the necessary powers.

The transportation system would be subject to the same conditions. It could either be predominantly by rail (if larger, denser cities are favored) or by automobile for relatively small, low-density communities. Mass transit would not be as necessary for commuting as it is now, and distant intercity communications could conceivably be handled by air.

The old central city might remain quite strong, for region-wide functions and highly specialized facilities, but it would have less employment and a relatively balanced population with mixed densities and dwelling types. There would be far less disruption and dislocation than in the Super-City alternative with a much greater chance to preserve the diversity and historic qualities which make for real "urbanity." Where dominant central cities do not now exist, there might be a tendency for the specialized regional functions to settle in various cities (Clarence Stein's model), strengthening their centers and differentiating their region-wide attractions. In general, the cities might vary greatly in size and character, and they could either become a fairly close-knit regional network with minimal space between or spread quite far out into a larger region, depending on variable purposes and conditions. For those who prefer them, there could be homogeneous, but only partly self-governing, enclaves. Except for the extremes of scatteration, concentration, and specialization, this pattern would probably offer the greatest choice in life-styles.

Costs would be relatively low, compared with any of the other alternatives, due to less scatteration on the one hand, and less high-density construction on the other. If rail mass transit is provided in addition to automobile circulation, this would add to costs but strengthen centers. Property values in the old central cities would have to be written down to some degree, but on the other hand, land for new development and big parks could be quite cheap if it were acquired in time.

In one form or another, this alternative would be feasible in almost any metropolitan area. It calls for no greater exercise of public power than is now applied to redevelopment, but basic innovations in policy and purpose would be required.

These are very sketchy and personal judgments as to the nature of the alternatives, the forces behind them, and their comparative significance. I would only argue that this *kind* of approach is needed to make both the science and art of environmental planning effective. Within a framework which poses a range of hypotheses as to the future form and structure of the urban complex, our pioneering efforts toward systematic understanding of the development process should be applied to the analysis of ends and means, and the weighing of costs and benefits, in particular situations. The same framework can, I think, enhance the art of public communication, which is a major responsibility of both planner and researcher. With creative imagination based on scientific analysis, the big choices open to public decision can be clearly presented.

Cities in Latin America are swelling at double the population growth rate, and "the slums and shanty towns ringing many of these cities become as much as twelve to fifteen percent larger every year." Each week about five thousand people increase the population of Rio de Janeiro.

Recognizing the enormous problem, David Owen asserts that in planning cities "we must reexamine our premises before making our decisions." Above all, we must "try to regain some of our original feelings toward the city as the cradle of civilization as we know it, an essential and inescapable part of our present lives, and worthy of our fullest attention."

Owen is right. But I fail to see how any fundamental reexamination is possible, or how the underdeveloped nations can avoid our mistakes, without massive doses of international aid and cooperation especially from wealthy advanced industrial societies. Struggling to survive, underdeveloped nations rarely have the time and resources necessary for proper planning. And these nations will never have them unless they receive humane help in solving their population and economic problems.

From Urbanization in the Developing World
—David Owen

. . . all the problems of urbanization which beset the economically-advanced countries are found in the less developed regions of the world, where special characteristics add weight to their difficulty and urgency. Solution calls for a tremendous interdisciplinary effort engaging the resources and intellect of research workers in many fields and countries.

Reprinted from *Goals For Urban America,* edited by J. L. Berry and Jack Meltzer, by permission of Prentice-Hall, Inc. Copyright © 1967 by Prentice-Hall, Inc., Englewood Cliffs, N. J.

Most of the problems of urbanization which Heckscher has argued beset the economically more advanced countries are to be found, full-fledged or in embryo, in the less developed regions of the world, whose people account for two-thirds of the population of our planet. There, however, they exhibit special characteristics born of climate, geography, social history and economic realities, which often add sharpness and weight to their difficulty and urgency. A discussion of urbanization in the developing world will thus provide perspective to subsequent discussion of American urban problems, and will, simultaneously, highlight the role of the United Nations in international urban development.

Population increase is a much more serious factor in the less developed world than it is in most advanced countries. The countries and territories of Africa, Asia and Latin America already account for 68.3 per cent of current world population. In the last five years alone, their combined populations grew by over 150 millions—more than three-quarters of the global increase. It is anticipated that these same countries will account for 85 per cent of the increase in the next thirty-five years—or approximately 2.6 billion additional people. If the projections hold true, the density of people per square kilometre will triple in Latin America, almost triple in Africa and double in Asia.

The spread of family planning practices helped by urbanization, as well as by education, social incentives, and the revolutionary cheapness and simplicity of modern techniques, will eventually exercise a significant braking action on this population growth, but is likely to be at least partially offset by far-reaching improvements in public health and a consequent reduction in mortality rates. To add to the problem, the age structure of the population is such that the number of family units will almost certainly increase at a higher rate than that of the population as a whole and this will intensify the need for housing.

Probable changes in population distribution are likely to be even more important than population growth itself. In addition to facing a vast increase in the total number of people in the world we are undoubtedly at the beginning of an era of tremendous changes in the distribution of people as between city and countryside. This is a process which is largely (though not entirely) completed in more highly industrialized countries, but in the developing world it has hardly begun.

To those accustomed to presenting the case of increased resource development in the world, the fact of the growth of the world population from 600 millions to 3200 millions in the years between 1800 and 1965 is a commonplace. What is perhaps less well-known is that the population living in cities with more than 100,000 inhabitants increased from 15 millions to 314 millions in the same period—a twenty-fold increase, of which most was localized in the West. If we use a more recent point of departure, we once again see the special problems of the developing areas. While European cities grew by less than 20 per cent in the period 1950–60, urban growth in the less developed countries averaged more than 60 per cent. In Latin America, cities have been swelling at an annual rate of between 4 and 6 per cent (double the population growth rate), while the slums and shanty towns ringing many of these cities become as much as 12 to 15 per cent larger every year. About 5000 newcomers move into Rio de Janeiro each week. São Paolo has tripled in size since 1940. In this same period, Caracas grew five times over, Lima more than trebled, Mexico City almost trebled as did Bombay; the populations of New Delhi, Karachi, Peking, Bogotá and Santiago doubled. In a decade, Dar es Salaam doubled, while Accra and Luanda grew three times as large. It took Conakry only five years to quadruple in size.

The urban problems created by this phenomenal increase plague our generation in every land, and our failure to discover and apply adequate solutions for these problems does not augur well for our capacity to deal with the next stage of the process which will be infinitely vaster in scale. The movement of people from the countryside to urban centers throughout the world during the next five decades is likely to result in an increase in urban population greatly in excess of the increase in the population as a whole. On a very conservative estimate there are likely to be as many people living in large urban complexes by 2000 as were living in the world as a whole in 1950. Things are going to be difficult enough in the highly industrialized world where the pace of rural-urban migration has slowed down or even reversed, and where economic circumstances will permit the appropriation of resources on the scale required to deal with the problems of urban concentration. How much more difficult are they going to be in the developing world where rural-urban migration has yet to run its full course, and where the means to cope with tasks hardly conceivable in their magnitude are certainly beyond the capability of most countries without help from outside.

Older models of city growth are not applicable to the developing world of today. The cities of Europe and North America were established in a period of rapid expansion of world trade, when their products were eagerly sought after on the world market. This, as we can now see, earned them the capital with which they could house the newcomers, pave the streets, and service the city with water, gas, and later on, sewers. The new cities of the world have no such boon: they are desperately ill-equipped to receive the migrants who are flooding into them, to whom they can barely offer shelter, far less regular employment. The main characteristic of the Dickens portrait of Coketown in *Hard Times* is its description of unremitting and heart-rending toil: but any account of cities like Calcutta or Karachi or Jakarta must focus on the very opposite characteristic—the hopeless and equally heart-rending search for work. Even countries which have been blessed by discovery of oil and the wealth which follows in its train are finding it essential to look to outside help in grappling with their urbanization problems.

Venezuela is a good example. In Venezuela, about a third of the total population of the country in 1936 was living in centers of more than 1000 inhabitants (34.7 per cent of 3,360,000). By 1964, this figure had risen to 70 per cent, so that no less than 5,940,000 people out of a total of 8,430,000 were so located. Moreover, 4,230,000 of these people were to be found in thirty-nine settlements of 20,000 population or more—50 per cent of the total population of the country. It is expected that some 6 millions will be living in such settlements by 1970. This kind of increase exerts tremendous pressures on the whole structure of the society; and the Venezuelan government asked the United Nations Development Program to assist it in examining the basic causes of the growth of cities, and propose new policies aimed at mitigating their worst effects. This project, which commenced in 1966, is an interesting case study in the development of new methodologies to examine these problems.

These things having been said, it must be added that there are some elements in the social condition of many of the less developed countries which make it possible to find simpler and less costly solutions to urban problems than elsewhere. The developing world is, for the most part, an equatorial or sub-equatorial world, where the average man makes fewer demands on his shelter than his brother in the north. In the north, a man's dwelling must provide him with shelter from a variety of elements, it must keep him warm in winter, and because of the long winter nights, it must serve as a focus for social existence which is largely centered around the family. The same is not true of the tropics, where, because of the more equable climate, men spend much more of their time out of doors—in the streets and bazaars if they live in cities. For this reason, their attitude toward shelter is not the same as in the north, until (of course) they reach a stage of affluence when their house becomes more of a symbol of their status than it is today. This point should be borne in mind when appraising the standards of accommodation prevalent in many of the cities of the developing world today: for reasons of status, ten square meters per person might provide palatial accommodation for a family in Singapore, but be very cramped quarters for a family in the United States.

It is clear that in tackling the appalling urban problems of the developing world we have to clear our minds of many preconceptions, and search for new models and new solutions. Attitudes of the Westerner who advises on solutions to urban problems elsewhere are too often developed in the first encounter with slums whose squalor far surpasses anything in the industrialized world of today. The common reaction is to try to do away with them at all costs, and to try to create—usually in the outskirts of the city—a new environment thought to be more acceptable to the erstwhile slum-dwellers. And so the world is full of well-intentioned slum clearance projects of this kind, whose main characteristic is that they ignore—often brutally—essential patterns of living that have developed in these same slum areas.

A start is now being made with the study of the ecology of these areas, and this may well throw a new light on urban development policies. One sensitive study of a major African metropolis has shown how the physical environment of the densely developed "down-town" area—which was being actively demolished under a slum clearance scheme—was a perfect response to the way of life—both social and economic—of its inhabitants. The demands of these people for covered living space were minimal. They affronted the consciences of the city authorities, but their need to be close to the city's heart, where their means of livelihood lay, was essential to their survival. The solution of providing tidy individual houses for these people some miles away from the city center was not, in their minds, the best possible! A similar study of housing in Lima, Peru, shows that the inner ring of city-center slums of the city—bad though conditions are in them—are an important staging place in the progress of the migrant in his cultural transformation from a countryman to an accepted resident of a city. For these areas, lying close to the city's heart, permit the newcoming resident to exploit every chance of casual employment that the city may offer at a time in his life when survival is more important than the quality of his shelter. Only later, when his foothold on metropolitan life is less precarious, does the newcomer turn his attention towards bettering his environment—and then comes the impetus to squat.

This existence of squatter settlement is, in itself, a characteristic feature of modern city environments throughout the developing world. People do not, as a rule, commit this illegal act of squatting merely for the sake of flouting the law. To them it is an act of despair against policies which are simply not geared to meeting their dilemma. Only in a very few countries of the developing world are there public housing programs which provide shelter for the lowest income groups which, however, constitute the majority of the city populations. And so, the newcomer, with the characteristic self-reliance of the countryman, fends for himself, and adapts his forms of rural cooperation to self-help building in the towns. Viewed in this light, the squatter settlements are not so much an act of defiance against the law as an enterprising solution to a very real probler

In discussing these problems in this detached way, it must not be thought that I am blind to the sheer enormity of the task involved in providing a satisfactory environment for the people living in these new cities, or lighthearted about illegal acts. We cannot forget that the stark reality of these cities is, all too often, inadequate shelter and community services, almost complete absence of sanitation and safe drinking water, filth and squalor in ever expanding areas, and a growing rate of disease and mortality. At the same time, gang activity, juvenile delinquency, crime and vice, the most conspicuous manifestations of personal and social disorganization, have become part of the social setting of blighted communities in which marginal populations must live. My point is rather that this task ahead of us is not simply one of allocating more resources based on systems of priority that we have evolved in the past, but that we must re-examine our premises before making our decisions. And of these, the foremost premise should be that, in cutting out the canker from our cities, we should not destroy its life.

The task of the city planner in this context, is to design a total environment for people whose present means are modest, but whose expectations are great. Because of the scarcity of finance, it is likely that a large proportion of the dwellings in the new cities of the developing world will have to be constructed of traditional materials—wood, bamboo, brick and tile—and because of the structural limitations imposed by these materials, the dwellings themselves are likely to be predominantly of one or two stories in height. In designing such communities, it will be important to allow for them to improve with the improving social and economic status of their inhabitants. The houses themselves may be minimal in size now, but their plots must be of sufficient size to allow them to expand; there may not be enough money for roads now, but the space for them should be reserved.

Possible use of new technologies should also be identified. There are several possibilities here: traditional methods can be improved by better uses of raw materials, by improved designs, and by the prefabrication of certain elements, all of which could lead to the lowering of costs for this kind of house. There is also the possibility that new materials may be developed to replace or supplement existing materials.

The implications of this kind of low density city are only now beginning to be appreciated. For if our assumptions on the future form and growth of urban centers are correct, we shall have to anticipate new urban forms—or at least, forms of urban development which are logical extrapolations from existing forms. Cities might well take the form of collections of planned "urban villages" whose aggregate populations could reach tens of millions of people. How to design for such conglomerations of people, whose level of technology is comparatively low, may well prove to be one of the foremost problems of our age, making corporate demands on the skills of many kinds of people.

A key issue in these new cities will be the location of work places close to homes, so that the need to move about in them will be minimized. If this can be accomplished whilst avoiding the chaos of the industrial towns of the nineteenth century, much will have been achieved. This, of course, is not an issue which is peculiarly applicable to the developing world. It is universal. Every major city in the world is suffering from this traffic thrombosis, and no certain solution is yet in sight; but whereas the richer countries have the financial means to try out new solutions, no such alternatives are available to the developing countries. In these countries, people will initially be dependent on non-power driven means of transport to a much greater extent than in any city of America or Europe. Even if they were as mobile, the problem of providing for mobility in areas of comparatively low densities is notoriously difficult to solve.

Clearly, much more thought will be necessary to devise a shape for the metropolis of the future in the developing world. Nor is there much time at our disposal for this, for we are in the midst of crisis, which could threaten the breakdown of these cities as *economic units,* much as New York tended to break down during its transit strike or its great "blackout."

It is time that the tools of economic evaluation were applied to the analysis of environmental conditions. What is the cost to the community of an unhealthy environment in terms of productivity losses? Of course, in the context of the developing world, this question is virtually meaningless, because most people are under-employed anyway. Furthermore, even the spectacle in some tropical cities of people bathing, washing clothes, and excreting in the same open canal does not always prompt public action because there are no apparent epidemics. But the debilitating effects of endemic disease are insidious enough to prompt our urgent attention. Rising concern over this matter was manifested in the choice by the World Health Organization of the topic "Man and his Cities" as the theme for World Health Day in 1966.

It is only in this way that we can place the high capital costs of servicing these new cities in a correct perspective. In the past, it has been all too customary for economists to regard such expenditures as "social overheads" which can be justified only on social grounds, therefore deserving the lowest priority in the Government's capital works budget. But, as a recent World Health Organization Expert Committee states: "from the point of view of economic development, the provision of social overhead capital is not an end in itself; it is rather a basic investment to provide the services needed to support the directly productive activities such as mining and manufacturing." It is on this basis that the International Bank for Reconstruction and Development—the World Bank—has agreed to provide finance on an increasingly large scale for this kind of development.

Another important policy issue is at present stultifying metropolitan growth throughout the world. Even if we manage to solve all of the problems so far ventilated on a technical level, we will still be faced with legal and administrative questions which, even in America, defy an easy solution. Outmoded legal systems are often left like debris on the shore when the colonial tide has receded: a system of planning law which, for example, seeks more to regulate the efforts of the private developer than to promote action plans in the cities which need them, obviously has little relevance in the developing world today. For, not only does such an approach stress the negative side of the planning process to an unnecessary degree, but also makes demands on trained staff which are quite outside the potential of developing countries to provide.

In addition, there is the question of the city's relationship to its region. The physical limits of many cities in the world today extend beyond the administrative limits of their jurisdictions; it is essential to devise policies which will encompass this wider area. In the case of New York, although the origins of regional thinking go back at least forty years, a metropolitan transportation policy has yet to appear. The same applies to many cities in the developing world—in Lagos, for example, where all attempts to prepare a metropolitan plan have been frustrated so far because of the difficulty of bringing together two autonomous regional authorities—even though the scale of its problems commands immediate attention.

There is, of course, no universal panacea for the solution of these problems, since they are so often embedded in the political structure of the countries concerned. In one country, the solution might best be sought by means of a boundary change—as has been done recently in London; in another, a federation of local authorities might best serve the needs of the situation. But, as a necessary first step, United Nations Development Program policy is stressing the importance of establishing, where politically possible, a central agency in the governments of the developing countries whose concern is entirely that of promoting and regulating the development of adequate local government machinery.

Nobody today will dispute the fact that the problems of city development today cannot be solved within the limits of their physical growth. After all, Daniel Burnham's plan for Chicago, published in 1909, extended to a distance of 30 miles from the center of the city. But there is a complementary approach, which involves a consideration of the part that the city plays in the economic structure of the country as a whole. Up until very recently this has been a field neglected by economists, who have been more concerned with the specification of a country's development goals by simply evaluating available resources and economic opportunities, and then suggesting policies to achieve these goals. To quote from a recent seminar on New Towns sponsored by the United Nations:

> National development policies do not fully recognize the spatial and locational aspects of economic growth, and, as a consequence, these aspects are generally neglected in development programs.
>
> The participants at this seminar saw the need to establish a physical planning unit at the central level in government . . . to assist in the translation of national economic and social policies into plans for the development of regions and of urban and rural communities . . . (and) also help to correct the excessive emphasis now placed on aggregative and sectoral analysis in current planning policies and programs. . . .

There are, of course, signs that governments are recognizing this. In the first United Nations project of this nature, a team was appointed to assist the Ghanaian Government to draft a national physical plan which became the basis for development policy.

Now the Government of Pakistan is about to receive substantial assistance from the United Nations Development Program in an audacious undertaking to locate and plan new cities in East Pakistan. This project presents a challenging problem of determining the sites for new cities in a country the size of Michigan State with a population of some 50 millions, whose three largest cities have populations of about 1,000,000, 300,000, and about 150,000.

This instance is a particularly good example of a country that has resolutely put the horse before the cart. The latter has too often been the case, and industrial location has been decided with very little regard to its social and physical consequences. Even in hard economic terms, the cost of a new industrial establishment cannot be reckoned simply in terms of the installation alone: it has to be serviced with power, water, and a transportation network; its workers have to be housed, fed and transported; their families have to be educated and cared for. Although studies on these matters are at present practically nonexistent, the indications are that the costs of these so-called social overheads are several times higher than the basic cost of installing the industry. Whether this cost is borne by the government concerned, or by the industrialist himself, or by the workers individually, it is still a levy against the total resources of the country and cannot be ignored by national planners.

The issues concerned in this discussion are thrown into sharp relief by considering a typical problem in a developing country: if the government is able to exert any measure of choice over the location of a new factory, should it be sited in the major metropolis, or in some other location either nearby or at a distance from the metropolis? Conventional economic thought on this problem will state that, if all the alternative sites are equally good from the siting standpoint, the metropolis should be chosen because there the industry will enjoy economies of scale. But this argument ignores the fact that this very policy makes the metropolis the more attractive to the migrant, and thereby adds to its difficulties. In Lloyd Rodwin's words, "the question that constantly faces responsible officials is how to channel investments so that they will not be frittered away throughout the country, or else expended in the big cities on costly urban services that could well be postponed. Ideally, the decision makers should husband this capital so as to create opportunities for investment and thus stimulate selected growing points, or impulse sectors." The growth point philosophy is gaining ground in many countries. The United Nations Development Program is, for example, assisting the Irish government in identifying such points as a basis for a national physical development program to relieve, in part, some of the pressure on Dublin.

Rodwin's point about the husbanding of resources is an important one, for recent studies are showing that building construction accounts for more than 50 per cent of the gross domestic capital formation in most countries. Furthermore, figures on building productivity indicate that either the value added per person employed in the construction sector is lower than for the economy as a whole, or that the labor-to-capital ratio in construction is higher than average, or both. There is, therefore, a clear need to focus our attention on this large and vital sector of the economy, and seek ways of increasing its efficiency.

In a recent paper prepared for the United Nations Committee on Housing, Building and Planning, estimates on a world basis have been made of the additional cost—that is the additional finance needed over and above present outlays—of eliminating the housing deficit for 80 per cent of the urban population over a period of 30 years. This estimate comes to $2,250 millions, or about 1.5 per cent of the aggregate national incomes of the developing countries in the analysis. If one adds to this the costs of providing basic utilities for such people, the total cost may be set at $5,465 millions or about 3.6 per cent of the aggregate national incomes. Although these figures are very rough, they give some indication of the magnitude of the problem, leading to the conclusion that:

> in order to meet their urban housing needs, even within the lower cost range, developing countries as a group would have to increase the funds invested in middle and low cost housing and related facilities by approximately 50 per cent. . . .

Clearly the greater part of this financial burden must fall on the countries themselves; the role which external capital can play is a limited one, but vital, nevertheless, to the future of the countries concerned. Unfortunately, it cannot be said that external capital has made up to now an impressive contribution to housing development (though I should make an exception to this generalization in the case of Latin America, where the Latin American Development Bank has done some splendid work in recent years).

A United Nations study last year on the financing of housing and community programs in the developing countries showed that a very modest amount of approximately $400 millions was *disbursed* annually between 1963–65 by multilateral, bilateral, public or private sources. If we can take this approximation (which includes the Eastern European donors) as a basis, it means that only 3.5 per cent of the total flow of aid and investment in the developing countries was applied to housing and urban development. The Inter-American Development Bank is still the leading source of public funds, with some $338 millions in loans for housing, urban water supply, and sanitation between 1961 and 1963. The International Development Association has granted some credits for water supply and sewerage systems and the International Bank for Reconstruction and Development, only recently, has made loans in connection with municipal water supply systems. The major bilateral programs, taken together, provided some $240 millions in housing financing in each of the last few years, while private investors accounted for an additional $60 millions.

The United Nations is not itself in a position to assist in capital financing. But it can assist in the provision of financial consultant services in mobilizing the necessary capital. It can also assist in the strengthening or regulation of the institutional framework within which investments are made. This includes housing finance agencies and credit cooperatives. The organization also recognizes the importance of investigating sources of international capital for this purpose and making proposals for an increasing flow. A study group shortly to be appointed under the auspices of the Center for Housing, Building and Planning will be studying this whole problem and making recommendations to governments on it.

The Center has also been the main vehicle for providing United Nations assistance to the developing countries in housing, building and planning. The process began fifteen years ago with technical assistance programs. In 1959, these were joined by the United Nations Special Fund bringing a new impetus and greater resources to this work. Now that the Expanded Program of Technical Assistance and the Special Fund have been brought together to form the United Nations Development Program, the available resources can be applied with a greater degree of flexibility, imagination and forward planning.

Under technical assistance, over 15 years, some 240 experts have assisted 70 governments in a variety of ways. A number of (major) cities of the world have benefited from impartial advice from United Nations town planners:

Rangoon, Singapore, Jakarta, Karachi, Kabul, Amman, Lagos, and Caracas, to mention but a few. The men who worked in these places, often alone under conditions of some difficulty—this is the nature of United Nations service— have succeeded in imparting skills to their counterparts, and establishing the beginning of an orderly approach to the problems of city development in the places concerned.

Experts in housing have assisted in developing pilot project programs in a number of African countries such as Somalia, Ethiopia, Rwanda, the United Arab Republic, and Guinea. The objects of these programs are to demonstrate new ways of building cheap houses, to assist in the development of institutions to finance such construction, and to help them to manage the houses once they are constructed.

A third major prong in U.N. efforts is to help countries to improve existing ways of building houses. This has been tackled in a variety of ways—by providing men who will develop research programs, or assist governments in establishing research institutes, as in Korea, Indonesia, Pakistan, Togo, or by providing specialists in such matters as bamboo construction, brick development, light weight concrete, ceramics and so on.

Over and above this, the effort has been to improve local skills, by providing fellowships for training abroad and by assisting in the development of educational institutions at all levels. In Ghana, for example, a successful program was established for educating planners up to sub-professional level. This school is now attracting students from other countries in Africa.

The establishment of the Special Fund has enabled much of the work begun under technical assistance auspices to be raised to a much higher level of significance. Support not only can be sustained over a longer period—usually of five years—but it can be provided in a larger volume making available expert services, fellowships and equipment. It also has proved successful in mobilizing government counterpart support on a much larger scale than had previously been possible.

There are U.N.-supported projects in Ireland, Singapore, Pakistan and Venezuela. Major efforts are now being directed to carrying forward urban development programs in Afghanistan, Argentina and Taiwan.

The first Special Fund project to be completed is one in Skopje, Yugoslavia, under which the government was assisted massively in the replanning and reconstruction of a city which suffered serious damage during an earthquake in 1963. Skopje will rise again from its ruins as a true example of international cooperation, the work of specialists from America, USSR, France, Britain, the Netherlands, Italy, Hungary, Czechoslovakia, Greece, Poland and Japan.

With the experience accumulated in modest but far-ranging programs, a more significant role can be expected from the United Nations Development Program.

As long as its activities remain essentially of a pre-investment character, there are four main areas in which available resources can be concentrated.

Pre-investment surveys can assist in providing the groundwork for public and private investment in urban development by helping central or local authorities to carry out planning surveys, prepare urban and regional plans and undertake specific pre-investment surveys. One result is advice to governments on appropriate strategies for the future development of their cities, what forms of transport would be most appropriate and how to distribute their growing populations in an orderly way throughout the metropolitan areas.

Pilot housing schemes may also be supported. These would include site planning, house design, provision of all basic services, building of houses and a full range of community buildings. Such projects would include financing and housing administration. Pilot schemes that best respond to local needs and conditions by demonstrating new techniques and processes of building and construction, making use of new materials, are preferred. They should also provide training on the spot in housing administration and management. In certain situations the World Food Program can provide food aid as a useful underpinner to projects of this kind, relieving the government of some of the financial burden.

It is already U.N. policy to assist governments in setting up or strengthening a Central Physical Planning Agency. Such bodies are by nature policy-making. The timely injection of a team of specialist-advisers to assist such agencies can result in the drawing up of development plans and targets and the implementation of properly-phased action programs. With such assistance, the often awkward and always delicate task of drawing together the various departments and agencies of government concerned with physical plans and their execution can be attempted.

Non-capital participation in the preliminary stages of the investment process is also an area where the UNDP can fill a gap in the developing countries. Assistance is often needed in the preparation of blueprints and master plans involving the terms and specifications of capital lending, particularly in housing development with its own special requirements and even more so in the developing countries where international or bilateral capital participation is so often necessary.

Last but not least, the UNDP can make an important contribution to the creation of an international climate of opinion favorable to large-scale aid and capital investment in housing programs throughout the developing world.

The problems associated with the future of cities in the developing world are extremely complex, demanding a much greater research effort than is at present being devoted to them. Whatever the solutions which research will come up with, the task of improving our present cities is likely to be extremely costly in terms of manpower, material resources and finance. There is an imperative need to tackle these problems urgently because the future well-being of billions of fellow humans is at stake. We are in a state of crisis: let us match our actions to the gravity of it.

In the past, there has been a tendency on the part of policy makers to regard city development as a kind of economic mill-stone round their necks: a nonproductive investment which has to be made to improve worsening social conditions. We must somehow seek to break out of these confining fetters to our thinking, and try to regain some of our original feelings towards the city as the cradle of civilization as we now know it, an essential and inescapable part of our present lives, and worthy of our fullest attention. The very least that we can say is that it is the creation—or re-creation—of cities as effective economic organisms which must command attention; but the true nature of the problem goes far beyond this. It is the creation of an environment in which men can truly realize their true potential—for who can say at present what is the effect on peoples' urge to develop, on their morale, on their whole attitude towards life, of a decent home and a healthy environment? Might this not perhaps be the very key that we are looking for, which unlocks the door to economic take-off?

We therefore stand at the very threshold of a new era for city development everywhere, and in the developing countries in particular, an era which is going to make enormous demands on us from every point of view. That it is a major challenge to governments and to international organizations needs no further emphasis. It is also a major challenge to the universities of the world. In all our countries our systems of higher education are based on fragmented knowledge, each department neatly compartmentalized, each with its own bureaucracy and academic definition. Yet the great task which I have been defining calls for a tremendous interdisciplinary effort engaging the resources of intellect and imagination of research workers in many fields and in many countries.

14

Poverty and Racism

Jim Hoagland sees little hope for any major changes in South Africa's inhuman social structure. However, it is interesting to consider the speech of the young black leader, Steven Biko, for his attitude resembles that of American black activists. When he criticizes white liberals and demands a future acceptable to blacks, Biko is embracing the themes and pleas of men like Malcolm X. In South Africa, too, "black is beautiful"; in South Africa, too, whites must change or risk the bitter conflict that is certain to come.

But similarities, however notable, between South Africa and America should never be allowed to obscure the great contrasts that exist between the two racial situations. Tribal barriers separate whites from blacks in a way that the U.S. has never experienced, and other "colored" groups, such as Indians, complicate the South African problem. The most important reason for Hoagland's pessimism is the almost total white control of South Africa's social, economic, and military resources. He believes that "violent manifestations of frustration and despair will probably be necessary to force any significant concessions out of the white rulers . . . ," and he doubts that blacks have the power to exhibit such manifestations in the near future. So unless whites change, or a superpower intervenes, the prospect in South Africa is inhumanity in the short-run, and certain bloodshed in the long-run.

From South Africa
—Jim Hoagland

. . . There are no apparent and truly satisfactory conclusions for the immense and tragic problems of [South Africa]. The violence, injustice, and deprivation of the past and present seem certain to continue into the future, whether it is whites or blacks who are in control of the southern part of the continent. Like the characters of Sartre's *No Exit*, the different tribes and nations of Southern Africa seem condemned to torture each other without hope of cessation. Only the positions of perpetrator and victim are mutable. Those of us who would make judgments about the future of South Africa can do little more than state a preference for the group we wish to see harmed, and for whose profit.

. . . The failures [that have created these problems] are those of English liberalism transferred to the Southern Hemisphere, African nationalism, Portuguese multiracialism, economic forces, and others. They have not substantially affected the successful white counterrevolution of the 1960s that continues today. Although there may be dramatic change in Rhodesia and Portuguese Africa, I do not see much hope that in the coming decade there will be a change in the fundamental condition of South Africa, which remains the key to the region. That condition is accurately described as white tyranny—complete white control, exercised as harshly as the whites feel is necessary to maintain their economic advantage and their false notion of racial superiority.

The two alternative courses of development that are most frequently proposed are the hope that multiracialism will be resurrected from the ashes of apartheid or that black revolution will succeed. . . . I do not see either as a likely prospect for South Africa in the 1970s, and perhaps not in this century.

Multiracialism, a cooperative sharing of political power and economic benefits among races in a single polity, was stillborn in South Africa. The whites never wanted it, and the blacks no longer do, if they ever did. Chief A. J. Luthuli's 1958 assertion that Africans aspire to "a truly multiracial country" where "democracy should by the nature of things be colorblind" is an echo from the past. The voice of the future comes from Africans like Steven Biko, a young medical student. As leader of the South African Students Organization, an all-black student group that had been recently set up, Biko delivered a remarkable speech to an educational workshop arranged by the Abe Bailey Institute in Cape Town in January 1971. His cool and analytical view of young black South Africa's response to the various forms of white domination is worth considering in some detail for its implications on the coming two decades:

"The major mistake the Black world ever made was to assume that whoever opposed apartheid was an ally. For a long time the Black world has only been looking at the governing party and not so much at the whole power structure as the object of their rage.

". . . It never occurred to the liberals that the integration they insisted upon as an effective way of opposing apartheid was impossible to achieve in South Africa . . . The myth of integration as propounded under the banner of the liberal ideology must be cracked and killed because it makes people believe that something is being done when in actual fact the artificial integrated circles are a soporific on the Blacks and provide a satisfaction for the guilt stricken Whites . . . who possess the natural passport to the exclusive pool of White privileges . . .''

Speaking of whites in general, Biko added: "Not only did they kick the Native but they also told him how to respond to the kick. For a long time the Native has been listening with patience to the advice he has been receiving on how best to respond to the kick. With painful slowness he is now beginning to show signs that it is his right and duty to respond to the kick *in the way he sees fit.*'' [Biko's emphasis]

''. . . Over the years we have attained moral superiority over the White man; we shall watch as Time destroys his paper castles and know that all these little pranks were but the frantic attempts of frightened little people to convince each other that they can control the minds and bodies of indigenous peoples of Africa indefinitely.''

White liberals in the National Union of South African Students (NUSAS), the multiracial group from which the Africans had split, reacted much as the white liberals did in the United States at the beginning of the black power movement. They were hurt, but they were unable to offer any convincing alternative. As Biko and others insisted, the growing black "awareness" and determination to go it alone did not represent a victory for apartheid. It reflected more the failure of liberal white attitudes, based largely on the assumption that class differences would continue to protect white privilege (except for the unfortunate poor whites, who would have to be sacrificed in the name of multiracialism). With some notable exceptions, the non-Communist "left" in South Africa has not advocated the elimination of white privilege, but merely a change in its form and a reduction of its worst excesses. The English-speakers of South Africa and Rhodesia, and the Portuguese, have stood for a permissive multiracialism. Blacks who can emerge from tribal society should be left unfettered. But in societies where the gap between the advanced minority and the majority are as great as they are in Southern Africa, that again constitutes having no policy. It is a wish, an idea, a good intention that has no substantial effect. Without courageous national leadership, it falls easily before the force of organized prejudice, for liberal attitudes are more concerned with the preservation of class structures than with race. For many self-described liberals, the racial issue is a blind, one on which they will make concessions, while to the others it is a real and decisive human issue. This has been shown to be the case not only in South Africa, but also in the Northern United States in recent years.

The stirrings of black awareness, and the skillful use of apartheid's institutions by Buthelezi and others, should not be taken as heralding the long-delayed black revolution, however. All available evidence indicates that the threat of revolution is not a realistic prospect, for lack of method, not for lack of cause. There will probably be outbreaks of mass racial violence over the next decade in South Africa, but they will resemble America's Watts and Newark in scale and result—stacks of black bodies in a charred ghetto inhabited by blacks, white policemen blowing smoke from their gun barrels, and a few token dead whites. It is reasonable to assume that without major outside intervention, which would probably have to come in the course of a general war between the superpowers, the whites will continue their control of the country's technology and armaments and will increase that control at least in proportion to the population increases that are supposed to spell doom for the whites by the end of the century. More hungry Africans may give increased reason to riot, but will not necessarily increase their effectiveness in fighting the whites.[1]

Despite this, African violence to come should not be unquestioningly viewed as "counterproductive," to use the American bureaucratic cover word for the argument for maintaining the status quo. Violent manifestations of frustration and despair will probably be necessary to force any significant concessions out of the white rulers, who now operate on the assumption of African apathy and acquiescence. Only if there is credibility to the threat that they run the risk of losing everything will the poor whites be convinced to yield anything.

This is not a call to the barricades. Only a moral coward would sit outside and urge the Africans to get themselves killed in a battle that they can win only if they are committed to fight to the last man. That is a decision they have to make. But if it is made, only a charlatan will deplore it. Violence has been under way some time in South Africa. It is the white government that is currently perpetrating it. The government's policies make counterviolence justifiable *if it is the only way to alter the status quo.* The uncertainty of the consequences of such counterviolence is a terrible consideration, but the continuation of what is happening in South Africa today cannot be justified on that basis.

Violent upheaval can possibly still be avoided, if white South African leaders will grasp the opportunity. To suggest that the opportunity exists does not mean that I assume they will.

There have always been a great number of solutions for South Africa. Nearly everyone seems to have one. What is impossible to get people to agree on is a definition of The Problem. For the Afrikaner, it is preserving his identity, his sense of mission, his grasp on power and his institutions. He does not want to be done unto as he has done. For the English-speaker, The Problem is more one of preserving material welfare and the establishing of guarantees that black advancement will not be at his expense. For Coloreds, The Problem is simply how to be treated fairly by either whites or blacks, since they will always be an in-between group. For the blacks, The Problem is a three-tiered one: first, to break the present cruelties and humiliation inflicted upon them; second, to achieve majority political control; third, to adopt a unified approach on the exercise of political control once it has been achieved.

---

[1] See *Politics and Law in South Africa,* by Julius Lewin (Monthly Review Press, 1963) for an application to South Africa of Crane Brinton's theory on prerevolutionary conditions, as outlined in Brinton's *The Anatomy of Revolution.* The application seems to me to be valid.

The failures of the two grand theoretical solutions—multiracialism and apartheid—have caused many thinking white and black South Africans to begin to examine the prospects for some form of racial coexistence, achieved through a restructuring of South African society that would take into consideration a compromise of all these goals. Compromise will undoubtedly mean a continuation of much of the worst injustice in the present system, but in the absence of the means of revolution, it may be necessary for the black majority. The search for compromise will be a difficult one, and the following discussion of some seminal ideas is intended more to indicate particularly troublesome areas rather than to draw a blueprint that will resolve the problems of Southern Africa, problems that can be resolved only by the peoples of Southern Africa, white, brown, and black.[2]

If it were turned into a sincere program for change, grand apartheid could offer some impetus for such a compromise by allowing the creation of independent black governmental bodies that could then seek greater international involvement in the problems of the region. It would also unfreeze the present situation by promoting the redrawing of boundaries in the region (and perhaps even in other areas of sub-Sahara Africa, which are also bedeviled by the colonial juxtaposition of hostile nations and tribes inside artificial borders). As a theoretical exercise, at least, the idea of a federation of South African states, in which there would be a system of checks and balances operating to guarantee rights for each of the ethnic groups in the different federated states, has a certain validity.

There should be no more than four or five governmental bodies formed on the basis of ethnic identification. The four million whites would constitute one, the four million Zulu another, the Xhosa a third, other African tribes one or two, and the Coloreds one. Each would have its own political parties and would elect leaders to deal from a position of equality with the white leaders. Treatment of Africans and Coloreds by white employers and other whites would be regulated by agreements between the units, judicable in federal courts.

For this arrangement to be a starting point in the search for a more equitable compromise, however, there must be present two elements that are currently absent in the formulation of apartheid. As long as they continue to be absent, the world can be certain there will be no meaningful peaceful change in South Africa.

The first is that the arrangement of South Africans into tribal and racial groups must be acknowledged to be a transitional phase, to be followed by a regrouping of the African population into larger governing units not based on tribalism. The white government must acknowledge that tribalism

---

[2]The tribal system seems to be inimical to the process of reaching compromise outside of small, well-defined groups. This is seen not only in South Africa, where Afrikaner and Zulu have never been able to compromise with other groups, but also across the rest of the continent. It is one of Africa's gravest difficulties.

is a dying political force in Africa. It must concentrate the help it has promised the black states to achieve the eradication of tribalism. It must stop trying to turn the clock back for its own advantage and must begin moving with the currents of history. Such a change in the public position of the South African government in this decade would be a key indication that there is suil some hope of avoiding violent confrontation. Without it, apartheid remains a transparent confidence trick.

Secondly, the black South African federation units have to be able to bargain with the whites on the shape of what will follow the racial and tribal federation. The only bargaining power they can have is their labor, which they must be able to withhold and yet survive. In the transitional phase, the black states will in fact resemble large labor unions. For this, the units will have to be economically self-sufficient in the sense that they will not have to depend on white South African industry and commerce to survive.

The South African government can contribute to this. It should implement the recommendations made on agricultural development by the Tomlinson Commission a generation ago. The 87-13 division of the land must be altered. Until it is, the concept of Africans being given "their" rights outside a central political unit will remain a hoax. The land must be divided on a basis other than the distorted and deceitful version of the ownership of land used by the present government. Finally, the white South Africans should let the Free Enterprise system they so warmly endorse function in their country. They should test the myth that Africans are in fact so different, so inferior, that they cannot do white man's work. If this is so, there is no need for apartheid's economic restrictions. If it is not so, there is no possible justification for them. In coordination with this, the government should expand its social welfare plans for whites who will be affected, to reduce the backlash this will cause, and make more equal educational opportunities for all races.

Equally important would be the role of foreign governments. Providing enough economic aid to the federation's black states to make sure they would be in a position to bargain should be an area of joint effort by the United States and the Soviet Union. It should be a priority program for both, and for Europe, especially if, as I assume, the South African white government continues to refuse to take seriously the prospect of dividing up South Africa.

These actions would help end the dangerous practice of the Vorster government of keeping a double set of books. While assuring the white electorate with a big wink that the promises of change and "freedoms" for Africans mean nothing, the government also tries to convince trade and investment partners that it can be shown to be working for justice, if it is just given a little time. Vorster is lying to one or the other, or perhaps both simultaneously. If he is interested in partitioning South Africa into viable units, then he should go at it in a serious manner, not as a game. And he should be prepared for major international involvement in working out an agreement between black and white that would be a compromise. Perhaps the only way majority rule could ever be achieved peacefully in a unified South

Africa would be through an arrangement guaranteed by the major powers, including the Soviet Union, who would be bound to intervene to protect carefully drawn and equitable guarantees for the white minority that would come into effect after majority political rule.

In the present context of regional and world politics, these suggestions sound utopian, although they fall far short of complete justice. I would be the first to admit that. It is easy to draw up political structures and alternatives in a vacuum, difficult to make them work when they collide with the human realities. The most glaring weakness in the ideas that I have been setting down is the simple fact that they have little if anything to offer the white working class, which will be required to make most of the sacrifices. Unless this class becomes convinced that sacrifices will enable it to head off a potentially successful uprising or an invasion, there is no reason at all for it to support such changes. Only moral pressure from strong leadership could prod the whites into changes. There are men capable of doing this in South Africa, but it is inconceivable to me that any of them can rise through the stultifying machine that now runs the country.

Those expecting grand turning points in South Africa in the next decade, then, are likely to be disappointed. Change will be incremental and will not mean any fundamental alteration of harsh white domination. . . . Four [trends] are likely to bring some amelioration in the condition of the non-white majority. They are the growth of class structure in the Afrikaner society, the Verligtes' moral arguments against petty apartheid and their discomfort at the plight of the Coloreds, the rejection by young, urban Afrikaners of the most extreme expressions of racism, as indicated by the 1970 campaign, and the increasing use of the institutions of apartheid by blacks and Coloreds for their own ends. But none of these forces is likely to bring more than marginal change to the racist status quo.

Nor is the movement of young whites out of South Africa's colleges onto the beginning rungs of the ladder of the establishment. There does not seem to be any significant generation gap in white South Africa today. Several days spent on the campus of Stellenbosch University indicated to me that the laager mentality has not been significantly weakened in young Afrikaners. Afrikanerdom's brightest and more liberal young people attend Stellenbosch, located in the Cape Province. "No, we know that we cannot afford to be irresponsible," a pretty young coed told me when I asked if there was any chance of student unrest in South Africa. "If we want to continue to survive, we must have discipline and authority." She said it was pointless to fight English-speakers now, but indicated she did not trust them. "They are part of the permissive society." Another Afrikaner graduate student, in a representative comment, said; "Nobody has been able to formulate a realistic alternative that would protect us from black domination. We have grown up while Africa to the north was in chaos, and we don't want it here."

The English-speakers' feeling of powerlessness in the country was mirrored at Witwatersrand University in Johannesburg. "Yes, I'm leaving the country,'' Ken Costa, president of the student council in 1970, told me. ''They [the Afrikaners] wear you down. There is no point in staying anymore.'' Lee Hayden, a journalism major, spoke of the two worlds she was trapped between: ''I talk to Afrikaners and they say they want to get rid of all the black men, however they have to do it. And I talk to the few Africans I know as friends, and they say they've given up, all they want to do is cut the white man's head off and throw it back into the ocean. God, do I feel trapped.''

Perhaps the best hope for change in the attitude and values among the young whites lies in the still uncertain impact of science and technology on South Africa in the coming decade. The often unforeseen social and political side effects of technical improvements in transportation, communications, medicine, and other areas can be enormous, as many nations have begun to realize. Automobiles in America shift political power from city to suburb, television makes new demands on political candidates, and I think it will soon be widely accepted that the birth-control pill has reshaped political as well as social attitudes in America and Europe within the last decade, especially among the young. The even more fundamental (and less fortunate) changes the computer will make in our political and social choices are still not clear. The possibilities, of course, are enormous.

South Africa lags at least five to ten years behind America and Europe in widespread acceptance of many of these technological changes. It is still conceivable that the country will not prove to be immune from the apparently deep and sudden shifts in the attitudes of the young seen elsewhere in the past ten years. But the South African government does better than most in controlling such influences. The Vorster regime was ridiculed for dragging its feet on establishing a national television network, but I think it is one of the few governments in the world that has given the effect of television its due. But it must be remembered that the increase in technology that brings the possibility of these changes in the white population also adds to its store of repressive strength. Like most forces at work in South Africa, this is a double-edged one.

My presentiment that white tyranny will continue unabated in the foreseeable future is a frustrating one, representing in some ways a surrender to the notion that life is, after all, absurd. I would feel much easier if I could report that there are signs in South Africa that history has an inevitable morality, that there will be justice in a society that almost completely lacks it today, that man is a rational and moral being, or, at the very least, that there will be retribution for his not being so. Those ideas are refuted daily in South Africa, as well as elsewhere.

For all of its mighty flaws, however, South Africa retains mighty potential for proving prophets of doom wrong. It is a magnificent land that is worth the unending struggle to master it. There is a vibrancy of life, and therefore a demand for hope, for a coming to terms with the absurdity of existence. The result is a strange, attractive mixture of exuberance and melancholy in the people who live in this Elysian setting, where beauty and betrayal set off each other in dazzling contrast. South Africa is Eden after the fall but before the expulsion. As man came to know the terrible joys of his own humanity, the full limits and determinate nature of earthly existence only through the fall, perhaps South Africa can come to know its full human potential only by passing through the dark night that currently envelops it. Like Camus, we must leave Sisyphus at the bottom of the mountain, where hope seems most futile but also most necessary. Perhaps in watching the South Africans shoulder their heavy burden of racial conflict we will all learn something. If not, that burden will surely crush first them, and then us.

Willard Johnson shows that industrial growth is so far from helping the poor that "the gulf between the richest twenty percent of families and the poorest twenty percent (as measured in constant 1969 dollars) widened from $10,565 in 1947 to $19,071 in 1969." These are American statistics, but the gap has widened throughout the world. The ratio between industrialized societies and those in the rest of the world was two to one in 1850, nearly fifteen to one in 1960, and if present trends continue it may reach thirty to one by the year 2000.

Although Johnson foresees no simple solutions, he is aware of the limits of industrial growth and suggests that the only practical option is a redistribution of wealth. Johnson develops a strong case for such redistribution but clearly presents the opposite side of the coin: "The deepest pitfall of all for redistribution programs" is the *belief*—held by poor and rich alike—"that to receive some direct benefit from a transfer system is to get something for nothing, and to get something for nothing makes one dependent and therefore less than a man, certainly less than an American." Here we have another belief that may have to be dealt with before constructive change can be effected.

Should the Poor Buy No Growth?
—*Willard R. Johnson*

No-growth societies—those that experience very little increase in population or per capita income or production—have, historically, been bottom heavy with poor people. The so-called "traditional societies" are the only examples we know. They have emphasized ecological balance and man's accommodation to the forces of nature. Many people consider rapid expansion of production and reproduction to require some special (cultural if not racial) blessings such as the Protestant Ethic, the Spirit of Capitalism, and the Industrial Revolution. Are we now to have a no-growth society composed of rich people or of some mixture of economic classes that includes a substantial number of rich people? The noted British socialist, Anthony Crosland, has stated that the current champions of the no-growth society

Reprinted by permission of *Deadalus,* Journal of the American Academy of Arts and Sciences, Boston, Mass. Fall 1973, *The No-Growth Society*.

are often kindly and dedicated people. But they are affluent; and fundamentally, though of course not consciously, they want to kick the ladder
down behind them. They are militant mainly about threats to rural peace
and wildlife and well loved beauty spots; but little concerned with the
far more desperate problem of the urban environment in which 80 per
cent of our citizens live.[1]

Is the superindustrial society going to be like the "traditional society"?
Is such a society now, for the first time in history, to be the social condition of
the wealthy instead of the poor? What is the proper response of the poor to
the call for a return to a no-growth society? Should the poor buy no growth?

In truth, practically nobody, rich or poor, argues for absolutely zero population or economic growth on a universal basis. Interests are not coherent in
these matters any more than in most others. Changes in population and income
are not always clearly related, certainly not in a consistently positive or negative way, and not in the same way for the aspiring as for the already affluent.
Rich people desire no population growth for the poor, but continued money
growth for themselves and perhaps even for the poor if it does not dampen their
own. The poor want to expand the ranks of the rich by at least their own number, but they do not want further income growth for the already rich. Some
poor people think increases in their own numbers enhance their chances of
becoming richer through political advantage in developed countries, through
increased productive labor resources in developing countries. They may regard efforts to reduce their rates of population growth as motivated by geno-
cidal or antidemocratic intentions. Of course, many of the poor do wish to
have fewer children; they recognize the grain of truth in the adage, "The rich
get richer and the poor get children." They may therefore prefer selective
growth policies which favor growth in the numbers but not necessarily in the
per capita wealth of the rich, and growth in the per capita wealth of the poor
but not in their numbers.

In any case, the question of which policies the poor should prefer is irrelevant.
The poor can't "buy" what the rich won't "sell," and the rich hoard all the
really effective roles in determining the outcome of such policy debates. It
will take power to alter the direction of fundamental economic trends and patterns of resource utilization in the United States and in the world. The numbers
of poor do not amount to a sufficient resource to offset the power of wealth.
Not yet. Perhaps the rich fear that someday they may and thus, in these debates, they stress population control as a starting point.

NO GROWTH DEFINED IN TERMS OF POPULATION

Population increase is not the real issue, however, at least not in America.[2]
Our projected population profile suggests that the American population will

---

[1]Mobil Oil Corporation, "Growth Is the Only Way America Will ever Reduce Poverty," Advertisement, *New York Times,* April 13, 1972.
[2]Glen C. Cain, "Issues in the Economics of a Population Policy in the United States," *American
Economic Review,* 61, No. 2 (May 1971).

double in about sixty years. While this will obviously put some strain on our resources, it will not overburden them. With only 6 percent of the world's population using perhaps 50 percent of its material resources, there is plenty of room for population growth in the United States. A more important reason to control population growth would be to reduce the level of our resources utilization in order to permit the rest of the world to achieve a standard of living nearer to what current standards call decent. Nonetheless, many Americans are concerned that if we limit population increase to near the zero point, the present basically young U.S. population will grow older without replenishing the youth, and the society will come to resemble a Florida retirement colony.

There is evidence that American women no longer want to have more children than would permit the population to approach nearly zero growth.[3] It seems safe to say that the technology of preventing unwanted births will improve and that soon it will be safe and fairly painless, even morally, to reduce the rate of childbirth to the level desired by the women concerned. It may be that poorer women desire more children than richer ones,[4] or that, in any case, they desire more than the rich wish to see them have. Even so, population growth among the poor will not soon overburden our national resource base; it will, however, strain the resource base that those who control social policy allow to the poor. Thus the real population issues to the poor are the incompatibility of their values and desires with those of the rich, and their lack of power to protect and satisfy their own values. With regard to the population of the domestic United States, though perhaps not to that of the world, it is a ruse to couch the issue in the language of population explosion or overburdened resources.

NO GROWTH DEFINED IN TERMS OF PRODUCTION OR INCOME

Mancur Olson has suggested in the introduction to this issue that we define "no growth" as zero increase in per capita net national product (NNP). Such a definition, however, is basically irrelevant to the real issues involved in the no-growth debate. As he himself has pointed out, there are a number of items that would augment per capita NNP that would also enhance the quality of life, even to the no-growth advocates. Indeed many of the controls that would be required to eliminate threats to ecological balance, controls which most no-growth advocates desire, involve money transactions, and thus contribute to an increased per capita NNP. Furthermore, as we assign money values to householding services, or increase our expenditures on education, keeping other things constant, we increase per capita NNP without putting any additional strain on ecological balance.

The real issue is to avoid the type of growth that threatens the future life of the human species and that hampers optimum satisfaction of human wants

---

[3]*Ibid.*
[4]Paul R. Ehrlich and Anne H. Ehrlich, *Population, Resources and Environment: Issues in Human Ecology* (San Francisco: W. H. Freeman, 1972).

and needs. No-growth advocates do not arouse the concern of the poor as effectively as they might by calling for stable per capita net national product or even for zero population growth, when so many people still lack so much of what they want and need and of what their countrymen already have. It would be more relevant for them to emphasize the threatened depletion of resources fundamental to everybody's survival and health and to the survival of civilization itself—threats to life support systems and to ecological balance for the species.

Do the poor people in the United States or in the poor countries of the world have any special stake in defending against these threats that the richer populations do not have? Will they suffer sooner or to any greater extent? Are their survival resources any better or worse than those of the richer groups? These are questions well worth returning to. First, however, I will join the debate by discussing the issue that is generally argued, that of the impact of general per capita growth in national product or income on the elimination of poverty.

THE PROPAGANDA WAR IN FAVOR OF GROWTH

The industrial enterprises that are most directly threatened by the depletion of nonrenewable mineral and fuel resources are seldom found among the ranks of the no-growth advocates. In fact, they are in the forefront of a propaganda campaign to convince the poor that their best hope for eliminating poverty is continued economic growth. This seems curious. The most blatant example is provided by the Mobil Oil Company which has invested an impressive sum to sponsor advertisements designed to convince the poor that economic growth is a requisite to the elimination of poverty in the United States. One such ad, quoted by Peter Passell and Leonard Ross in "Don't Knock the $2-Trillion Economy,"[5] runs as follows:

GROWTH IS THE ONLY WAY AMERICA WILL EVER REDUCE POVERTY. . . . While the relative share of income that poor people get seems to be frozen, their incomes do keep pace with the economy. It's more lucrative to wash cars or wait on tables today than 20 years ago. Even allowing for inflation, the average income of the bottom 10th of the population has increased about 55 percent since 1950. Twenty more years of growth could do for the poor what the Congress won't do.

The problem with the logic of this argument is that it fails to give due consideration either to alternative ways of eliminating poverty (such as transfer payments) or to the changes that occur in consumption needs. Things such as telephones and television sets that were not considered necessities twenty years ago are seen as such today. Another Mobil Oil advertisement in the series says:

We can have full employment and true equality of opportunity only in an economy that creates new jobs and new opportunities. We can have

---

[5]Peter Passell and Leonard Ross, "Don't Knock the $2-Trillion Economy," *New York Times Sunday Magazine,* March 5, 1972.

decent homes and a decent environment only with proper land use, continuing technological innovation and an adequate and dependable supply of energy.

Still another asserts in a headline, "Growth is not a four-letter word." It quotes British socialist Anthony Crosland:

Even if we stopped all further growth tomorrow, we should still need to spend huge additional sums on coping with pollution. We have no chance of finding these huge sums from near-static GNP, any more than we could find the extra sums we want for health or education or any of our other goals. Only rapid growth will give us any possibility.

The fact that it is Mobil Oil, which admits that "The United States will consume more than twice as much oil in the next 30 years as it has consumed in the entire history of the country's oil industry," that spent the thousands of dollars for these advertisements to convince the poor that their hope lies in economic growth makes the argument suspect in itself.

ECONOMIC GROWTH AND ELIMINATION OF
OFFICIALLY DEFINED POVERTY

Can we really count on continued increases in per capita GNP or NNP to substantially reduce if not eliminate poverty in the United States? However indignant we might be over the fact that the owners and managers of Mobil Oil or General Motors will benefit more from growth than the poor, we might comfort ourselves if poverty were being eliminated, even if inequality were not. But there is no clear evidence that poverty is or can be eliminated as a consequence of the processes of general economic growth.

It is quite clear that the ranks of the poor have thinned recently during years of significant economic growth. In 1959 there were nearly 40 million people who would be classified as poor by today's Census Bureau standards. This number had fallen to 25.6 million in 1971, a decrease of 14.4 million in twelve years, or nearly 1.2 million a year. It is tempting to conclude that, if similar trends could be maintained, all the poor could be moved out of official poverty in twenty-one years. Alan Batchelder has, in fact, noted that "the drop in the incidence of poverty was so great between 1961 and 1968 that if the 1961 to 1968 trend were to continue through 1981 America would have no poverty."[6] It is not, however, that simple a matter. There have been some important fluctuations in the rate of poverty elimination, as Batchelder's comments indicate. The seven-year rate was higher than the eleven-year rate. The trend may reverse itself. The number of poor rose from 1959 to 1961, and again from 1969 to 1970, and it did not change from 1970 to 1971.[7] Perhaps, despite economic growth, we are now entering a period of increasing numbers of poor. (Some

[6] Alan B. Batchelder, *The Economics of Poverty* (New York: Wiley, 1971), pp. 25ff.
[7] U.S. Department of Commerce, Bureau of the Census, *The Social and Economic Situation of the Black Population in the United States (SESBPUS)*, Current Population Series, P-23, No. 42 (July 1972).

economists, however, feel that statistical techniques account for the rising number of people considered poor.[8])

Structural features of the American economy cause the relationship between growth and the rate at which poverty is eliminated to produce different results at different times. Features of general growth that had a significant impact on poverty twenty years ago have much less today. Batchelder and several others[9] have noted that structured-in poverty will be increasingly difficult to eliminate. The decline in poverty between 1961 and 1968 resulted from an expansion of aggregate demand and increased labor productivity. By 1968, however, the able-bodied poor who were capable of doing so had already worked their way out of poverty. But work, in itself, is not sufficient to remove a family from poverty. In 1970 the heads of nearly three million poor families were employed, but this did not protect them from poverty.[10]

Poverty is a feature built into the current American economy and social structure. It results from social, political and economic discrimination which thwarts needed investment in poor people.[11] It is not due to an abundance of bums who do not want to work but rather to an abundance of businessmen who won't or can't give jobs to those who need them, and of labor unions that won't allow people to acquire the credentials and skills they need to get jobs. Those most likely to be left out of the picture of general growth are blacks (except for young urban black families in the North in which both father and mother work), families headed by females, farm families, and the elderly. The poverty of these groups is relatively impervious to the benefits of general economic progress.[12] Economists are unable to agree as to the extent and reasons why these groups are isolated.

However, the fact is that we prevent old people from working and, in 1970, 4.7 million elderly persons, comprising 4.6 percent of all household units, accounted for 18.2 percent of the poor individuals in the country.[13] We keep blacks from getting jobs: in 1971 nearly one million blacks, or almost 10 percent of the national nonwhite work force, were officially classified as unemployed,[14] and unofficially the figures are probably much higher. In Massachusetts in mid-1972 the unemployment rate for inner city blacks was over 22 percent and among the black youth it was over 35 percent. The black poor are more likely than the white poor to be employed, but both their employment and their education work less well for them. In 1971, nearly 10 percent of the black male heads-of-families with some college education were impoverished, as compared to only 3 percent of whites.[15]

---

[8]Herman P. Miller, "Changes in the Number and Composition of the Poor," *Inequality and Poverty,* ed. Edward C. Budd (New York: Norton, 1968), pp. 152–166.

[9]*SESBPUS;* Theodore W. Schultz, "Public Approaches to Minimize Poverty," *Poverty Amid Affluence,* ed. L. Fishman (New Haven, Conn.: Yale University Press, 1966).

[10]U.S. Office of Economic Opportunity, Office of Planning, Research and Evaluation, *The Poor in 1970: A Chartbook* (Washington, D.C.: U.S. Government Printing Office, 1972).

[11]Schultz, "Public Approaches to Minimize Poverty."

[12]Miller, "Changes in the Number and Composition of the Poor."

[13]OEO, *The Poor in 1970.*

[14]*SESBPUS,* p. 51.

[15]*Ibid.*

Improving the industrial structure, providing tight labor markets, and holding down inflation would be important public policy objectives in order to improve black incomes. However, economic growth has not and will not improve the situation very much, though recession may aggravate it considerably as it did between 1969 and 1970. Poverty seems to be built into our current social and economic structure. As Theodore Schultz has noted, our most important declines in poverty have been due to increases in income from labor, which are in turn due to increases in the demand for high skills and to the responsiveness of the labor force to this market situation. But blacks, agricultural workers, women, older people and workers in the South have generally been kicked out or held out of these labor markets.[16]

Growth, defined as rising per capita NNP, can have some positive effect on the incidence of poverty for some blacks, less so for whites. Lester Thurow, a leading analyst of measures of poverty, has determined that "General growth results in higher incomes for both blacks and whites," but the key element for blacks in this is the availability of jobs, especially of full-time jobs in the government service and industrial sectors.[17] These are the types of jobs that blacks have been able to get and to benefit from most fully. In the future, however, there is likely to be more flexibility in the service than in the industrial sector, especially if ecological balance becomes a more potent influence on our economic policies.

There are special implications here for the zero economic growth advocates. The industries in which blacks have a foothold and a potential for economic improvement are precisely those where we find the greatest ecological hazards. Blacks are particularly entrenched in the auto industry and many of the industries and services peripheral to it. Blacks constitute 23 percent of nonfarm, nonconstruction laborers.[18] Black workers form substantial contingents in industries which deal with chemicals, fabricated metals, primary metals, and nonelectrical machinery and transportation equipment. Industries like these are closely identified with the problems of poisoned lakes and streams, and with overuse of material resources, especially of nonrenewable resources such as petroleum, natural gas, and other fuels that will become increasingly important as energy sources in the future. Traffic problems, overcrowding, noise, and other invasions of psychic domains are also rooted in these industrial activities. Those whose predominant objectives are ecological may threaten economic progress for blacks as well as for great numbers of nonblack and nonminority poor.

An equally important if not more serious threat to these industries is the fact that the raw materials that feed them are close to exhaustion. This is particularly threatening to patterns of industry in the United States because we account for such high percentages of total world usage. Paul and Anne Ehrlich note, for example:

[16]Schultz, "Public Approaches to Minimize Poverty," pp. 165–181.
[17]Lester Thurow, ed., "Analyzing the American Income Distribution," *American Economic Review,* 60, No. 2 (May 1970), 261–269.
[18]*SESBPUS,* p. 68.

Estimates of the total American utilization of raw materials currently run as high as 50 percent of the world's consumption, with a projection of current trends to about 80 percent around 1980. Probably 30 percent and 50 percent would be more realistic figures, but in any event our consumption is far beyond our "share" on a basis of population. We number less than 6 percent of the world's people![19]

The Club of Rome's *The Limits of Growth* presents an even more dire picture. Taking into account rates of utilization that are growing exponentially, and even assuming that, somehow, five times the known reserves of needed raw materials will be found, they predict that we will exhaust those materials most crucial to present patterns of industrial civilization within 173 years.[20]

The other way to relate per capita NNP and officially defined poverty is to ask: Would a slackening of growth or a lack of growth especially hurt the poor? Would it wipe out the gains that have already been made? Certainly the periods of stagnation and decline in 1958, 1961–1962, and 1969–1970 have tended to do so. Especially among the black population there were income reversals in each of these periods. The economic progress that poor people, especially blacks, made in the 1960's essentially ended with the Nixon Administration. The percentage of white and black families and individuals in poverty has remained virtually constant since 1968.[21] A lack of continued growth, without substantial change in national policies to facilitate the transfer of wealth and income through transfer payments, tax reform and job development, or vigorous antidiscrimination efforts would probably have disastrous consequences for blacks, and perhaps for the poor more generally.

ECONOMIC GROWTH AND ELIMINATION OF UNOFFICIAL POVERTY

The statistical improvements we have been examining are, to an alarming degree, merely a matter of definition. The minimal income level established in 1969 by the Federal Interagency Committee reflects the interest of federal agencies that are supposed to reduce the incidence of poverty. They are more concerned about statistical results than about human needs. In 1971 they considered $4,137 to be the annual income figure beyond which the typical American family (an urban family of four composed of a thirty-eight-year-old husband, a nonworking mother, a boy of fifteen and a girl of eight) was no longer in the "low income" or poor group. Other federal bureaus, with different clientele and interests, define the problem according to other sets of criteria. The Department of Labor has announced that this "typical" American family needed $7,214 a year to maintain the lowest "reasonable and decent" standard of living as of the autumn of 1971.[22] This minimum is far

---

[19]Ehrlich and Ehrlich, *Population, Resources and Environment,* p. 58.
[20]Dennis L. Meadows, Donella H. Meadows, Jorgen Randers, and William W. Behrens, III, *The Limits of Growth,* A Report for the Club of Rome (New York: Universe Books, 1972), Table 4, pp. 56–57.
[21]*SESBPUS,* pp. 38–39.

below the $10,971 that they estimated would be needed for an intermediate standard of living, or the $16,000 for a high standard. But it is about twice the average family welfare allowance awarded in mid-1972 in Boston.

No doubt the poor aspire to comfort. We need not argue here whether the "American way" gives one a right to a comfortable level of income. It is apparent, however, that many needs for healthy and sane living in peaceful social settings must go unmet at the levels of income officially used to define poverty. Oscar Ornati has indicated criteria for defining various levels and types of poverty.[23] L. Fishman summarizes his position as follows:

> Ornati defines poverty generally as the lack of command over goods and services sufficient to meet minimum needs. These needs are different as seen from different perspectives. The most often used poverty calculations approximate those which Ornati bases on eligibility guidelines for public assistance programs. This level he calls the "minimum subsistence" poverty budget. The federal government makes use of another set of budgets to determine "living wages" requirements. Ornati calls this poverty level "minimum adequacy." Yet a third poverty line can be established on the basis of guidelines that have been used to settle various wage disputes. This level he calls "minimum comfort." All three levels are of "poverty."

The minimum adequacy and minimum comfort budgets reflect the demands and pressures of the population to which they are applied, the organized and working poor, more than does the subsistence budget which is administratively determined for welfare and other public assistance recipients. These budgets have grown over the years in response to rising prices and needs more than the subsistence budget. Thus the number of people with incomes falling below the subsistence budget poverty line has tended to decline without any real lessening of misery or greater satisfaction of need.

Another influence on measurements of the incidence of poverty is the use of constant dollar and value standards to define poverty. Projecting 1960 standards of poverty in 1960 dollar values backwards thirty years would define more people as poor than were considered so at the time. Similarly, if we used the standards of thirty years ago and projected them forward to today, we would find that some of the poverty had dwindled for statistical reasons alone. Ornati concludes that it is more fair and accurate to compare amounts of poverty in terms of contemporary standards.[24]

It seems that the best we can hope for from recent economic trends is to reduce the number of people who live under conditions of abject poverty, below the level of income by which the Census Bureau officially defines poverty. But how long would we have to wait for those trends to eliminate poverty even at this unrealistically low level? Lowell Galloway, writing in 1965, attempted

---

[22]*The Boston Globe,* May 7, 1972.
[23]Oscar Ornati, "The Poverty Band and the Count of the Poor," *Inequality and Poverty,* ed. Edward C. Budd, as summarized by Fishman, ed., *Poverty Amid Affluence.*
[24]*Ibid.*

to strengthen the case for using growth as a tool to eliminate poverty.[25] He criticized the projections of poverty reduction made by the Council of Economic Advisers on the basis that they assume that a linear relationship exists between rates of economic growth and poverty elimination, and that all families are either completely unresponsive or equally responsive to economic change. He assumed instead a nonlinear relationship which enabled him to claim a higher poverty elimination rate although one that declines with additional economic progress, leaving a residual group who are increasingly impervious to the benefits of economic progress, including blacks, female-headed families, farm families, and the like. He makes his own projections, which can be compared to the CEA ones, based on the differing rates of economic growth and levels of unemployment in the periods 1947–1956 and 1956–1963. In addition, he varied his assumptions about the level of unemployment.

FIGURE 1

Actual and Projected Percent of
Families Below Poverty Line

	GALLOWAY			COUNCIL
Unemployed	*4%* *(1947–1956)*	*5%* *(1970)*	*6%* *(1957–1963, 1971)*	
1956 actual	22.2%			22.2%
1963 projected	16.6			18.5
1963 actual			18.5	
1970 projected	12.6		14.2	
1970 actual		10.0		10.0
1971 actual			9.9	9.9
1980 projected	6.4		8.7	10.0

Galloway concluded that growth could not eliminate poverty much below the 6 percent level but would get us to that level sooner than the Council had estimated. The actual level of unemployment in 1970 was 5 percent and since early 1971 has been around 6 percent, and the actual percentage of all families represented by the poor was 10 percent in 1970 and 9.9 percent in 1971, so perhaps the figures of the Council of Economic Advisers are closer to the correct ones. It is clear that the rate of poverty elimination is now virtually zero. Perhaps we have already reached Galloway's impervious hard core, but at 10 percent rather than 6.4 percent of all families. Poverty is going to continue to be a problem, even as officially defined, for more than another decade, despite projections of growth. John Hardesty and others predict that in 1990 there will still be 2.5 million families and 5 million unrelated individuals living in poverty compared to the 5.3 million families and 5 million individuals who were poor in 1971.[26]

[25]L. E. Galloway, "The Foundations of the 'War on Poverty,' " *American Economic Review,* 55, No. 1 (March 1965), 122–131.
[26]John Hardesty, "An Empirical Study of the Relationship Between Poverty and Economic Prosperity," *Review of Radical Political Economy,* 3, No. 4 (Winter 1971), 93; current figures from U.S. Department of Commerce Current Population Reports, Series P-60, No. 86, Table 5.

RELATIVE STANDARDS OF INCOME AND WEALTH

We have discussed several concepts of poverty, all of them absolute, based that is, on definite fixed budgets defined almost exclusively in terms of what it costs to meet certain selected needs. There are also relativistic concepts which define poverty in terms of the incomes of other groups. The absolutistic approach is akin to the legal concept of due process, a minimum standard to which everyone has a right, while the relativistic approach accords with the legal doctrine of equal protection or equity, which seeks to avoid extreme differences in the way the system deals with people. The absolutistic is the less controversial of the two. Since we can predetermine consumption patterns and supply and calculate the cost of living, being poor or rich has, according to this standard, a precise and stable meaning. Ironically, however, a competitive free enterprise system that spurs individualism and egotism makes it harder, not easier, to ignore relative standing. People in our society, especially the poor, value keeping up with the Joneses. Thus it is perhaps more realistic to define poverty in relative terms that take into account the changes in income and expenditures patterns of the general society.

The most common relative standard of poverty is arbitrarily pegged at 50 percent of the median income. Perhaps we accept this standard only out of aesthetic appreciation for its symmetry—half of half. But, defined this way, poverty is less tractable than it is when defined by any but the most generous absolutistic standards. Here we are really talking about reducing income inequality. In the postwar period income inequalities have increased in the American society, a fact which may take on increasing importance because of the exalted place equality has occupied in American myth.

Let us look first at the nation's performance with respect to reducing income inequality. Herbert Gans has observed that in the United States between 1960 and 1970, when the median family income rose from $5,260 to $9,820, the proportion of families earning half the median dropped only 1 percent—from 20 to 19 percent.[27] This is a far less striking improvement than can be claimed when poverty is defined according to the absolutistic measures used by the Census Bureau. The disparity of results produced by techniques of accounting is revealed with great clarity in this example: in 1960 the poverty line did fall at 50 percent of median individual income, but the poverty line was not permitted to rise as median income rose so that by 1970 the poverty line came to only 40 percent of the median. As Gans notes, "During the decade the poverty line rose far more slowly than the median income, and the inequality gap between the poor and the median earners actually widened by a full twenty percent."[28] This permitted officials to claim that the number of poor had declined when almost the same proportion of households had incomes below 50 percent of the median income.

Thurow and Lucas have measured the retrogression of the poor when their income is measured against that of others, especially of the decidedly rich:

---

[27]Herbert Gans, "The New Egalitarianism," *Saturday Review,* May 6, 1972.
[28]*Ibid.*

they note that the gulf between the richest 20 percent of families and the poorest 20 percent (as measured in constant 1969 dollars) widened from $10,565 in 1947 to $19,071 in 1969.[29]

The picture is worse for blacks, a point of particular importance. Blacks have a special interest in the matter of eliminating poverty, not because they are the only poor people—they are a minority even among the poor—but because about a third of all blacks are poor, even in terms of the arbitrarily low official poverty line. Poverty is no less frequent, and no more welcome in black households now than before the antipoverty programs. Since 1948, non-white income has made what appear to be spectacular gains, going from $7.9 billion to approximately $46 billion in 1971. But any comparison of black income to white income, whether in terms of aggregate income, or of median level, or of percent of total income compared to percent of total population, shows that blacks have not made much headway; Negroes held 5.1 percent of the total white income in 1948, a mere 6.4 percent in 1963, and only about 6.6 percent in 1971.[30] There is, however, a widening span between the aggregate income by race calculated in dollar amounts: in 1948 white income was $146.2 billion, nonwhite $7.9 billion—a difference of $138.3 billion; by 1963 white

FIGURE 2

*Median Income of Nonwhite Families as a Percent
of White Median Family Income, 1950–1971.*[31]

Year	Nonwhite	Year	Nonwhite
1950	54%	1961	53%
1951	53	1962	53
1952	57	1963	53
1953	56	1964	56
1954	56	1965	55
1955	55	1966	60
1956	53	1967	62
1957	54	1968	63
1958	51	1969	63
1959	52	1970	64
1960	55	1971	63

income had climbed to $347.5 billion while the Negro's rose to $23.6 billion— a difference which had also expanded to $232.9 billion; by 1971 white income was $649 billion and black income was $46 billion, a difference of $603 billion.[32]

The same picture of lack of progress emerges from a comparison of black and white median family income. Patterns of distribution within each racial group have augmented the disparity between blacks and whites on the lower

---

[29]*The Boston Globe,* March 20, 1972, p. 1.
[30]Sidney M. Wilhelm, *Who Needs the Negro?* (Garden City, N.Y.: Doubleday, 1971), p. 163; U.S. Department of Commerce Population Report, Series P-60, No. 86, Table 37.
[31]*SESBPUS,* Series P-23, No. 42, Table 16, p. 29.
[32]*Ibid.*

end of the income scale. Sources since 1950 differ in specifics, but they indicate that in general black median family income has fluctuated in the area of 50 to 60 percent of white median family income. Figure 2 gives the available figures. In addition, the gap in absolute dollar figures between white and non-white median family income is actually widening: in 1947 it was $2,174; by 1966, it was $3,036; and by 1971, it was $4,270, more than double the 1947 figure.[33]

Wealth inequalities may be a more significant factor in the no-growth debate than income inequalities: not only are they greater, but they also have long-range effects on income, and are likely to increase with growth. Furthermore, because of the power of wealth, they are less subject to change as a result of politics. Given the lack of strong redirecting forces in the economy, some growth probably gets absorbed into wealth: even the superrich can only spend so much on current consumption. This absorbed capital acts as a corrective, however, because, by limiting consumption, it dampens growth.

The disparities between white and black family wealth, or net family worth, are very stark. They have been calculated in a tentative fashion by Andrew Brimmer, who indicates an average gap of $16,214.[34] The disparities within the general society, ignoring racial differences, are even greater. Whites have as much cause as blacks to be concerned about them because wealth is highly concentrated in the United States, and is becoming ever more so. Brimmer reports that, in the late 1960's, over half of all private assets were owned by about 9 percent of American families.[35] Gans reports that the country has always had an unequal distribution of wealth: "In 1774, among the minority of Philadelphians affluent enough to pay taxes, 10 percent owned fully 89 percent of the taxable property."[36] While we have made some headway in reducing inequality since 1774, things have not changed very much in this century.

The landmark Lampman study found that in 1953 more than 30 percent of the assets and equities of the personal sector of the economy (about 20 percent of all wealth was government owned) were held by only 1.6 percent of the adult population.[37] They held all ownership of state and local (tax exempt) bonds, more than 82 percent of all stock, 38 percent of all federal bonds, 29 percent of all cash, 16 percent of the real estate holdings, 13 percent of life insurance reserves, and 6 percent of pension and retirement funds. R. J. Lampman's data generate the chart of wealth in Figure 3. Notice how much of the total held by the top 1 percent is actually held by the top 0.5 percent.

[33] Andrew F. Brimmer and Henry S. Terrell, "The Economic Potential of Black Capitalism," paper presented at the 82nd Annual Meeting of the American Economic Association (New York: December 1969) for 1947 and 1966 data; *SESBPUS*, p. 1, for 1971 data.

[34] Brimmer and Terrell, "The Economic Potential of Black Capitalism."

[35] *Ibid.;* Michigan Survey Research Center confirms in 1972 that the top 10% own 56% of all wealth. Cf: Michael Brower, "Some Issues of Economic Structure, Policy and Politics in Latin America and the U.S.," paper presented to the Annual Meeting of the American Political Science Association (Washington, D.C.: September 5–7, 1972).

[36] Gans, "The New Egalitarianism," p. 44.

[37] R. J. Lampman, *The Share of Top Wealth-Holders in National Wealth, 1922–1956* (Princeton, N.J.: Princeton University Press, 1962), p. 23.

FIGURE 3

Concentration of Wealth in the United States[38]

Year	½ of 1% of Adults (Percent of All Wealth)	1% of Adults
1922	29.8	31.6
1929	32.4	36.3
1933	25.2	28.3
1939	28.0	30.6
1945	20.9	23.3
1949	19.3	20.8
1953	22.7	24.2–28.7[39]
1954	22.5	n.a
1956	25.0	26.0
1958	n.a.	30.0[40]
1962	n.a.	31.0[41]
1969	n.a.	28.0–34.0[39]

In the recent years of renewed economic growth, the number of very wealthy has increased: in 1966 there were over 90,000 millionaires, for example, whereas in 1953 Lampman recorded only 27,000. Part of this is due to inflation which boosts the money value of holdings more than consumption power.[42] But the concentration of wealth has also been increasing, as Figure 3 shows. Gans asserts that the top 1 percent of wealth holders currently own more than a third of all wealth.

In terms of the position of the poor in the no-growth debate, the type of wealth that is concentrated is more important than the degree of concentration. The superrich hold even larger portions of investment wealth than of general wealth, and it is investment wealth which directs the activities of productive corporations; which determines levels of expansion, job creation, prices, reinvestment, etc.; and which has such a profound effect on politics. It has been asserted that the top 200,000 wealth holders own 32 percent of all investment assets,[43] and that 2 percent of individual stock holders own about two-thirds of all stock held by individuals.[44]

---

[38]R. C. Edwards, M. Reich, and T. E. Weisskopf, *The Capitalist System* (Englewood Cliffs, N.J.: Prentice-Hall, 1972), Table 4-E, p. 170.

[39]The lower figure was computed by James Smith of the University of Pennsylvania, based on estate holdings net of debt, a methodology different from that used by Lampman. The higher figure is what I understand that the Internal Revenue Service has calculated, taking into account certain actuarial estimates. Smith has calculated the concentration of wealth for 1953 as well, which is the higher figure reported for that year. His figures show no substantial change since that time, although all the intervening years have not yet been calculated.

[40]*Ibid.*, Table 5-E, p. 211.

[41]*Ibid.*, p. 172.

[42]Lampman's 27,000 1953 dollar value millionaires would have numbered only 17,611 in terms of 1944 dollar values.

[43]Edwards, *et al.*, *The Capitalist System*, p. 173.

[44]Gans, "The New Egalitarianism."

The impact of that control is amplified by the extent to which a few corporations dominate the business sector. One-tenth of 1 percent of the almost two million corporations in this country control 55 percent of the total corporate assets; 1.1 percent control 82 percent of those assets.[45] William Buckley has pointed out that the 200 largest firms in America command 58.7 percent of the market place. This is up from the 48 percent in 1948.[46] What does this domination mean? Perhaps it is what leads the federal government to subsidize businesses to the level of $63 billion, a fact determined recently by William Proxmire's Joint Economic Committee; or perhaps it supports the tax loopholes which cost the government $77 billion, according to economists Benjamin A. Okner and Joseph A. Pechman; or perhaps it is responsible for what populist Fred Harris points to: an estimated $60 billion in overcharges made by shared monopolies which can set prices without much regard to laws of supply and demand.[47]

With this kind of concentrated economic power, perhaps it really doesn't matter whether the poor want to buy no growth or not. The basic decisions are made by the superrich, and can only be moderated by political forces. To the relatively poor, the debate as it is currently argued ignores the real issues. Neither side can offer much relief, certainly not sufficient relief, without resorting to policies calling for a substantial redistribution of income, and perhaps of wealth as well.

REDISTRIBUTION

As we have seen, no trends allow us to predict in a clear-cut manner just when recent patterns of economic activity will eliminate poverty in the United States. Moreover, those debating growth or no-growth policies disagree about their implications for the poor. Mobil Oil echoes Passell and Ross in asserting that "Growth is the only way America will ever reduce poverty," while noted economist Lester Thurow asserts that "poverty cannot be eliminated without direct income transfers."[48]

A decade of impressive economic growth but meager improvement in the poverty situation makes it an act of wisdom to side with Thurow. The real issue then is to determine the relationship between achieving effective income transfers and economic growth. Is it easier or harder to get redistribution with no growth as the goal of public policy or as the condition of the economy?

It is useful to distinguish the import of the no-growth debate as a debate or clash of values and preferences from the implications of impending real limits to growth. Often the debate is argued as if both sides could assume the possibility of continued growth and thus dispute only the costs of such growth.

---

[45]Ibid., p. 43.
[46]William F. Buckley, Jr., "A Look Back: ITT Pulled In," The Boston Globe, Friday, July 7, 1972, p. 17.
[47]Fred Harris, "The Real Populism Fights Unequal Wealth," New York Times, Op-Ed, May 25, 1972.
[48]Passell and Ross, "Don't Knock the $2-Trillion Economy"; Thurow, Poverty and Discrimination, p. 151.

The "no growthers" point to the problems of continued growth: fouling of the atmosphere, dangers to health, offense to the senses, rising prices for scarce nonrenewable resources and the products that use them, crowding, ugliness, and loss of recreational resources and beauty spots. The "growthers" point to the dangers of no growth: the lack of improvement in economic well-being and the resultant increases in social turmoil among the poor as their convictions that they play in a zero sum game are confirmed; the increased rigidity and more forceful political control on the part of the superrich who neither wish nor feel the need to accept a more slender slice of the economic pie.

Stuart Chase has called this debate over growth an antagonism between partisans of the gross national product on the one hand and partisans of the quality of life on the other, between green-money men and green-earth men. Put this way, I again question whether either side has solace to offer the poor. The money men are holdovers from the days of what Charles Reich calls Consciousness II: a society which contains the seeds of its own destruction and will be replaced by Consciousness III. Consciousness III types are now busy organizing earth days and holding ecology marches; they would rather be honey-seekers than money-seekers, but then they can be both. The revolution they pursue is not likely to involve the partisans of the black revolution who find it hard to drop the concerns of Consciousness II, lest they leap-frog history altogether. The black and white youth of the counterculture quickly fell out with each other.

To be relevant to the needs of the poor, those who advocate growth will have to talk more specifically and effectively than they have to date about specific types and rates of growth that would alleviate the misery of the underclass. Merely saying that growth is good and has not done all it can do to eliminate poverty is not enough. On the other hand, they could take some of the heat off themselves by pointing out the failure of no-growth advocates to deal directly with the problems of the poor.

British economist E. J. Mishan, a no-growth advocate, is guilty of debating the issues in terms of values that, for all their humaneness, ignore the concerns of the poor. He challenges economic growth policies because he questions values deeply rooted in Western society. The trouble with growth, according to him, lies with the materialistic nature of a social order that piles up more and more material goods. He sees this as destructive to humane values and antithetical to human happiness. Growth, to him, is a potentially unbalanced, misdirected, and destructive force in itself. No doubt his concerns feed on a genuine consideration for the quality of life, but they seem to me mistaken about the contribution material goods can make to it.

John Kenneth Galbraith, sometimes counted in Mishan's camp on the growth question, is more concerned about the failure of the post-Keynesian synthesis on which we once relied, at least in terms of expectation, to harness growth to the interest of the general good, including the reduction of poverty. That synthesis coupled Keynes' policies for promoting high levels of employment and high rates of growth with Alfred Marshall's policies for allocating resources and distributing incomes in order to respond to social needs within a private, essentially market-oriented economy. The synthesis was effected by Paul Samuelson, who was not unconcerned about poverty and other socially disturbing imperfections in the economy, but who did not believe that a police state was required to protect advantage, or that fundamental redistribution of income and wealth was necessary to eliminate severe disadvantage. Fusfeld has characterized Samuelson's system:[49]

> Much of the system rested on the assumption that competition would prevail and concentrated economic power could not control markets for its own benefit. To ensure competition and prevent monopolies from building up, the post Keynesian synthesis required strong anti-trust legislation, and where natural monopolies existed . . . vigorous regulation by government . . . to ensure full employment and growth by the proper mix of spending, taxation, and monetary policy. . . . Even poverty might be ended by a growing economy.

Galbraith's analysis has revealed the failure of these assumptions to accord with reality. Monopolies did develop in the mature industrial societies, and are continuing to develop at an ever more rapid rate. Big business aided and abetted big government, and vice versa. Inflation became an overwhelming problem, even carrying over into periods of rising unemployment. Galbraith, like Mishan, now attacks economic growth itself; it doesn't work either as a goal or as a safety valve. An economy dominated by private decisions about consumption and production, he argues, tends to starve its public sectors.[50] The society's needs for long-term development, social betterment and general welfare get slighted in favor of luxuries and entertainment. It seems apparent today that big business can pretty much mold consumer tastes and spending patterns to its own needs.

Galbraith and Mishan call for a new synthesis, a reconstruction of economics to move us toward more humane goals, and to permit us to analyze more realistically the obstacles to that movement. Perhaps they reject less the values growth produces than the values that produce growth.

At this point I should specify what I mean by redistribution, for there are several redistribution schemes, most of which promise great improvement, and it is quite possible to misunderstand their character and their promise. Initially we might, as a nation, choose simply to eliminate what is officially defined as poverty; in 1971 this would have meant eliminating incomes lower than $4,137 for the modal family of four. Later, more humane floors for income might be established. We might also choose to transfer money directly only from the very richest of the population to the very poorest, rather than to spread the burden evenly among the nonpoor. To have done this in 1971 would have required that about $12.1 billion be added to the aggregate incomes of those officially designated by the Census Bureau as low-income families and individuals. To have taken this entire amount from the richest 5 percent of the

---

[49]Donald Fusfeld, "Post-Post Keynes: The Shattered Synthesis," *Saturday Review*, January 22, 1972.
[50]J. K. Galbraith, *The Affluent Society* (New York: New American Library, 1970), Ch. 22.

population would have reduced their pretax money incomes from all nonpublic transfer sources[51] only by 8.2 percent. Their share of the nation's total income would have dropped from 21.6 percent to 19.8 percent. Surely such a restriction of income would be economically and morally, if not politically, feasible.

More far-ranging proposals might reach substantially up into the ranks of those who find it virtually impossible to support their families adequately. These are not broken families, save perhaps in spirit. Heading these families, typically, is a working male, but, although they contain the clear majority of the country's population, they receive considerably less than a majority of the aggregate annual income.

Dr. Harold W. Watts of the University of Wisconsin proposed to the Democratic Party Platform hearings in St. Louis on June 17, 1972, one of the simplest plans yet advanced to aid not only the poor, but also the middle class that is under such financial stress. He proposed to replace the present public assistance and individual income tax programs, as well as all other means-tested programs with a "credit income tax" scheme. Each taxpayer would pay the same basic tax, at the rate of one third of all income received before the benefits derived from the redistribution scheme itself. There would be an additional 6⅔ percent surtax on any annual income in surplus of $50,000, and still another 10 percent surtax on income in surplus of $100,000. Money would then be redistributed back to *everybody* on an equal footing, regardless of income. Each aged and disabled person would receive a payment of $1,560 a year, able-bodied adults eighteen to sixty-four would receive $1,320 a year, children ten to seventeen would receive $660, and younger ones $420. The modal family of four could not have an income less than $3,720. Such a family would break even, that is, receive back as much as it paid in taxes, at an annual income of $11,160. Work incentives would operate all along the road: any person earning $3.00 would keep $2.00 as long as his total income were less than $50,000 a year, and no person, however rich, would lose more than 50 percent of any dollar.

The impact such a scheme would have on the current distribution of income seems startling. Seventy percent of the entire population would benefit, ending up with more money than they did in 1970. The poorest 20 percent of the population would have 10 percent of the total final income, compared to between 7.7 and 7.9 percent in 1970. The next 50 percent of the population would enjoy an increase of 5 to 7 percent over their 1970 income. Perhaps equally important, in terms of the political feasibility of the scheme, the total revenue available to the government would *increase* by about $3 billion over that generated by the present system.[52]

With 70 percent of the populace, as well as the government, coming out ahead under such a scheme, why does it not command the support of the coun-

---

[51]Excluding social security, direct public assistance, unemployment insurance, workmen's compensation and income-conditioned veterans' benefits.

[52]Watts' calculations utilize Brookings Institution (Schultz) estimates for 1975. They assume a population of 214 million, total incomes of $1,046 billion, tax yield of $361 billion, less credits of $232 billion plus $18 billion in replaced public assistance programs. Total for government, $147 billion, as against present projections of $144 billion.

try? Of course the scheme was mauled in the infighting of the Democratic primary candidates and McGovern's other liabilities were involved, but there was more to the opposition than that. As Passell and Ross state, "On the face of it, there should be an easy solution to poverty in the United States. A redistribution of only 5 percent of the national income could bring every family up to a minimum $5,000 income." But they point to the fate of the President's Family Assistance Program as evidence that the idea of "explicit redistribution of income is still political anathema."[53]

Part of the handicap of such proposals, as McGovern discovered, is public confusion about their "costs." Such proposals involve taking money away from some people, perhaps from all income receivers at one stage or another of the operation. That which is taken away is popularly regarded as a cost. The confusion lies in the notion that it is a cost to "the country." Actually the money is taken from some people and given to others. It does not cost the country anything, except the quite limited expenses of the administrative system that supervises the transfers. The important question is whom does it cost? Watts' scheme costs only the 30 percent who receive the highest incomes, and them not very much. But there is an apparent inclination for most people to believe the extremely wealthy, who are in fact threatened, when they scream that the program would cost "the country" the nearly $44 billion in net losses that they themselves would suffer. Such "costs" should properly be measured against the costs of social control, the losses incurred through crime and social turmoil to the extent that it is rooted in poverty and needless deprivation, or even against the $40 to $45 billion that the present system transfers among our people with far less positive results.

Perhaps we have not touched on the deepest pitfall of all for redistribution programs, the attitudes held as much if not more fervently by the poor than by the rich: that to receive some direct benefit from a transfer system is to "get something for nothing" and to get something for nothing makes one "dependent" and therefore less than a man, certainly less than an American.

Here, both the motive for and the failure of Nixon's Family Assistance Plan are most instructive, as brilliantly analyzed by one of its chief authors, D. P. Moynihan.[54] Far less bountiful than the plans we have already discussed, FAP would nonetheless have provided direct cash payments to the poor. Providing a maximum of $2,400, it would have eliminated only 60 percent of poverty but it would partially have covered the need of every poor child and concentrated on the working poor. The crisis to which Nixon was responding was seen in terms of welfare reform, and the issue of welfare, argues Moynihan,

is the issue of dependency. . . . Being poor is often associated in the minds of others with admirable qualities, but this is rarely the case with being dependent. . . . It is an incomplete state in life—normal in the child, abnormal in the adult. In a world where completed men and women

---

[53]Passell and Ross, "Don't Knock the $2-Trillion Economy," p. 70.
[54]Daniel P. Moynihan, *The Politics of a Guaranteed Income,* serialized in *The New Yorker,* January 13, 20 and 27, 1973.

stand on their own feet, persons who are dependent—as the buried imagery of the word denotes—hang.

It is one of the perversities of American life that only those who receive direct cash payments from government, not related to earnings from work, are considered dependent, and thus despicable; while those who receive services, benefits, and credits against costs they would otherwise pay, especially against taxes in the form of government guarantees, overruns, tax shelters, tax-free dividends, depreciation allowances, and the like, are considered independent, self-reliant embodiments of the work ethic. To add insult to injury, the welfare system has been designed and operated to ravish the family, degrade and deny the adult, and defeat the child. Thus, Moynihan admits, the system, seemingly deliberately to the victims, makes welfare recipients dependent in fact, unable to organize or utilize social resources of self-assertion or development in order to profit and progress, rather than slowly die as a result of the inadequacy of the payments in money and kind they receive. They are in a position analogous to that of the colonized and, in the words of Albert Memmi, "the colonized is not free to choose between being colonized or not being colonized."[55]

What is the source of such pernicious attitudes and practices? Perhaps it is the insistent strain of individualism in American culture. The exaltation of self-help, self-development, and rags-to-riches hopes certainly seems to play a part. Moynihan set the Family Assistance Plan against this background by asserting that its uniqueness derived from its assertion of "income by right." How odd that this concept should be unique—given the faith of the founding fathers in the "inalienable right" to "life." Life, but not the means to life? In a society where it is impossible to return to nature, and which cannot offer either enough work or enough pay for the work there is, one cannot sanely or justly assert the right to life without the right to the means for life.

These values of self-assertion and heroic individualism—each American making his own declaration of independence—are deemed to be a source not of pernicious outcomes, but of productivity. Productivity is considered perhaps the prime virtue; it defines the success of the individual and of the system; Eric Fromm takes it as the measure of virtue itself, although he charges the society that wishes to make people virtuous to make the unfolding and growth of every person the aim of all social and political activity. Instead, we have made it the prerequisite. Today productivity is preempted by technology, access to which is unequal. Virtue is assigned, then, only to those who control that access, a lessening proportion of the whole society. But people continue to live with their illusions, and thus to seek production, and the ordinary worker's growing sense of redundancy generates only vague anxieties. He will turn hardest against any initiative to distribute products to those who have lost or never gained any nexus with production at all. This outlook fits more easily with overall economic growth than with no growth. Times of growth justify

---

[55] Albert Memmi, *The Colonizer and the Colonized* (Boston: Beacon Press, 1965), p. 86.

a faith in the availability and even the meaningfulness of work. No growth threatens to awaken us to the prospect not simply of having less (which is not really necessary), but of *being* less, and without illusions. Opponents to the Family Assistance Program played on these confusions and fears: they riddled the plan with work requirements and "incentives" until the "costs" were made to appear prohibitive.

Another cause of the demise of FAP was racism. However much one wishes to be able to discuss the sources of the failure of efforts at social justice in the United States without invoking that abused word, one cannot in this case. American political life is marvelously consistent in these matters. In American mythology the bottom of the social heap is defined by blackness, and thus, despite the fact that a majority of the poor, even a majority of the "dependent poor" are white, welfare and dependency are thought of as "black problems." Efforts to improve the lot of the poor and of those on welfare are popularly characterized as "more for the blacks." Anathema!

Moynihan prefers to ascribe the greater responsibility for the failure of FAP to the liberals and to the blacks themselves. They failed, according to him, to appreciate that "the public wanted to help the poor but not to encourage dependency." He calls Nixon's term, "workfare," a mere public relations ploy, but the work requirements were compulsory. Moynihan seeks refuge from the sting of this fact by pointing to the work incentive program embodied in the 1967 Social Security amendments which had equally compulsory requirements that were not and presumably could not be implemented, because there weren't enough suitable jobs. But he notes that "Congressmen would rail against the measure, asking who was going to iron shirts once FAP was enacted," and it was in response to such criticisms that the work requirements were put in.

In a far less spiteful analysis of these proposals, James Welsh noted[56] that Wilbur Mills had provided the relevant defense against white Southern criticism in their first Congressional test, when he said, "Yes, a disproportionate number of welfare recipients are black, but most of the working poor are white, and live in the South."

Delaware's Senator John Williams, not National Welfare Rights Organization's George Wiley, was most responsible for killing FAP—although Wiley is considered the archvillain by more than Moynihan—for Williams knew that the work incentives he valued most would drive the "costs" of the program beyond the $4 billion limit Nixon had affixed for it.

Nixon wanted to win the respect of black Americans, but also of those other Americans whom Moynihan characterizes as "white wage earners in big cities, alarmed by the fantasies of the Black Panthers and such, hard enough pressed themselves, and focusing on welfare as a symbol of how government had abandoned the interests of the working class." Nixon's attention was apparently arrested by Peter Hamill's article, "The Revolt of the White Lower Middle

---

[56]James Welsh, "Welfare Reform: Born August 8, 1969; Died October 4, 1972—A Sad Case Study of the American Political Process," *New York Times Sunday Magazine,* January 7, 1973.

Class,'' which argued that men, mostly Catholic, who earn their living with their hands or back and who ''do not live in abject, swinish poverty, nor in safe, remote suburban comfort . . . earn between $5,000 and $10,000 a year. And they can no longer make it in New York.'' A lot of them and their kind supported George Wallace. ''That should have been a warning, strong and clear,'' argued Hamill. ''If the stereotyped black man is becoming the working class white man's enemy, the eventual enemy might be the democratic process itself.'' Moynihan thinks that the President agreed.

Precisely these elements of the lower middle class would stand to benefit in greatest numbers from the tax credit or negative income tax type redistribution plans we have already discussed, or even the demogrant plan so ill proposed by George McGovern. Nevertheless, popular attitudes of racism and individualism, and a mistaken belief in the uniqueness and purity of our good intentions concerning matters of social policy conspire to stifle any real action to eliminate poverty. Rather than accept the claims, which Moynihan records, that FAP was ''uniquely American,'' or ''the most important social legislation in history,'' or ''unique in boldness,'' we should evaluate the plan and popular reaction to proposals for redistribution in the light of the observation Moynihan made when first advancing FAP, that the United States is the only advanced industrial state without a family assistance plan. As my erstwhile colleague Hugh Heclo has pointed out:

> Today it is still easy to overestimate the role of U.S. national government in what are generally regarded elsewhere as standard welfare programmes. Old age pensions and unemployment insurance, initiated in 1908 and 1911 in Britain awaited national action in the U.S. until 1935; the British sickness benefit scheme of 1911 finds no American counterpart until Medicare in 1966: the family allowances instituted in Britain in 1945 have never been accepted; lagging over a generation behind Britain, U.S. benefits for the non-aged disabled began only in 1956, and for their dependents only in 1958.[57]

There are important differences in basic attitudes about welfare programs between the people of other industrial societies and Americans: they desire to spread the benefits and we to limit them; they see a sudden rise in the number of people drawing cash relief as a deficiency in their system of services while we blame the individual recipients; they seek to maximize the participation of the eligible and we to minimize it.

CONCLUSION

American prejudices are deeply rooted. They are not likely to be turned over by the weak commitment to the values that promote redistribution exhibited so far by prominent spokesmen for no-growth policies. For example, in the famous report of The Club of Rome Project on the Predicament of Mankind,[58] of the seven policy alternatives considered in simulating a condition of

---

[57]Hugh Heclo, ''The Welfare State: The Costs of Self-Sufficiency,'' *Lessons from America*, ed. Richard Rose (London: Macmillan, forthcoming in 1974).

social equilibrium at "a decent living standard," only one related directly to the needs and conditions of the very poor elements of the world's population:

> Since the above policies alone would result in a rather low value of food per capita, some people would still be malnourished if the traditional inequalities of distribution persist. To avoid this situation, high value is placed on producing sufficient food for *all* people. Capital is therefore diverted to food production even if such an investment would be considered "uneconomic."[59]

The authors did not suggest any basic tampering with the distribution system itself. It is therefore an open question whether some people would not go hungry even if sufficient aggregate food production were achieved to supply all people. That this danger is a distinct possibility is discernible from their own comments about the existing Green Revolution.

> Where these conditions of economic inequality already exist, the Green Revolution tends to cause widening inequality. Large farmers generally adopt the new methods first. They have the capital to do so and can afford to take the risk. . . . On large farms, simple economic considerations lead almost inevitably to the use of labor-displacing machinery and to the purchase of still more land. The ultimate effects of this socio-economic positive feedback loop are agricultural unemployment, increased migration to the city, and perhaps even increased malnutrition, since the poor and unemployed do not have the means to buy the newly produced food.

The authors of the report did voice a concern about poverty and inequality and they devoted cogent but few words to attack "one of the most commonly accepted myths in our present society," namely, "the promise that a continuation of our present pattern of growth will lead to human equality." They demonstrated in the report that present patterns of population and capital growth are increasing the gap between rich and poor on a worldwide basis. They felt that "the ultimate result of a continued attempt to grow according to the present pattern will be a disastrous collapse."

They were most concerned about the general collapse they could foresee for industrial society, although presumably this would leave few pickings for any survivors. The compelling feature of the argument is not that it may be undesirable to continue present patterns of growth, but that it may be impossible to do so, and preserve society as we know it. The report is entitled, after all, *The Limits of Growth*. We may guess that, if the food resource limits are the first to be reached, then the developing countries would suffer first and perhaps most. If material resource limits are the first reached, the developed world would be hardest hit. But, either way, everybody would find the results disastrous. These absolute limits of growth, at least for industrial society, may well be reached in less than a century and a half. If they are real, approaching

---

[58]Meadows, *et al.*, *The Limits of Growth*.
[59]*Ibid.*, p. 164.

them will hurt people in tangible ways. Fuel costs will mount until present patterns of industrial activity and even home heating are disrupted, businesses close, and people discover neighborliness or freeze. Mineral resources will be coveted more by producers and users alike, exacerbating international tensions and driving the prices of finished products even further out of the range of the poorer elements of society. Substitutes and the production innovations necessary to use them will be searched out, but there is some question whether these will be available on a general basis, or reserved for the wealthy elements or countries. Some nonsubstitutable resources will be exhausted and we will have to adjust our life styles to do without them.

Such changes and the forces they set in motion will perhaps make less credible the appeal so often made to growth itself as a way to bring economic improvements to the poor. The social costs of continuing to deny the poor may then be such that those who pay them will be forced to take the question of direct redistribution of income, and perhaps of wealth, more seriously. Present indications are, however, that improvements for the poor are likely to result not from a shift in attitude to one which values no growth for itself, but rather from alliances between the very poor and the middle class. Both will have a direct interest in gaining a larger share of the economic pie, and together they would have the political power to wrest what they want and need from the superrich, who, constituting as little as 5 percent of the population, or at most 30 percent, will have to resort to direct police state tactics to deny their claims.

15

Biological Research

Erwin Lausch's selection provides detailed explanations of the kinds of brain research now taking place. Although one doctor admits that he is "a little horrified at the idea of a society in which some men walk about with other men's heads and vice versa," the research continues; Japanese scientists may soon be the first to keep a severed head "alive" in a laboratory.

Are these experimenters Frankensteins or rather researchers boldly doing the basic research needed if we are ever to understand the workings of the brain? It is very difficult to answer these questions with an unqualified yes or no. However, the basis for an answer is furnished by Ellul's and Roszak's articles (Part One). First, some of the research now being undertaken is happening only because it is possible—a further example of the philosophy that "if we have the technology, we must use it." When such research is dangerous, I think it should be stopped. Second, and more important, the values of science and objectivity are and should be secondary to ethics on our list of priorities. The questions we must consider very seriously are many: Does this research promise great danger to humankind? Should anyone ever engage in such experiments as head grafting? Do we want to know how to electronically manipulate each other's brains?

Like those above, the answers to these questions are not black and white. But if we wish to avert the dangers posed by biological research, we must keep firmly in mind that the touchstone of any answer is that science is subordinate to ethics, and that objectivity must be subordinate to the welfare of human life.

From Manipulation
—Irwin Lausch

INVESTIGATIONS ON ISOLATED LIVE BRAINS

The operation had already lasted five hours, but the most difficult part was still to come.

On the operating table lay a young rhesus monkey deeply anaesthetised. He was mercifully spared, at least for the time being, any awareness of what was happening to him. Robert J. White, neurosurgeon at the Western Reserve University in Cleveland, Ohio, had set himself the task of isolating the monkey's brain, completely separating it from the rest of the body, and then examining it—examining it live, that was the problem.

For no other organ in the body perishes so quickly as the brain if there is failure in the blood supply. It needs a fifth of the whole amount of oxygen which the blood carries, from the lungs into the body. If the blood supply to the brain is interrupted, the functions of life are extinguished after only a few minutes. In contrast to the heart, attempts at resuscitation are futile.

So even a minor piece of clumsiness while operating could have wrecked the ambitious project. But White had sensitively and patiently worked his way to the crucial stage of the operation. He had severed the spinal cord in the region of the animal's neck, inserted a small T-shaped tube in each of the two cephalic veins, and (as he laconically wrote afterwards in a scientific report) removed in succession 'all the anatomical structures surrounding the brain'. The tubes were then closed. Later the blood would flow through them from the heart-lung machine into the brain.

A brief pause heavy with tension—then everything went very fast. White first tied off the spinal arteries, which contribute only one-fifth to the brain's blood supply, and cut through them below the tie. Now and also afterwards the brain could do without them, if the machine functioned smoothly. Spinal cord and spine were also cut through. Then he tied the cephalic arteries under the inserted T-tube. He opened the connections to the heart-lung machine and severed the cephalic arteries below the ties.

He had now completely severed the brain from the body with which that morning it was still linked in an apparently inalienable unity. The body lay lifeless on the operating table, unnoticed, until an assistant eventually carried out the headless corpse. But the brain lived.

It needed oxygen and energy-giving dextrose from the blood which the machine supplied to it, and it discharged carbon dioxide into the blood. But the main thing was: it worked. That the nerve cells were active was shown by the electroencephalograph (EEG): the jagged lines registered by this machine proved that the brain's functions were intact.

WHAT DREAMS MAY COME?

It was in 1963 that White first succeeded in this spectacular isolation of a live brain. Since then he has peeled over a hundred brains of rhesus monkeys from their skulls and severed them from their bodies. He has kept them alive for hours, sometimes for days. He has also severed dogs' brains and transplanted them into other dogs. Experiments with isolated brains have long been made in other places besides Cleveland.

In September 1963 White published in *Science,* the American scientific journal with by far the widest circulation, an account of his neurosurgical *tour de force*. Almost at once there was a storm of protest. The question under debate was whether he had overstepped a border which scientists too ought to respect. The arguments on this point have continued till the present day.

I myself, writing now about the isolated brain, am prey to the same medley of conflicting emotions and ideas which flooded my mind when I first read about White's experiment. While I admire the boldness, skill and determination with which he went about it, it also fills me with anxiety and makes me shudder. It is a tricky problem for our human brain, so thirsty for knowledge, to decide what ought and what ought not to be done to other brains, including those of animals. (The whole question of experiments on animals is, of course, a thorny and complex one, which I have no space to discuss in this book.)

Perhaps the most disturbing thing is that we do not know what goes on in an isolated brain; when it wakes from the anaesthetic, is it in any sense aware of the grotesque situation into which the operator has brought it? What does such a solitary brain think of? Is it tormented by fears, does it want to escape? Is it filled with rage at its impotence or sunk in resignation? 'What dreams may come to a disembodied brain,' asked a writer in the British magazine, *New Scientist,* 'and what pain, that the mute organ is unable to express?'

We do not know. The brain on the laboratory table might also have quite different feelings. Perhaps it feels joy to be free for good from its ordinary work. Perhaps it feels an amazed exhilaration that it can now for once consider only itself.

'I suppose,' said Lee Wolin, experimental psychologist in White's team, 'that waking, he [the monkey] would feel like an individual subjected to complete paralysis, because when a man is paralysed, he is aware of the senses' absence. Yes, I assume that this monkey knows the absence of the flesh. But with no physical pain, because all the nerves have been cut off. Psychological suffering, I don't know. I have no idea if he would feel happy or unhappy or lonely.'

We have no instrument so far which can give information about this. The graph of brain current registered on EEGs can offer various conclusions regarding healthy and sick brains. But scientists have not yet read off feelings and thoughts from the jagged lines.

Anyhow, White and his colleagues succeeded in gaining contact with isolated brains. Through a probe, which produced minute electrical currents, he stimulated the stumps of the nerves for seeing and hearing. In the intact organism these nerves lead to quite definite areas of the cerebral cortex, and they pass on to these areas what the eyes and ears register. They do not, however, transmit light or sound waves to the cerebral cortex, but electrical signals, into which the perceptions of the sense organs have immediately been transformed. It is only these electrical signals, after they have been processed in the cerebral cortex, which enable us to experience the world of colour and sound we know.

White's isolated brains no longer possessed eyes and ears, so they could no longer react to light and sound waves. But the electrical signals entering the nerve stumps were immediately transmitted into the brain. Measurements at the cerebral cortex showed that the signals arrived. Very probably the solitary brains 'saw' and 'heard' something—without eyes and ears.

That isolated brains react also to normal sense perceptions was shown by A. J. Blomquist and D. D. Gilboe, two scientists in the neurosurgical department at the University Clinic in Madison, Wisconsin, who severed dogs' brains from their bodies and connected them to a heart-lung machine. But the isolated brains were left two possibilities of contact with the outside world: an ear, and a small piece of nose with the nerves which led from there into the brain. Whether stimuli from the outside world arrived 'correctly' was to be shown by electrodes positioned at the places on the cerebral cortex where the brain normally processed them. The experimenters gently touched the remains of the nose with an electrically driven apparatus which vibrated fast, and the recording from the first electrode promptly showed a strong deviation: the part of the brain responsible for sense stimuli from the nose area had registered the touch stimulus. Normally, of course, the brain would not have confined itself to registering the stimulus; it would have told the muscles, withdraw the head at once!

Blomquist and Gilboe made a loud clicking come from a loudspeaker set up about a yard from the dog's intact ear. They immediately saw the reactions on the EEG machine with which a second electrode placed on the cortex was connected. The jagged line registered by the machine shot up to form a huge indentation. So the brain had listened accurately.

There is impressive evidence, then, that the isolated brain does actually function. But while for all our knowledge it may suffer terrible fears and torments, should such experiments not be abandoned? The question is clearly justified, the answer extremely difficult and complex.

For White and other brain researchers do not, of course, plan their drastic operations in an overweening sense of human omnipotence; they are not merely concerned in doing whatever looks technically possible, nor are they motivated by pure scientific curiosity. Their essential interest is to be able in the future to help patients who are at present beyond their help or who could be more fully helped. For that they must know more about the brain.

The isolated brains offered the possibility for the first time of making exact examinations of certain processes of metabolism in the brain. There is no other way of establishing so precisely what enters the brain with the bloodstream and what quantities of what substances the blood discharges again. Researchers can study on the exposed brain what the central organ of the organism needs for nourishment besides oxygen and dextrose, and what chemicals it produces which are normally carried away into the body. There is a completely unprecedented chance to follow up, for instance, the effects on the brain cells which can be produced by drugs, changes of temperature, infections, etc. According to White:

> The direction of research marked out by the existence of such preparations will in future put us in the position of being able to analyse exactly the biochemical and neurophysiological functions which take place in the brain and which may be considered the physical basis of specialised psychic functions like memory, consciousness and intelligence. . . . For the neurosurgeon the possibility is also of great importance that with this method he can study more exactly the mechanisms which after surgical operations so often lead to brain oedema (the collection of fluid into the brain), to brain failure and so finally to the patient's death.

Experiments in which White and other brain researchers 'froze' isolated brains cut off from all blood supply, proved particularly illuminating as regards possible benefits for patients. At normal bodily temperature a brain dies irrevocably, if the blood supply is interrupted longer than a few minutes. But a brain cooled down just above freezing-point, White discovered, would survive several hours without blood supply.

The brain's electrical activity ceases; but the brain itself is only in suspended animation. When at the end of the experiment he had blood warmed to body temperature flow through the brain, the electrical activity started up strongly again, directly the temperature of the brain rose above 30°C (86°F).

The results of such experiments encouraged White to carry out operations which only seemed conceivable if the blood supply to the patient's brain could be temporarily interrupted. After his experiences with frozen, isolated brains, he dared to freeze the brains of patients needing operations—where the brain remained excluded from the circulation of blood for up to half an hour.

Even more astonishing results were achieved by three Japanese scientists, I. Suda, K. Kito and C. Adachi, at the Physiology Department in the University of Kobe. They froze live cats' brains, and kept them in the deep freeze for months—at −20°C (−4°F). The brains' electrical activity had already ceased far above freezing-point. But when they carefully thawed out the petrified brains, and a heart-lung machine pumped in fresh, warm cats' blood, it started again. The EEG registered lines which showed no signs of any brain damage. One brain which could later be restored to life from its petrified state spent 203 days in the deep freeze.

However, for it to survive its stay there, the Japanese scientists found, a special preparation was needed. Before they freed the live brain from the anaesthetized cat, they replaced its warm blood by a sodium solution cooled to 10°C (50°F), to which they had added dextran, a synthetic substitute for blood plasma.

While the blood substitute was pulsing through the body, they severed the brain from the body and attached it to a heart-lung machine. Then they gradually added to the sodium solution fifteen per cent glycerine, which had proved an effective antifreeze with other live tissue. Finally they put the brain into a plastic container filled with the same fluid consisting of sodium solution, dextran and glycerine, and put the whole thing in the deep freeze. For resuscitation they first let the brain slowly thaw out, and replaced the glycerine fluid first by sodium solution, then by warm blood.

The significance of these Japanese experiments lies not only in the proof that the brain, master organ of the body, considered so delicate, possesses under certain conditions an almost incredible resistance to cold. An equally exciting result is that it is evidently possible to exchange the blood completely for a substitute fluid—which casts doubt on the widespread doctrine that nerve cells are specially liable to damage from lack of oxygen.

This doctrine rests on medical experience that, of all organs, the brain reacts most sensitively to an interruption of the blood supply, and that only a few minutes after such an interruption it is irreparably damaged and perishes. In his experiments White, too, took account of this apparently irrefutable fact. But the Japanese researchers replaced the blood with a fluid which could not transmit any oxygen to the nerve cells (as it does not contain any). Before the refrigeration, sodium solution alone was pulsing through the cat's brain for over two hours. Even allowing for the fact that the solution was cool and the tissue cooled by it had a relatively small need for oxygen, nerve cells could not be all that sensitive to the lack of oxygen if they survived this test without damage.

The researchers also reached the conclusion that the cause of the brain damage constantly observed, instead of being extreme sensitivity to lack of oxygen, was a very marked vulnerability in the fine blood vessels in the brain. Even after a brief interruption of the blood stream the venules (small veins) could no longer open and so caused a continuous loss of oxygen. Obviously it may be very important medically to know the real cause of the brain's sensitivity to circulatory troubles

BRAIN TRANSPLANTS

Understandably, the experiments with isolated brains immediately aroused speculations as to whether they would one day lead to brain transplants. If a man's brain was incurably damaged, for instance by a car crash, might the body not be equipped with the healthy brain of another man, who has been carried off, say by a heart attack? If live brains can be kept fresh for months in the deep freeze, why not establish brain banks which would keep a suitable brain ready for all requirements?

Brains have in fact been connected already with a foreign organism. As early as the fifties the Soviet surgeon Vladimir Petrovich Demichov in Moscow carried out a series of experiments in transplanting brains, with results which made headlines all over the world as 'Dogs with Two Heads'. But actually it was the whole front half of a small dog which was transplanted, brain, head, neck and front paws. Demichov sewed it into a big dog's neck. The transplanted head, after coming out of its anaesthesia, could smell and see, eat and bark. The big dog found the unwonted burden in its neck uncomfortable, and tried to shake it off. This caused pain to the small dog-head. It resisted and bit its carrier in the ear.

Demichov's dog-head transplants, which lived for up to twenty-nine days, were ingenious if creepy experiments, which showed great surgical skill. But they contributed little to transplant research. Speculations about real brain transplants were only possible after White in Cleveland had isolated the brains of rhesus monkeys. For these brains severed from their bodies, he did more than supply them with blood through the heart-lung machine. He often selected a 'live blood-pump'. He connected the solitary brain with the circulation of an anaesthetised rhesus monkey; the monkey's heart easily managed the extra task. A 'transplantation', White wrote, had thus taken place from one live animal to another.

The quotation marks are his. Clearly he realised himself that the expression 'transplantation' was rather too bold for an experimental arrangement whereby one monkey had for a period merely supplied another monkey's brain with blood. In fact, he described an experiment he carried out in 1965 as 'the first successful brain transplantation'. In this experiment, which he repeated several times, he severed a dog's brain from its body, in the same sort of way as he had done before with a monkey's brain. It was much harder with a dog for anatomical reasons, and it took him eight to nine hours; but it had the advantage that dogs cost much less than monkeys. In another dog's neck he prepared a pocket of skin which was to take the isolated brain.

The brain was attached to the receiver dog's cephalic artery and neck vein. After he had lined it with electrodes and equipped it with devices which later allowed him to follow the temperature, blood pressure and composition of the blood, he sewed up the skin pocket. He continued such experiments for up to three days. The transplanted brains functioned splendidly right to the end— as the measuring instruments showed—so far as they were in a position to function when cut off from all nerve connections.

Such a transplant is not in the least like a heart or kidney transplant. A transplanted brain, which carries out no function in the body but just quietly and inscrutably 'thinks its own thoughts', does not signify any progress from a medical point of view. The brain transplant which leads to a close connection between body and brain, which would be considered a far greater sensation than heart transplants, is not likely to come about all that soon.

The 'immunity barrier' which has wrecked so many transplants of other organs—the organism's tendency to attack alien bodily tissue as a cause of sickness—is possibly less marked with the brain, it is true, than with heart and kidneys. After the conclusion of his experiments with the transplanted dogs' brains, White found no indication of any damage through an immunological defence reaction of the receiver animal.

That need not mean, however, that a foreign brain would also be tolerated over a longer period, although the brain itself is known to suffer foreign substances readily. Experimenters have deposited skin, fatty tissue, nerve fibres and cancerous growths in the brains of live animals, and such foreign matter has always survived there longer than in any other organ.

The main problem, therefore, facing specialists in organ transplants, would perhaps play a smaller role with the brain. But other problems, both medical and moral, seem in the long view insoluble. There would, of course, be no difficulty in isolating a live human brain, as White has done with monkeys and dogs. It would even be easier, he says. He has not yet tried it, though he admits he 'would like to study an isolated human brain'. But for the moment he sees no chance of getting such an object of study in his laboratory. 'What family', he sadly asked the journalist Oriana Fallaci, 'would ever authorise me to use a relative from the moment in which his heart stopped? We are locked in traditions, often in the most despicable hypocrisy; one prefers to know that his relative's brain is decaying in the ground rather than to know it's living in a laboratory.'

Various interesting experiments could certainly be carried out with a human brain on a laboratory table, but it is not clear what insights they might bring for a brain transplant. Even the most skillful surgeon is not capable in the available time of attaching all the nerves and blood vessels, which must be cut through in isolating the brain, to the nerves and blood vessel stumps of the proposed receiver, after the latter's dead brain has been cleared out. Even if the impossible were to succeed, the *tour de force* would be useless: the nerve endings once severed would not grow together again.

Assuming the brain could be accommodated in the skull and attached to the receiver's circulation, it would be well provided with blood supply and capable of functioning. But without intact nerve endings it would remain an isolated brain, cut off from its environment, and could not itself make any communication. The brain-receiver's eyes, ears and mouth could not see, hear or say anything; the body would be completely paralysed. The situation would be different, of course, if a surgeon wanted to transplant not only a brain but a whole head. 'That', said White, 'is altogether possible and infinitely easier than isolating a brain as I am doing.' Only relatively few large blood vessels would have to be patched up; but what about the nerves?—the stumps of millions of nerve fibres in the spine could not be united to make them function properly. The person with the new head would remain sectionally paralysed.

Perhaps one day a trick will be discovered to overcome this obstacle as well. But what would be gained by it, and who would benefit? In the last resort, when you think about it, it is quite wrong to talk about a head transplant, for the body without the head is nothing. Our consciousness and our personality are enclosed in the head. Should it ever come to the point that someone's head is combined with someone else's body, then the body will have been transplanted, not the head.

There is a short-story 'black comedy' by Roald Dahl about the brain isolation of an Oxford don with cancer, whose wife blew cigarette smoke in the eye attached to his brain; and in the *Deutsches Ärzteblatt* (German Medical Journal) in 1969 Dr Bernd Leineweber described the consequences of such a transplant experiment in a science-fiction story. The narrator finds the note-book of a man of fifty-five called Peter Nieburg, who in the first entries com-plains of troubles with his vision and balance, maddening headaches and symptoms of severe paralysis. He is to have an operation, and reports on this a few days afterwards: 'A young man's head is to be transplanted! I tremble at the idea. What possibilities! Shall I really do it? What shall I think? Shall I think as I would like to, or as my predecessor thought?'

The operation takes place. Soon there are entries from a student of twenty-five who introduces himself as Klaus Koller, complains at having to make entries in a diary which belongs to one Peter Nieburg, hasn't any idea how he came into the hospital, can only remember jumping from a thirty-foot tower, and is amazed at how old his body has become: 'Grey, flabby!' Bit by bit he learns the truth. With Nieburg's body he is now to continue his life as Nieburg, who lived on his own without relatives. Koller moves into Nieburg's flat and gives himself out to be Nieburg's unknown son. But he cannot come to terms with his body. Continual heart pains intensify his despair: 'I am an old man!' The last entry: 'Have made up my mind. Refuse to bear this filthy fifty-five-year-old body any longer. I shall throw myself in front of a car.'

White's thoughts about this are no different. 'I am a little horrified at the idea of a society in which some men walk about with other men's heads and vice versa.' For the moment there will not be such people, if only because at present the technical difficulties cannot be solved. But something else would already be technically possible today. 'Could a severed human body be kept alive?' Oriana Fallaci asked White, who replied: 'Yes, it isn't difficult. It can be accomplished now with existing techniques.' But he would not be the first to do it. 'I haven't resolved as yet this dilemma: is it right or not?' The Japanese, he thought, would be the first to keep a severed human head in a laboratory.

*   *   *

ELECTRICAL MANIPULATION

George Orwell's 'Big Brother' in 1984 keeps his subjects under constant watch by television cameras. In 1949, the year when Orwell wrote his grim vision of the future, W. R. Hess was awarded the Nobel Prize for medicine for his pioneering experiments in brain stimulation, which had already been going for some time but had not received much public notice. His work re-vealed the possibilities of such stimulation; and the ideas developed since then make Orwell's fantasies look quite old-fashioned.

Already in the 'fifties the American electronic engineer Curtiss R. Schafer found it 'economically quite worth considering' to plant hundreds of electrodes into the brains of children directly after birth and thereafter direct the children by radio signals. Such radio-controlled children would be far cheaper to pro-duce and maintain than robots: 'to construct a simple mechanical machine man on present standards costs about ten times as much as the birth and breeding of a child up to his sixteenth year.' And in 1968 the magazine *Newsweek* com-mented: 'In 1984 it seems Big Brother will no longer have to watch. He'll just tune in and turn people on or off.'

We are coming closer to 1984 without the menacing aspects of brain stimulation looking in too great danger of being realised. All the same José Delgado reported in 1970 having given a computer at Yale the task of taming a self-assertive and aggressive young chimpanzee called Paddy with the aid of brain stimulations, and making him quiet and obedient. After a few days the computer had fulfilled its assignment, and it took about a fortnight after it was switched off before Paddy had recovered his spirit.

The principle was simple. Delgado installed on Paddy's head a transmitter and receiver the size of a cigarette lighter, which he called a 'stimoceiver'. This was connected with electrodes leading deep into Paddy's brain, and he was in radio contact with the computer. He fed it with the pattern of electric currents from Paddy's brain, and in return received signals which he transmitted into the brain. The computer received a special input from an area of the limbic system which the anatomists have christened the *amygdala* (from the Latin for walnut) because of its shape. These currents showed a typical pattern when Paddy behaved aggressively. The computer, programmed accordingly, analysed the currents, and directly it discovered signs of aggressiveness, sent signals to the stimoceiver which transmitted the signals into a particular area of the brain stem. This brain stimulation produced an unpleasant feeling, and Paddy's brain soon grasped the connection between that feeling and his aggressive behaviour: he became mild as a lamb.

A model for future efforts to turn young thugs into peaceful members of society? Why not, if it can help both the victims by stopping the violence and the thugs who are now outlawed because of it? But where do you draw the line? Brain-stimuli suppressing aggressiveness for sons who oppose their fathers? Definitely not. For rebellious students more concerned with 'demos' than with their studies? For political extremists with respectable motives whose ideological fanaticism may have even more brutal effects than are caused by the thugs? For psychopaths—clockwork oranges galore? Who is to decide?

Plans to make the agents and advocates of violence pacific, on the model of Paddy or by other operations, are likely to produce more aggressiveness (between supporters and opponents of the idea) than will be removed by the treatment of those who need it or are deemed to need it. Early thought is essential on how such unwanted effects might be eliminated.

ELECTRODES TO FIGHT AGGRESSION

Many other impressive demonstrations have been given, besides Paddy's taming, of aggressive animals suddenly becoming peaceful through deliberate brain stimuli. Unmanageable monkeys, who usually could not be fed without safety precautions being taken, directly the current flowed into the brain would even allow the food to be taken out of their mouths. At the University of California in Los Angeles Carmine D. Clemente got cats to let go of rats they were just about to kill. A burst of current into the right centre made the cats completely forget their intention. Without taking any further notice of their victims, they crept away and lay down to sleep in a corner of the cage.

José Delgado, a Spaniard by birth, a neuropsychologist with great physical courage and a flair for causing sensations, went into the bull-ring at Cordoba armed only with a mini-transmitter, and let the bull charge him. He had previously planted an electrode in its brain, and when the bull was only two yards away, he pressed the transmitting knob. It immediately stopped in its tracks.

In another experiment he planted an electrode in the brain of a monkey called Ali, the tyrannical head of a family of four. Ali's mate Elsa, the most subordinate member of the family, quickly learnt to mollify the tyrant by working an electric switch near the manger. In the end she reached the point of deliberately defying him and only checking him in his fury at the last second with the aid of the switch.

Such a pacifier switch would no doubt seem desirable to many who suffer under an insupportable boss or a dictatorial parent. Obviously the method with which Elsa protected herself from Ali offers no practical solution for human relations; but doctors have begun to use electrical brain stimulation at least on patients with extreme inclinations to violence.

Over two hundred men and women who were continually making unnecessary attacks on other people were investigated and treated at Massachusetts General Hospital in Boston, where Frank R. Erwin is director of a centre for psychiatric research. In a number of cases electrical stimulation of the brain was a considerable help in discovering the cause of the unwarranted violence and cutting it out.

One of the patients was a young woman who without any reason had already made twelve attacks on others, including a woman who accidentally touched her arm in the cloakroom of a restaurant and whom she almost killed. By brain stimulation with electrodes Erwin found out which place in the brain was responsible for this unrestrained aggressiveness. When the electrode was in the right place, she promptly became worked up as soon as the current was switched on. The excitement ended abruptly when a point was stimulated adjacent to the centre which produced the aggressiveness. Once recognised, the dangerous brain tissue, a tiny region, could be destroyed, and the tendency to violence disappeared.

There was also a very talented engineer who had fits of rage in which he sometimes hurled his wife across the room. Erwin planted in his head an electrode through which a small place deep in the brain could regularly be stimulated—with the result that the fits stopped. An operation seemed indicated for a permanent solution, and this had the success desired: it was some years ago, and since then no outbursts of uncontrollable rage have occurred. A similar operation stopped a mother in Boston from periodically beating her twelve-year-old son almost unconscious in her frantic rage. Dangerous aggression has also been damped down in other cases. Ten seconds of brain stimuli at the right place, Delgado reported on one patient, suppressed aggressive behaviour for up to forty-eight hours.

WHAT CHANCE FOR DICTATORS?

Knowledge about pleasure centres has also been used clinically. Robert Heath in New Orleans and other researchers after him have planted into many people's heads brain electrodes leading to these centres. The patients have included schizophrenics resistant to all attempts at treatment, sufferers from persistent depressions and compulsion neuroses, but also cancer patients with unrelievable pain. Directly the current is switched on, they feel the beneficial effect: despair and hopelessness disappear, intolerable pain dissolves or at least is alleviated. The feeling of well-being varies according to which pleasure centre is touched. In extreme cases the brain stimulus, as one depressive patient said, is 'better than sex'.

A dictator who was put in the position of rewarding 'good behaviour' by granting pleasure feelings could easily achieve whatever he wanted. An idea of the possibilities is given by an experiment carried out in America with a monkey, which had an electrode in its brain leading to a pleasure centre. The current for stimulating the centre was provided by a photo-cell buckled on to the monkey. Thus equipped, he was sent off to a destination unknown to him. He arrived there safely.

The photo-cell was in fact attached to his body in such a way that the sun shone on it while the direction was right. If the monkey strayed from his course, no more sunlight came on to the photo-cell, no more current flowed into the electrode, and the pleasure centre remained unstimulated. The monkey, 'hooked' on pleasure feelings, reverted as quickly as possible to the right direction.

Understandably, no medical application has yet been found for the possibility of stimulating aversion centres in the brain and so producing discomfort, pain or fear—although this could of course be used as a form of aversion therapy to make alcoholics, for instance, dislike drinking. In any case such feelings can undoubtedly be produced by stimulation of these centres. Experiments on monkeys subjected to it have shown how extremely effective the stimuli are for punishment purposes. The monkeys could pull a lever to switch on the stimulus themselves, and soon afterwards the current began to flow. They were then constantly occupied with fruitless attempts to get rid of the tormenting discomfort. After three hours they were completely distracted and irritable. They refused to eat or to cooperate any further. Several died. But when a pleasure centre was stimulated afterwards, the monkeys which had been made ill regained their health and spirits within a few minutes.

Like most animals, man lives in groups. Anyone who wanted to manipulate people by brain stimuli could start at this point too. For, as researchers have repeatedly found in experiments with animals, influencing a single member of the group by brain electrodes can drastically alter the behaviour of others in the group—especially when brain stimulation produces aggressiveness.

Delgado put a cat and a kitten together on a platform. They got on well until a brain stimulus made the kitten aggressive. Directly the current was switched on, it began to spit, showed its claws, and attacked the cat, which responded, after a moment of surprise, by defending itself. The fight broke off at once when the brain stimulus was stopped, and restarted when the current flowed again. After the kitten, under the compulsion of some current, had several times repeated its sudden attack, the good relations between the two cats were shattered. From then on they watched each other with hostility.

R. Apfelbach at the University of California in Berkeley upset the social life of a gibbon family by using a succession of electrical stimuli at short intervals to make one of the gibbons howl loudly and behave aggressively. 'If struc-

tures which generate aggressive behaviour and noise-making are stimulated,'
he reported, 'normal group behaviour disintegrates.'

Electrical stimuli can dethrone leaders and bring to power previously obedient followers. In Yerkes Regional Primate Research Centre, Bryan W. Robinson stimulated the sexuality of a lower-ranking chimpanzee in such a way that
the former underling asserted himself against the chimpanzee lord and forced
him into the role of a spectator. It is hard to say whether this procedure could
be adapted in human society for humiliating paladins fallen from grace or rivals
beaten in the fight for power; no doubt there are simpler methods already available for carrying out such purposes.

But suppressing aggressiveness, producing feelings of pleasure or of fear
and pain, destroying the normal fabric of unpopular groups—such attacks on
the human psyche, technically quite possible today by brain stimulation, might
be very attractive to a dictator. Two of the possibilities of manipulating minds
could even be praised as philanthropic ideas: who would deny that it is a worthy
aim to give people more peace and well-being?

The experts are divided on the expediency and necessity, and advantages
and disadvantages, of electrical brain manipulation in human society. Many,
like Nobel prize-winner Sir John Eccles, fear it more than the atom bomb;
others are concerned that efforts to civilize the human psyche might come too
late. The former see a wide extension of brain stimuli as the end of human life,
the latter as the beginning.

Delgado, called by the British scientific journalist Nigel Calder 'the prophet
in chief of a better world through brain electrodes', thinks there are great prospects from mind manipulation. He looks forward to a human society 'psycho-
civilized' for the very first time through brain stimulation and other influencing
techniques. Considering human aggressiveness, Arthur Koestler has said,
such a development cannot start soon enough.

Most researchers, however, do not believe it will be possible to carry out on
a large scale such controversial incursions into the human brain. Pessimistic
predictions that whole populations might be enslaved through 'soul manipulation' are rejected as futile by Seymour Kety of Massachusetts General Hospital
on the grounds that 'anyone influential enough to get an entire population to
consent to having electrodes put into their heads would already have achieved
his goal without firing a single volt'. But this reflection starts from the premise
that a dictator would suddenly try to introduce soul manipulation with a people
unprepared and unmotivated for the innovation.

Kety does not take into account that it would probably creep in, starting in
hospitals, and then perhaps going on to prisons, where brain stimulation might
also be shown to be desirable. Brain electrodes, positioned in pleasure centres
by specialized pseudo-doctors, might in fringe zones of society compete as
fashionable joy-bringers with hashish, LSD and heroin. Once established,
brain stimulation might gradually become acceptable, to a degree which would
eventually allow the dictator to take the plunge into total manipulation.

This also, of course, is mere speculation. We know today the uses to which
electrical brain stimulation can be put. No one knows what the future may hold;
only vigilance can protect us from unpleasant surprises.

16

Pollution

The issue of whether or not environmental pollution will eventually result in catastrophe is an unsettled one, but the signs are ominous. In *The Limits of Growth* (Meadows et al.), the authors make a deliberately frightening point: "Virtually every pollutant that has been measured as a function of time appears to be increasing exponentially." We would seem to have little to gain from waiting to see what the outcome of this situation will be.

Marshall Goldman's article focuses specifically on pollution in the Soviet Union, but it also has a broader focus. In addition to discussing the benefits and faults of socialism as a means of dealing with pollution problems, Goldman echoes Heilbroner (Chapter 2) with his argument that Soviet pollution problems, like everyone else's, are rooted in industrial growth. Economic and political systems obviously have their effects on the growth and control of environmental pollution, but at bottom the villain is still the worldwide commitment to industrial growth. And since many scholars argue convincingly that there are definite limits to the extent of industrial growth that the earth can bear, we would be wise to begin the slowdown now rather than find out in a very unpleasant way just what those limits are.

From The Convergence of Environmental Disruption
—Marshall I. Goldman

By now it is a familiar story: rivers that blaze with fire, smog that suffocates cities, streams that vomit dead fish, oil slicks that blacken seacoasts, prized beaches that vanish in the waves, and lakes that evaporate and die a slow smelly

Reprinted from *Science*, Vol. 170, October 2, 1970, by permission of *Science*. Copyright ©1970 by the American Association for the Advancement of Science.

death. What makes it unfamiliar is that this is a description not only of the United States but also of the Soviet Union.

Most conservationists and social critics are unaware that the U.S.S.R. has environmental disruption that is as extensive and severe as ours. Most of us have been so distressed by our own environmental disruption that we lack the emotional energy to worry about anyone else's difficulties. Yet, before we can find a solution to the environmental disruption in our own country, it is necessary to explain why it is that a socialist or communist country like the U.S.S.R. finds itself abusing the environment in the same way, and to the same degree, that we abuse it. This is especially important for those who have come to believe as basic doctrine that it is capitalism and private greed that are the root cause of environmental disruption. Undoubtedly private enterprise and the profit motive account for a good portion of the environmental disruption that we encounter in this country. However, a study of pollution in the Soviet Union suggests that abolishing private property will not necessarily mean an end to environmental disruption. In some ways, state ownership of the country's productive resources may actually exacerbate rather than ameliorate the situation.

THE PUBLIC GOOD

That environmental disruption is a serious matter in the Soviet Union usually comes as a surprise not only to most radical critics of pollution in the West but also to many Russians. It has been assumed that, if all the factories in a society were state-owned, the state would insure that the broader interests of the general public would be protected. Each factory would be expected to bear the full costs and consequences of its operation. No factory would be allowed to take a particular action if it meant that the public would suffer or would have to bear the expense. In other words, the factory would not only have to pay for its *private costs,* such as expenses for labor and raw materials; it would also have to pay for its *social costs,* such as the cost of eliminating the air and water pollution it had caused. It was argued that, since the industry was state-run, including both types of costs would not be difficult. At least that was what was assumed.

Soviet officials continue today to make such assumptions. B. V. Petrovsky, the Soviet Minister of Public Health, finds environmental disruption in a capitalist society perfectly understandable: "the capitalist system by its very essence is incapable of taking radical measures to ensure the efficient conservation of nature." By implication he assumes that the Soviet Union can take such measures. Therefore it must be somewhat embarrassing for Nikolai Popov, an editor of *Soviet Life,* to have to ask, "Why, in a socialist country, whose constitution explicitly says the public interest may not be ignored with impunity, are industry executives permitted to break the laws protecting nature?"

Behind Popov's question is a chronicle of environmental disruption that is as serious as almost any that exists in the world. Of course in a country as large as the U.S.S.R. there are many places that have been spared man's disruptive incursions. But, as the population grows in numbers and mobility, such areas become fewer and fewer. Moreover, as in the United States, the most idyllic sites are the very ones that tend to attract the Soviet population.

Just because human beings intrude on an area, it does not necessarily follow that the area's resources will be abused. Certainly the presence of human beings means some alteration in the previous ecological balance, and in some cases there may be severe damage, but the change need not be a serious one. Nonetheless, many of the changes that have taken place in the Soviet Union have been major ones. As a result, the quality of the air, water, and land resources has been adversely affected.

WATER

Comparing pollution in the United States and in the U.S.S.R. is something like a game. Any depressing story that can be told about an incident in the United States can be matched by a horror story from the U.S.S.R. For example, there have been hundreds of fish-kill incidents in both countries. Rivers and lakes from Maine to California have had such incidents. In the U.S.S.R., effluent from the Chernorechensk Chemical Plant near Dzerzhinsk killed almost all the fish life in the Oka River in 1965 because of uncontrolled dumping. Factories along major rivers such as the Volga, Ob, Yenesei, Ural, and Northern Dvina have committed similar offenses, and these rivers are considered to be highly polluted. There is not one river in the Ukraine whose natural state has been preserved.[1] The Molognaia River in the Ukraine and many other rivers throughout the country are officially reported as dead. How dangerous this can be is illustrated by what happened in Sverdlovsk in 1965. A careless smoker threw his cigarette into the Iset River and, like the Cuyahoga in Cleveland, the Iset caught fire.

Sixty-five percent of all the factories in the largest Soviet republic, the Russian Soviet Federated Socialist Republic (RSFSR), discharge their waste without bothering to clean it up.[2] But factories are not the only ones responsible for the poor quality of the water. Mines, oil wells, and ships freely dump their waste and ballast into the nearest body of water. Added to this industrial waste is the sewage of many Russian cities. Large cities like Moscow and Leningrad are struggling valiantly, like New York and Chicago, to treat their waste, but many municipalities are hopelessly behind in their efforts to do the job properly. Only six out of the 20 main cities in Moldavia have a sewer system, and only two of those cities make any effort to treat their sewage.[3] Similarly, only 40 percent of the cities and suburbs in the RSFSR have any equipment for treating their sewage. For that matter, according to the last completed census, taken in 1960, only 35 percent of all the housing units in urban areas are served by a sewer system.[4]

[1]*Rabochaia Gaz.* 1967, 4 (15 Dec. 1967).
[2]*Ekon. Gaz.* 1967, No. 4, 37 (1967).
[3]*Sovet. Moldaviia* 1969, 2 (1 June 1969).
[4]V. G. Kriazhev, *Vnerabochee Vremia i Sphera Obslyzhivaniia* (Ekonomika, Moscow, 1966), p. 130.

Conditions are even more primitive in the countryside. Often this adversely affects the well-water and groundwater supplies, especially in areas of heavy population concentration. Under the circumstances it is not surprising to find that major cities like Vladimir, Orenburg, and Voronezh do not have adequate supplies of drinking water. In one instance reported in *Pravda,* a lead and zinc ore enriching plant was built in 1966 and allowed to dump its wastes in the Fragdon River, even though the river was the sole source of water for about 40 kilometers along its route. As a result the water became contaminated and many people were simply left without anything to drink.

Even when there are supplies of pure water, many homes throughout the country are not provided with running water. This was true of 62 percent of the urban residences in the U.S.S.R. in 1960.[5] The Russians often try to explain this by pointing to the devastation they suffered during World War II. Still it is something of a shock, 25 years after the war, to walk along one of the more fashionable streets in Kharkov, the fifth largest city in the U.S.S.R., and see many of the area's residents with a yoke across their shoulders, carrying two buckets of water. The scene can be duplicated in almost any other city in the U.S.S.R.

Again, the Soviet Union, like the United States, has had trouble not only with its rivers but with its larger bodies of water. As on Cape Cod and along the California coast, oil from slicks has coated the shores of the Baltic, Black, and Caspian seas. Refineries and tankers have been especially lax in their choice of oil-disposal procedures.

Occasionally it is not only the quality but the quantity of the water that causes concern. The Aral and Caspian seas have been gradually disappearing. Because both seas are in arid regions, large quantities of their water have been diverted for crop irrigation. Moreover, many dams and reservoirs have been built on the rivers that supply both seas for the generation of electric power. As a result of such activities, the Aral Sea began to disappear. From 1961 to 1969 its surface dropped 1 to 3 meters. Since the average depth of the sea is only about 20 to 30 meters, some Russian authorities fear that, at the current rate of shrinkage, by the turn of the century the sea will be nothing but a salt marsh.[6]

Similarly, during the past 20 years the level of the Caspian Sea has fallen almost 2½ meters. This has drastically affected the sea's fish population. Many of the best spawning areas have turned into dry land. For the sturgeon, one of the most important fish in the Caspian, this has meant the elimination of one-third of the spawning area. The combined effect of the oil on the sea and the smaller spawning area reduced the fish catch in the Caspian from 1,180,400 centners in 1942 to 586,300 centners in 1966. Food fanciers are worried not so much about the sturgeon as about the caviar that the sturgeon produces. The output of caviar has fallen even more drastically than the sea level—a concern not only for the Russian consumers of caviar but for foreigners. Caviar had been a major earner of foreign exchange. Conditions have become so serious

[5]*Ibid.*
[6]*Soviet News* 1970, 6 (7 Apr. 1970).

that the Russians have now begun to experiment with the production of artificial caviar.

The disruption of natural life in the Caspian Sea has had some serious ecological side effects. Near Ashkhabad at the mouth of the Volga a fish called the
belyi amur also began to disappear. As a consequence, the mosquito population, which had been held in check by the belyi amur, grew in the newly formed
swamps where once the sea had been. In turn, the mosquitoes began to transmit
malaria.[7]

Perhaps the best known example of the misuse of water resources in the
U.S.S.R. has been what happened to Lake Baikal. This magnificent lake is
estimated to be over 20 million years old. There are over 1200 species of living
organisms in the lake, including freshwater seals and 700 other organisms that
are found in few or no other places in the world. It is one of the largest and
deepest freshwater lakes on earth, over 1½ kilometers deep in some areas.[8]
It is five times as deep as Lake Superior and contains twice the volume of water.
In fact, Lake Baikal holds almost one-fortieth of all the world's fresh water.
The water is low in salt content and is highly transparent; one can see as far as
36 meters under water.[9]

In 1966, first one and then another paper and pulp mill appeared on Lake
Baikal's shores. Immediately limnologists and conservationists protested this
assault on an international treasure. Nonetheless, new homes were built in the
vicinity of the paper and pulp mills, and the plant at the nearby town of Baikalsk
began to dump 60 million cubic meters of effluent a year into the lake. A specially designed treatment plant had been erected in the hope that it would maintain the purity of the lake. Given the unique quality of the water, however, it
soon became apparent that almost no treatment plant would be good enough.
Even though the processed water is drinkable, it still has a yellowish tinge and
a barely perceptible odor. As might be expected, a few months after this effluent had been discharged into the lake, the Limnological Institute reported
that animal and plant life had decreased by one-third to one-half in the zone
where the sewage was being discharged.

Several limnologists have argued that the only effective way to prevent the
mill's effluent from damaging the lake is to keep it out of the lake entirely.
They suggest that this can be done if a 67-kilometer sewage conduit is built
over the mountains to the Irkut River, which does not flow into the lake. So far
the Ministry of Paper and Pulp Industries has strongly opposed this, since it
would cost close to $40 million to build such a bypass. They argue that they
have already spent a large sum on preventing pollution. Part of their lack of
enthusiasm for any further change may also be explained by the fact that they
have only had to pay fines of $55 for each violation. It has been cheaper to
pay the fines than to worry about a substantial cleanup operation.

Amid continuing complaints, the second paper and pulp mill, at Kamensk,
was told that it must build and test its treatment plant before production of

---

[7]*Turkm. Iskra* 1969, 3 (16 Sept. 1969).
[8]O. Volkov, *Soviet Life* 1966, 6 (Aug. 1966).
[9]L. Rossolimo, *Baikal* (Nauka, Moscow, 1966), p. 91.

paper and pulp would be allowed. Moreover, the lake and its entire drainage basin have been declared a "protected zone," which means that in the future all timber cutting and plant operations are to be strictly regulated. Many critics, however, doubt the effectiveness of such orders. As far back as 1960, similar regulations were issued for Lake Baikal and its timber, without much result. In addition, the Ministry of Pulp and Paper Industries has plans for constructing yet more paper and pulp mills along the shores of Lake Baikal and is lobbying for funds to build them.

Many ecologists fear that, even if no more paper mills are built, the damage may already have been done. The construction of the mills and towns necessitated the cutting of trees near the shoreline, which inevitably increased the flow of silt into the lake and its feeder streams. Furthermore, instead of being shipped by rail, as was originally promised, the logs are rafted on the water to the mill for processing. Unfortunately about 10 percent of these logs sink to the lake bottom in transit. Not only does this cut off the feeding and breeding grounds on the bottom of the lake but the logs consume the lake's oxygen, which again reduces its purity.

There are those who see even more dire consequences from the exploitation of the timber around the lake. The Gobi Desert is just over the border in Mongolia. The cutting of the trees and the intrusion of machinery into the wooded areas has destroyed an important soil stabilizer. Many scientists report that the dunes have already started to move, and some fear that the Gobi Desert will sweep into Siberia and destroy the taiga and the lake.

AIR

The misuse of air resources in the U.S.S.R. is not very different from the misuse of water. Despite the fact that the Russians at present produce less than one-tenth the number of cars each year that we produce in the United States, most Soviet cities have air pollution. It can be quite serious, especially when the city is situated in a valley or a hilly region. In the hilly cities of Armenia, the established health norms for carbon monoxide are often exceeded. Similarly Magnitogorsk, Alma Ata, and Chelyabinsk, with their metallurgical industries, frequently have a dark blue cap over them. Like Los Angeles, Tbilisi, the capital of the Republic of Georgia, has smog almost 6 months of the year. Nor is air pollution limited to hilly regions. Leningrad has 40 percent fewer clear daylight hours than the nearby town of Pavlovsk.[10]

Of all the factories that emit harmful wastes through their stacks, only 14 percent were reported in 1968 to have fully equipped air-cleaning devices. Another 26 percent had some treatment equipment. Even so, there are frequent complaints that such equipment is either operating improperly or of no use. There have been several reported instances of factories' spewing lead into the air.[11] In other cases, especially in Sverdlovsk and Magnitogorsk, public health

[10] I. Petrov, *Kommunist* 1969, No. 11, 74 (1969).
[11] *Rabochaia Gaz.* 1969, 4 (27 June 1969); *Ekon. Gaz.* 1968, No. 4, 40 (1968); *Lit. Gaz.* 1967, No. 32, 10 (1967).

officials ordered the closing of factories and boilers. Nevertheless, there are periodic complaints that some public health officials have yielded to the pleadings and pressures of factory directors and have agreed to keep the plants open "on a temporary basis."

One particularly poignant instance of air pollution is occurring outsiue tne historic city of Tula. Not far away is the site of Leo Tolstoy's former summer estate, Yasnaya Polyana, now an internationally known tourist attraction with lovely grounds and a museum. Due to some inexcusable oversight a small coal-gasification plant was built within view of Yasnaya Polyana in 1955. In 1960 the plant was expanded as it began to produce fertilizer and other chemicals. Now known as the Shchkino Chemical Complex, the plant has over 6000 employees and produces a whole range of chemicals, including formaldehyde and synthetic fibers. Unfortunately the prevailing winds from this extensive complex blow across the street onto the magnificent forests at Yasnaya Polyana. As a result, a prime oak forest is reported near extinction and a pine forest is similarly affected.

LAND

As in other nations of the world, environmental disruption in the U.S.S.R. is not limited to air and water. For example, the Black Sea coast in the Soviet Republic of Georgia is disappearing. Since this is a particularly desirable resort area, a good deal of concern has been expressed over what is happening. At some places the sea has moved as much as 40 meters inland. Near the resort area of Adler, hospitals, resort hotels, and (of all things) the beach sanitarium of the Ministry of Defense collapsed as the shoreline gave way. Particular fears that the mainline railway will also be washed away shortly have been expressed.

New Yorkers who vacation on Fire Island have had comparable difficulties, but the cause of the erosion in the U.S.S.R. is unique. Excessive construction has loosened the soil (as at Fire Island) and accelerated the process of erosion. But, in addition, much of the Black Sea area has been simply hauled away by contractors. One contractor realized that the pebbles and sand on the riviera-type beach were a cheap source of gravel. Soon many contractors were taking advantage of nature's blessings. As a result, as much as 120,000 cubic meters a year of beach material has been hauled away. Unfortunately the natural process by which those pebbles are replaced was disrupted when the state came along and built a network of dams and reservoirs on the stream feeding into the sea. This provided a source of power and water but it stopped the natural flow of pebbles and sand to the seacoast. Without the pebbles, there is little to cushion the enormous power of the waves as they crash against the coast and erode the shoreline.

In an effort to curb the erosion, orders have been issued to prevent the construction of any more buildings within 3 kilometers of the shore. Concrete piers have also been constructed to absorb the impact of the waves, and efforts are being made to haul gravel material from the inland mountains to replace that which has been taken from the seacoast. Still the contractors are disregarding the orders—they continue to haul away the pebbles and sand, and the seacoast continues to disappear.

Nor is the Black Sea coast the only instance of such disregard for the forces of nature. High in the Caucasus is the popular health resort and spa of Kislovodsk. Surrounded on three sides by a protective semicircle of mountains which keep out the cold winds of winter, the resort has long been noted for its unique climate and fresh mountain air. Whereas Kislovodsk used to have 311 days of sun a year, Piatagorsk on the other side of the mountain had only 122.[12] Then, shortly after World War II, an official of the Ministry of Railroads sought to increase the volume of railroad freight in the area. He arranged for the construction of a lime kiln in the nearby village of Podkumok. With time, pressure mounted to increase the processing of lime, so that now there are eight kilns in operation. As the manager of the lime kiln operation and railroad officials continued to "fulfill their ever-increasing plan" in the name of "socialist competition," the mountain barrier protecting Kislovodsk from the northern winds and smoke of the lime kilns has been gradually chopped away. Consequently, Kislovodsk has almost been transformed into an ordinary industrial city. The dust in the air now exceeds by 50 percent the norm for a *nonresort* city.

Much as some of our ecologists have been warning that we are on the verge of some fundamental disruptions of nature, so the Russians have their prophets of catastrophe. Several geographers and scientists have become especially concerned about the network of hydroelectric stations and irrigation reservoirs and canals that have been built with great fanfare across the country. They are now beginning to find that such projects have had several unanticipated side effects. For example, because the irrigation canals have not been lined, there has been considerable seepage of water. The seepage from the canals and an overenthusiastic use of water for irrigation has caused a rise in the water table in many areas. This has facilitated salination of the soil, especially in dry areas. Similarly, the damming of water bodies apparently has disrupted the addition of water to underground water reserves. There is concern that age-old sources of drinking water may gradually disappear. Finally, it is feared that the reduction of old water surfaces and the formation of new ones has radically altered and increased the amount of water evaporation in the area in question. There is evidence that this has brought about a restructuring of old climate and moisture patterns.[13] This may mean the formation of new deserts in the area. More worrisome is the possibility of an extension of the ice cap. If enough of Russia's northward-flowing rivers are diverted for irrigation purposes to the arid south, this will deprive the Arctic Ocean of the warmer waters it receives from these rivers. Some scientist critics also warn that reversing the flow of some of the world's rivers in this way will have disruptive effects on the rotation of the earth.

---

[12]*Izv.* 1966, 5 (3 July 1966).
[13]*Soviet News* 1969, 105 (11 March 1969).

REASONS FOR POLLUTION

Because the relative impact of environmental disruption is a difficult thing to measure, it is somewhat meaningless to say that the Russians are more affected than we are, or vice versa. But what should be of interest is an attempt to ascertain why it is that pollution exists in a state-owned, centrally planned economy like that of the Soviet Union. Despite the fact that our economies differ, many if not all of the usual economic explanations for pollution in the non-Communist world also hold for the Soviet Union. The Russians, too, have been unable to adjust their accounting system so that each enterprise pays not only its direct costs of production for labor, raw materials, and equipment but also its social costs of production arising from such byproducts as dirty air and water. If the factory were charged for these social costs and had to take them into account when trying to make a profit on its operations, presumably factories would throw off less waste and would reuse or recycle their air and water. However, the precise social cost of such waste is difficult to measure and allocate under the best of circumstances, be it in the United States or the U.S.S.R. (In the Ruhr Valley in Germany, industries and municipalities are charged for the water they consume and discharge, but their system has shortcomings.)

In addition, almost everyone in the world regards air and water as free goods. Thus, even if it were always technologically feasible, it would still be awkward ideologically to charge for something that "belongs to everyone," particularly in a Communist society. For a variety of reasons, therefore, air and water in the U.S.S.R. are treated as free or undervalued goods. When anything is free, there is a tendency to consume it without regard for future consequences. But with water and air, as with free love, there is a limit to the amount available to be consumed, and after a time there is the risk of exhaustion. We saw an illustration of this principle in the use of water for irrigation. Since water was treated virtually as a free good, the Russians did not care how much water they lost through unlined canals or how much water they used to irrigate the soil.

Similarly, the Russians have not been able to create clear lines of authority and responsibility for enforcing pollution-control regulations. As in the United States, various Russian agencies, from the Ministry of Agriculture to the Ministry of Public Health, have some but not ultimate say in coping with the problem. Frequently when an agency does attempt to enforce a law, the polluter will deliberately choose to break the law. As we saw at Lake Baikal, this is especially tempting when the penalty for breaking the law is only $55 a time, while the cost of eliminating the effluent may be in the millions of dollars.

The Russians also have to contend with an increase in population growth and the concentration of much of this increase in urban areas. In addition, this larger population has been the beneficiary of an increase in the quantity and complexity of production that accompanies industrialization. As a result, not only is each individual in the Soviet Union, as in the United States, provided with more goods to consume, but the resulting products, such as plastics and detergents, are more exotic and less easily disposed of than goods of an earlier, less complicated age.

Like their fellow inhabitants of the world, the Russians have to contend with something even more ominous than the Malthusian Principle. Malthus observed that the population increased at a geometric rate but that food production grew at only an arithmetic rate. If he really wants to be dismal, the economist of today has more to worry about. It is true that the population seems to be increasing at accelerated rates, but, whereas food production at least continues to increase, our air, water, and soil supplies are relatively constant. They can be renewed, just as crops can be replanted, but, for the most part, they cannot be expanded. In the long run, this "Doomsday Principle" may prove to be of more consequence than the Malthusian doctrine. With time and pollution we may simply run out of fresh air and water. Then, if the damage is not irreversible, a portion of the population will be eliminated and those who remain will exist until there is a shortage once again or until the air, water, and soil are irretrievably poisoned.

INCENTIVES TO POLLUTE UNDER SOCIALISM

In addition to the factors which confront all the people of the earth, regardless of their social or economic system, there are some reasons for polluting which seem to be peculiar to a socialist country such as the Soviet Union in its present state of economic development. First of all, state officials in the Soviet Union are judged almost entirely by how much they are able to increase their region's economic growth. Thus, government officials are not likely to be promoted if they decide to act as impartial referees between contending factions on questions of pollution. State officials identify with the polluters, not the conservationists, because the polluters will increase economic growth and the prosperity of the region while the antipolluters want to divert resources away from increased production. There is almost a political as well as an economic imperative to devour idle resources. The limnologists at Lake Baikal fear no one so much as the voracious Gosplan (State Planning) officials and their allies in the regional government offices. These officials do not have to face a voting constituency which might reflect the conservation point of view, such as the League of Women Voters or the Sierra Club in this country. It is true that there are outspoken conservationists in the U.S.S.R. who are often supported by the Soviet press, but for the most part they do not have a vote. Thus the lime smelters continued to smoke away behind the resort area of Kislovodsk even though critics in *Izvestiia, Literaturnaya Gazeta, Sovetskaia Rossiia, Trud,* and *Krokodil* protested long and loud.

At one time state governments in our country often reflected similar one-sidedness. Maine, for example, was often cited as an area where industry did what it wanted to do to nature. Now, as the conservationist voting bloc has grown in size, the Maine state government finds itself acting as referee. Accordingly it has passed a far-reaching law which regulates the location and operation of all new industry. Failure to have voted for such legislation may have meant defeat at the polls for many politicians. No such device for transmitting voting pressure exists at present in the U.S.S.R.

Second, industrialization has come relatively recently to the U.S.S.R. and so the Russians continue to emphasize the increase in production. Pollution control generally appears to be nonproductive, and there is usually resistance to the diversion of resources from productive to nonproductive purposes. This is even reflected in the words used to describe the various choices. "Conserve" generally seems to stand in opposition to "produce."

Third, until July 1967, all raw materials in the ground were treated by the Russians as free goods. As a result, whenever the mine operator or oil driller had exploited the most accessible oil and ore, he moved on to a new site where the average variable costs were lower. This has resulted in very low recovery rates and the discarding of large quantities of salvageable materials, which increase the amount of waste to be disposed of.

Fourth, as we have seen, it is as hard for the Russians as it is for us to include social costs in factory-pricing calculations. However, not only do they have to worry about social cost accounting, they also are unable to reflect all the private cost considerations. Because there is no private ownership of land, there are no private property owners to protest the abuse of various resources. Occasionally it does happen that a private property owner in the United States calculates that his private benefits from selling his land for use in some new disruptive use is *not* greater than the private cost he would bear as a result of not being able to use the land any more. So he retains the land as it is. The lack of such private property holders or resort owners and of such a calculation seems to be the major reason why erosion is destroying the Black Sea coast. There is no one who can lay claim to the pebbles on the shore front, and so they are free to anyone who wants to cart them away. Of course private landowners do often decide to sell their land, especially if the new use is to be for oil exploitation rather than pebble exploitation. Then the private benefits to the former owner are high and the social costs are ignored, as always. The Russians, however, under their existing system, now only have to worry about accounting for social costs, they lack the first line of protection that would come from balancing private costs and private benefits.

Fifth, economic growth in the U.S.S.R. has been even more unbalanced, and in some cases more onesided, than in the United States. Thus, occasionally change takes place so rapidly and on such a massive scale in a state-run economy that there is no time to reflect on all the consequences. In the early 1960's, Khrushchev decided that the Soviet Union needed a large chemical industry. All at once chemical plants began to spring up or expand all over the country. In their anxiety to fulfill their targets for new plant construction, few if any of the planners were able to devote much attention to the disruptive effects on the environment that such plants might have. We saw one result at Yasnaya Polyana. In fact, the power of the state to make fundamental changes may be so great that irreversible changes may frequently be inflicted on the environment without anyone's realizing what is happening until it is too late. This seems to be the best explanation of the meteorological disruption that is taking place in Siberia. It is easier for an all-powerful organism like the state than for a group of private entrepreneurs to build the reservoirs and reverse the rivers. Private enterprises can cause their own havoc, as our own dust bowl experience or our use of certain pesticides or sedatives indicates, but in the absence of private business or property interests the state's powers can be much more far-reaching in scope. In an age of rampant technology, where the consequences of one's actions are not always fully anticipated, even well-intentioned programs can have disastrous effects on the environmental status quo.

ADVANTAGES OF A SOCIALIST SYSTEM

Amidst all these problems, there are some things the Russians do very well. For example, the Russians have the power to prevent the production of various products. Thus, the Soviet Union is the only country in the world that does not put ethyl lead in most of the gasoline it produces. This may be due to technical lag as much as to considerations of health, but the result is considerably more lead-free gasoline. Similarly, the Russians have not permitted as much emphasis on consumer-goods production as we have in the West. Consequently there is less waste to discard. Russian consumers may be somewhat less enthusiastic about this than the ecologists and conservationists, but in the U.S.S.R. there are no disposable bottles or disposable diapers to worry about. It also happens that, because labor costs are low relative to the price of goods, more emphasis is placed on prolonging the life of various products. In other words it is worthwhile to use labor to pick up bottles and collect junk. No one would intentionally abandon his car on a Moscow street, as 50,000 people did in New York City in 1969. Even if a Russian car is 20 years old, it is still valuable. Because of the price relationships that exist in the U.S.S.R., the junkman can still make a profit. This facilitates the recycling process, which ecologists tell us is the ultimate solution to environmental disruption.

It should also be remembered that, while not all Russian laws are observed, the Russians do have an effective law enforcement system which they have periodically brought to bear in the past. Similarly, they have the power to set aside land for use as natural preserves. The lack of private land ownership makes this a much easier process to implement than in the United States. As of 1969, the Soviet Government had set aside 80 such preserves, encompassing nearly 65,000 square kilometers.

Again because they own all the utilities as well as most of the buildings, the Russians have stressed the installation of centrally supplied steam. Thus, heating and hot water are provided by central stations, and this makes possible more efficient combustion and better smoke control than would be achieved if each building were to provide heat and hot water for itself. Although some American cities have similar systems, this approach is something we should know more about.

In sum, if the study of environmental disruption in the Soviet Union demonstrates anything, it shows that not private enterprise but industrialization is the primary cause of environmental disruption. This suggests that state ownership of all the productive resources is not a cure-all. The replacement of private greed by public greed is not much of an improvement. Currently the proposals for the solution of environmental disruption seem to be no more advanced in the U.S.S.R. than they are in the United States. One thing does seem clear, however, and that is that, unless the Russians change their ways, there seems little reason to believe that a strong centralized and planned economy has any notable advantages over other economic systems in solving environmental disruption.

Shirley Foster Hartley focuses "on how pollution problems are compounded by population pressures." For example, she points out that while more and more acreage is constantly put to plough in an effort to support the nutritional needs of the growing world population, "the salts deposited with irrigated water threaten the ultimate destruction of soil productivity." Although it is possible to drain the water off, the costs are great, and "neither the press of population nor immediate profit incentives will allow the world the luxury of holding extensive acreage out of maximum production." Thus, while trying to feed people today, we may be destroying the soil needed to feed people tomorrow.

So we return to the question of crisis. Safe irrigation is a realizable possibility, but like many other ecologically sound procedures, it will require more time, money, and effort than our immediate "practical" goals deem feasible. As long as speed and efficiency are more important to us than the long-term health of our environment, our chances of effecting safe irrigation—and many other changes—are slight.

From Population: Quantity v. Quality
—Shirley Foster Hartley

POLLUTION

A great many books have been written on the causes and consequences of pollution. I want to touch only briefly on how pollution problems are compounded by population pressures. We will review some of the causes of pollution, examine some of the differences in pollution between underdeveloped and developed countries, and, finally, survey the way in which different parts of the biosphere are affected by pollutants.

Pollution is the accumulation, in the air, the waters, and the soils of the biosphere, of substances harmful to living things. Since, by definition, substances in the air, water, or soil are not pollutants until they are of sufficient quantity to be harmful to living things, man is still discovering specific pollutants. Furthermore, since the chemical composition of the parts of our biosphere is very complex, it is not always clear which substances, in what concentrations, over what period of time, become harmful and to what extent.

The population explosion and the technological explosion together cause the increasing pollution of our environment. It has become commonplace to note that the increasing affluence of persons in advanced countries has contributed more to pollution than a simple rise in population numbers. Recognizing the truth of the statement, however, does not close the issue. People are not overwhelmingly eager to give up the niceties recently acquired. And, as we are trying to eliminate or reduce pollution from some sources, it increases from other sources (note the increase in camper-wagons, power boats and motorcycles as well as newsprint and educational materials). It is precisely because we hope to raise the level of life for *all* that population numbers are a major concern in relation to pollution. It is no coincidence that pollution has been recognized as a very real problem in the last few years. The population explosion and implosion are very recent phenomena. Not only people themselves, but all sorts of activities and products related to the maintenance of people contribute to the spoiling of our natural resources and of the environment in general. Twice as many people at a constant standard of living would produce twice as much garbage, whether the waste were discharged into the air, the waters, or dumped on land. If the number of "things" people possess or use up increases, so does the potential destructive power of the useless remains. Old automobiles don't just fade away, and the metallic content is seldom recycled. They have been piling up in ugly heaps.

Pollution occurs, then, partially as a result of the population increase and the rise in standards of living. It is also a consequence of the time lag in our recognition of the problems created by people pollution and our lack of concern or inability to remedy the problems.

A COMPARISON OF THE DEVELOPING AND DEVELOPED COUNTRIES

In the less developed countries pollution is more directly a result of the population explosion. Although there were instances of water and soil pollution in the past, the problem on a broad scale is a very recent phenomenon. No one who has seen the rivers flowing through some of the more populous underdeveloped countries of the world can doubt that people are polluting these rivers directly. Anyone who watches people bathe and brush their teeth in water from the river that carries the sewage past Bangkok knows that increased population means increased pollution.

Chemical pollutants have several interrelated effects upon the people of the less developed nations. Many of these products have been introduced in recent years to destroy disease-carrying agents or crop pests. Pesticides have helped save crops from destruction by insects, and chemical fertilizers have helped increase crop yields. The chemical products have helped lower the death rate, resulting in the population explosion. In addition, many people who would otherwise have died at an early age are able to add their waste products to the ever-expanding disposal problem. The same chemicals have polluted the air, the water, and in some cases the soils of the countries involved.

In the developed countries, where population has been growing less rapidly than in the underdeveloped nations, there has been an explosion in the number of "things" produced for use by people. They have contributed far greater quantities of pollutants to the biosphere than have the less developed countries, generally.

There is some logic to the argument that to insure continued increases in their standards of living, the affluent nations should be working toward a *negative population growth rate*. The North American standard of living is impossible for the overpopulated, impoverished areas of the world. The 6.5 percent of the world population presently living in the United States and Canada are using up approximately one half of the world's yield of resources. Philip Hauser has computed that *at our standard of living the total products of the world would support about a half a billion people:* only one-seventh the number presently alive.

It serves no one's interest to add to the number of world consumers. The affluent create one problem by consuming more than their share of the world's resources and another problem by throwing away so much waste. Solid wastes now average over four pounds per American per day. Urban areas especially are having real problems trying to dispose of these wastes. Yet most city governments, Chambers of Commerce, and citizens at large still plan for and encourage expansion. Without great and immediate effort the continued growth of cities will lead to increased pollution of all kinds. . . .

. . . A part of the problem in the developed countries is that the substances which pollute the environment are usually the residue from some product or service. It would be easy to halt pollution if those products or substances had only negative consequences. However, driving a car is usually more convenient than walking, riding a bicycle, or taking a train or bus. It is less trouble to throw bottles and newspapers into the garbage can than to save them for recycling. Pesticides, fertilizers, and even defoliants have positive uses, not merely negative consequences.

The effects of pollution, moreover, are no longer confined merely to the region of pollution. Developed countries are increasingly banning the use of DDT, but they will receive the residues from its use in less developed countries. DDT, which now threatens lives indirectly, has been saving millions of lives directly. The leaders of certain United Nations agencies (the World Health Organization and the Food and Agricultural Organization) are unwilling to ban DDT and other persistent pesticides on the basis of probable future harm to human beings, because of its immediate life-saving capacity in malaria control. They argue that holding off on the use of DDT as a caution against the possible and even probable long-term effects is a luxury that the less developed nations cannot afford. Time will certainly tell.

POLLUTION IN VARIOUS PARTS OF THE BIOSPHERE

Many different agents are involved in the pollution of water, air, soil, and living species. The same hazardous chemical agents often permeate several or all of the areas of the biosphere. DDT is the best-known example: it is carried by air and in the waters and soils of the earth and affects insects (the target), grazing animals that eat the same grasses and grains as the insects, fish that eat the green plants of the ocean, birds, animals, and human beings who eat the fish, the grazing animals, or the grains that have been sprayed.

WATER POLLUTION

Soil erosion may be aggravated by a lack of care of the land or by the mass clearing of forests. Precious topsoil may fill streams that were once clear with mud that is carried downstream to dammed areas, natural lakes, and the ocean.

These water sources may become overloaded with mud and silt and the land, meanwhile, has lost some of its initial richness. Knowledgeable farmers typically use fertilizers to restore the agricultural yield. The fertilizer itself results in another type of pollution. As the fertilized land is watered by rain or irrigation, nitrate nitrogen from the fertilizer is carried by the water to streams and lakes, killing the living species of those waters. The amount of nitrate nitrogen entering Lake Erie from the farm lands in the Erie watershed is equal to the amount of pollution entering from Detroit and all the other major cities that have been dumping sewage into the lake. Lake Erie has been widely publicized as a dead lake, its natural species having been killed by pollution. It is also dangerous for swimming and human enjoyment.

The increased use of Lake Tahoe in California by the expanding population of that state and by visiting tourists has endangered the life of that lake. The increase in seasonal and year-round population at Tahoe has caused pollution, silting, and algae to mar the natural beauty of the lake. Although construction that would add more raw sewage to the lake has been halted, there is no way to retract the previous contamination. A new $3 million experimental sewage treatment plant at the south end of the lake pumps treated water 14 miles to the Indian Creek reservoir. It arrives colorless, odorless, tasteless, and stripped of harmful wastes. The plant is an expensive experiment and serves only a portion of the lakeside population. However, if the purification procedure proves itself over time, the costs for future treatment facilities could be cut by pumping pure water back into the lake.

Most people have assumed that the *oceans* are too big to pollute, but marine biologists say that the oceans too are becoming polluted at an increasing rate. Lead is one of the substances which man is dumping into the sea in unprecedented quantities. The lead used in antiknock gasolines is discharged into the atmosphere, is drained out, and eventually finds its way to the ocean. Lead is found in the upper layers of the entire ocean, in greatest concentration near the coastlines. Since lead is toxic to most living things (including human beings) even in minute amounts, it is threatening in the portions of the oceans near the shoreline, which normally carry the greatest variety and quantity of living species.

Dr. Edward I. Goldberg of the Scripps Institution of Oceanography has said that an estimated one million tons of oil a year are leaked or spilled into the Atlantic Ocean from tankers and other ships. Seamen have reported finding oil droplets all along the Atlantic route from the Middle East to Central America.

Vast amounts of dry cleaning fluid and freon, the gas used in aerosol cans, may be finding their way into the oceans. Dr. Goldberg said there is no idea what the effects might be on the life of the sea.

Ocean pollution affects everyone. What one nation or group does affects many others. President Nixon proposed recently that the United Nations be allocated the management of resources and the income from the oceans of the world (beyond the 12-mile limit claimed by most nations). Presumably the plan would not only provide the U.N. with an independent source of income, but would invest the organization with responsibility for the protection of a world resource.

AIR POLLUTION

Mankind is now taxing the capacity of our atmosphere to absorb and carry away the enormous amount of emissions from areas of high population density. Almost every major city of the world has serious air pollution problems. Even more important, the entire atmosphere of our planet is now afflicted to some degree. Pollution at times reduces the amount of sunlight reaching New York City by nearly 25 percent, and that reaching Chicago by approximately 40 percent.

There is a growing recognition of the problem (most people cannot escape seeing, smelling, and tasting the smog) and the Air Quality Act of 1967 states that the U.S. goal is not only to protect the nation's air shed from further harm, but to *enhance* the quality of air. However, new pollutants are being added faster than the old ones can be controlled.

Some appreciation of the problem of trying to halt air pollution may be gleaned from a review of the sources of air pollution (see Table 1). Over 140 million tons of air pollutants were estimated to have been released by Americans in 1968. Motor vehicles contribute about 60 percent of the total and an even greater proportion of carbon monoxide and hydrocarbons.

TABLE 1

Sources of Air Pollution (in millions of tons annually)

	CARBON MONOXIDE	SULFUR OXIDES	NITROGEN OXIDES	HYDRO- CARBONS	PARTIC- ULATE MATTER	TOTALS
Motor vehicles	66	1	6	12	1	86
Industry	2	9	2	4	6	23
Power plants	1	12	3	1	3	20
Space heating	2	3	1	1	1	8
Refuse disposal	1	1	1	1	1	5
Totals	72	26	13	19	12	142

SOURCE: Population Reference Bureau. "The Thin Slice of Life." *Population Bulletin* 24 (December 1968), 117.

All of the pollutants are deadly in greater amounts, but even in small doses they are believed to contribute to deaths from lung cancer, pneumonia, chronic bronchitis, and emphysema. Dr. John T. Middleton, Director of the National Air Pollution Control Administration, says:

> On any busy thoroughfare you'll certainly breathe in lead . . . nitrogen oxide . . . carbon monoxide and organic matter such as the polynuclear hydrocarbons, . . . sulfur oxides, a variety of particulates and oxides of iron, aluminum and other metals. . . . Both the gases and particulates can be harmful by themselves. But what greatly disturbs us is the fact that a mixture of them is often even more harmful. It's not just an additive effect—it's an enhancing one (*Population Bulletin,* 1968, p. 118).

Wherever and whenever *thermal inversion* (a warm layer or "lid" over a cooler layer of air) occurs, the pollutants cannot rise and dissipate, so they build up close to the ground. Thermal inversions are very frequent around Los Angeles and account for much of the difference between the kinds of pollution on the East and West Coasts.

The Los Angeles Air Pollution Control District, one of the most able in operation anywhere, has established and enforced strict standards of control. Yet, although it has been possible to keep the density of smog from increasing, the volume of heavily polluted air has continued to increase in area and height. While the per capita amount of pollution has declined, the continued growth of population in the area leads to an ever-increasing total pollution. The geographical spread of the area and the lack of an adequate public transportation system, together with increasing numbers of people, mean that increasing numbers of automobiles are on the roadways. The United States as a whole has one motor vehicle registration for every two persons of all ages (United States Bureau of the Census, 1970). Los Angeles has more than its share.

The smog generated in the Los Angeles basin is destroying 100,000 acres of Ponderosa and Jeffrey pine trees 60 miles from the city. The smog oxidants destroy the leaf tissue that carry on the vital process of photosynthesis by which the trees are nourished. Smog levels near Santa Cruz in northern California are now sufficient to damage the Monterey Pines. It is suspected that trees in many other areas are also being damaged.

SOIL POLLUTION

Among the factors that cause deterioration of productive soils is erosion. The soils harbor a very complex system of interconnected species and erosion destroys the entire network at once. Man cannot re-create the living organisms of the soils once they are gone. Yet, deforestation continues to expose additional topsoil to erosion by wind and water. Borgstrom estimates that "in many parts of the globe the available [farm] land should be shrunk (reduced) in order to save the topsoil. More than half of India's tilled land is afflicted by soil erosion, one-third so seriously as to jeopardize the future of the topsoil".

In his attempt to renew some of the exhausted nutrients of the soil, man has developed all sorts of soil additives. Most of these have already proved to be helpful in increasing crop yields when they are added over great acreage, but not all are helpful to the soil itself. Fertilizers are likely to be used if they increase yields per acre. Yet it is not known how often the fertilizer, or the accompanying chemicals, are likely to be harmful to the soils, especially over a long period of time.

While both the total acreage and the proportion of agricultural land under irrigation are increasing yearly, the salts deposited with irrigated water threaten the ultimate destruction of soil productivity.

Rainwater is essentially salt-free, but water for irrigation having come in contact with the minerals and fossil salts of soils and geologic materials may contain several tons of dissolved salts per acre foot. Plants grown by irrigation absorb and transpire the water but leave nearly all of the salt behind in the soil, where it accumulates and eventually prevents plant growth unless removed by leaching and drainage.

An annual leaching by heavy rainfall can be counted on in only 4 of the 21 countries having more than one million hectares of irrigated land. In the other countries, salinity of the soil is a potential hazard.

Several civilizations that flourished in the distant past left evidence of irrigation systems that failed because they did not provide for salinity control.

On the basis of his acquaintance with salinity literature, contact with foreign salinity specialists, and travel in Latin America, the U.S.S.R. and the Near and Far East, Dr. C. A. Bower, Director of the U.S. Salinity Laboratory in Riverside, California, estimates that "salinity reduces crop yields on one-fourth to one-third of the world's irrigated land." He notes further that:

Designers of irrigation developments during the last 50 to 75 years have usually been aware of salinity hazards but in many cases they failed to provide control measures, particularly artificial drainage. This has led to the development of much salt affected soil in presently irrigated areas and has necessitated extensive remedial measures. Fortunately, there is scarcely an irrigation development planned today that does not take into account the need for salinity control.

The $250 million agricultural empire in Southern California's Imperial Valley is an excellent natural laboratory for the study of salt-poisoning of the soil. Farmers are postponing the destruction of the soils via a vast network of underground drainage tubes to carry off saline water before it destroys the roots of the crops. The tubes have already been installed under 400,000 acres at a cost of from $100 to $490 per acre. In all, more than 16,000 miles of tile have been laid, enough to go through the center of the earth to the other side and back again. Farmers who laid tubes 200 feet apart five or ten years ago are already going back to lay tubes 100 feet, 50 feet, or even 25 feet apart.

Others could learn from this natural laboratory in order to prevent a repetition of the same mistakes all over the globe. However, neither the press of population nor immediate profit incentives will allow the world the luxury of holding extensive acreage out of maximum production. Long-term results may well increase the problems of feeding the peoples of the earth. If deserts continue to be created faster than new acreage is put under the plow, there will be no long-term human solutions.

DEFOLIANTS

Chemical weed-killers have been used for many years. Treatment of small spots and larger areas with light amounts of defoliants is an acceptable means of eradicating unwanted plant growths. When used under controlled conditions and in very light concentration, there do not seem to be any long-term negative effects.

However, for the first time, high concentrations of herbicides are being used over wide areas as a part of U.S. military policy in Viet Nam. Most of the defoliation has occurred along roads and rivers, around military establishments, and along the Cambodian and Laotian borders. The mangroves along the Nha Bo River, the main shipping channel to Saigon, have been heavily defoliated.

Observations on the ground indicate that one application leads to a modest kill of canopy trees, but not seedlings. A year after spraying, the timber could still be harvested for commercial use. The smaller trees then could continue to grow in the area.

Since the program began in 1962 the acreage defoliated has increased so rapidly that by the end of 1968 the Department of Defense estimated that 3.5 million acres had been defoliated. As much as 20-25 percent of the forests of Viet Nam have been sprayed *more than once* so that all seedlings are also destroyed.

The targets and concentrations of poisons have been pinpointed positively, which will allow the future study of the consequences of different rates of application. Agriculturalists, biologists, and zoologists should be immediately involved in studying the effects not only on the trees themselves, but also on other plant life, and on the birds, fish, and wildlife of the areas.

The problem of defoliation lies in the fact that *no one knows the long-term effects.* Military goals must be balanced by other long-term considerations. If, as Orians and Pfeiffer suggest, the attitude of the South Vietnamese toward Americans has soured because of defoliation, the war could be lost even though, and perhaps because, some battles have been made easier to fight.

Defoliation is a drastic measure in a world whose population is increasing so rapidly that it needs every bit of useful acreage. Even during the war in Viet Nam, the populations of both the north and the south have almost doubled. Although short-term military advantage is possible, the long-term effects of defoliation are not known, but are likely to be detrimental.

CHEMICAL POLLUTANTS AND THE FOOD CHAIN

"Persistent" pesticides are those that do not break down and disappear in time. A light spray each year builds up over time and may be carried by wind and water. It is concentrated by many organisms and passed up the food chain to higher animals. The last species in the food chain is man.

The best known of the "persistent" pesticides is DDT. It was introduced commercially only 26 years ago (in 1946) to control malarial mosquitoes and various insects that are harmful to crops.

DDT is actually less toxic than many newer poisons. Endrin is estimated to be 50 times more harmful than DDT, with dieldrin, aldrin, chlordane, and toxaphene ranging between the two.

The United States Department of Agriculture has been criticized by the Rienows for claiming that it cannot set up recommendations on most poisons because it knows too little about them. The Department had in fact for years registered dieldrin and aldrin as safe. Then in 1966 they canceled its registered use. How can the widespread use of *any* poisons be allowed if too little is known about them?

DDT was once hailed as a marvelous find, but only the immediate advantages were known. Now some of the relatively long term disadvantages are appearing, even though not enough time has lapsed to *maximize* their intensity in human beings.

The increasing dangers of DDT may be seen by considering its concentration in the food chain within a single estuary. Only 70 parts per billion in drifting microscopic plants of the water eventually resulted in 800 parts per million in the fat of porpoises, a 10,000 fold concentration. A few parts per million can kill, and food fish, shrimp, and crabs die in several weeks. No one knows how often or in how many places these food sources may be disappearing without our being able to identify the cause of loss.

Birds of prey also concentrate the persistent poisons, since they feed upon species which have themselves concentrated small amounts. Eagles, ospreys, and some great hawks have been laying infertile eggs or eggs whose membranes are too thin to protect their delicate interiors. It is now established that DDT has been traveling through the insect-fish-bird feed cycle, accumulating in greater density at each link in the chain and impairing the birds' ability to reproduce. Several species are now threatened with complete extinction.

The same build-up occurs on land. Hay and grasses that have been sprayed are eaten by grazing animals, chickens, and so forth. Human beings then consume the milk and meat, as well as the original grains. The concentration multiplies in each link in the food chain—and becomes most highly concentrated in the last link—man. The DDT intake of infants around the world is now about twice the daily maximum deemed safe by the World Health Organization. Concentrations of more than 12 parts per million have been found in human fat and as high as 5 parts per million in human milk (though the usual range is some 0.05 to 0.26 parts per million). The DDT concentrations in mothers' milk in the United States now exceeds the tolerance levels established for foodstuffs by the Food and Drug Administration.

Because the heavy and widespread use of the persistent pesticides is a very recent phenomenon, the long-term effects are still unknown. Biologists have every reason to believe that these biologically active molecules are dangerous. One study, the results of which were obtained by autopsies, showed a correlation between DDT levels in human fat and cause of death. Concentration of DDT and its breakdown products, DDE and DDD, were significantly high in the fat of patients who had died of softening of the brain, cerebral hemorrhage, hypertension, portal cirrhosis of the liver, and various cancers than in groups of patients who had died of infectious diseases. Neurophysiologist Alan Steinbach of the University of California at Berkeley claims that DDT is an irreversible nerve poison. Experiments with animals indicate that exposure to chlorinated hydrocarbons, of which DDT is one, caused changes in the central nervous system.

As more is learned about chemical pollution of the environment, perhaps man will become more cautious. Perhaps too, mankind will recognize that it is the basic population pressure that encourages the use of products that provide immediate results, but may have numerous long-term hazards.

17

Population

This selection needs little commentary. The figures are stark and there for all to see. We must either make population control our highest world priority, or we race a future that will add two billion people to the earth's population within the next twenty-five years.

And even if we make the drastic changes necessary to feed two billion more people, how will we house or feed them, or deal with the vastly increased pollution they will cause? If population growth is allowed to continue, can we imagine a future that will tackle all these problems together?

Finally, a suggestion: If the advanced industrial societies began to reevaluate their cultures, perhaps underdeveloped nations would follow suit. Right now the developing countries seem eager to confront their growing populations with societies that promise to become technostatist. What is the human prospect if that occurs?

From World Population: The View Ahead
—*Milos Macura*

TABLE 1

Expectancy of Life ($\acute{e}_0$)

	1960-65	1980-85	1995-2000
Europe	68.7	73.7	73.9
U.S.S.R.	70.2	73.9	73.9
Northern America ...	71.7	73.9	73.9
Oceania	61.0	64.9	66.7
Eastern Asia*	46.3	55.8	62.7
Southern Asia	46.4	56.6	64.6
Latin America	57.9	65.0	68.7
Africa	41.1	48.8	54.7

SOURCE: Population Division of the United Nations (work sheets).
*Japan: 68.2, 1960-65; 73.0, 1980-85; 73.9, 1995-2000.

TABLE 2

Sex- and Age-Adjusted Birth Rates

	1960-65	1980-85	1995-2000
Europe	19.3	18.0	18.0
U.S.S.R.	20.3	22.0	22.0
Northern America ...	26.7	24.0	24.0
Oceania	28.7	27.3	27.5
Eastern Asia*	34.1	24.5	19.4
Southern Asia	44.6	36.9	26.6
Latin America	42.1	37.3	30.8
Africa	48.8	47.0	43.0

SOURCE: Population Division of the United Nations (work sheets).
*Japan: 14.9, 1960-65; 15.5, 1980-85; 15.8, 1995-2000.

TABLE 3

Female Population 15-44 Years Old

	(IN MILLIONS)		
	1960	1980	2000
Europe	88.8	99.6	106.6
U.S.S.R.	50.7	60.6	72.9
Northern America ...	39.8	55.9	75.5
Oceania	3.2	4.7	6.6
Eastern Asia	174.8	236.4	298.7
Southern Asia	185.9	299.1	513.6
Latin America	45.6	79.2	142.9
Africa	58.0	94.3	164.3

SOURCE: Population Division of the United Nations (work sheets).

*   *   *

TWENTIETH CENTURY POPULATION TRENDS

. . . The variety in growth pattern of the world's populations in the twentieth century is such that it can be generalized only with major reservations. The beginning, the intensity, and the combination of changes in fertility and mortality and their relationships to structural changes, as well as to their economic, social, and cultural correlates, do not encourage their being interpreted by a single hypothesis or a simplified set of hypotheses as generally valid. But for a broad understanding of the changes that have already taken place and that are anticipated for the next thirty-five years, a distinction between demographic trends in developed and less-developed countries may be useful.

This distinction is understood, indeed, to indicate the importance that is attributed to the association between the levels of development and the pattern of population growth. The distinction should not be understood as static.

Reprinted from *World Population: The View Ahead,* edited by Richard Farmer, John D. Long, and George Stolnitz, by permission of Indiana University.

though it classifies the same areas of the world into two basic groups over the whole of the twentieth century[1]—a long century in character, witnessing most profound demographic, economic, social, and political changes that affect the tempo of over-all development and the speed of transformation of less-developed areas into developed ones. This dual distinction should not under-rate the importance of diversity in the pattern of population growth, especially in the less-developed stratum; this diversity may have, of course, a significant influence on many aspects of future life and relevant policy considerations (see Table 4).

The segment of the history of world population that is under discussion has been studied by many authors and under different circumstances. Nothing new can perhaps be added to what has already been stated or organized in a synthesis.[2] However, the fact that humanity has entered the last third of the last century of the second millennium suggests that this particular period be further considered. If the assumptions on future fertility and mortality could be accepted *grosso modo* as suggested in *World Population Prospects,* both the increment and the tempo of growth of population during the next thirty-five years would be expected to exceed those occurring during the last sixty-five years (see Table 5). Obviously, a strong accent is on all growth indices of the less-developed regions, where six-sevenths of the next thirty-five years' increment in world population will take place. This period's population growth will be more than double that of the last sixty-five years.

The upward trend of the world population growth rate, which has been in general the main characteristic of the last sixty-five years, will probably continue until the middle of the period under consideration. Then it will gradually take the reverse direction. As encouraging as this turn may seem, its practical value would be diminished by the continuous absolute growth of population over the period, with a marked increment in each successive decade.[3]

The main changes in the reproductive pattern of world population, as regards both the relations between the developed and less-developed regions, and mortality and fertility, have taken place—broadly speaking—since World War II. Of course, during the first half of the century, there were some short periods when the growth rates of population in less-developed regions exceeded the ones in the developed regions. These were the periods of wars and of the

---

[1]A "nonstatic" classification which would reclassify each area from the less-developed to the developed group as soon as it reaches the criterion of developed would better satisfy some analytical needs. It could contribute to the study of the demographic transition of the world and to a better description of its particular stages. However, for the present analysis it seems that the classification of areas as published in *World Population Prospects* . . . meets the main purposes. It should be noted that level of fertility was used in this study as the criterion for defining the dichotomy between the developed and less-developed areas *(World Population Prospects* . . . , p. 3 and *Population Bulletin of the United Nations* (No. 7; New York: United Nations), pp. 1–3.

[2]Compare, for example, relevant chapters providing syntheses in *Determinants and Consequences of Population Trends* (New York: United Nations), the summary volumes of proceedings of the first and second World Population Conference; *Population Bulletin* No. 7; and others.

[3]The absolute growth of world population is estimated for the 1960's to be about 590 million; for the 1970's about 740 million; for the 1980's about 860 million; and for the 1990's about 940 million.

TABLE 4

Population Trends in Developed and
Less-Developed Regions, 1900–2000

	POPULATION IN MILLIONS			ANNUAL RATE OF GROWTH (%)		
	WORLD	DEVELOPED	LESS-DEVELOPED	WORLD	DEVELOPED	LESS-DEVELOPED
1900*	1,650	550	1,100	. . .	. . .	. . .
1910†	1,740	600	1,140	0.53	0.87	0.36
1920	1,861	674	1,187	0.67	0.17	0.41
1930	2,070	759	1,311	1.07	1.20	1.00
1940	2,296	822	1,474	1.04	0.80	1.18
1950	2,516	858	1,658	0.92	0.43	1.18
1960	2,998	976	2,022	1.77	1.30	2.01
1970	3,592	1,082	2,510	1.82	1.04	2.19
1980	4,330	1,194	3,136	1.89	0.99	2.25
1990	5,187	1,318	3,869	1.82	0.99	2.12
2000	6,129	1,441	4,688	1.68	0.90	1.94

SOURCE: *World Population Prospects as Assessed in 1963* (Population Studies No. 28; New York: United Nations, 1958), p. 23.
*J. D. Durand, "World Population Estimates, 1975–2000," *Proceedings of the World Population Conference, 1965*, II (New York: United Nations, 1967), p. 21.
†Interpolated between 1900 and 1920.

TABLE 5

Increment in Population in Two Periods

PERIOD		WORLD	DEVELOPED REGIONS	UNDEVELOPED REGIONS
		INCREMENT (MILLIONS)		
1900–65	. . . .	1,630	482	1,148
1965–2000	. . . .	2,849	410	2,440
		AVERAGE DECENNIAL INCREMENT (MILLIONS)		
1900–65	. . . .	250	74	176
1965–2000	. . . .	815	117	700
		PERCENTAGE INCREASE OVER THE PERIOD		
1900–65	. . . .	99	88	104
1965–2000	. . . .	87	40	108
		AVERAGE RATE OF GROWTH (IN PER CENT)		
1900–65	. . . .	1.1	1.0	1.1
1965–2000	. . . .	1.8	1.0	2.1

SOURCE: *World Population Prospects . . .* , p. 134.

Great Depression, with substantial demographic consequences for many advanced countries. But, as a rule, the rates of population growth of developed regions were relatively higher, owing to the effects of differential fertility and mortality in both developed and less-developed regions.

A fast decline in mortality in less-developed regions, combined with almost stable fertility in the late 1950's and in the 1960's, was in sharp contrast to the declining fertility and mortality in developed regions. "La reprise démographique" in the postwar years brought the rate of births in developed regions to its peak at about 23 and the rate of natural increase to about 13 per 1,000, but this was substantially lower than the respective rates in the less-developed regions. The decrease in mortality in the latter was such (and will continue to be such) that it easily offset the slow decline in fertility. The peak of the rate of natural increase in less-developed regions may therefore be expected in the 1970's; by that time, it may reach 22.5 per 1,000 for the less-developed regions as a whole.

The interplay of fertility and mortality and of the sex and age structure may result in unexpected demographic features, as indicated by levels, trends, and relations of crude birth and death rates in the two regional categories (see Table 6). This interplay may be even more pronounced for smaller regional groupings where the factors involved may form a particularly unusual constellation[4] with different growth effects. The attainment of highest rates of population increase in the less-developed countries may be dispersed over a period of fifty years and at varied levels. The peak increase of population (in terms of percentage decennial increase) was achieved in mainland Eastern Asia in the 1950's with

---

[4]The crude death rates do to some extent contribute to the "unexpected features." Standardized rates obviously give a different picture; for example, in Latin America the crude rate for the 1990's is estimated as about 6 and the standardized rate (using the age distribution of developed regions) at about 12. These may be compared with the standardized rate for Northern America, which is about 9.

TABLE 6
Crude Birth and Death Rates
(Per 1,000)

YEAR	WORLD		DEVELOPED		LESS-DEVELOPED	
	BIRTHS	DEATHS	BIRTHS	DEATHS	BIRTHS	DEATHS
1965–70	32.9	14.4	18.5	8.5	39.4	17.3
1970–75	32.4	13.6	18.7	8.6	38.2	15.7
1975–80	31.6	12.8	19.4	9.0	36.5	14.4
1980–85	29.6	11.5	19.3	9.1	33.9	12.5
1985–90	28.5	10.7	19.0	9.2	31.8	11.2
1990–95	26.9	9.9	18.5	9.4	29.7	10.0
1995–2000	25.7	9.3	18.3	9.6	28.0	9.2

SOURCE: *World Population Prospects . . .* , pp. 34, 35.

an increase of 16.2 per cent. In Tropical South America and South East Asia it is anticipated at levels of 36.8 and 29.3 per cent, respectively, for the 1960's. At least seven regions may have their peak increase in the 1970's, ranging from 44.0 to 26.4 per cent (Polynesia and the Caribbean). Southern Africa may reach its peak increase of population in the 1980's (30.4 per cent), and the rest of South-of-Sahara Africa after the 1980's.[5]

The contribution of the areas of European settlement to the twentieth century population growth may not substantially differ from the contribution of the developed areas, for "European" and "developed" are rather close, and their geographical coverage overlaps. The assessment of the importance of the areas of European settlement for the growth of world population had primarily a theoretical value, and Professor Durand is right when he states that they were not a dominant factor in the world population trend over the last two centuries. As for the future, the share in world population of areas of European settlement may well drop from 35 per cent in 1965 to 31 per cent in the year 2000. This is because their contribution to the increment of population may diminish from 35 per cent over the period 1900–65 to 26 percent for the last third of the century.[6]

REGIONAL PROSPECTS FOR END OF CENTURY

The geographical distribution of the world's resources and world population, together with the regions' nonsynchronized trends. bring the regional aspects

[5]*World Population Prospects . . .* , pp. 21 and 138.
[6]Taking Professor Durand's estimates for the early periods and the UN estimates for the twentieth century, the long-range trends (in millions) are as follows:

Year	World	European Settlement	Share, in per cent
1750	750	165	22
1800	960	230	24
1850	1240	330	27
1900	1650	575	35
1965	3280	1146	35
2000	6129	1903	31

It may be observed that the 1750 figure differs somewhat from estimates made by Carr-Saunders and Willcox in *Proceedings of the World Population Conference*.

of world population growth into focus. The publication, *World Population Prospects*, has made data available on the world, the less-developed and developed regions as a whole, eight major areas of the world, and twenty-four regions up to the year 2000, and for all countries and some geographical areas to 1980. This is, perhaps, the most comprehensive source for the study of population trends and prospects. According to the medium variant of the UN projections, the last third of the century may bring the demographic changes in eight major areas indicated in Table 7.

The biggest absolute addition to the present population is anticipated in Southern Asia, which has almost one-third of the world population. The three largest countries are the main contributors to this huge growth of population: India, whose population is expected to increase from 483 million in 1965 to 981 million in the year 2000; Pakistan, with an increase from 115 million to 288 million; and Indonesia with a growth of population from 105 million to 152 million in 1980. It should be noticed that the volume of growth of population in this area is closely related to its tempo. The next in importance to Southern Asia is Eastern Asia, where the pace of growth is estimated as very moderate but with an impressive absolute increase. This is due to the slow growth of the population of Japan (from 97 million in 1965 to 122 million in the year 2000), and also the relatively slow but large growth of population of China (from 695 to 1,034 million). It is evident that the bulk of the increment in population of this area is due to the growth of China's population, and that future demographic changes in the area will closely follow the changes in that country's population.

Latin America and Africa are both expected to have large increases in population, coupled with a very fast rate of growth. In fact, the relative growth of the Latin American population may be the highest, followed immediately by the relative growth of population in Africa. Brazil and Mexico will probably contribute the largest share to the growth of population of Latin America (Brazil, from 81 million in 1965 to 211 million in the year 2000). In Africa the largest increase is anticipated for Nigeria, from 58 million in 1965 to 91 million in 1980. But in contrast to the two areas discussed above, neither Latin America

TABLE 7
Population of Major Areas, 1965 and 2000
(IN MILLIONS)

AREA	1965	2000	INCREMENT	IN PER CENT
Europe	440	527	87	20
U.S.S.R.	231	353	122	53
Northern America	213	354	141	66
Oceania	17	32	15	88
Eastern Asia	852	1,287	435	51
Southern Asia . . .	976	2,171	1,194	122
Latin America . . .	245	638	393	160
Africa	306	768	462	151

SOURCE: *World Population Prospects* . . . , p. 134.

nor Africa may be dominated by the growth pattern of a particular country or of a couple of countries.

A substantial growth in population is also estimated for Northern America (in which the estimated growth for the U.S.A. is from 194 million to 322 million) and for the Soviet Union. The relative growth of these regions is moderate but much higher than the growth of European population, which is in relative terms the lowest.

Among the countries that were mentioned in the preceding analysis, no fewer than six have many common signs of serious economic underdevelopment, though their social structure and political organization differ greatly. Their aggregate population was about 1.5 billion in 1965, representing 47 per cent of the total world population. On the other hand, not more than three of the countries listed may be considered highly industrialized and technologically advanced. Again, they differ substantially in social structure and political organization. Their aggregate population was about 520 million in 1965 or one-seventh of the world's population, and one-third of the population of the six large economically less-developed countries.

ANTICIPATED STRUCTURAL CHANGES

Emphasizing the structural and qualitative problems of the future "development" of population perhaps has its strongest justification in the fact that there is no growth of population that does not have its own structural features.[7] As a matter of fact, all or almost all economic, social, cultural, and political functions have their "demographic framework," which is the stratum of population that is supposed to perform a given function; this is also how population becomes defined and structured economically, socially, educationally, and so forth. Differentiation of the functions is usually related to differentiation among sex and age groups; this is why the sex and age-structure of the population has not only demographic but also economic and social meaning. This differentiation is also a province in which many changes may be expected during the next thirty-five years (see Table 8).

According to the medium variant, all regions may face a more or less marked relative decline in the young-age group (0-14 years) by the end of the century, while the share of the old-age group (65 years and over) may increase.[8] The Soviet Union and Europe particularly may have a high relative growth of old-age population; perhaps the aging of population will acquire the most imposing characteristics of the growth trend in these two areas. An important relative

---

[7]"Development" of population is understood as a process which is simultaneously quantitative and qualitative, consisting of the growth of population (natural increase and migration) and of its structural changes (changes in biological structure as well as in economic, social, educational, and other relevant structures). For additional comments see Milos Macura, "Réflexions sur les éléments de la théorie démographique," *Economie et Société, publication jubilaire éditée à l'occasion du 70ème anniversaire de M. Le Prof. D. E. Kalitsounakis*, Athens, 1961, pp. 439–62.

[8]The proportion of young and old age groups in Northern America and Oceania is somewhat unexpected; it may be understood, however, if assumptions on fertility and mortality are taken into consideration.

TABLE 8
Age Structure, 1965 and 2000
(in per cent)

AREA AND YEAR		0–4	5–14	15–24	25–44	45–64	65
Europe	1965	8.5	16.6	14.9	27.6	21.8	10.6
	2000	7.7	15.2	14.5	27.0	22.5	13.1
U.S.S.R.	1965	10.3	20.6	13.8	30.7	17.7	6.9
	2000	9.3	17.8	15.8	26.3	19.6	11.2
Northern	1965	10.6	20.4	15.8	24.2	19.9	9.1
America	2000	10.6	19.2	17.1	26.3	17.9	8.9
Oceania	1965	11.1	20.1	16.5	25.7	18.9	7.7
	2000	11.5	20.1	17.1	25.4	17.4	8.5
Eastern	1965	12.9	22.7	18.0	26.6	15.3	4.5
Asia	2000	9.0	17.5	17.2	29.7	19.2	7.4
Southeast	1965	16.8	25.3	17.8	24.5	12.4	3.2
Asia	2000	12.0	22.5	20.0	27.7	13.2	4.6
Latin	1965	16.6	25.7	18.3	23.8	12.2	3.4
America	2000	13.8	24.2	19.8	25.6	12.3	4.3
Africa	1965	17.1	26.0	19.4	33.9	10.9	2.7
	2000	16.4	25.9	19.5	23.8	11.2	3.2

SOURCE: *World Population Prospects* . . . , pp. 127–31.

increase in the working-age group is evident in all regions, but with emphasis on the younger or more mature working-age population, depending on the stage of demographic maturity of particular areas.

Expressed in functional contingents, the anticipation of a change in age structure is, no doubt, very instructive. For lack of space, only estimates for the two large groupings of regions will be given, though they might have more meaning if estimates for an eight-area world breakdown could be given. As the expected growth of the female contingent of reproductive age has already been discussed (Table 3), only other major functional contingents will be considered here (Table 9).

The fastest expansion, far beyond what is anticipated for the total population, may be reached by the old-age contingent. Its growth in the less-developed areas, if compared to the present situation, may be particularly fast; but it probably will not constitute more than 6 per cent of the increment in total population between the years 1965 and 2000. In the developed stratum, the relative growth of this contingent is moderate, but economically and socially very important, since it will constitute almost 18 per cent of the increase in total population.

Slower, though even more serious, may be the growth of the working contingent—for well-known reasons arising both from the present employment situation and the capital requirement for new openings. In the less-developed regions, this contingent may rise from 1.2 billion in 1965 to 2.8 billion by the end of the century. Since the already overpopulated agricultural sector could not provide additional employment opportunity, the nonagricultural sector

TABLE 9
Functional Contingents, 1965 and 2000

	WORLD	DEVELOPED REGIONS	LESS-DEVELOPED REGIONS
PRESCHOOL CONTINGENT (0-4 YEARS)			
1965 (millions)	452.0	97.0	355.0
2000 (millions)	705.0	127.0	578.0
Increment (millions)	253.0	30.0	223.0
Per cent increment	55.8	30.9	62.8
Average annual rate of growth	1.28	0.77	1.40
SCHOOL-AGE CONTINGENT (5-14 YEARS)			
1965 (millions)	751.0	191.0	560.0
2000 (millions)	1,284.0	242.0	1,042.0
Increment (millions)	333.0	51.0	482.0
Per cent increment	71.0	26.7	86.1
Average annual rate of growth ..	1.55	0.70	1.77
WORKING CONTINGENT (15-64 YEARS)			
1965 (millions)	1,908.0	652.0	1,256.0
2000 (millions)	3,751.0	908.0	2,843.0
Increment (millions)	1,843.0	256.0	1,587.0
Per cent increment	96.6	39.3	126.4
Average annual rate of growth	1.95	0.95	2.36
OLD-AGE CONTINGENT (65 YEARS AND OVER)			
1965 (millions)	169.0	91.0	78.0
2000 (millions)	389.0	165.0	224.0
Increment (millions)	220.0	74.0	146.0
Per cent increment	130.2	81.3	187.2
Average annual rate of growth	2.41	1.73	3.06

SOURCE: Population Division of the United Nations (work sheets).

would have to give employment to over 1.2 billion new workers within the next thirty-five years, on the assumption that 80 per cent of the working contingent will enter the labor force.[9] It should be added that, in the developed regions, the working contingent may grow at a slightly lower rate than total population, and that its increase of 260 million amounts to only 60 per cent of total population increment to the end of the century. This, as well as the fact that the structural reserves of labor are almost exhausted in developed countries, may contribute to a growing demand for labor, which may be partly met outside the developed regions. If this happens, it may be a stimulus either for an increase in interregional migration or for growth in mobility of capital.

The next structural problem of population prospects—the fast growth of school-age population—is again concentrated in the less-developed areas. It is true that its relative growth is under what is anticipated for total population. But the absolute number of new students in primary and secondary schools

[9]Compare with the average relative increase in nonagricultural employment as suggested by Ansley Coale on the assumption that the increment in the labor force is to be employed outside agriculture—Ansley Coale, "Population and Economic Development," in Philip Hauser, ed., *The Population Dilemma* (Englewood Cliffs, N.J.: Prentice-Hall, Inc.), pp. 66–68.

may exceed 1 billion; this would call for a tremendous extension of education facilities, which even now fall far short of needs. No doubt the developed countries may also encounter new educational problems, but their demographic component may be far smaller, even almost negligible.

As an illustration only and without any intention to discuss the complex issues of future education further, the growth of illiteracy will be briefly mentioned. According to the latest UNESCO estimates, the rate of illiteracy was reduced from 43 per cent to 39 per cent from 1950 to 1960. At the same time, the number of illiterate adult population increased from 700 million to 740 million. Allowing for deaths, among which the aged illiterate population is a large proportion, an estimate of 290 million new illiterates was made for the period under consideration.[10]

If a broad generalization concerning demographic prospects over the next thirty-five years is permitted, it could be said that the average annual rate of growth of population of 1.8 per cent would call for a faster expansion of all kinds of consumption than during the last twenty years. It might also be suggested that the long-range problems of the employment and investment complex would need an even speedier and more energetic solution, since the working contingent is expected to grow by almost 2 per cent. A faster expansion in education and training may also be needed to meet not only a high 1.5 per cent rate in growth of school-age population, but also to accommodate the large numbers of new students emerging from the large increments in population. An extremely high growth of the old-age contingent, over 2.4 per cent, would open new questions both of an economic and a social nature. A final general observation must underline the fact that the greatest and most profound changes, not only in numbers but also in the structure of population, will take place in the less-developed parts of the world, where needs and resources are even now considerably out of balance with one another.

The joint authors concentrate on the consequences rapid population growth will probably have in the areas of politics, education, and health. In general, their analysis is quite restrained, but they draw attention to the great number, as well as the varying nature and magnitude of the problems attendant upon rapid population growth. For example, in countries that have high fertility rates, health services of necessity concentrate their efforts on the care of mothers and children. Because medical care for the young requires a higher doctor-patient ratio than care for people aged fifteen to forty-five, population growth increases the burden on doctors even more by demanding the allocation of additional money to health services. If there is no money for adequate care, infant mortality rates will increase, and the fertility rate will climb even higher. For in societies with high infant mortality rates, people tend to reproduce frequently in the hope that two or three of their children will live to be adults.

---

[10]*Statistical Yearbook, 1965* (New York: United Nations, 1966), pp. 32–33. Critical situations are being encountered in Africa, where the illiterate population grew by 20.3 million in ten years; Eastern Asia by 16.9 million; and Southern Asia by 7.2 million.

From Rapid Population Growth
—The National Academy of Social Sciences

POLITICAL AND SOCIAL CONSEQUENCES

. . . High population density and rapid growth are blamed for many disturbing features of a changing world: urban violence, political instability, poverty, pollution, aggressive behavior, revolution, and hypernationalism. Nevertheless, empirical attempts to relate population growth to these political pathologies have been uniformly unsuccessful. There is no evidence that population growth decreases the level of political stability or increases the probability of conflict and violence and aggressive behavior.

One reason for what may be myths about population and political pathology is that population change is ordinarily associated with socioeconomic change, and change carries with it the high likelihood of at least some disruption. Some of the characteristic forms of behavior associated in the public mind with high population density may, in fact, be much more significantly related to the prevalence of poverty and discrimination.

Another reason is the neglect of the subject by serious scholars. In the presence of ignorance, the intellectual gap has been filled by opinion. For example, there is a feeling, quite unsupported by evidence, that people in densely populated countries are more prepared to behave in irrational ways and to seek remedies by violence for internal and external problems, because they value human life less. This feeling is supported sometimes by crude biological analogy and oversimplification of the complexities of the interdependency of demographic and social change.

Nevertheless, the beliefs concerning real or imagined political consequences of demographic behavior are of great political importance in themselves. Hearsay knowledge and ignorance are available to politicians, and, as in the case of *lebensraum,* can be used with great effect to convince people to adopt policies espoused by politicians for entirely other reasons. Clearly the only antidote to unverified hypotheses applied as guides to public policy or as sources of propaganda is to increase the sophistication of tested knowledge and to disseminate the results through public education.

In the following discussion of the political and social consequences of rapid population growth it is essential to bear in mind that the current concern about the negative consequences of this growth are set against the backdrop of powerful pressures to achieve new and higher levels of income, health, education, and well-being. These goals are given differing shades of emphasis depending on the society from which they spring, but it is safe to predict that in the developing countries of the world the great mass of people would happily embrace them all, sure in the knowledge that they need and want more of whatever they are. In an atmosphere of rising expectations political "solutions" have an ineluctable glamour.

POLITICAL ADMINISTRATION AND GEOGRAPHIC DENSITY

It is difficult to govern a large territory with a small and dispersed population. The high per capita costs of governing underpopulated regions increase the likelihood of conflict between central and subordinate government units when justice, health, and education remain locally based (as is usually the case) because of the difficult problems of transportation and communication associated with attempts by the central government to have continuing contact with the citizenry. This suggests that the larger the population, the more effective its government can be, because the per capita costs of government are reduced. However, difficulties of another kind emerge as density increases. The larger the population, the greater the total cost of government, the less feasible the participation of the individual in the government—except for voting—and the greater the variety of interests seeking to influence the choice among options. With an increase in density, and in economic and social development, the organizational structure necessarily becomes more expensive and more elaborate and the people more subject to regulation, although the increased services government renders may compensate for this aspect.

No matter what the geographic density of people, it is clear that the strains upon the administrative resources of government are increased by the numbers of people that government must serve—just in terms of meeting the increasing demands for public services, such as public security, judicial processes, and legislation. Added to this are the specialized needs such as education, health, housing, transportation, communication, and whatever sort of regulatory devices seem needed to make the system operate with minimum friction. There is a high potential for conflict between central authority located in densely populated urban areas and local authority centered in rural, sparsely settled regions.

DIFFERENTIAL POPULATION GROWTH

Population growth is unlikely to be the same for all parts of a nation's population, partly because the mortality decline that creates growth is likely to be different from one sector of society to another, but principally because growth is ordinarily associated with socioeconomic changes that promote migration from one geographic and/or occupational sphere to another. Population redistribution has major political consequences: the breaking of old ties and forming of new ones on the part of the migrants, the dislocation costs for the sending and receiving populations as well as for the movers, a decline in the importance of systems of local political and social control. As development proceeds, populations tend to concentrate rather than disperse, and regional inequalities tend to become greater. One consequence of this process is that concentration in cities makes political organization more feasible.

Numbers and Political Power. Since numbers constitute an element in the relative political power of social groups, it follows that differential growth rates affect the distribution of political power within a society. This differential may be of less import for social classes than for ethnic groups, since the former are less visible and they gain and lose population by the process of social mobility associated with economic change. Conflicts between ethnic groups, on the other hand, are the counterpart within a nation of the kinds of conflicts between nations—conflicts that may be pursued by means of policies to gain demographic advantage. Ethnic groups are subpopulations with their own patterns of natural increase. Differential size and growth, and the perception of this, are important political facts in all political systems, and perhaps particularly in democratically oriented systems. Population policy may be explicitly or implicitly employed to extend the dominance of one ethnic group over another, or to extend political control over an area not previously well populated, or more generally to influence public policy decisions in discriminatory ways. Intergroup relations may be exacerbated by the migration that generally accompanies population growth and economic development. If low-fertility groups advocate a general policy of low fertility, the policy may be perceived by the targets of the policy to be politically motivated!

From an international viewpoint, political or other social elites may see population growth as a measure of the strength of the nation. Military manpower is still regarded by some as an index of political power despite the lessons of current history. Thus one consequence of rapid population growth may be to stir dreams of political, military, or economic expansionism.

IMPLICATIONS OF CHANGING AGE STRUCTURE

An outstanding characteristic of a rapidly growing population is the tendency of different age groups to increase at different rates, with the younger ages expanding at a greater rate than the older ages. Conversely, a dampening of the growth rate affects the younger first and only later the older ages. There are three reasons for this pattern of increase by age: The largest decline in mortality is registered in the age group with the highest mortality level, the infants. Second, fertility changes are by definition modifications of the ratio of those aged 0 to those in the childbearing span. Finally, any change at younger ages is passed on with the passage of time to the reproductive ages and is reflected back through the process of reproduction.

A stationary population with high fertility and high mortality is a young population. With mortality decline and the resulting positive rate of growth, the population becomes younger—the more so the higher the rate of growth. When fertility declines, the population becomes older, reaching a maximum age when it becomes stationary at a low mortality level. Thus the typical sequence in a demographic transition is that a young population becomes even younger as a consequence of mortality decline, but then becomes older as a consequence of fertility decline.

This transformation of the age structure has many important ramifications for the body politic. Different age groups make different kinds of demands upon the state—for health services for children and mothers, for the various levels of public education, for employment opportunities for entrants into the labor force, for medical services and social security for the old. For example, with an increase in the number of school-age children, the government may be pressured to divert investment funds from industry to education. More generally, different parts of the social system, to the extent that their membership is age-defined, take on a different relative configuration as a consequence of population growth, and change the power balance of the society. As with the assessment of the consequences of other demographic changes, there are two levels of consideration: a change from a previous equilibrium situation is disturbing to the status quo, and a new stable pattern fails to emerge, so that continual adjustment rather than merely adjustment to a new equilibrium is required.

One outstanding consequence of the modification described is an increase in the dependency ratio as a consequence of an increase in the rate of growth. (The dependency ratio is the ratio of that part of the population unable to produce sufficiently to meet its own needs—say those under age 15 and over 65—to those in the intermediate ages.) Although this is clearly an increased burden on the society, it may be more bearable, because of three associated circumstances: first, the mortality decline that produces the change in the age distribution may be associated with morbidity decline and better health; because the producing population is healthier it is likely to be more productive. Second, the labor force, as the key subpopulation, will, like the general population, be younger. Finally—a more subtle point—it is possible that a decline in mortality, representing as it does a decrease in the role of chance and unpredictability in human affairs, may diminish the sense of fatalism, strengthen the feeling that it is feasible to control the environment and make meaningful long-range plans, promote a sense of future-orientation, and generally increase the prominence of secular rather than sacred attitudes.

One characteristic of a high-mortality society, in toto and within its constituent groups, is a strong correspondence between respect, authority, status, and power, on the one hand, and age, on the other—to some extent irrespective of performance. In a low-mortality, high-fertility society with great numbers of young people, the respect for age and the status quo may sharply decline and those organizations unprepared for this phenomenon may be subjected to great stress.

A final point concerns the possibility that a society will experience change because individual characteristics are a function of age. If, for example, it could be demonstrated that youth is linked with liberalism and age with conservatism, as is commonly believed, then a growing population, because of its more youthful age structure, would be a more liberal population. In apparent support of this proposition, many modern revolutionary movements have been associated with, and have utilized, an increase in the number of young adults. It is difficult to differentiate in this situation the consequences of youthfulness, per se, and the extent to which the brunt of the disadvantages of change falls predominantly on the young adults, or, from another perspective, the extent to which their concentration in urban centers makes them more available for political organization.

In point of fact, little can be said with confidence about the meaning of age for individual behavior in some abstract causal sense, because of two confounding circumstances: (a) Most research on the subject has unavoidably confused its significance as an identifier of the person's location in historical time. Do the political and social attitudes of those over age 70 show the consequence of an inevitable aging process, or are they the result of birth in the 19th century? (b) Behavior in an age is only partly a consequence of the characteristics the individual brings into the situation. Societies are organized to expect particular kinds of behavior, and are ordinarily successful in bringing performance into line with those expectations. One of the most likely accompaniments of a process of social and economic development is a modification of age norms.

SOME SPECIAL POLITICAL PROBLEMS

Although the evidence is indeed thin, there is reason to speculate that rapid population growth contributes to (but does not create) certain unique types of politico-legal problems in less developed countries. For example, it appears reasonable to inquire about the size of the bureaucracy as a tool of administrative management in those countries in which there are pressures on the government caused by underemployment and unemployment.

Rapid population growth in rural areas can place remarkable strains on a legal system that presents real or perceived barriers to economic well-being; for example, the way land is held, its passage from generation to generation, and inheritance laws—all influence political decisions. Here the mix of political and economic consequences becomes blurred, and it is abundantly clear that not enough is known about the ways people react to and perceive these problems.

Finally, there is one clear political consequence of rapid population growth that has deliberately been excluded from this analysis: the sometimes exciting politics of fertility control—or family planning. This would be the subject of another entire volume, to say the least. It is possible to expect that education, information, and understanding of the consequences of rapid population growth will in the near future substantially decrease the volatility of this issue in most countries. Nonetheless, a different frame of reference and method of analysis would be required to make any definitive statements on this subject.

SOCIETY AND THE FAMILY

The consequences of rapid population growth for the family depend heavily upon the associated changes that may be occurring in the society and the economy. For example, the arithmetic of child dependency would be very much altered if the society were to prescribe child education and proscribe child labor. Both developments would institutionalize the rights of individuals, specifically the new generation, over the claims of family obligation, specifically to the older generation, and modify drastically the familism that has been so congenial to high fertility. Occupational opportunities outside the family farm would be another blow to the parent-child relationship, particularly since most such opportunities require migration of the child and allegiances to extra-familial organizations. Such changes would bring into question the pattern of traditional obligations of children to parents and place particular strain on the pivotal parental generation, which feel bound by the traditional demands of their parents without any compensating claims on their children.

In summary, the new demographic situation of mortality decline and rapid growth may represent a severe structural strain on relationships within the family. From one standpoint this situation may be viewed as a grave consequence of population growth; from another standpoint it may be regarded as a necessary step in transforming the social structure in order to make the new equilibrium one of low fertility and mortality. The obstacles to such a new equilibrium are considerable, because of likely opposition from those with a vested interest in the traditional structure—from some heads of governments, of armies, of religions, and of families, and from certain of the privileged and the property-owning. The outcome is obviously problematic, and will differ in detail from one culture to another, but it seems unlikely that the tide of social transformation that is sweeping the world can be more than postponed, whatever the current strength of tradition in any particular society.

*   *   *

EDUCATION AND POPULATION GROWTH

. . . There is considerable evidence from recent economic research that factors other than the amount of capital investment in the means of production or growth in the quantity of labor are of major importance in economic growth. Such growth requires much more than an accumulation of capital and an increase in the number of workers. New types of productive instruments have to be created, new occupations generated and learned in new contexts and locations, new types of risks have to be assumed, and new social and economic relationships have to be forged.

Hence, the development factors include: (a) improvement in the quality of labor through education and other means of skill acquisition, as well as better health and welfare; (b) more favorable conditions for the introduction of innovation and technical change; (c) institutional changes leading to more effective organization and management at both governmental and private levels; and (d) a better environment for entrepreneurs. These factors are interrelated, and all depend to some extent on improvements in education.

RECENT EDUCATIONAL EXPANSION

The number of children enrolled in the primary schools of the less developed countries rose 150 percent during the 15 years from 1950 to 1965, and the percentage of all children 6 to 12 years old who were in school rose from less than 40 percent to more than 60 percent. This marked increase in enrollment ratios (the fraction of the total age group who are in school) reflected in large measure the value placed on education by people of all classes and income groups in the developing countries.

Public pressure for more education probably came in part from increasing economic returns to skill and education as industrialization proceeded and in part from the widening disparity between the incomes of people who had some formal education and those who were illiterate. This disparity in turn came from the growing demand for skilled labor and the stagnation in demand for uneducated and unskilled workers, whose numbers were rapidly increasing because of high rates of population growth. Studies in four Latin American countries and in India show that the earnings of people with 5 to 6 years of schooling are double or triple those of persons who have spent less than 2 years in school. Persons with 11 years of education earn three to six times as much as functional illiterates.

EDUCATION OF CHILDREN AS A FORM OF SAVING AND INVESTMENT

Educational expansion means that many parents have been spending more to improve the education and skills of children even though this has become more difficult as the number of children in each family increased. These investments in the "quality" of children may be taking place at the expense of savings by households and corresponding capital investment in the physical means of production. Statistical analysis of a large number of less developed countries shows that the level of savings measured in terms of national income remains, over time, a relatively constant fraction of per capita incomes. This fraction does not increase as per capita incomes rise, but from country to country it shows a strong inverse correlation with child dependency ratios, that is, the proportion of children less than 15 years old to adults 15 to 65 years old.* (As we have seen, these dependency ratios depend directly on birth rates and rates of population growth.) Total savings, including those invested in human capital through education and better nutrition and child care, though still low in absolute terms because of low per capita incomes, are considerably higher than monetary savings or investments in physical capital and may be rising more rapidly than per capita incomes.

LIMITATIONS ON EXPENDITURES FOR EDUCATION AND DEVELOPMENT

Allocating expenditures for education presents difficulties on the government, as well as the family, level. In low income countries public investments in education reduce the amount that can be spent by governments on capital investments for short-term increases in production. The proportion of the gross national product (GNP) that can be drained off in taxes by all levels of government is limited by the necessities of human survival. In India, for example, 60 to 90 percent of personal incomes must be used to meet the physiological needs of the people for calories, protein and other nutrients, clothing, and shelter. Governments also face other difficulties in raising sufficient direct and indirect taxes to provide the revenue that must be shared among education, health and welfare services, and capital expenditures for development. These difficulties arise from the low levels of exports and imports available for customs revenue and the frequently deteriorating terms of trade, the prevalence of family morality rather than public morality, and the lack of effective political and economic controls.

---

*Nathaniel H. Leff, "Dependency Rates and Savings Rates," *Amer Econ R,* Vol. 59, No. 5, Dec. 1969. pp. 886–896.

The situation of average households in low income countries is similar to that of governments. There are difficulties even when per capita incomes rise. The ratio of total savings to income cannot be increased very rapidly as per capita incomes grow, even if strong incentives exist, simply because the necessities of life require that a high proportion of income be used for food, clothing, and shelter. Increasing numbers of children in the average family keep this proportion high even when total family income rises. In economic terms, the "elasticity" of savings to rising incomes tends to be close to one. This means that consumption needs are not adequately met by present income and the bulk of any increase in per capita income will be used for increasing consumption rather than savings.

EDUCATIONAL COSTS PER CHILD IN DEVELOPED AND LESS DEVELOPED COUNTRIES

On the average the developed countries with their high per capita incomes are able to spend both a greater percentage of national income and far greater amounts of money on public education than the poor countries. This contrast is widened by the large proportion of children in the developing countries, a result of high birth rates and low death rates. Therefore, even if the level of educational expenditure were the same, expenditures per child would be much less than for low-fertility countries. For example, in 1965 the United Kingdom used 6 percent of its GNP for education, while Ghana used 5 percent. But the school-age population (5 to 19 years) was about 37 percent of the total population in Ghana and 22 percent in the United Kingdom. Thus Britain used nearly twice as large a percentage of its GNP per head of the school-age population as did Ghana. In absolute terms, the United Kingdom, with a GNP per capita of $1,800, spent about $500 per child for education, and Ghana, out of a total GNP per capita of $300, spent $15 per capita, or about $40 per child.

Education in the developing countries is further handicapped by the fact that educational costs per child in schools, in terms of per capita incomes, tend to be relatively high. The differential in incomes between educated and uneducated people is much larger than in the developed countries, and consequently the ratio of teachers' salaries (which constitute 60 to 80 percent of educational costs) to per capita incomes is commonly two or three times this ratio in developed countries.

PERCENT OF NATIONAL INCOME THAT CAN BE DEVOTED TO EDUCATION

The low incomes of developing countries are not in themselves a fixed barrier to the channeling of substantial proportions of income into education, provided governments give education a sufficiently high priority and are able to raise the necessary taxes. There is a wide variation among countries, but on the average they spend about 3.5 percent of national income on education. But there does not appear to be much correlation between per capita GNP and the percentage of national income devoted to education. At all levels of per capita GNP, this percentage varies widely, from 1.5 to 2 percent in Ethiopia, Pakistan, Nicaragua, and Portugal to about 6 percent in Kenya, Ivory Coast, Cuba, and Libya, and more than 8 percent in Zambia and Tunisia. Expenditures per child of school age have an even greater range, from less than $5 to more than $75.

In spite of the rapid expansion of education in the less developed countries, the absolute numbers of illiterates in these countries increased from 1950 to 1965 because of the population factor; the number of children in the primary age group rose more rapidly than the number being educated. Educational planners in Africa, Asia, and Latin America are aiming at a reversal of this situation in the future by raising enrollment ratios to above 90 percent as rapidly as possible.

Time Required to Raise Enrollment Ratios. In many countries such an increase in enrollment ratios would be extremely difficult and perhaps impossible to accomplish in less than 15 to 20 years. One reason is that accelerating rates of population growth and the low levels of secondary and higher education during the past 2 decades have resulted in a small proportion of potential teachers relative to the numbers of potential students. Teachers must be recruited from the smaller and more poorly educated cohorts of these past years, in some regions in the face of competition from industry and other sectors. Moreover, the increase in the percentage of the GNP used for education that is required to raise enrollment ratios can be attained only rather slowly in many countries, because it requires a reorganization of fiscal and tax procedures that may not be possible until the GNP becomes much larger than at present.

Savings in Enrollments Resulting from Reductions in Fertility. If the desired rise in enrollment ratios takes place over 20 years or more, the rate of growth of the school-age population will greatly affect the total numbers of children in school. This can be seen by analyzing the situation of a typical developing country in which the population of children 5 to 14 years old is increasing by 3 percent per year, and educational plans call for a rise in enrollment ratios from 40 percent at present to 95 percent after 20 years. If fertility remains constant over these 2 decades, the number of children in school at the end of the period will have increased by 338 percent. With a steady decline in fertility at a rate of 1.7 percent per year the increase will be 270 percent. If fertility declines by 3.3 percent per year for 15 years, the numbers of children in school will have increased only 206 percent. Thus the savings in enrollments resulting from sharply reduced fertility will be about 30 percent after 20 years. The effect after the first 10 years would be much smaller however—about 3 percent—because of the 5- to 6-year lag in the effect of a reduction in fertility rates on school-age population.

If the rise in enrollment ratios from 40 percent to 95 percent takes place over 30 years, the constant fertility projection gives a 517 percent rise in enrollment at the end of this period, whereas for a rapidly declining fertility the increase would be only 200 percent. A 51 percent saving in enrollment would be attained at the end of this period by the assumed rapid reduction in fertility. Fertility reduction would give a saving of only 3 percent at the end of the first 10 years, and 30 percent at the end of 20 years, just as in the previous case.

Effects of Declining Fertility on Costs of Education. The effects on future educational costs of declining fertility rates versus continuance of present high fertility are more difficult to visualize than the effect on future enrollments. A rise in enrollment ratios with continuing high fertility will require that an increasing percentage of GNP be devoted to education, even if GNP increases more rapidly than population. This results from the fact that the costs of education per student increase about as rapidly as per capita incomes. Most of these costs represent teachers' salaries, and these rise as per capita incomes rise.

Moreover, if the school system is to be expanded and improved, the proportion of expenditures for buildings and equipment and the nonteacher component of recurrent costs must be raised. To create a more balanced system the ratio of students in secondary and higher education, relative to those in primary school, must be increased, even to ensure a sufficient number of primary teachers. In Africa and Asia, secondary education is six to fifteen times more expensive per student than primary education, and university education twenty-three to thirty-nine times more. Finally, improvement in the quality of education must be attained primarily through raising teacher qualifications, and this means both greater costs and a lengthening of the time for teacher education, and a rise in salaries more than proportional to the increase in per capita incomes, if education has to compete for personnel with industry and other sectors.

For a given increase of GNP, per capita incomes will be higher if fertility declines and population growth is slowed. Hence the cost of education per student will increase more than if fertility had remained constant. Consequently, the effect of a fertility decline on educational costs will be less than proportional to the reduction in the number of children to be educated. But calculations for a typical case—Pakistan—show that whether or not enrollment ratios and educational quality are improved, total educational costs would be significantly smaller if present fertility rates were rapidly lowered than if fertility were constant. This is basically due to the fact that the proportion of children to adults in the population would diminish. In 1985 the percent of GNP required if fertility remained high would exceed that required for rapidly declining fertility by 13.9 percent if enrollment ratios held constant, by 10.4 percent if enrollment ratios are raised, and by 9.4 percent if, in addition, pupil/teacher ratios are lowered. In 1995, the excess in the high-fertility case would be 38.5 percent, 29.9 percent, and 27.5 percent respectively. By 1995, the amount saved each year would be about 900 million dollars, more than four times the *total* expenditures for education in Pakistan in 1970.

High Rate of Economic Growth Required to Increase Enrollment Ratios. The calculation for Pakistan assumes a growth in GNP of 6 percent per year, or about 350 percent by 1995. Even with this very high rate of growth, more than 8 percent of national income would have to be devoted to education in order to accomplish the planned increase in enrollment ratios, unless there is a marked decline in fertility. Practically no country today allocates such a high percentage of resources to education. If the economy grows at a slower rate, the increase in enrollment ratios would probably be impossible to attain without a sharp reduction in fertility.

URBANIZATION AND EDUCATION

Another consequence of high rates of population growth that affects education is the rapid urbanization that is occurring in most less developed countries because of migration of redundant workers and their families from the countryside. Both enrollment ratios and educational standards are usually higher in urban than in rural areas. Therefore, educational planners need to keep these differences in mind and to take into account the rates of urban migration both in planning the allocation of educational resources and in budgeting additional funds for raising enrollment ratios and improving educational quality.

ALLOCATION OF EDUCATIONAL RESOURCES

Without greatly increased educational expenditures, the necessity of providing primary education for rapidly growing numbers of children inevitably diverts resources away from technical, vocational, and higher education, all of which are required in many countries to provide the skilled technical manpower essential for economic growth. One of the most difficult problems faced by educational planners and administrators is to strike an optimum balance between the two kinds of education, in the face of public pressures for expanding school enrollment ratios and for a broader geographic distribution of schools.

THE ROLE OF EDUCATION IN REDUCING FERTILITY

The quantity and quality of education affect fertility rates, and hence population growth, in several ways:

1. Education postpones the age of marriage. Educational opportunities for women, particularly secondary and vocational education, tend to raise the age of marriage. This is clearly seen in the Khanna District of the Punjab in northwestern India, where the age of marriage of women has risen from less than 17 to more than 20 during the past decade as education and employment in teaching, nursing, and other occupations have become available. This postponement of marriage is one of the contributing causes to the decline of the birth rate from 38 per 1,000 in 1957–59 to 32 per 1,000 in 1966–68.

2. Educated women have fewer children. Evidence from several countries shows that women with 7 or more years of schooling have fewer children and smaller families than women who have had little or no education. The reasons are complex and not entirely understood, but among them are probably the greater access to information and to communications media possessed by educated women; the alternatives to childbearing available to them in the form of jobs and opportunities for service; their increased role in family decision-making; their greater ability to provide adequate nutrition and better health for their children, with the result that they are faced with less uncertainty about

their children's survival; and their realization that a small family will make it easier to provide education and social mobility for the children.

3. Educational costs to the parents lead to smaller desired family size. Even when the costs of teacher salaries and the capital and equipment costs of education are paid by the state, children in school are a considerable expense to their parents. Their material needs are greater and they are less able to contribute to family income. Hence parents perceive their interests are better served by having fewer children.

4. Economic and social development resulting from education tends toward a reduction in fertility. As we have pointed out, an increase in the quality and skills of the labor force, together with other individual and social characteristics related to education, are probably the most important elements in economic and social development. At the same time, there is evidence that a certain level, or rate, and character of development are necessary conditions for a marked decline in fertility under the present circumstances of less developed countries. Although both these propositions rest largely on statistical grounds and are difficult to quantify or state in any rigorous fashion, the empirical relationships seem clear. We may say with some conviction that an increase in the quantity, an improvement in the quality, and a raising of the average level of education in most developing countries would promote economic development and thus a slowing down of population growth.

TIME LAGS IN EDUCATIONAL AND ECONOMIC DEVELOPMENT

Both high rates of population growth and the poverty that is synonymous with underdevelopment severely impede a rapid expansion of education. The time lags for interaction between population and economic change and educational improvement are long. A reduction in fertility would significantly improve educational prospects only after about 10 years; there is also a lag of about 10 years in the effects of education on economic development and on fertility. Neither the developed nor the less developed countries can afford to relax their efforts to bring about a reduction in fertility by all acceptable means or to take advantage of every opportunity for capital investment and institutional change that offers a possibility of speeding up the development process.

CONSEQUENCES FOR PUBLIC HEALTH AND HEALTH SERVICES

Public health technology applied on a mass scale in the developing countries has reduced death rates dramatically. Yet the level of personal health services for the individual and the community varies widely and, in general, remains far below the levels of the more developed regions. National leaders and the public aspire to a level of health services that will reduce mortality still further and increase the health and well-being of the people. However, as with education and other public services, high fertility forces health ministries to run fast to stay in the same place—let alone improve services. Unlike other services, however, personal health services can have a direct effect upon population growth by reducing mortality and by providing family planning services.

Governmental health expenditures in most developing countries are between 0.3 and 2.5 percent of GNP, ranging from less than 30 cents to several dollars per person per year. In most developed countries these expenditures are between $13 and about $75 per person and the fraction of GNP is usually between 1 and 4 percent.

POPULATION GROWTH AND PERSONAL HEALTH SERVICES

For the next 20 years at least, the demand for health services will outrun the supply—by any measure such as doctor/population ratios or number of hospital beds. Rapidly growing population combined with higher aspirations make this inevitable. A study of doctor manpower needs from 1955 to 1965 in thirty-one developing countries illustrates the problem of numbers.* To maintain the doctor/population ratios of 1955, 25 percent more doctors were needed because of rapid population growth. To increase the doctor/population ratio by 3.3 physicians per 100,000 people, from 17.9 to 21.1, 50 percent more doctors were needed by the end of the 10-year period. At zero population growth, only 18.5 percent more doctors would have been needed.

The age and geographical distribution of the population also affects the health services. In a high-fertility community the primary stress on health services will be the care of mothers and children. The problems of medical treatment for infants are substantially greater than the problems of treating young adults, and hence care of the young requires a higher doctor/population ratio than the care of people aged 15 to 45. The levels of personal health services are usually much higher in urban areas than in rural ones, both in terms of numbers of physicians per capita and in facilities.

In a high-fertility region many women have several pregnancies very early in their childbearing years and continue to bear children up to the time of menopause. Very young mothers, older mothers, mothers with closely spaced pregnancies—all high-parity mothers—face risks. Except in most favored socioeconomic groups, evidence suggests that a short interval between pregnancies depletes the mother's capacity to give her baby a good start. She also carries a higher risk for her own health and safety, especially if she has several pregnancies very early in her childbearing years. Fetal loss rate under such circumstances is higher, infant survival is lower, and malnutrition and some impairment of growth and development are found in the surviving children. Mothers not only suffer from illnesses associated with pregnancy and childbearing, but are more vulnerable to other health hazards of a more general nature. They bear the burden of caring for the children, often under unfavorable circumstances and frequently with fewer opportunities to avail themselves of any health services that may exist.

With closely spaced pregnancies, or high parity, or the combination thereof, there is also greater risk of early interruption of pregnancy and of prematurity. Where breast feeding is the only chance a child has to survive, early birth of another infant curtails the benefit from the mother's lactation and predisposes the child to Kwashiorkor or other types of malnutrition. Studies from the United

*World Health Statistics Report, Vol. 21, No. 11, Geneva, 1969.

States and the developing countries reveal the not surprising fact that, as family size increases, per capita spending for food goes down. As a result, corresponding diet inadequacies and nutritional deficits are common. Malnutrition in childhood is usually not clearly identified in mortality statistics, for it is largely reflected in deaths from dysentery, measles, pneumonia, etc. to which undernourished children have lessened resistance.

ABORTION

Rapid population growth is usually paralleled by a lack of community experience in the use of contraceptives. The result is a large number of unwanted pregnancies, and, in many countries, frequent resort to induced abortion, particularly when the desirability and feasibility of limiting family size become recognized.

Abortion is widely considered both a social and a medical (or health service) problem. The sociocultural aspects of this problem are so varied and so intimately associated with the historical, legal, and religious patterns of individual countries that it is difficult to attempt any brief analysis of their complexity or to generalize about the way rapid population growth affects specific situations. It is possible, however, to assemble an impressive amount of evidence to give weight to two generalizations about abortion.

First, it appears that as traditional societies (no matter where) begin to make the transition from high to low fertility, the popularity of induced abortion as a method of fertility control rises markedly. It may even reach what has been termed epidemic proportions in some societies. Second, lawmaking bodies are becoming increasingly convinced by the argument that the costs and dangers of illegal and unskilled abortions outweigh whatever other arguments are advanced in behalf of restrictive abortion laws. Arguments for community health and safety, and for women's personal freedom, are carrying the day in many communities, although the acceptance of legal abortion is far from uniform from one society to another or within societies.

To the health planner this situation presents some very serious questions, whether abortion is a legal or extra-legal means of fertility control. The prevalence of induced abortion beyond the law (particularly if in epidemic proportions) results in serious demands on health services for medical salvage procedures. In some hospitals in developing areas, from one fourth to one third of hospital maternity beds are used for postabortion cases. Yet low-cost legal abortion service cannot be provided unless there is a realistic resource base of facilities and trained personnel. This must be one element in the decision whether to provide legal abortion facilities as a major component of a fertility control program designed to contribute to social and economic development. Insofar as possible, the need for abortion should be minimized by providing women who wish to avoid pregnancy with easy access to contraceptive materials and information.

However, the complete elimination of abortion through the effective use of contraceptives is a distant and probably not attainable goal. In those societies in which the drive to limit family size is strong, the use of abortion tends to rise. It also tends to rise after the inception of effective and extensive contraception programs which help to inculcate a small-family norm. Nonetheless, experience in Japan and the USSR shows that the goal of eventually decreasing the rate of induced abortion by the use of other family planning methods is feasible when accompanied by intensive education and information programs.

FAMILY PLANNING

The leaders of many developing countries see high natality levels as a handicap to overall development. During the next 20 years the trend toward expanded and intensified family planning programs will undoubtedly increase. In some societies, there are already attempts to achieve specific lower levels of population growth. In others the emphasis is more general—to improve maternal and child health and to alleviate the poverty that is associated with large families.

A national family planning program and government health services can interact in three ways:

(1) Particularly where a variety of fertility-control methods is offered, and especially if these include sterilization or abortion, the family planning program will often be a part of the personal health services provided by the government. The requirements for frontline workers are different for some kinds of family planning programs than for other health services; the program management should have a high and semi-autonomous status; and the costs should be considered as new and additional to those for other services.

(2) If a drop in birth rates results from the family planning program, the need for personal health services will be less than it would be with continuing high fertility. For example, in a country in which the level of health services is being doubled, a 25 percent decline in average rate of population growth would produce a 15 percent saving in annual health expenditures at the end of 20 years, compared to the expenditures required if the rate of population growth is unchanged. The effect on maternal and child health services will be proportional to the decline in birth rates and will be felt as soon as a decline occurs.

(3) The family planning program may compete with the personal health services for scarce medical facilities and personnel, including physicians and trained nurses. Where family planning programs and health services are combined, there may also be a direct competition for funds; the budget for an effective family planning program is likely to be at least half the health services budget in those developing countries that spend less than 1 percent of GNP on health. Competition for personnel, facilities, and funds will arise as soon as the family planning program is initiated, before it has had an appreciable effect on fertility. The extra demand for physicians can be minimized by employing family planning workers who are not physicians, but who have been especially trained to carry out the necessary physical examinations and other activities required in the family planning program. This has been tried successfully in Pakistan. Modern techniques for induced abortion greatly reduce the time requirements for physicians to perform abortions, and the number of days spent in hospitals by abortion patients.

HEALTH CONSEQUENCES OF DENSITY AND CROWDING

The commonly held view that crowding and population density, per se, have deleterious effects on health probably derives largely from four empirical observations: (a) Traditionally the densely populated (i.e., urban) areas have *reported* higher death and morbidity rates. (b) Industrialization and urbanization have frequently been followed by dramatic increases in death rates attributable to infectious diseases. (c) Studies of military training camps have reported exceptionally high rates of virus diseases. (d) In some laboratory studies, deleterious health consequences are noted as the number of animals housed together is increased.

The orthodox explanation for these observations is that crowding increases infectious disease, mainly through a greater opportunity for the spread of infection. For example, outbreaks of upper respiratory infection among recruits in military training camps are explained as the result of the herding together of large numbers of susceptible young men with a few infected individuals. But there is evidence that crowding also has other injurious health effects, which occur primarily during the period when the degree and extent of crowding is rapidly increasing. The effects appear to be much less serious when the rate of crowding is slow and the crowded population has sufficient time to become adapted to its environment.

Thus rapid population growth and its accompanying rapid urbanization are probably more injurious to health than actual population density. In many cases, however, it is difficult to isolate the effects of crowding, as such, from other conditions, such as poverty, poor nutrition, poor housing, and pollution, which formerly characterized all cities and still prevail in the rapidly growing cities of the poor countries, and in the "inner cities" of the United States.

Before the modern era, cities were often called "eaters of men"—their birth rates were usually lower than their death rates, and the population was maintained by continuing migration from the countryside. Even as late as 1950, urban death rates in the United States were slightly higher than rural ones. But by 1960 the situation had reversed, and in 1966 death rates in cities and towns were only half as high as those in rural areas. The incidence of infectious illness was much lower. This was at least partly the result of better sanitation and health facilities in the cities and suburban towns, relative to the rural areas, plus the fact that migration of younger people to the cities had left an older, more susceptible population behind in the countryside. Low morbidity and mortality also characterize crowded areas in other countries with high levels of health services and sanitation. For example, although Hong Kong and Holland have very high population densities, they are said to enjoy two of the highest levels of physical and mental health in the world. The levels of mortality and morbidity in the densely populated cities and towns of Great Britain are about the same as those in rural areas.

Both animal experiments and experience with human beings indicate that social stresses due to crowding produce physiological disturbances. In turn, these increase susceptibility to both infectious and noninfectious disease. The effects are most severe before individuals have had time to become adapted to the crowded conditions. In animals, physiological changes occur during the period when the size of the population in the same space, that is, the population density, is increasing. These changes include increased adrenal and other endocrine secretions and a higher level of activation of the central nervous system. It is believed that they result from increased social interactions which enhance emotional involvement and produce excessive sensory stimuli. Animals in subordinate positions within the group tend to respond in a far more extreme fashion than those at the top of the social hierarchy, both in the volume of endocrine secretions and in manifestations of disease and pathology. After the population has reached its maximum size and has become adapted to the crowded conditions, the level of physical pathology drops to that of animals living in an uncrowded environment.

Some of the ameliorating effects of urban adaptation in human beings are suggested by the death rates from lung cancer in the United States. When controlled for the degree of cigarette smoking, these death rates are considerably higher in farm-born people who have migrated to cities than in life-long city dwellers. In a study of Appalachian mountaineers working in an urban factory, it was discovered that the first generation suffered from a high rate of illness and absenteeism; their sons did not.

In the rapidly growing cities of developing countries, the newcomers can be expected to be at the highest risk for another reason as well. A frequent accompaniment to urbanization is the atomization or destruction of the family and kinship groups that provide protection and emotional support to rural individuals. In the course of time, new types of groups develop in the cities to fulfill some of these functions, but it is often difficult, particularly for newcomers, to become effectively integrated into these groups. Individuals who are deprived of such meaningful group relationships, exposed to ambiguous and conflicting demands for which they have had no previous experiences, and frustrated at achieving their goals and aspirations, may be more likely to become victims of both infectious and noninfectious disease. Insofar as this effect exists, it is difficult to distinguish from the direct consequences of a rapid increase in the level of urban crowding.

It should be evident from this discussion that the magnitude and nature of the effects of crowding on human beings are highly uncertain. Much research is needed to clarify and quantify them. . . .

While acknowledging the energy crisis, Geoffrey Baraclough places a large share of the blame for our present food crisis on "neocapitalism." I believe he is correct. But in reading his article, keep at least three points in mind. First, in making his case, I believe Baraclough underestimates the effects and strains of population growth. Second, although it will be possible to feed the population of the present and even that of the future, we must still promote population control for at least one reason: Throughout his article, Baraclough ably stresses the social and political changes that must be made if underdeveloped peoples are to eat. Inevitably, those changes will bring conflict and crisis, and there is no reason to subject children to a future filled with misery. Third, and most important, this article is included in the "population" chapter because it highlights the major value shifts that are required if *today's* underdeveloped peoples are not to starve. The prospect that these changes will occur is doubtful, and complicated by the fact that Baraclough himself fails to consider the pollution effects of his proposals. Our future becomes even more dim if population continues to grow and even more people are forced to endure terrible housing, unemployment, rapid social change, and authoritarian governments of the right and left.

From The Great World Crisis
—Geoffrey Baraclough

. . . Most of the facts about the food situation are assembled in Lester Brown's new book [*By Bread Alone*]. Two seem to me to be particularly illuminating. The first, cited also in the useful report from the Management Institute for National Development,[1] is that it was only in 1974 that the U.S. government ceased to pay farmers not to grow crops (in 1973 the bill was over $3 billion), thus bringing about 50 million unproductive acres back into use. The second, reported by the Transnational Institute in Washington,[2] is that in the Sahelian region of Africa, where drought and famine are rampant, thousands of the best acres and a large share of the scarce water resources are assigned by "multinational agribusiness corporations" to the production not of foodstuffs for the native population but of raw materials and other products for marketing in the developed world.

What this can mean in practice is shown by the World Bank report on Mali, one of the Sahelian countries worst affected by the drought. In Mali, the World Bank tells us, "production of food for domestic consumption . . . has declined steadily" from 60,000 tons handled by official marketing channels in 1967 to a current 15,000 tons—but "export crops—notably peanuts—have increased during the same period, despite the ravages of the recent drought."

Add one further fact, again from the Transnational Institute, and the real dimensions of the food question become apparent. During the famine of 1965–1966 in India, we are told, food aid was withheld until the Indian government agreed to "the penetration of US capital" in other words, of the petrochemical industries headed by the Rockefeller group—"into the field of fertilizers."

What this means in practice scarcely needs underlining. "Modern fertilizer," Henry Kissinger told the Rome food conference, is "the most critical single input for increasing crop yields," but its production and marketing are controlled by international corporations which have no interest in eliminating shortages and reducing prices and no evident incentive to help the developing

From Geoffrey Baraclough, "The Great World Crisis." Reprinted with permission from *The New York Review of Books*. Copyright © 1975 Nyrev, Inc.
[1]*World Food Supply: A Global Development Case Study*, p. 18.
[2]*World Hunger: Causes and Remedies*, p. 31.

countries when they can unload their products at good prices at home. In addition, as Lester Brown points out, they have shown great reluctance to invest in new plants in the underdeveloped world or to "provide technical assistance for plant management and repair." When we are told that fertilizer plants in developing countries are inefficient and "many are now producing at below two-thirds their capacity," we have every right to ask whether one reason may not be what the World Bank disarmingly calls "the structure of the international fertilizer market."

The first necessity, in discussing the food question, is to get rid of the misconceptions in which it is currently bogged down. If the energy crisis has been deliberately misrepresented, the misrepresentations in regard to food are immeasurably worse. Two myths, in particular, have befogged the whole issue. The first is the persistent legend that food shortages are the consequence of inexorable population pressures. The second is that there is an over-all shortage of foodstuffs. Neither will bear serious scrutiny. The problem "is not simply a shortage of food" but "inequity of distribution"; or, as the Transnational Institute more trenchantly puts it, at the conclusion of its impressive report: "hunger is caused by plunder and not by scarcity."

The argument that hunger is the result of a burgeoning world population is particularly pernicious, because it is only too likely to breed a spirit of defeatism. There is, indeed, already a vociferous lunatic fringe, led by MIT professor Jay Forrester, which argues that "no matter how much food you have, population will overrun it," and advocates a policy of "directing aid to those countries with the greatest chance of survival, while abandoning others to famine."[3]

This, not to mince matters, is unsavory rubbish, with about as much theoretical justification as the Nazi Final Solution. As Paul Demeny has pointed out, the constantly reiterated references to "soaring birth rates" in the underdeveloped world "have little factual basis and in many instances no basis at all."[4] In any case, every reputable demographer knows that the only historically proven way of reducing population growth is to improve living standards, beginning with adequate feeding, and that it is the hungry, indigent, and despondent who have large families. No one is going to practice birth control if he expects five out of six of his children to die of starvation before the age of three.

The other fashionable remedy for the food crisis, for those too squeamish to advocate starvation, is birth control. In itself, this is common sense, though as Lester Brown, a powerful advocate of contraception, freely admits, "there will be little chance of bringing birth rates down rapidly enough to avert disaster" without "a more equitable distribution of income and social services." It would, in other words, be disastrous if the view took hold that population control, in itself, was a sufficient answer. As the Transnational Institute points out, "population could decrease and production increase, but if the great

---

[3]"Hunger: The Clock Ticks on," *Boston Globe,* November 24, 1974.
[4]Paul Demeny, "The Populations of the Underdeveloped Countries," *Scientific American,* September, 1974, p. 152.

majority of the population lacked purchasing power to pay for its food," the only result would be that "the minority will continue to live in luxury while the great masses of the people live in misery, as the case of Brazil demonstrates today.

The simple fact is that, contrary to popular preconception, there is ample land available to provide food for a burgeoning world population. Properly used, according to Roger Revelle's calculations, the world area of potential arable land (about 2.3 times the currently cultivated area) could support between 38 and 48 billion people—that is, between ten and thirteen times the present population of the earth. "The limiting factors," he concludes, "are not natural resources but economic, institutional and sociopolitical restraints."[5] This is a polite way of saying that what is at fault is the economic system and the political system it underpins.

When we are told—by Robert McNamara among others—that the troubles of Latin America are due to overpopulation and that the only remedy is birth control, the answer is that Latin America, with a population of only 265 million, covers an area three times as large as the United States, and has a far lower population density. It has also the largest amount of arable land of any continent, and yet it imports most of its food and 60 percent of the arable lies fallow, largely because the landowners find it more profitable to grow cash crops, such as sugar and coffee, for export than subsistence crops to feed their own people.

Not surprisingly, therefore, the developing countries view the current campaign for contraception with a certain skepticism. Even if we leave out of the picture the United States, the great consumer and leading advocate of birth control for blacks, browns, and yellows, it is only necessary to look at France, a country with a population density nine times that of Brazil, one-third more than Nigeria, and greater even than that of Indonesia, and with a ratio of arable land to population not greatly different from that of India, to see the anomalies; for France not only satisfies the food needs of its population but also produces considerable surpluses for export.

There are, it is true, great discrepancies from country to country and from continent to continent in the availability of agricultural land. Argentina, with 7.69 hectares per capita, can absorb a substantial population growth; Haiti, with only 0.16, evidently cannot. But the question is not simply the availability of land. The phenomenal increase in French productivity between 1955 and 1967—corn up from 11 to 41 million tons, for example, and barley from 27 to 97—was achieved virtually without increasing the area under cultivation.

If France, with 0.34 hectares of arable per person, can do this in only twelve years, it is hard to think of any good economic reason why India, with an equivalent ratio of arable land to population, should not be able to do likewise, if it is provided with adequate supplies of fertilizer and modern machinery. We should not, in short, be surprised if the underdeveloped countries see the population-control proposals put forward by the developed countries of the

[5]Roger Revelle, "Food and Population," *Scientific American*, September, 1974, pp. 168–169.

west as "self-interested substitutes for confronting the real issues" or even as "instruments . . . to preserve their political and economic supremacy."[6] They may well be right.

The truth, of course, is that the so-called food crisis is due not to population growth but to affluence; it is, in other words, a side product of the artificial prosperity which the industrial West whipped up in the 1950s and 1960s by lavishly squandering Middle East oil. Although world population increased by less than 50 percent between 1951 and 1971, world production of cereals doubled, but the bulk of the surplus went not to the poor but to the rich.

At least one-third of the increased demand for food reflected increases not in population but in the diet of the affluent countries. In North America alone consumption of cereals per head rose from 1,000 pounds a year to nearly 1,900 pounds. This formidable increase was due, as is now well known, to the emergence of meat eating as one of the symbols of affluence—an ironic development when we recollect that the English soldiers sent to conquer Wales at the close of the thirteenth century mutinied when, instead of their customary bread and ale, they were given meat and milk, food in their view only fit for savage Welshmen.

The fact remains that consumption of beef per person doubled in the United States between 1940 and 1972. And in other industrial countries the increase was steeper and quicker. In West Germany, according to figures quoted by Lester Brown, meat consumption rose by one-third per person between 1960 and 1972; in Italy it almost doubled and in Japan it increased over three and a half times. Dazzled by the rising prices, cattle raisers in the United States, Canada, Australia, Argentina, Ireland, and New Zealand hastened to cash in on the growing demand. The ironic result, by the end of 1974, was a "beef glut," while elsewhere in the world people were dying of starvation.

This depressing situation has obviously nothing to do with food shortage and a great deal to do with the way commercial agriculture operates in a capitalist economy. What has happened, quite simply, is that grain surpluses that were once available for consumption in the poorer countries are now sold to farmers in rich countries, at prices which poor countries cannot afford, to feed their livestock. Meat is notoriously the most wasteful of all foodstuffs, requiring an input of four to seven pounds of cattle feed for every pound of meat produced, and the consequence is that over 60 percent of US grain output—or something like 140 million tons a year—is consumed entirely by cattle, sheep, pigs, and poultry.

We have only to recall that the total world shortfall of cereals in 1972–1973 amounted to no more than 60 million tons to see the significance of this in relation to what Kissinger has called "the desperate struggle for sustenance." According to one calculation, the livestock population of the United States alone (leaving out dogs and cats) consumes enough food material to feed 1.3 billion people.

---

[6]*World Hunger: Causes and Remedies.*

Since 1965, Barbara Ward tells us, Americans have added 350 pounds per head to their annual diet, largely in the form of beef and poultry—an amount very nearly equivalent to an Indian's entire diet for a whole year.[7] Whether it has done them anything but harm from a health point of view may be open to debate; but no one in his right mind would suggest that most Americans, or the peoples of other industrialized states, were seriously undernourished in 1965.

Once again, as in the squandering of energy, it is a case of that conspicuous consumption which has become a status symbol of affluent society. But the reason why it has become a status symbol, as John K. Galbraith long ago pointed out, is that it is sold to the public as a status symbol through lavish, incessant advertising campaigns paid for by corporations which can think of no other way of keeping the wheels of business profitably turning. It is worth remembering, as we gloomily inspect the soaring prices in the supermarket, that over 90 percent of the rise is due not to increases in the price of the food itself but to the elaborate system of processing, packaging, advertising, and distribution, which is where the lion's share of the profit lies.

All of this goes far to explain why the underdeveloped countries are unable to import the food they require; but it does not explain why they need to. Thirty years ago the underdeveloped countries as a whole had a large surplus of food. "Net grain exports from Latin America," Lester Brown tells us, "were substantially higher than those from North America." Today the developing countries are net importers. How has this reversal come about?

The reasons, needless to say, are complicated and controversial, but at the risk of simplification it can be said that, in the last resort, the failure of agriculture in the tropical, underdeveloped world to provide adequate supplies of food for domestic consumption is the result of its subordination to the needs of the developed world. It responded, in the economist's more neutral language, to "impulses generated by temperate industrial production."[8]

For some eighty years, in other words, the tropical countries put practically all their research and effort into export crops like cocoa, tea, and rubber, and virtually no effort into food production. This was, of course, originally a consequence of colonial rule, and the historian can easily trace the way in which the colonial powers—the British, for example, in Burma or Malaya—fostered these developments. Moreover, there is little doubt that for forty or fifty years they were beneficial. But what was true in 1910 was no longer true in 1960. The reason, essentially, was the immense advance in agricultural productivity, through the use of fertilizers, mechanization, and the introduction of improved strains of coffee, rubber, and other plants. As a result, the underdeveloped countries found themselves saddled with increased crops of tea, cocoa, coffee, which they could not sell at a profit, and at the same time with the need to import foodstuffs which had been sacrificed to the production of these, and other, cash crops.

It would be absurd to suggest that the governments of the newly emancipated ex-colonial countries were innocent victims of these developments. Nothing

---

[7]Barbara Ward, "The Fat Years and the Lean," *The Economist,* November 2, 1974, p. 24.
[8]W. Arthur Lewis, *Aspects of Tropical Trade* (Stockholm: Almquist & Wiksell, 1969), p. 7.

compelled them, as their terms of trade got worse, to try to compensate by increasing their output of commercial crops. In theory, at least, they could have switched over to a policy of raising domestic food productivity. If they didn't (and for the most part they didn't), it was for two reasons. First, they swallowed lock, stock, and barrel the old dogma, so dear to Western economists, and to multinational corporations, that the prosperity of underdeveloped countries depends upon what they can sell to industrial countries. Secondly, and more practically, they were faced from the 1950s onward by the huge American grain surpluses, which the United States was prepared to unload at prices that deterred them from embarking on expensive programs for building up home production.

It is scarcely an exaggeration to say that, until the shortages of 1972, the underdeveloped world served as a regulator enabling the United States to keep its agricultural production more or less in balance. There were also a number of secondary consequences resulting from colonialism and from lopsided development subordinated to the purposes of the industrial world. Among the more notorious are the stranglehold established by foreign financial institutions— American, British, French, and now Japanese—which, by granting or withholding loans and credit, largely determine the economic climate of most underdeveloped countries; the power wielded by the so-called multinational agribusiness corporations; and the role in all developing countries of the sector of wealthy hangers-on of foreign business, usually not more than 5 percent of the population, who have done exceedingly well out of the existing disparities and have no intention of surrendering their privileges.

There is no doubt that the existence of these deeply entrenched vested interests makes any radical attack on the basic causes of world hunger extremely difficult. Only wide-ranging social reforms, involving land tenure, income distribution, and marketing, will enable the miserable, poverty-stricken peas-. antry, scratching a bare living from inadequate plots of land, to abandon a hapless subsistence agriculture and turn to production for the market. But such reforms are bound to impinge on the privileged position of powerful interest groups, which are unlikely to accept them without fighting back. One has only to recall the fate of Arbenz in Guatemala or of Allende in Chile to see what can happen to a political leader who takes agrarian reform seriously.

This is probably one of the reasons why, so far, there is little evidence that the world is coming to grips with the deep, underlying causes of the food crisis. There is, it is true, now a wide measure of agreement that only a radical increase in food production in the developing countries can provide a real solution to the world food problem, and that this will not occur until, in the words of the director-general of the Food and Agriculture Organization, they "get rid of antiquated and often oppressive agrarian structures."[9] But how this is to be achieved is left tantalizingly vague. It is easier, and politically less explosive, to concentrate on measures to alleviate the worst consequences.

In countries where, as the Indian minister of agriculture and food alleged in 1969, the large landowners, representing no more than 3 or 4 percent of

---

[9]*The World Food and Energy Crisis*, p. 8.

the farming population, "exert all political power" and "make all the decisions," reform is easier to advocate than to accomplish. The World Bank has announced that, in future, it will "give priority" to countries putting through land reform policies, but in almost the same breath it admits that "where the political will for reform is lacking, the Bank can do no more than offer advice." The United Nations, also, agrees that "profound transformations of the present socio-economic structures" are necessary, but concludes resignedly that this is "a very complex long-term process," which is tantamount to saying that it expects little or nothing to be done.

In fact, if we look in detail at current proposals, the most striking thing about them is that even those which correctly identify the essential problem immediately proceed, in practice, to give it the lowest priority or no priority at all. The points emphasized are population control, increased food production by the industrialized countries, technical improvements in agriculture in the developing world, and the rebuilding of food stocks to meet future contingencies; but the question of fundamental land reform ("more aid in changing agricultural institutions and practices that presently impede productivity," as the report sponsored by the Institute on Man and Science cautiously puts it) figures only as an afterthought. The result, as the Transnational Institute caustically observes, is that "the only priorities which could trigger a steady growth in food production are excluded."

This tendency to evade the fundamental issues is strikingly evident in the proposals submitted by Henry Kissinger at the Rome food conference on November 5.[10] Here again, the highest priority was given to increasing the output of the agriculturally advanced industrialized countries. So far as the developing countries are concerned, all the emphasis falls on technical improvements—·"new technologies . . . to increase yields and reduce costs," expanded fertilizer production, improved storage—and on investment, but the social and political problems impeding productivity are simply ignored. Kissinger notes, it is true, that "farmers have no incentive to make the investment required for increased production"; but this is attributed not to poverty, insecurity, uneconomic smallholdings of two or three acres, and the other disadvantages which afflict the peasants of backward countries, but to unremunerative prices, shortage of credit, and inadequate transportation and distribution facilities.

Kissinger's proposals—which are fairly representative of current high-level thinking—not only fall short of immediate requirements but, taken alone, could make the long-term situation worse rather than better. To give priority to stepping up the export surplus of the United States and other advanced countries could only perpetuate the dependence of the underdeveloped upon the industrial world and ensure that the poor countries will remain, as at present, beggars at the rich man's table. Naturally, it will help if more productive strains of rice and wheat can be raised, or if losses through inefficient storage can be

---

[10]"The Global Community and the Struggle Against Famine," address by Henry A. Kissinger before the World Food Conference, Rome, Italy, November 5, 1974 (Department of State, Washington, DC).

eliminated. There is no dispute about that. The mistake is to suppose that technical improvement alone is the answer. As the Transnational Institute observes, "Anyone who knows anything about the agrarian problem in the underdeveloped countries knows that there are structural factors which would prevent success, even if they possessed the knowledge of a thousand encyclopedias, a legion of experts and unlimited quantities of tractors, fertilizers and pesticides."

This is also the reason why the much-publicized "Green Revolution" has disappointed expectations. On a technical level it has achieved much. In India alone it made possible an expansion of wheat production from 11 million to 27 million tons between 1965 and 1972, an increase "unmatched by any other country in history." But instead of producing a general improvement of living standards, it is generally agreed, the benefits have flowed to a privileged minority. It is the rich farmers who can afford chemical fertilizers, agricultural machinery, and the rest, not the 70 percent of poor peasants with less than an acre of land each. Moreover, it is much easier for rich landowners than it is for small farmers to get bank credit with which to carry out irrigation programs and build up large mechanized agricultural estates.

One result of modernization, therefore, has been to drive large numbers of peasants off the land to swell the ranks of the unemployed living in squalor in the slums around the cities. Examples abound throughout Latin America, Africa and Asia, from oil-rich Venezuela, with the highest per capita income in Latin America ($1,260 in 1973), where 78 percent of the population lives at starvation level in squalid urban hovels, to booming oil-rich Nigeria, where GNP per capita is still only $130 a year.[11] In Persia, some 17,000 Iranian farmers were displaced when the Shah leased hundreds of thousands of acres of newly irrigated land to multinational agribusinesses, such as Shellcott and Hawaiian Agronomics. The productivity of these concerns, it is said, is below that of medium-sized Iranian farms, but it is easier for the government to collect rent from foreigners than to help to put its own small farmers on their feet.[12]

The position is admirably summed up by the authors of the Transnational Institute report when they write that "no sustained agricultural development can be achieved without social progress, and social progress is impossible without sustained progress in agriculture." The practical question is whether the industrial world, which calls the tune, wants or is even prepared to contemplate the only sort of social progress which can make a long-term solution of the world food problem possible.

Its feasibility is beyond doubt. In Japan, where the modernization of agriculture reaches back to the early years of the century, the eight-acre farmer, using family labor, has been highly successful in food production, and the agrarian revolution in China, which banished the age-old cycle of famine in twenty years, was based on labor-intensive techniques. Taiwan, also, has employed similar methods with great success; and the Venezuelan minister of

---

[11] For Venezuela, see *The New York Times*, October 25, 1974; for Nigeria (and a number of other examples) see *World Bank Annual Report 1974*, pp. 24–25.

[12] Frances FitzGerald, "Giving the Shah Everything He Wants," *Harper's Magazine*, November, 1974, p. 78.

finance recently calculated that, given the necessary social reforms, it would require only three years to make the country self-sufficient in agriculture. In Europe, there is the example of Bulgaria, whose 12 million impoverished small farmers were as backward and depressed as any in Asia or Africa. Not only did Bulgaria become self-supporting within a dozen years, but it also produced a surplus for export which is now its major source of foreign exchange earnings.

But these results were only achieved through far-reaching social changes, and here is the rub. Everyone, naturally, would be delighted if the developing countries could become self-sufficient in foodstuffs, and no one objects to limited measures of peasant self-help. But what if the necessary reforms go further and threaten the existing social and economic balance, including the privileged position of the great landowners and foreign concessions? Henry Kissinger's failure at Rome to mention social reform may have been more than accidental; for a radical program of reform, starting in India or Pakistan, in Venezuela or South Vietnam, may spread like an infectious disease until eventually the mansions of the rich as well as the hovels of the poor are threatened. That is why the West, confronted with the choice, may opt to pay ransom in the form of food shipments and concessionary aid whenever a particularly severe crisis arises, rather than face up to the only sort of measures that can make the developing countries self-supporting.

Meanwhile, we are left with the current emergency, 400 million people or more "barely surviving" (in Robert McNamara's words) "on the margin of life." Common sense, to say nothing of common humanity, would suggest that the first priority would be emergency measures to rescue them from their plight. Instead, to everyone's consternation, the Rome food conference spent its time discussing measures to obviate food shortages in 1985, not how to forestall the imminent catastrophe, and President Ford refused to sanction an immediate doubling of American assistance. "It's absurd," declared Senator Clark of Iowa, "to sit here talking about a problem of hunger ten years from now, and ignore the fact that millions are going to die this winter." It might have been nearer the truth if he had said "It's criminal."

Nevertheless, as McNamara has emphasized, "the world has not suddenly lost its wealth," the affluent nations have not "suddenly lost their capacity to assist those countries most in need." Barbara Ward is surely right when she says that "the issue is squarely political." When, at the time of President Ford's refusal of increased food shipments, an "Administration source" said there would be "no problem if financing can be obtained," and another "Washington bureaucrat" promised that the United States would "do its share," the cat was out of the bag. For the problem, as everyone knows, is that financing cannot be obtained, and when it comes down to defining each country's share the way is open for interminable haggling and no action. The starving millions of Asia and Africa, in short, have become the playball of international politics.

This is a disagreeable but not, perhaps, a surprising conclusion. I am not, of course, propounding a conspiracy theory of history, still less conducting a witch-hunt for villains and scapegoats. No governments are blameless. If the United States is prepared to play politics with food, the Arab and Iranian governments are equally ready to play politics with oil. And the governments of the developing countries, instead of giving priority to their urgent economic problems, devote a disproportionate part of their resources to military spending, which, according to the Institute for World Order, "has grown more than twice as fast as population and one and one half times as fast as GNP since 1960."[13] As Professor Richard N. Gardner of Columbia observes, no one can be expected to go on donating "endless amounts of food to an Indian government that cuts its family planning budget, mismanages food production and distribution, and invests scarce resources in the testing of nuclear devices."

Nothing is more certain than that the food and energy crises will get worse, rather than better, if they become the object of political bargaining in which each country seeks its own immediate advantage. They can also no longer be left to take care of themselves, as they have been left to take care of themselves for the last twenty-five years, without a catastrophe in which we shall all be engulfed. The essential question is whether they can be solved within the framework of the existing economic and political system. If the foregoing analysis has demonstrated that they are not self-contained problems, which can be isolated and dealt with separately, but are part of a wider crisis still, it would seem that what we are faced with is the breakdown of the industrial system built up in the West since 1950 and of the international order it created. This does not necessarily mean, as many people assume, the collapse of Western civilization. The resources, accumulated wealth, scientific achievements, and human endowment upon which our civilization is based are still intact. The question . . . is how to achieve alternative social and economic arrangements that will enable us to ride out the crisis and build a better world.

---

[13]*World Military and Social Expenditures 1974,* by Ruth Leger Sivard, published under the auspices of the Institute for World Order, 1140 Avenue of the Americas, New York, 30 pages, $2.00.

Epilogue

Dictionaries define an epilogue as a summary speech ending a play, poem, or book. Although this epilogue is not a speech, it is an attempt to summarize *The Future as A Social Problem* by making three points.

First, assuming some agreement with my general argument, how does a society begin a basic reevaluation of its cultural assumptions? In any precise sense, I have only one answer to this question: I don't know. No plan exists for a process that ends in a radical, yet voluntary, reanalysis of culture. No plan exists that tells us how to convince millions of people that the world urgently requires a conscious reevaluation and change of values. In fact, not only can advocates of change expect fierce resistance to their efforts, they must—if they are honest—warn their listeners that major change will require sacrifice and pain.

If a precise plan is lacking, advocates of change have one major advantage: The world's survival depends on radical change. Naturally, we need not admit that a crisis exists. Black can be white if people say so, and in recent years many have criticized those who forecast disaster. The argument goes something like this: "Since the dawn of time, dissidents have forecast the world's end and it has never happened. So what's different now? We agree that there are major problems, but none that we can't handle. In the long run everything will work itself out."

Perhaps the optimists are correct. But the articles in this volume furnish a body of evidence that is difficult to refute. For our situation *is* unique. Unlike those living in every other period in history, we do have—in fact and probability—the capacity to destroy ourselves and our planet. This is the argument that advocates of change must disseminate as widely as possible. For time is short, and our problems are great.

I believe that advocates of change must *argue* their case. Ethics notwithstanding, violence is only likely to frighten people back into the shell of the past. As Ortega demonstrates, change promises pain, and for that reason people normally resist it. Violence and self-righteousness can only alienate many moderate people who might otherwise have seen the truth in our argument, and that will only hasten the disaster we seek to avoid.

Conceivably, arguing our case—in schools, in churches, in clubs, any-where—might prove that disaster is not imminent, which would be marvelous. But if our argument is sustained, then advocates of change can create the sense of awareness needed to mobilize people for the radical social change that will be required. For example, studies of social movements indicate that these movements arise out of social unrest; and that unrest has three ingredients: a collectively induced rejection of present social arrangements, a collective cultivation of grievance and dissatisfaction with the present, and a "shared chafing" in having to live with a present that promises a worse future.[1]

So, the task is to make people chafe by rubbing them against the arguments in favor of change. It is hoped that, in order to obtain relief from the chafing, they will seek solutions, and together make the 1980s a "decade of mobiliza-tion" in which "proposals for new world-order systems will begin to be taken seriously in various political arenas and will be discussed within all major types of societies."[2]

My second point concerns the relationship between ideological and institu-tional change. Although we seek both simultaneously, our aim is to attack problems at their roots; our focus must, therefore, be on shifting cultural be-liefs and values. This, in turn, has two effects on institutional—practical— change. First, it will take time to create the kinds of support needed for such reforms as the international control of environmental pollution. Of course, this does not mean neglecting pollution control in the meantime, but it does require the realization that meaningful organizations for international pollution con-trol will not be formed until enough people have altered their present views *and* are willing to act on their new opinions. Second, because we are trying to treat the causes of our problems, we must avoid superficial institutional changes. Crises may put a brake on major changes, or political leaders may try to silence criticism via promises or investigatory commissions. However, advocates of change must resist attempts to undermine their efforts by insist-ing that there is little sense in grounding new institutions in worn-out values. Above all, practical change must be rooted in a thorough reevaluation of our present social systems.

The last point relates to communes. I have already disagreed with Charles Reich's opinion that the best way to foster radical social change is to "opt out" of society. Withdrawing is silently sanctioning a continuation of the status quo. Few of those in power care if people live in the wilds, so the commune represents no significant challenge to our present values. In fact, departure lets those in power to escape the criticism of some of society's brightest young

---

[1] These remarks appear in an unpublished paper by Herbert Blumer.
[2] Richard Falk, *This Endangered Planet* (New York: Vintage Books, 1972), p. 433.

people. Recall, also, the observation made by Peter and Brigette Berger (cited in the Introduction to Chapter 7): Somebody has to fill the positions of power left vacant by those who flock to the commune. If those positions are filled by people committed to yesterday and today, then one result of "opting out" will be a future that is even worse.

To my mind, the best way to foster radical change is to seek it within advanced industrial societies. Struggling to stay alive, most underdeveloped nations lack the will and resources to reevaluate values (e.g., industrialization) they have just or are just accepting. Only the more advanced societies have lived with modernity long enough to understand its problems and possibilities; and among them, America has the greatest chance to achieve radical social change. This is so for several reasons: First, reasonable amounts of freedom exist in the U.S.—social movements like feminism are already asking questions that touch the heart of traditional values. Second, with a large number of educated citizens, the chances that the arguments will be heard and understood are good. Third, America's natural resources and economic wealth constitute a source of influence in the battle for change; if America should decide to effect the radical changes we have been discussing, other countries might have to follow suit.

Of course, no guarantees exist that the U.S. or any other nation can accomplish these changes. Our stockpiles of nuclear weapons could easily destroy even the best-laid plans. But recall, once again, Ortega's warning against despair. Although reality may breed pessimism, it is the world that is actually there, the world that can be changed. For if only people make social reality, only people can change it. The choice is a human one. The choice is ours.